ARCHITECTURE OF SOLITUDE

ARCHITECTURE OF SOLITUDE

Cistercian Abbeys
in Twelfth-Century England

PETER FERGUSSON

PRINCETON UNIVERSITY PRESS, PRINCETON, NEW JERSEY

Copyright © 1984 by Princeton University Press
Published by Princeton University Press, 41 William Street,
Princeton, New Jersey 08540
In the United Kingdom:
Princeton University Press, Guildford, Surrey

All Rights Reserved
Library of Congress Cataloging in Publication Data will be
found on the last printed page of this book

ISBN 0-691-04024-9

This book has been composed in Linotron Garamond
Clothbound editions of Princeton University Press books
are printed on acid-free paper, and binding materials are
chosen for strength and durability. Paperbacks, while satisfactory
for personal collections, are not usually suitable for library rebinding.
Printed in the United States of America by Princeton University Press
Princeton, New Jersey

FOR MY MOTHER,
URSULA MABEL FERGUSSON
AND IN MEMORY OF MY FATHER
ALFRED MILNTHORPE FERGUSSON

CONTENTS

FIGURES

PLATES

Photographs are the author's unless otherwise indicated.

ABBREVIATIONS

AASRP   *Associated Architectural Societies Reports and Papers*

AB   *Art Bulletin*

AC   *Analecta Cisterciensia* (formerly, until 1965, *Analecta sacri Ordinis Cisterciensis*)

Ann. F.   T. A. Beck, *Annales Furnesienses* (London, 1844).

Ann. W.   H. R. Luard, ed., *Annales monastici*, Rolls Series 36, part 2 (London, 1865).

Ant. Jnl.   *The Antiquaries Journal*

Arch.   *Archaeologia*

Arch. Ael.   *Archaeologia Aeliana*

Arch. Camb.   *Archaeologia Cambrensis*

Arch. Cant.   *Archaeologia Cantiana*

Arch. Jnl.   *Archaeological Journal*

ASOC   *Analecta sacri Ordinis Cisterciensis* (changed in 1966, to *Analecta Cisterciensia*)

B. Mon.   *Bulletin Monumental*

BoE   *Buildings of England*

Cam. Soc.   *Camden Society*

CCC   *Cîteaux—commentarii cistercienses* (formerly, until 1958, *Cîteaux in de Nederlanden*)

Chart. F.   A. W. Crawley-Boevey, *The Cartulary and Historical Notes of the Cistercian Abbey of Flaxley* (Exeter, 1887).

Chart. N.   J. T. Fowler, ed., *Chartularium abbathiae de novo monasterio, The Publications of the Surtees Society* 66 (Durham, 1876).

Chart. R.   J. C. Atkinson, ed., *Cartularium abbathie de Rievalle, The Publications of the Surtees Society* 83 (1887).

Chart. Ruf.   C. J. Holdsworth, ed., *Rufford Charters*, in *Thoroton Society Record Series* 29 (1972); 30 (1974); 32 (1980).

Chart. S.   J. McNulty, ed., *The Chartulary of the Cistercian Abbey of St. Mary of Sallay in Craven*, in *Yorkshire Archaeological Society Record Series* 88 (1933); 90 (1934).

Chart. T.   H. F. Salter, ed., *The Thame Cartulary*, in *Oxfordshire Record Society* 25 (1947); 26 (1948).

Chart. W.   E. H. Fowler, ed., "Cartulary of the Abbey of Old Warden," *Bedfordshire Historical Record Society Publications* 13 (1930).

Chron. LP.   E. Venables, ed., *Chronicon abbatie de Parco Lude, Lincolnshire Record Society* 1 (1891).

Chron. M.   E. A. Bond, ed., *Chronica monasterii de Melsa*, Rolls Series 43, parts 1-3 (London, 1866-1868).

Col. C.   *Collectanea Cisterciensia* (formally, until 1964, *Collectanea Ordinis Cisterciensium reformatorum*)

CN   *Cîteaux in de Nederlanden* (changed in 1959 to *Cîteaux—commentarii cistercienses*)

COCR   *Collectanea Ordinis cistercensium reformatorum* (changed in 1964 to *Collectanea Cisterciensia*)

CR   *Calendar of Close Rolls Preserved in the Public Record Office* (London, 1902, and forward).

DoE   *Department of the Environment*

Fund. K.   E. J. Clark, ed., *Fundacio abbathie de Kyrestall, Publications of the Thoresby Society* 4 (1895).

L. and P. Henry VIII   *Letters and Papers, foreign and domestic, of the reign of Henry VIII: Preserved in the Public Record Office*, 32 vols. (London, 1862-1932).

Jnl. BAA   *Journal of the British Archaeological Association*

Jnl. SAH	*Journal of the Society of Architectural Historians*		*Cisterciensis ab anno 1116 ad annum 1786*, 9 vols., *Bibliothèque de la Revue d'histoire écclésiastique* (Louvain, 1933-1941).
Jnl. WCI	*Journal of the Warburg and Courtauld Institutes*		
Med. Arch.	*Medieval Archaeology*	*Trans. BGAS*	*Transactions of the Bristol and Gloucester Archaeological Society*
Mem. F.	J. R. Walbran, ed., *Memorials of the Abbey of St. Mary of Fountains, The Publications of the Surtees Society*, 42 (1862); 67 (1876).	*Trans. CWAAS*	*Transactions of the Cumberland and Westmorland Antiquarian and Archaeological Society*
Mon. Angl.	Sir William Dugdale, *Monasticon Anglicanum*, 6 vols. (London, 1846 ed.).	*Trans. ERAS*	*Transactions of the East Riding Antiquarian Society*
Mon. Ebor.	J. Burton, ed., *Monasticon Eboracense* (York, 1758).	*Trans. LCAS*	*Transactions of the Lancashire and Cheshire Antiquarian Society*
PL	J.-P. Migne, *Patrologiae cursus completus, series latina*, 221 vols. (Paris, 1844-1864).	*Trans. RIBA*	*Transactions of the Royal Institute of British Architects*
Proc. SAS	*Proceedings of the Somerset Archaeological and Natural History Society*	*Trans. WNFC*	*Transactions of the Woolhope Naturalists Field Club*
		T. Soc.	*The Publications of the Thoresby Society*
RCHM	*Royal Commission on Historical Monuments*	*VCH*	*Victoria County History*
		WANHM	*Wiltshire Archaeological and Natural History Magazine*
S. Soc.	*Publications of the Surtees Society*	*YAJ*	*Yorkshire Archaeological Journal*
Statuta	J. M. Canivez, ed., *Statuta Capitulorum Generalium Ordinis*	*YASRS*	*Yorkshire Archaeological Society Record Series*

ACKNOWLEDGMENTS

The writing of this book was made possible by a grant in 1978-1979 from the Howard Foundation and from the faculty research fund of Wellesley College. I also gratefully acknowledge additional financial support from Wellesley College for travel, the drawing of maps, and the preparing of an index.

My first introduction to Cistercian architecture came in Professor Eduard Sekler's classes in the School of Design at Harvard, and much of the vivid interest generated by his teaching remains alive for me. I am also deeply grateful to Professors James Ackerman and John Coolidge of the Fogg Museum, Harvard, for their painstaking efforts to make an architectural historian of me. In putting together the material for this book, I have been helped by many people; some listened to my ideas (and often corrected them), others gave me specific information or kindly answered letters, a few slogged through murky drafts of chapters. I wish to thank Professors Maurice Beresford of the University of Leeds; François Bucher of the University of Florida; and Madeline Caviness of Tufts; Mrs. Bridget Cherry of *The Buildings of England*; Mr. John Cherry of the British Museum; Professor William Clark of Queens University, New York; Mrs. Nicola Coldstream of the University of Reading; Professor Michael Davis of Mount Holyoke College; Mr. Peter Draper of Birkbeck College, University of London, and particularly, for many helpful conversations and visits; Vice President Frances Fergusson of Bucknell University; for hospitality and much kindness, Miss Ruth Fergusson of Leeds; Dr. Eric Gee, formerly of the Royal Commission on Historical Monuments, York; Mr. R. Gilyard-Beer, formerly Assistant Chief Inspector of Ancient Monuments; Mr. Alasdair Glass of London; Professor D. Greenway of the Institute of Historical Research, the University of London; Miss Barbara Harbottle of the University of Newcastle; Professor M. F. Hearn of the University of Pittsburgh; Father S. F. Hockey of Quarr Abbey; Professor Christopher Holdsworth of Exeter University; Mr. J. Hopkins of the Society of Antiquaries, London; Professor Walter Horn of Berkeley; Mr. John James of Wyong; Dr. Peter Kidson of the Courtauld Institute; Dr. T. Kinder of Scottsville; Professor Arnold Klukas of Oberlin College; Professor B. Layman of Wellesley College; Dr. Kevin Leddy of London; Lord Leigh of Stoneleigh Abbey; Professor Meredith Lillich of Syracuse University; Professor Carolyn Malone of the University of Southern California; Mr. Robert C. Moeller III of Wayland, Mass.; Dr. Kenworth Moffett of Cambridge, Mass.; Sir Nikolaus Pevsner of London; Professor Colin Platt of the University of Southampton; the late Mr. E.V.C. Plumptre; the late Mr. Stuart Rigold; Professor J.R.S. St. Joseph of the University of Cambridge; Mr. A. D. Saunders, Chief Inspector of Ancient Monuments and Historic Buildings of England; Mr. Gyde Shepherd of Ottawa; Dr. Roger Stalley of Trinity College, Dublin; Professors Raymond Starr and Ann Stehney of Wellesley College; Mr. Neil Stratford of the British Museum; Father Chrysogonus Waddell, O.C.S.O. of Gethsemani Abbey; Mr. F. B. Watkins of Flaxley Abbey; Dr. Christopher Wilson of the University of Hull; Miss Joan Woodward of Oxford. My dog, Wyatt, would also like a mention; taking him for walks through the landscape of Wellesley College has allowed me the time and space to sort out scholarly issues that would have otherwise remained compacted.

I am particularly indebted to three colleagues in Cistercian studies, though in acknowledging their help I do not wish to implicate them in the book's shortcomings. Professor David Walsh of the University of Rochester spent many hours explaining the Bordesley excavations to me and kindly showed me through them (in the pouring rain). Dr. Glyn Coppack, Inspector of Ancient Monuments for Southeast England most generously kept me fully informed on his recent excavations at Fountains. He made three site visits in the north with me and was ever willing to discuss scholarly issues. Pro-

xviii   ACKNOWLEDGMENTS

fessor Caroline Bruzelius of Duke University gave me particular help at many stages of writing. She improved a large number of my ideas, shared her unrivaled knowledge of the French Cistercian abbeys, and provided timely and gracious encouragement.

At Princeton University Press Christine Ivusic and Anna Mitchell made the production and design of the book a graceful and learning experience. Through the various stages that transform a manuscript into a book, I was most fortunate to have as editor Miss Tam Curry. Her alert reading eliminated many errors, and she made numerous improvements to the text and other invaluable suggestions.

My deep and abiding thanks go to the Department of Art at Wellesley College. During my association with it I have received what can only be described as a paid education—and I feel privileged to have been part of its distinguished tradition. In particular, I wish to thank the late Professor John McAndrew whose teaching and conversations helped me to learn a great deal about architecture; Professor Eugenia Janis for her interest and helpful criticism in a field of specialization far distant from her own; and Professor Lilian Armstrong for numerous constant and long-standing kindnesses and support.

My greatest thanks go to Miss Katherine Galbraith of Birkbeck College, University of London. Over nearly two decades I have learned much about medieval art in the north of England from her and have benefited greatly from her rigorous scholarly standards. Not only has she shared ideas, read and criticized drafts of certain chapters, sent me in search of books and sources, but her unselfish interest in the project encouraged me to finish it.

WELLESLEY, 1981

"What is the reason," at length Miss Wardour asked the Antiquary, "why tradition has preserved to us such meagre accounts . . . of these stately edifices, raised with such expence of labor and taste, and whose owners were in their times personages of such awful power and importance? The meanest tower of a freebooting baron or squire who lived by his lance and broadsword is consecrated by its appropriate legend, and the shepherd will tell you with accuracy the names and feats of its inhabitants; but ask a countryman concerning these beautiful and extensive remains—these towers, these arches and buttresses and shafted windows, reared at such cost three words fill up his answer—"they were made by the monks lang syne."

—Sir Walter Scott, *The Antiquary*

PREFACE

IN THE LATE SUMMER of 1535 Thomas Cromwell's commissioners rode out through the English countryside to begin their examination of the monasteries. Five years later more than eight hundred religious institutions had been dissolved, their assets and goods appropriated by the king, Henry VIII. The process of closure was erratic, crude, sometimes brutal, with visitations that included bullying and humiliating interrogations of the communities. For the Cistercian order these years saw more than four centuries of unbroken monastic practice come to an end. As the monks were dispersed, the rhythms of work and worship that had shaped their buildings disappeared forever. Where recently had stood church or cloister, warming room or workshop, barns or guest house, there now lay deserted and shattered ruins. It is these skeletal remains, despoiled by man and weathered by time, that form the basis for this study of the order's architecture in England.

Though less dramatic than their departure, the arrival of the Cistercians in England was marked by events unprecedented in that country's religious life. In little more than twenty years, between the early 1130s and 1150s, the Cistercians established or brought under their control forty-five monasteries, including Rievaulx and Fountains in Yorkshire and Furness in Lancashire, which quickly numbered communities of several hundred men. Nothing on this scale had ever before been attempted. Giving form and expression to this expansion was the work of the Cistercians as builders. Isolated and sometimes untamed sites rapidly became thriving building complexes, some extending over more than ten acres and dominated by churches of cathedral scale. Throughout the twelfth century the sounds of the masons working echoed across the secluded valleys chosen by the order for its settlements. Although only a small proportion of this prodigious enterprise survives, the haunting beauty and superb craftsmanship of the remains document the great energies and high ideals that marked one of the most extraordinary phases of medieval history.

The simplicity and power of the early Cistercian abbeys appeal greatly to modern tastes. Leading architects of the twentieth century such as Le Corbusier have drawn inspiration from them, and they are visited yearly by tens of thousands.[1] Popular interest has been matched by scholarly attention, and in recent years studies have appeared on the abbeys in Denmark (1941), France (1947, 1979), Switzerland (1947, 1957), Spain (1954), Ireland (1955-1960), Italy (1956, 1958, 1981), Germany (1957, 1973), Poland (1958), Sweden (1967), Belgium (1971, 1975) and Greece (1979).[2] Conspic-

---

[1] Most notable was Le Corbusier's interest in the twelfth-century abbey Le Thoronet (Var), which he studied in the course of forming the design for the Dominican house of Ste. Marie de la Tourette near Lyons. See M. Purdy, "Le Corbusier and the Theological Program," in R. Walden, ed., *The Open Hand: Essays on Le Corbusier* (Cambridge, MA, 1977), 286-321.

[2] See V. Lorenzen, *De danske cistercienserklosters bygninghistorie* (Copenhagen, 1941). For France, see M. Aubert, *L'Architecture cistercienne en France*, 2 vols. (Paris, 1947); and C. A. Bruzelius, "Cistercian High Gothic: The Abbey Church of Longpont and the Architecture of the Cistercians in the Early Thirteenth Century," *AC* 35 (1979): 1-204. For Switzerland, see J. Gantner, *Kunstgeschichte der Schweiz*, 2 vols. (Frauenfeld, 1947); and F. Bucher, *Notre Dame de Bonmont und die ersten Zisterzienser Abteien der Schweiz* (Bern, 1957). For Spain, see H. P. Eydoux,

"L'Abbatiale de Moreruela et l'architecture des églises cisterciennes d'Espagne," *CN* 5 (1954): 173-207. For Ireland, see H. G. Leask, *Irish Churches and Monastic Buildings*, 3 vols. (Dundalk, 1955-1960). For Italy, see R. Wagner-Rieger, *Die italienische Baukunst zu Beginn der Gotik*, 2 vols. (Graz-Koln, 1956-1957); L. Fraccaro de Longhi, *L'Architettura delle chiese cisterciensi italiane con particolare riferimento ad un gruppo omogeneo dell'Italia settentrionale* (Milan, 1958); and D. Negri, *Abbazie cistercensi in Italia* (Pistoia, 1981). For Germany, see H. Hahn, *Die frühe Kirchenbaukunst der Zisterzienser* (Berlin, 1957); and W. Krönig, *Altenberg und die Baukunst der Zisterzienser* (Bergisch Gladbach, 1973). For Poland, see Z. Swiechowski and J. Zachwatowicz, "L'Architecture cistercienne en Pologne et ses liens avec la France," *Nadbitka z biuletnyu historii stuki* 20 (1958): 139-73. For Sweden, see I. Swartling, "Cistercian Abbey Churches in Sweden and the 'Bernardine Plan,'" *Nordisk*

uous by its absence is an up-to-date treatment of the English houses. In fact, more than a century has passed since the publication of the sole book on them, Edmund Sharpe's *The Architecture of the Cistercians*.[3] To some extent the lacuna is misleading, however. Much has been written about the history of individual houses in England, going all the way back to accounts by the monks themselves long before the Dissolution. What is lacking is a book that collects this scattered material and studies it in the light of recent scholarship on architecture and related historical matters like patronage, economics, and the complex growth of the order's legislation.

To define the goals of this study, three principal stages of scholarship on the architecture of the Cistercians in England may be outlined. The first originated in the early nineteenth century in response to the curiosity of antiquarians and travelers about individual sites. It included descriptive guides, collections of measured drawings, reports of amateur clearances, and scholarly monographs. Among the last were important books by Beck on Furness (1844), Potter on Buildwas (1846), Guillaume on Netley (1848), Woodward on Bordesley (1866), Aveling on Roche (1870), and the superb work of Reeve on Fountains (1892).[4] These incorporated selections of documents, broad narrative histories, lists of abbots, catalogs of finds, and fine line engravings of the remains. Analysis of the architecture was omitted, however; what remained was presented and left to speak for itself.

Edmund Sharpe departed from this monograph approach. In handsome folio volumes like *Architectural Parallels* he published comparative details, of base moldings, for instance, from groups of Cistercian and non-Cistercian buildings. This greatly aided classification and dating and gave a broad overview of the order's architectural development, but the details were severed from their context in the history of the building and, a more serious weakness, their manner of presentation rigidified the architectural process. Arrayed like botanical specimens, the drawings form morphological sequences, and it is hard to resist seeing a determinism as the progress of a plinth molding or string course is followed across the page.[5] Although no one knew Cistercian architecture better than Sharpe, his book on the subject, written late in his career, is disappointing. Organized by building type, it provides elliptical definitions of each monastic structure: the church, refectory, dormitory, kitchen. Its thirty-seven brief pages do little justice either to the Cistercians or to Sharpe's knowledge of their buildings.

The major change in Cistercian studies occurred around 1900, first in the work of William St. John Hope (1854-1919), secretary of the Society of Antiquaries of London, and Sir Harold Brakspear (1870-1934), an architect. Under their direction a series of rapid excavations—eight sites were cleared and findings published in just over a decade—greatly expanded the base on which knowledge of the order's buildings had previously rested.[6] Much of this

Medeltid: Konsthistorska Studier Tillägnade Armin Tuulse (Stockholm, 1967). For Belgium, see S. Brigode, "L'Abbaye de Villers et l'architecture cistercienne," *Revue des archéologues et historiens d'art de Louvain* 4 (1971): 117-40; and S. Brigode, "L'Architecture cistercienne en Belgique," *Aureavallis: Mélanges historiques remis à l'occasion du neuvième centenaire de l'abbaye d'Orval* (Liège, 1975), 237-45. For Greece, see B. K. Panagopoulos, *Cistercian and Mendicant Monasteries in Medieval Greece* (Chicago, 1979).

The early body of this literature is reviewed by J. A. Schmoll, "Zisterzienser-Romanik: Kritische Gedanken zur jüngsten Literatur," *Formositas Romanica* (Basel, 1958), 153-80. Treatments other than by national boundary have been far rarer. Notable is the work of Hahn on the early churches, of Krönig on the Romanesque and Gothic phases, and of Schneider on subject topics: see above for Hahn and Krönig; A. Schneider et al., *Die Cistercienser: Geschichte, Geist, Kunst* (Cologne, 1974).

[3] The book appeared in two parts: part 1 in 1874 and part 2 in 1876. The year following the publication of part 2 a fifty-seven-page supplement was issued to be inserted between parts. In this, Sharpe gives brief descriptions of twenty-one abbeys in France, England, Germany, and Spain.

[4] See catalog entries for full citations.

[5] Sharpe's work was preceded by Paley's by two years, the latter including examples of Cistercian moldings (F. A. Paley, *A Manual of Gothic Mouldings* [London, 1844: new ed., 1845]). Paley, a versatile and prolific author, makes convincing the analogy between architectural history and natural history. He was also a classifier of wild flowering plants and published an important volume on the subject in 1860. For the English (and Continental) precursors of the study of architecture through detail, particularly Thomas Rickman, see P. Frankl, *The Gothic: Literary Sources and Interpretations through Eight Centuries* (Princeton, 1960), 506ff.

[6] The sites, in order, were: Fountains (1898-1899), Furness (1899-1900), Stanley (1905), Waverley (1905), Beaulieu (1906),

work involved the simple clearance and exposure of walls rather than archaeology as it is understood today. Hope and Brakspear established new standards of observation and accuracy, and their discoveries provided a wealth of fresh, reliable information.

The work of John Bilson, more important historically, remedied the lack of synthesis in these separate studies of individual monuments. In two pioneering articles (1907, 1909) he transformed the insular focus of the earlier scholarship.[7] An architect like Sharpe and Brakspear, Bilson brought an acute eye for detail and a rigorous knowledge of design to bear on Cistercian architecture, but he also recognized the international character of the order and the need to examine the early buildings in England in a European context. Bilson also established a comprehensive methodology disciplined by a powerful visual and intellectual control of the material. In one sense his publications brought to a close two decades of intensive scholarship on Cistercian architecture in England, which by the outbreak of World War I was better studied than that of any other country.

Thereafter, scholarly output declined. An entire generation was lost in the war, and in the postwar years chauvinism in England and Europe discouraged broader investigation. In addition, available manpower was directed toward large serial studies

such as the *Victoria County History* and the *Royal Commission on Historical Monuments*. There was as well the daunting authority of Bilson's work; all the important questions seemed answered. But most damaging, perhaps, was the halt of archaeological investigation, which under Hope and Brakspear had opened up so much new material. A shift in ownership largely accounts for this. Whereas from the Dissolution through the nineteenth century monastic remains were privately owned, after World War I sites began passing into government hands: Rievaulx in 1918, Byland in 1921, Roche in 1921, Furness in 1923, Buildwas in 1925, Croxden in 1936, Sawley in 1947, Kingswood in 1950, Cleeve in 1951, Rufford in 1959, Fountains in 1966, and Waverley in 1967. With three-quarters of the important sites guarded by the government Directorate (now the Department of the Environment), responsibilities of maintenance and public presentation preempted those of archaeology. Where work was done, such as that by Sir Charles Peers, it took the form of clearance and consolidation rather than full investigation of the site.[8] Only in the past decade has the inactivity of the preceding fifty years given way to promising new work.[9]

In the meantime, new initiative came from the universities. Archaeologists based in universities began work on five sites not owned by the Directorate: Kirkstall (in 1950-1954, 1960-1964, 1980

Kirkstall (1907), Pipewell (1909), and Jervaulx (1911). Work on a ninth, Coggeshall, was interrupted by the outbreak of war in 1914. Hope also contributed notes resulting from study visits to Louth Park (1891), Byland (1896), and Rievaulx (1914); Brakspear to Hailes (1901) and Forde (1913).

[7] The first and less well known is "The Architecture of Kirkstall Abbey Church, with Some General Remarks on the Architecture of the Cistercians," *T. Soc.* 16 (1907): 73-141. This issue of the journal was entirely devoted to Kirkstall, and Hope contributed the first seventy pages. With Bilson and Hope both discussing the same building, their contrasting methods emerge clearly. The second article, "The Architecture of the Cistercians, with Special Reference to Some of their Earlier Churches in England," *Arch. Jnl.* 66 (1909): 185-280, reused much of the material in the first but adapted it for a wider audience (see 185 n. 1).

Like Sharpe and Brakspear, Bilson was also a practicing architect. In one sense his approach is close to Sharpe's, and more than a third of each study is devoted to architectural details arranged under categories. The intellectual range of Bilson's work puts it in a different class, however. One lim-

itation of both studies is a leveling of distinctions between buildings, a result of the stress on architectural detail in which parts of a building can be shown in a formal relationship to parts from other buildings, regardless of their relation to other detailing and regardless of larger architectural qualities such as massing, articulation, or the handling of space.

Bilson's work bears comparison only with that of Rev. Robert Willis (1800-1878), and the two men rank as England's greatest medieval architectural historians. For a bibliography of Bilson's scholarly work, see A. H. Thompson, "John Bilson," *YAJ* 36 (1944-1947): 253-59.

[8] Peers cleared Rievaulx and Byland and wrote the handbooks on both abbeys. His influence on the appearance of sites in England under the care of the Directorate was far-reaching, a fact noted in his obituary, see *Ant. Jnl.* 33 (1953): 149-50.

[9] Concerning the study of the twelfth-century foundations, mention should be made of the work of Gilyard-Beer at Rufford in the mid-1950s and of the excavations of Coppack at Fountains from 1978 to 1981. See catalog entries for Rufford and Fountains.

and continuing), Newminster (1961-1963), Bordesley (1969 and continuing), Garendon (1969), and Boxley (1971-1972).[10] With better techniques and far wider interests they have produced a mass of new material, as shown for instance by the fourteen seasons at Bordesley under the direction of Philip Rahtz of York University. In addition, architectural historians, again in universities, have reassessed the remains of the order's buildings against developments elsewhere in England and on the Continent.

Broadly, then, three phases may be discerned in the scholarly literature, each of which has left impressions on attitudes and methodology. The first was dominated by architects such as Sharpe, Brakspear, and Bilson; the next, by the Directorate under men like Peers; the third and most recent, by archaeologists based in or trained by the universities, such as Rahtz, Lawrence Butler, and Glyn Coppack. For each phase the history of the Cistercians' buildings means something different, both in what is singled out for discussion and in how it is treated.

The present study seeks to build on this substantial body of work. It begins by pulling together for the first time the dispersed information from all of the sites, a collection that in itself reveals more about the order's architecture than might be anticipated; evidence survives, in fact, for over half of the fifty twelfth-century foundations. But no investigation could be justified without addressing broader matters like the overall pattern of development of Cistercian architecture in England in the twelfth century, the relations between the groups of buildings in different parts of the country, the sources from which new ideas came, the connections to the houses in France, the part played in the

introduction of Early Gothic particularly in the north, and the impact on older and very different architectural traditions within the country.

Two difficulties face the historian of Cistercian architecture and condition the present approach. Long before the late 1530s many of the twelfth-century buildings had been altered or replaced, and following the traumatic events of the Dissolution destruction of the former monasteries was widespread and thorough. Thus, basic to any study is the reconstruction of the original form of the buildings. Dating the buildings is equally difficult. None of the churches can be dated by documents, and in only one instance, at Fountains, has the sequence of construction been satisfactorily worked out. Yet a clear, or at least a clearer, understanding of dates must underlie attempts to discern the architectural development and its relation to the order's Continental traditions.

Countering these difficulties are sizable advantages. Work on individual sites is greatly facilitated by past scholarship. Plentiful comparative material comes from recent studies in Europe, crucial in distinguishing local from international trends. And in England the material aspects of Cistercian culture that bear on the architecture have been greatly elucidated; for instance, farming and economics have been studied by Donkin and Waites; patronage and its effects on settlement, by Hill; monastic charters of individual houses, by Holdsworth, Baker, Hockey, Denning, and others.[11]

The chronological boundaries imposed on this study can be justified on several grounds. Historically, the twelfth century was the period of the order's greatest flowering. Fifty of the sixty-four abbeys that it established in England in its four-hundred-year history were founded between 1128

[10] For bibliographies, see catalog entries under individual sites. One should also mention the work of L.A.S. Butler of Leeds University on the Welsh houses ("The Cistercians in England and Wales: A Survey of Recent Archaeological Work, 1960-1980," *Studies in Cistercian Art and Architecture* 1 [1982]: 88-101) and of R. A. Stalley of Trinity College Dublin on the Irish houses (*Architecture and Sculpture in Ireland, 1150-1350* [Dublin, 1971]).

[11] See R. A. Donkin, *The Cistercians: Studies in the Geography of Medieval England and Wales* (Toronto, 1978); B. Waites, "The Monastic Grange as a factor in the Settlement of North-

east Yorkshire," *YAJ* 40 (1959-1962): 627-56; B. Hill, *English Cistercian Monasteries and their Patrons in the Twelfth Century* (Urbana, 1968); C. J. Holdsworth, ed., *Rufford Charters. Thoroton Society Record Series* 29 (1972); 30 (1974); and 32 (1980); D. Baker, "The Genesis of Cistercian Chronicles in England: The Foundation History of Fountains Abbey," *AC* 25 (1969): 14-41; and pt. 2 in *AC* 31 (1975): 179-212; S. F. Hockey, *The Beaulieu Cartulary. Southampton Record Series* 17 (Southampton, 1974); S. F. Hockey, *Quarr Abbey and its Lands, 1132-1631* (Edinburgh, 1970); A. H. Denning, ed., *The Sibton Estates, Suffolk Record Society* 2 (1960).

and 1200. And although only one of a number of reform movements to originate during the century and often outnumbered in their foundations by other orders, the Cistercians eclipsed their rivals in the size of their monasteries, in their rapid assembly of estates, and in the immediate influence they exercised on English ecclesiastical and political life. As might be expected of an order led by Saint Bernard, the direction of their spiritual and secular affairs throughout these years lay in the hands of great if decidedly strong personalities. They included two archbishops—Murdac of York (1147-1153) and Baldwin of Canterbury (1184-1190)—and four saints—William of Rievaulx (died 1145), Robert of Newminster (died 1159), Waltheof of Melrose (died 1159), and Ailred of Rievaulx (died 1167).

Decisive changes discernible around 1200 define the termination of this study. For the first fifty years that the Cistercians were in England, their architecture was marked by developments independent of others in England; local influences were modest. But in the last decades of the century and particularly after 1200 much of this insularity was modified, and increasingly the order's architecture fell under the influence of English High Gothic. Style partly explains this, although often the changes went beyond style and involved the character of architecture. Another factor involved a shift in the pattern of patronage. Formerly, the local barons served as the monks' patrons, but they were now replaced in a number of important cases by the king. At Beaulieu in Hampshire, established in 1204, King John served as patron and an immediate alteration in the scale, ambition, and the sources of architecture can be discerned. Elsewhere, in older, existing foundations, architecture also assumed a different character. In the south at Waverley, the order's first abbey in England, the small early church was superseded by a vastly larger building begun in 1203; and in the north at Fountains work started in 1205 on a huge new choir and east chapel range, with lavish marble shafting and a spectacular handling of space and light that transformed the tight, dark east end of the Romanesque church.

Because architecture embodies ideas, reflects identity, and gives physical form and expressive meaning to values, a study devoted to Cistercian architecture during the order's greatest historical and spiritual period is self-justifying. Sensitivity to architecture's expressive power surfaces in Cistercian writing and legislation in the twelfth century, and it can also be inferred from the passionate attention given to planning and design in the order's buildings. No other monastic movement showed as great a preoccupation with architecture or implicitly acknowledged the powerful nature of its art.

The most important single building of the monastery, the church, becomes the focus of this study, although adjacent buildings will be considered when their histories shed light on dates, interpretation, or construction sequence. For the monks the church carried a profound significance; day after day throughout their lives it formed the backdrop for their most arduous and fulfilling work, the *opus Dei*. Shaped by the monks, the church in turn helped define their own character and lives. More than any other monastic structure, then, the church stands as a witness to the order's spiritual and temporal ideals.

To believe that these ideals remained fixed after their initial formulation, however, is to fail to grasp the living quality of twelfth-century monastic life, its openness to growth. As will be seen in the following pages, the physical history of the English abbeys in these years, far from being lock step in its development, was one of frequent revision and adjustment. Seen in context, these fabric changes register the passage of maturing concepts and new needs; as such they parallel the continual augmentation that recent research has shown to characterize the documents of Cistercian government.

ARCHITECTURE OF SOLITUDE

Cistercian monasteries in England in the twelfth century.

1

A Way of Life
In Search of an Architecture

SITUATED IN secluded valleys whose wooded slopes rise to form an enclosure of nature that echoes the man-made walls within them, the abbeys of the Cistercians rest in a compelling harmony with their surroundings. Basic to this harmony and a defining feature of their buildings is a pervasive simplicity of shape, placement, scale, and materials. Simplicity was the visible expression of much of what lay behind the order's reforming ideals, although concealed by it were the tough-minded and sophisticated attitudes, hard won and hard maintained, that led to its achievement. How did such ideals originate? And what governed their development and their wide-ranging consequences for architecture?

The early history of the Cistercians was considered straightforward until recent years. Since then research has turned up a number of complications. Some of the early documentary accounts and even basic facts have been shown to have been tampered with, many in the late twelfth century by partisans of Saint Bernard who sought to enhance his role in the order's history.[1] The events that led to the foundation of the order occurred in 1098, when a group of dissenting monks left the Cluniac abbey of Molesme in southern Burgundy, frustrated in their attempts to effect a more exact observance of the Rule of Saint Benedict. These men represented only one of a number of such movements, which sought a renewal of monastic life. Abandoning Molesme, the twenty-one monks led by Abbot Robert settled a site on swampy land at Cîteaux, fourteen miles south of Dijon.[2] They called their new community simply the *monasterium novum* and, following the tradition observed at Molesme, raised for their use buildings of wood.[3] In the following year, 1099, complaints from the benefactors of Molesme persuaded the pope to order the return of Abbot Robert, and with him went about half of the original monks. The controversy surrounding this episode threatened the new community's existence, but an indication of stability emerges in the early years of the new century from the fact that work began on a stone church and cloister to replace the earlier wooden ones. These lay just to the north of the original settlement and were consecrated in 1106 by the bishop of Châlons. Even then there was probably little idea of founding a new monastic order as such; the monks still thought of themselves as Benedictines attempting to live more in accordance with the letter of the Rule than was possible at Molesme.

In 1109 leadership of the community passed to an Englishman, Stephen Harding, abbot for the next twenty-four years. Born to noble Anglo-Saxon parents in Sherborne in the west country around

---

[1] The classic treatment is D. Knowles, *The Monastic Order in England*, 2d ed. (Cambridge, 1963), esp. 208-66. See also R. W. Southern, *Western Society and the Church in the Middle Ages* (London, 1970); A. Schneider et al., *Die Cistercienser: Geschichte, Geist, Kunst* (Cologne, 1974); L. J. Lekai, *The Cistercians: Ideals and Reality* (Kent, OH, 1977).

[2] The etymology of "Cîteaux" has been variously explained. The traditional derivation is from the site—namely, from *cisternae*, the Latin word for cistels or boggy ground. An alternative is that it originated from the abbey's position on the old Roman road that ran between Langres and Chalons-sur-Saône, where the monastery stood on "this side of the third milestone" (*cis tertium lapidem miliarium*).

[3] The phrase used was *monasterium ligneum*. For this and for the account of Molesme, see V. Mortet, *Recueil de textes relatifs à l'histoire de l'architecture en France au moyen age, XIᵉ-XIIᵉ siècles* (Paris, 1911), 1:296.

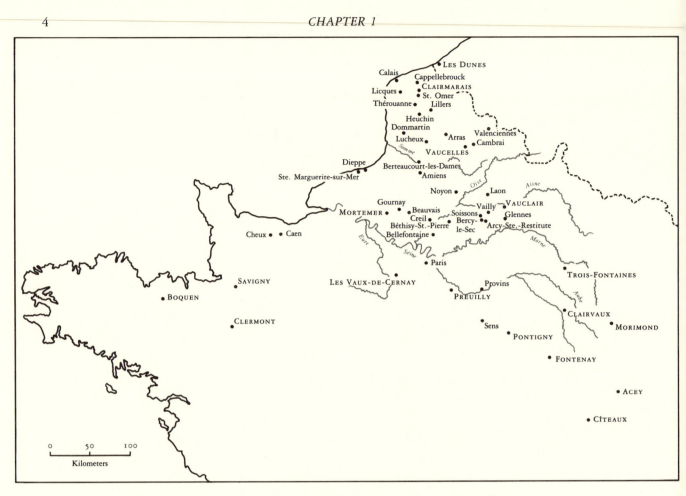

Northeastern France: Cistercian monasteries and related twelfth-century standing churches.

the time of the Conquest, Stephen had been pledged to the monastery there as a child. But he did not follow the normal pattern of a monastic vocation. He apparently abandoned monastic life altogether at one stage, deserted Sherborne, and moved first to Scotland, then to France, where he may have completed his education in Paris. After a pilgrimage to Rome he traveled to Burgundy and around 1085 found his way to Molesme. By the time of the secession he had risen to the rank of subprior. According to William of Malmesbury in the *Gesta regum Anglorum*, written in 1122-1123 and the earliest source on the matter, it was Stephen who provoked the upheaval within Molesme.

Under Stephen's leadership the new community at first almost perished; his interpretation of poverty

[4] See Knowles, *Monastic Order*, 199-200; P. H. Talbot, "An Unpublished Letter of St. Stephen," *COCR* 3 (1936): 66-69.

and work was so severe that disease and death seriously reduced the number of monks (although to picture Stephen in exclusively ascetic terms is misleading, for there is evidence, literary as well as artistic, of warmth of personality and humor).[4] Cîteaux's reputation for discipline and total withdrawal from the world, however, attracted attention and admiration and new recruits. By 1113 their number strained the physical resources of Cîteaux, and a colony was founded at La Ferté. Later that year the young Burgundian aristocrat, Bernard des Fontaines, and a group of his male relatives joined Cîteaux, though later falsifying of the order's documents moved the date of their arrival forward a year to imply that it had saved the struggling community from extinction.

In 1114 a second expansion became necessary, and Cîteaux sent out a colony to Pontigny. The following year the process was repeated, first with the establishment of the abbey at Morimond and then the abbey at Clairvaux (with the twenty-five-year-old Bernard as abbot). Together with Cîteaux these abbeys formed the so-called mother houses, although Cîteaux retained primacy, with its abbot bearing the title *Pater universalis ordinis*; all subsequent foundations were filiated, as daughter houses, to one of them. By 1119 five more houses had been established, and Stephen in that year turned to Pope Calixtus II, who as former bishop of Vienne had known Cîteaux well, to constitute all ten abbeys as a new order. The Cistercians' ensuing growth is without parallel in western monasticism; forty years after the foundation of the first colony Cistercian monasteries numbered 339, and by the end of the century the number had risen to 525.[5]

Although overshadowed by Bernard, Stephen Harding's impact on the Cistercians was fundamental. In particular, he possessed the rare ability to give legislative shape to the new community's spiritual ideals. Two of the order's seminal constitutional documents, the *Exordium cisterciensis cenobii* (also referred to as the *Exordium parvum*) and the *Carta Caritatis*, are largely by his hand, both written around 1119.[6] That they could well have been based on earlier legislative documents, however, is suggested by mention of the existence of well-ordered legislation in the pope's bull of authorization. Common to the documents and an essential feature of the Cistercians' reform was a single-minded return to the original sources of western monasticism, not only to the Rule of Saint Benedict but also, as modern scholarship has shown, to the ideals of pre-Benedictine monasticism as exemplified in the teaching of Saint Basil (d. 379) and John Cassian (d. 435).[7]

An uncompromising insistence on poverty was basic to the new movement. Identifying the economic forms upon which the monasteries rested as the root cause of the unsatisfactory state of monastic practice, the Cistercians enunciated a new socioeconomic system. They renounced all cash revenues common to established monasteries—from seignorial and ecclesiastical sources, for instance—because these transactions brought the monks into contact with the world outside the monastery. Instead, theirs was to be a land economy. To ensure seclusion, monasteries were to be located on isolated land, "far from the concourse of men" in the *Exordium*'s words, and to make this feasible, the abbey's lands were to be worked solely by and for the community.

Self-sufficiency without resort to feudal labor was to be achieved through the acceptance of lay brothers, or *conversi*. First fully integrated into monastic life by the Cistercians, the lay brothers were bound by a simpler discipline and undertook a greater share of manual work and a correspondingly smaller part in the *opus Dei*. One consequence of their integration into the monastery was a fundamental modification of the traditional monastic plan.[8] For centuries the cloister and church had been the exclusive realm of the monks; now they were shared to some degree with the lay brothers, who were assigned the west ranges of the cloister and the west bays of the nave. Inevitably, the process of reapportioning took time to work out architecturally. The idealism that led to the integration of the largely illiterate lay brothers with the monks partly accounts for the appeal of the Cistercian order: it offered a new vocation and a new status to men who were formerly accorded laborer or servant standing.[9]

---

[5] Eventually, in the seventeenth century, a total of 740 houses was reached. For the numbers and filiations of Cistercian abbeys, see L. Janauschek, *Originum Cisterciensium*, vol. 1 (Vienna, 1877).

[6] The *Carta caritatis* exists in two versions—the *Summa cartae Caritatis* and the *Carta caritatis prior*—both of which are probably amplifications of an earlier text (see J. de la Croix Bouton and J.-B. Van Damme, *Les Plus Anciens Textes de Cîteaux* [Achel, 1974]). For the influence of Stephen's views on art, see A. Dimier, "Saint Etienne Harding et ses idées sur l'art," *COCR* 4 (1937): 178-93.

[7] See Lekai, *The Cistercians*, 22. The same rigor to return

to sources marks Harding's revision of the Bible in 1109, for which he obtained the help of Jewish rabbis, and of the chant for which visits were made to Milan to seek pure texts and melodies of the Ambrosian hymns and to Metz in search of the authentic liturgical chant.

[8] As shown by C. Malone in W. Horn and E. Born, *The Plan of St. Gall*, Berkeley, 1981, vol. 2, 315-56.

[9] Knowles, *Monastic Order*, app. D, 754-55; J. Dubois, "L'Institution des convers au XIIᵉ siècle, forme de vie monastique propre aux laïcs," *I Laici nella "società christiana" de secoli XI e XII* (Milan, 1968); Schneider, *Die Cistercienser*, 46ff.; C. J. Holdsworth, "The Blessings of Work: The Cistercian

Cistercian reform effected far-reaching changes in the details and character of the life of a monk, many of which bore consequences for their architecture. The Rule of Saint Benedict divided the monastic day between the offices (*opus Dei*), spiritual reading (*lectio divina*), and manual work (*opus manuum*). But by the eleventh century this tripartite division had virtually disappeared; Ulrich's description of life at Cluny around 1090 shows that the monks had no time for manual work and only minimal time for reading.[10] Much of their day was devoted to a liturgy that had become progressively richer and more elaborate. Two examples from Cluny illustrate the extent of these accretions: before greater feasts the Night Office had to be started the preceding evening in order to conclude it before daybreak; and as many as 210 Psalms could be said daily, in contrast to their once weekly recital as directed by Saint Benedict.[11] Faced with this dense growth, the Cistercians ruthlessly pruned the monastic timetable. Beginning with the *opus Dei*, they cut all additions with the sole exception of the morning conventual Mass, leaving the offices in the skeletal form ordained by Saint Benedict. At the same time ceremonial was reduced and musical chant simplified. With large parts of the monastic day now freed, manual work and reading could be restored. The routine of Cistercian monks differed from that of the older orders in one other important respect as well; from the beginning, following the Rule of Saint Benedict, the founders provided the opportunity for private prayer.[12] Even during periods set aside for reading, a Cistercian monk was permitted to enter the church for prayer.

To facilitate these reforms, the *Carta Caritatis* provided a model for centralized government that ranks as one of the masterpieces of medieval planning. In an age complicated by labyrinthine systems of authority, the Cistercians created a single, clear line of command. One body of written legislation was made binding on all houses. Relations between houses were organized by a simple arrangement of affiliation. To ensure uniformity in all areas from art and architecture to farming and finances, each abbey was subject to a yearly visitation by the abbot of the founding house (Cîteaux was to be visited by the abbot of one of the other four mother houses). To preserve identity, wide freedom from local authority was insisted upon, underwritten by papal fiat. Finally, to maintain the order's centralized character, all the abbots were required to assemble once a year at Cîteaux to enforce discipline and enact new legislation. So successful was this system of government in practice that a century later, in 1215, the Lateran Council ordered that it be used as the model for the reform of other monastic orders.

It is difficult to grasp today how thoroughly the Cistercian reform changed established monastic practice. Whereas the habits worn by Cluniac monks were black, those of the Cistercians were undyed or white (hence the title, "White Monks"); undershirts and woolen breeches were forbidden, an unheard of austerity in northern climates; diet was strictly vegetarian; silence was enforced.[13] Nothing better illustrates how different the Cistercians were from other orders than the criticisms directed at the practices of the new movement. Around 1127,

View," *Sanctity and Secularity, Studies in Church History* 10 (1973): 59-76. It should be pointed out that despite this democratic character the Cistercians were fundamentally conservative. Bernard himself came from the Burgundian aristocracy and spent much time attracting to the order others from this same class.

[10] On the details of life at Cluny, see D. Knowles, "Cistercians and Cluniacs: The Controversy between St. Bernard and Peter the Venerable," *The Historian and Character* (Cambridge, 1963), 50-75, esp. 52.

[11] See Knowles, *Monastic Order*, 211, and app. 18, 714-15; also L. J. Lekai, *The White Monks* (Okauchee, 1953), 171ff.; and A. A. King, *Liturgies of the Monastic Orders* (London, 1955), 66-72.

[12] See P. Guignard, *Les Monuments primitifs de la règle cistercienne* (Dijon, 1878), 172.

[13] Specified in the *Summa cartae Caritatis*, article 11, and a detail mentioned in 1135 by Orderic Vitalis: ". . . all dispense with breeches and lambskins, abstain from eating fat and flesh-meat . . . maintain silence at all times and wear no dyed garments . . . they toil with their hands and produce their own food and clothing" (see M. Chibnall, ed., *The Ecclesiastical History of Orderic Vitalis, Vol. IV, Books VII and VIII* [Oxford, 1973], 325). The Cistercians were not the first to use undyed or white habits (see G. Constable, *The Letters of Peter the Venerable* 2 [Cambridge, MA, 1967]: 115-16; and J. Leclercq, *Bernard of Clairvaux and the Cistercian Spirit* [Kalamazoo, 1977], 13-14). The symbolism of white, signifying glory, can hardly have endeared the Cistercians to the older orders who adhered to the traditional black habits signifying repentance. At first, Cistercian habits were apparently a grey-brown, but white was established by *circa* 1115.

for instance, the abbot of Cluny, Peter the Venerable, asked how it was possible "for monks fed on poor vegetable diet when even that scanty fare is cut off by fasts to work like common laborers in the burning heat and showers of rain and snow and in the bitter cold? Besides, it is unbecoming that monks which are the fine linen of the sanctuary should be begrimed with dirt and bent down with rustic labors."[14]

A few years later Ailred of Rievaulx described the characteristics of Cistercian monastic life. He has one of his novices in Yorkshire say: "Our food is scanty, our garments rough; our drink is from the stream and our sleep often upon our book. Under our tired limbs there is but a hard mat; when sleep is sweetest, we must rise at bell's bidding. . . . Self-will has no place; there is no moment for idleness or dissipation. . . . Everywhere peace, everywhere serenity, and a marvelous freedom from the tumult of the world."[15] These words reveal one condition of the monk's life: the submission to a routine that both inhibited personal expression and was in many respects anti-intellectual. Around 1130, Bernard wrote to Henry Murdac, then a distinguished teacher in the school of York: "Believe us who have experience, you will find much more laboring amongst woods than ever you will amongst books. Woods and stones will teach you what you can never hear from any master."[16] Such statements reveal the conviction that the monk's quest for spiritual fulfillment and mystical enlightenment was the highest to which man could aspire. Of course, other outlets for expression existed. One uncalculated benefit of the withdrawal of educated men from secular life and occupation

with "rustic labors" such as land clearance, water control, sheep and cattle farming was that they quickly questioned established methods and revolutionized agricultural techniques. Giraldus Cambrensis could write with little exaggeration in the late twelfth century: "Give the Cistercian a wilderness or forest, and in a few years you will find a dignified abbey in the midst of smiling plenty."[17]

In addition to the *Exordium* and *Carta Caritatis*, a third body of documents, the *Statuta*, defined Cistercian life. These were the assembled decisions taken at the annual General Chapters at Cîteaux. Like the other early documents, they developed with the order's progressive experience and were subject to continual augmentation. The various versions of the statutes, with the different dates of enactment and the variation in text, pose historical problems that are still unsolved.[18] A collection of twenty *capitula* appeared in 1119, but the first codification did not occur until 1152.[19] They cover a wide range of issues and are inevitably proscriptive in character. Yet they need to be seen less as repressive measures than as attempts to give workaday form to Cistercian asceticism. They were not intended to be interlocking pieces of an integrated legislative program but *ad hoc* judgments responding to problems as they arose.

Among the first statutes are those concerned with the expansion of the order. Before a new monastery could be established, they ruled the population of the founding house had to reach sixty monks. The process of establishment then began with a general invitation from the patron for the monks to settle on land he provided; only isolated land was acceptable, and a minimum distance of twelve Bur-

[14] Constable, *Letters of Peter the Venerable* 1:52ff.; and on the date, 2:270-74. On the dispute between the two men, see A. H. Bredero, "The Controversy between Peter the Venerable and St. Bernard," in G. Constable and J. Kritzeck, eds., *Petrus Venerabilis, 1156-1956* (Rome, 1956), 53-71; and Knowles, "Cistercians and Cluniacs," 50-75.

[15] *PL* 195:562-63; the translation is Knowles', from *Monastic Order*, 258.

[16] B. S. James, *The Letters of St. Bernard of Clairvaux* (London, 1953), letters 107 and 156.

[17] J. S. Brewer, ed., *Itin. Camb., Rolls Series* 21 (London, 1861): 45.

[18] The statutes were published in nine volumes by the order's appointed editor, J.-M. Canivez, *Statuta capitulorum Generalium Ordinis Cisterciensis ab anno 1116 ad annum 1786. Bibliothèque*

de la Revue ecclésiastique, 9 vols. (Louvain, 1933-1941). Despite its recent date, subsequent research, particularly on the early legislation, has called into question the dates and wording of a number of the twelfth-century statutes. The literature is extensive. See particularly, J. A. Lefèvre, "Pour une nouvelle datation des Instituta Generalis Capituli apud Cistercium," *COCR* 16 (1954): 241-66; J. A. Lefèvre, "Les Codifications cisterciennes aux XIIᵉ et XIIIᵉ siècles d'après la tradition manuscrites," *ASOC* 15 (1959): 3-22; J.-B. van Damme, "Genèse des Instituta Generalis Capituli," *CCC* 12 (1961): 28-60. For a resumé of the more recent position, see Lekai, *The Cistercians*, 21-32, 407.

[19] Critical evaluation of the different versions of the early legislation now shows that the widely cited codification of 1134, published by Canivez, is suspect and probably false.

gundian leagues had to separate a new house from a neighboring one.[20] The approval of the local bishop was then sought, with great stress placed on cordial relations with him, and application for establishment was made to the General Chapter.[21] Prospective sites were next examined, and temporary buildings of wood or wattle and daub raised on the site chosen.[22] Site clearance and the construction of the wooden buildings were usually the responsibility of the founder and took place before the arrival of the founding community, which consisted of an abbot and twelve monks, an apostolic nucleus, and a party of lay brothers.[23] Abbeys were dedicated to the Virgin Mary; and because of their required remoteness, their names were usually drawn from a characteristic of the physical site: in the case of the English foundations, for instance, Forde, Fountains, Rievaulx (*Rie vallis*), and Roche (meaning "rocks"). Other names express the beauty of the place: Beaulieu, Byland (*Bella landa*), Strata Florida (Valley of Flowers). Sometimes the names witness the Cistercian view that the monastery was a foretaste of paradise: Vaudey (*Vallis Dei*), Glenluce (*Vallis lucis*), and Dieulacres (God's Fields); or in France, Clairvaux (*Clara vallis*) and Morimond (*Moriri mondo*).[24]

The picture of a well-ordered, thoughtful preparation that emerges undoubtedly represents an ideal. In reality, of course, new foundations frequently suffered from a lack of foresight. In England, for instance, half of the twelfth-century foundations

had to make at least one move.[25] Kingswood had four false starts; Byland, five. Where accounts survive, the abbot's role in site selection was usually central. At Meaux Abbot Adam single-handedly determined the monastery's location. At Kirkstall, after one failed attempt, it was Abbot Alexander who went out in 1152 in search of new land. Coming to the valley of the Aire, so the abbey's chronicler relates, "he began to ponder in his mind concerning the site of the place and its conditions, the pleasant character of the valley and the river flowing past, and the woods adjacent as being suitable for the erection of workshops. . . . And it seemed to him this place was fair enough and fit for building an abbey upon."[26] This account may, of course, be a truncated version of a more elaborate foundation procedure, and it may have been inserted to promote the abbot's role. But it provides a clue to the persistent failure of early settlements. A single man's judgment could easily err in the assessment of practical difficulties. On occasion a lay brother was charged with site selection. In 1171 land was offered to Buildwas for a new foundation at Dunbrody (Co. Wexford) in Ireland, and Abbot Ranulf dispatched Alan, a trusted lay brother, to assess it. Alan received a poor welcome, however; he was forced to take refuge in a hollow tree and surveyed the lands as quickly as possible. On his return he reported the property barren and the inhabitants barbarous, and the proposed gift was turned down.[27] Examples like these make it easier to see why the

---

[20] *Statuta* 1 (1135:6): 32-33; repeated in 1152 ([1152:1], 45). On the general matter of site selection, see R. A. Donkin, "The Growth and Distribution of the Cistercian Order in Medieval Europe," *Studia Monastica* 9 (1967): 257-86. The composite account of the foundation process given in the text is not arranged chronologically, nor does it consider the subsequent repetitions or augmentations of the statutes on foundation.

[21] The *Exordium* emphasized the need for close cooperation with the diocesan. The abbot of Revesby was censured in 1199 for failing to secure episcopal permission for establishment of a new house at Cleeve (*Statuta* 1 [1199:17]: 235). By the early thirteenth century there are cases where the General Chapter decreed that prospective sites should be examined by two abbots who were then to report back to the next chapter; for instance, see *Statuta* 2 (1226:33): 54.

[22] See P. J. Fergusson, "The First Architecture of the Cistercians in England and the Work of Abbot Adam of Meaux," *Jnl. BAA* 136 (1983), 74-86.

[23] Only the monks are mentioned in the *Exordium*, but the lay brothers can be assumed and are mentioned on occasion. At Sawley in Yorkshire, for instance, William de Percy, the abbey's patron, is credited by the *Chronicle* with building the first wooden architecture. He then summoned the founding community, from the mother house of Newminster, which consisted of the abbot, twelve monks, and ten lay brothers (see catalog).

[24] J. Laurent, "Les Noms des monastères cisterciens," *Association Bourguignonne des sociétés savantes* 1 (1928): 168-204; A. Dimier, *Les Beaux Noms des monastères de Cîteaux en France* (Lyon, 1944); M. Aubert, *L'Architecture cistercienne en France* (Paris, 1947), 1:92-93. For the expansion of the 1119 statute on church dedications in 1151, see Lefèvre, "Pour une nouvelle datation," 260.

[25] R. A. Donkin, "The Site Changes of Medieval Cistercian Monasteries," *Geography* 44 (1959): 251-58.

[26] *Fund. K.*, 176-78.

General Chapter mandated progressively more elaborate procedures for site selection.

Single-handed decisions aside, haste in establishing new abbeys in the order's early years may also account for difficulties being overlooked. Ignorant of local climatic conditions, for instance, the order accepted some sites that proved unsuitable for growing arable crops, a necessity for the vegetarian communities. At Sawley wet and cloudy weather resulted in the harvest repeatedly rotting on the stalk.[28] A similar problem caused the failure of Kirkstall's first settlement, as the *Fundacio* explains: "We remained there [at Barnoldswick] several years, suffering many discomforts of cold and hunger, partly because of the inclemency of the air and the ceaseless trouble of rain; partly because, the kingdom being in turmoil, many a time our possessions were wasted by brigands. The site of our habitations therefore displeased us . . . and through the advice of our patrons we migrated to another place."[29] Questions of subsistence that might be assumed basic were not infrequently overlooked, perhaps as Donkin suggested, out of an excess of asceticism and initial zeal.[30]

In any event, seclusion was easier to legislate than it was to find. Land completely empty of inhabitants was rare, despite the sparse population of twelfth-century England. But where such conditions did not exist, the Cistercians were not above creating them. Deliberate depopulation, or resettlement, became a Cistercian commonplace, a practice succinctly summarized by Walter Map in 1182: "they make a solitude that they may be solitaries."[31] As early as 1142 Revesby reduced three small villages to clear a space; in 1145 Woburn evicted the village of the same name; around 1150 in the Midlands, Combe destroyed Upper Smite, and Garendon wiped out Dishley. And in the north around 1175, Fountains ousted the inhabitants of Thorpe Underwood; Kirkstall, the residents of Accrington; and Rievaulx and Byland conducted similar evictions.[32] As might be imagined, such dispersals engendered fierce resistance; Coggeshall's depopulation of Rumilly involved the Essex abbey in an eight-year lawsuit (1152-1160) that reached the papal court in Rome.[33] Walter Map's attack on the Cistercians, for all its prejudice, contains an element of truth: "How gratefully do they enter on the lands that have been given to them . . . caring not so much how they get them as how they keep them. And because their Rule does not allow them to govern parishioners, they proceed to raze villages and churches, turn out parishioners, destroy the altars of God, not scrupling to sow crops or cast down and level everything before the ploughshare."[34] The heartlessness of such removals was moderated to some extent: at Old Byland the evicted were assigned new land, and a hamlet was built for them; at Rufford the dispossessed were compensated with cash and alternative land.[35]

A second category of statutes refers to liturgical objects and furnishings in the church. Some, such as those specifying what a church could possess, date from the early period and are first embodied in the *Summa cartae Caritatis*, then repeated in the statutes. Sculptures were prohibited (1119); paintings were permitted only on crosses, which in turn, could be made of no other material than wood (1119); altars could not be decorated (1134).[36] In the sanctuary a single candle in an iron candlestick

---

[27] See M. Chibnall, "Buildwas Abbey," *VCH: Shropshire* 2 (London, 1973): 51.

[28] *Chart. S.*, 1.

[29] *Fund. K.*, 176.

[30] R. A. Donkin, "The Cistercian Order and the Settlement of Northern England," *Geographical Review* 59 (1969): 403-16, esp. 406.

[31] For Map, see E. S. Hartland, ed., *Walter Map: De Nugis Curialium*, Cymmrodorion Record Series 9 (1923): 50. On Cistercian depopulation, see R. A. Donkin, "Settlement and Depopulation on Cistercian Estates during the 12th and 13th Centuries," *Bulletin of the Institute of Historical Research* 33 (1960): 141-65; also, C. Platt, *The Monastic Grange in Medieval England: A Reassessment* (New York, 1969), 91-93. The same was

true in France (see C. A. Bruzelius, "Cistercian High Gothic: The Abbey Church of Longpont and the Architecture of the Cistercians in the Early Thirteenth Century," *AC* 35 [1979]: 22).

[32] B. Waites, "The Monastic Grange as a Factor in the Settlement of Northeast Yorkshire," *YAJ* 40 (1959-1962): 627-56, esp. 652.

[33] For the dispute see B. Hill, *English Cistercian Monasteries and their Patrons in the Twelfth Century* (Urbana, 1968), 112.

[34] Hartland, ed., *Walter Map*, 49.

[35] M. W. Barley, "Cistercian Land Clearances in Nottinghamshire," *Nottingham Medieval Studies* 1 (1957): 75-89.

[36] *PL* 166, *Exordium*, cap. 17, col. 1509; and in *Statuta* 1 (1134:xx): 17; and (1134:x): 15. For a recent survey of the

was permitted (1119), except on special festivals when three were allowed (1195).[37] Relics could be placed on the altar, but it was forbidden to light candles before them (1185).[38] On the feast day of a saint, however, a lamp (not candles) might burn during the night before his altar (1189); in the church a lamp could burn continuously (1152).[39] Burial within the church was allowed only for kings and queens, for bishops and archbishops (1152), and for lay founders (1157).[40] Stained-glass windows of more than two colors were prohibited, as were painted images on them (1134, 1159, 1182); and the doors of the churches had to be painted white.[41] For the Mass, chalices could be of silver, or silver gilt, but not of gold (1119); censors had to be of iron or copper only (1119); vestments were limited in type and had to avoid rich decoration (1119).[42] Liturgical and other manuscripts were to be written in ink of one color and without historiated initials (1151).[43] Such proscriptions confined choice in the area of decoration, not architectural style, but they defined the internal appearance of the building and limited its embellishment.

The effective manner in which the statutes controlled the possessions of a monastic house is revealed by a curious episode at Kirkham in Yorkshire. A foundation of Augustinian canons established in the mid-1120s, Kirkham underwent a crisis some years later when a faction within the community

opted to join the Cistercians. The split was eventually avoided, and Kirkham remained Augustinian, but matters had gone far enough for an agreement to be drawn up dividing the house's goods and chattels. The Augustinians were to move out, to a new location at Linton, and were to take with them all movables: crosses, chalices, books, vestments, and all domestic utensils. The stained-glass windows were to be removed and replaced by windows of clear glass, and the departing monks were to leave at Kirkham one bell, whichever they pleased.[44]

Surprisingly few statutes refer directly to architecture. As already seen, the *Summa cartae Caritatis* (c. 1119) specifies the earliest wooden buildings that were to be provided before the site was occupied by the founding monks. But the statutes are mute about architectural practice after colonization, although tangentially they mention building labor. This was provided by a mixed work force from the early years forward. On the one hand, the monks and lay brothers worked on construction, a feature singled out for praise by the Norman historian, Ordericus Vitalis, in the mid-1130s;[45] transfer of such work crews within the monasteries of the order was permitted. But outside labor was also hired in. The needs of these workers are mentioned several times in the *Summa cartae Caritatis* and the *Exordium Parvum*, and later statutes in the 1130s

problems relating to the artistic statutes, see P. Policarpo Zakar, "La Legislazione Cistercense e le sue fonti dalle origini fino al 1265," in *I Cistercensi e il Lazio: Atti delle giornate di studio dell'Università di Roma, 17-21 Maggio 1977* (Rome, 1978), 127-34.

[37] *PL* 166, *Exordium*, cap. 17, col. 1509; and *Statuta* 1 (1195:25): 186. The *Consuetudines* speak of two candles, one on either side of the altar (see A.R.P.H. Séjalon, ed., *Nomasticon Cisterciense* [Solesmes, 1892], 125). According to King, *Liturgies of the Monastic Orders*, 120, the candle was not permitted to be placed on the altar in Cistercian churches until the thirteenth century and remained beside the altar in an iron candleholder. It was only in the sixteenth century that the custom of placing candles on the altar became universal.

[38] *Statuta* 1 (1185:4): 98.

[39] Ibid. (1189:12), 112; and (1152:5), 46.

[40] Ibid. (1152:10), 47; and (1157:63), 68. The statute was repeated in 1180 (1180:5), 87, at the same time assigning the chapter house as the appropriate burial ground for abbots. The lay founder provision was extended in 1322 to anyone who contributed to the construction of the church, ibid. 3 (1322:3):

358).

[41] Ibid. 1 (1134:lxxx): 31; (1159:9), 70; (1182:11), 91. For the doors, ibid. (1157:12), 61.

[42] *PL* 166, *Exordium*, cap. 17, col. 1509. On rare occasions, compromises resulted from the insistence of a donor and the fear of offense in the refusal of a gift. At Mellifont in Ireland in 1157, for instance, Devorgilla, wife of Tighernan O'Rourke, gave a chalice of gold for the high altar, together with costly furniture for nine other altars (see M. Archdall, *Monasticon Hibernicum* [London, 1786], 479). For the censors and vestments see *PL* 166, *Exordium*, cap. 17, col. 1509.

[43] *Statuta* 1 (1134:lxxx): 31. Neil Stratford has recently shown the date to be 1151 (see N. Stratford, "A Romanesque Marble Altar-Frontal in Beaune and some Cîteaux Manuscripts," in A. Borg and A. Martindale, eds., *The Vanishing Past: Studies for Christopher Hohler* [Oxford, 1981], 223-39, esp. 227).

[44] *Chart. R.*, 108.

[45] "They have built monasteries with their own hands in lonely, wooded places . . ." (Chibnall, ed., *Ecclesiastical History*, 327).

and 1150s regulate their diet, apparel, and attendance at certain offices.[46]

The only statute addressed directly to architecture was enacted in 1157 and forbade the construction of towers.[47] Why towers alone among all the elements of architecture were singled out for prohibition will be discussed in chapter 3; but the uniqueness of this statute does not signify the order's indifference to architecture. The prohibition suggests only that towers became a specific issue of disagreement in the late 1150s and so required discussion in the General Chapter. A related statute passed in the same year limited an abbey to two bells, directed that their weight not exceed five hundred pounds so that one person might ring them and ordered that they be rung only separately.[48]

But if statutes were not the means of formulating ideas on architecture, what was? No other written sources are known, although the similarities among Cistercian buildings strongly suggests their existence at one time. Lacking them, certain general, and some more well-defined ideas can be gleaned from sermons and other treatises.[49] Because the Cistercian reform was based largely on a return to the Rule of Saint Benedict, the Rule's references to building, brief as they are, exerted a profound influence. In chapter 52 Benedict says of the church: "Let the Oratory be what its name implies, and let nothing else be done or kept there"; and in chapter 4 he describes the monastery as a "workshop for the art of holiness."[50] Both images are utilitarian, and both underlie the section in the *Exordium* on

the church: "In the House of God, in which by day and by night they desired to offer devout service to God, nothing should be left that savored of pride or the superfluous, or such as could at any time corrupt the poverty, guardian of virtues, that they had voluntarily chosen for themselves."[51] The key phrase ("quod superbiam aut superfluitatem redoleret") is general, but its recurrence in Cistercian writing of the period suggests that it carried an explicit meaning that, although it may not have taken an extended critical or analytical form, was nevertheless widely understood.

As architectural concepts, the absence of pride and the avoidance of the superfluous require elaboration. On the simplest level they reveal the order's insistence on poverty in their building. But they also speak to the Cistercians' obsession with disengagement from the world of the senses as the primary way of reaching spiritual enlightenment. Divine contemplation could be achieved only through an environment with minimal sensory stimulus. William of St. Thierry wrote: "For what is within us is benefited in no slight degree by what is around us, when it is arranged to accord with our minds and in its own way to correspond with the ideas we have set before us . . . a spirit that is intent on interior things is better served by an absence of decoration and trimming in the things around it."[52] Similarly, the sermons and letters of Saint Bernard make frequent reference to the need for a neutral ambiance to aid in sensory disengagement.[53]

As has been often remarked, Bernard himself had a highly sensitive eye and wrote with a passionate

---

[46] *Statuta* I (1134:xxiv): 18; and (1157:56), 67; and (1157:47), 66.

[47] Ibid. (1157:16), 61.

[48] Ibid. (1157:21), 62.

[49] The most convincing attempts to define the spiritual ideals embodied in Cistercian architecture are F. Bucher, "Le Fonctionalisme de Saint Bernard et les églises cisterciennes Suisses," *Actes du XIXᵉ congrès international d'histoire de l'art* (1958), 49-56; and F. Bucher, "Cistercian Architectural Purism," *Comparative Studies in Art and Literature* 3 (1960): 98-105.

[50] "Oratorium hoc sit quod dicitur, nec ibi quiquam aliud geratur aut condatur" (J. McCann, ed., *The Rule of Saint Benedict* [London, 1952], 118). The connections with the Rule of Saint Benedict are discussed by A. Dimier in "Architecture et spiritualité cisterciennes," *Revue du Moyen Age Latin* 3 (1947): 255-74; see also A. Dimier, "La Règle de Saint Benoit et le

dépouillement architectural des Cisterciens," *L'Architecture monastique, Numéro spécial du Bulletin des relations artistiques France-Allemagne* (1951), no page numbers.

[51] "Ne quid in domo Dei in qua die ac nocte Deo servire devote cupiebant remaneret quod superbiam aut superfluitatem redoleret, aut pauperatem virtutum custodem, quam sponte elegerant, aliqundo corrumperet" (*PL* 166, *Exordium*, cap. 17, col. 1509). The condemnation quickly spawned a wider literature (see V. Mortet, "Hugue de Fouilloi, Pierre Le Chantre, Alexandre Neckam, et les critiques dirigées au douzième siècle contre le luxe des constructions," *Mélanges Bémont* [Paris, 1913], 105-37).

[52] *The Golden Epistle of William of St. Thierry, Cistercian Fathers Series* 12 (Kalamazoo, 1971): 61.

[53] For instance, his address to postulants at Clairvaux (see *PL* 185, col. 238).

intensity. These qualities inform much of his *Apologia*, written in the mid-1120s. Its importance as a primary source on a wide range of Cistercian attitudes and practices make the circumstances that led to the document's appearance important to consider. Around 1124 the supporters of Saint Bernard had attacked monastic practices at Cluny, drawing a dignified rebuke from its newly elected abbot, Peter the Venerable, who had come to office following the damaging rule of Abbot Pons de Melgueil (1109-1122). It was to this rebuke that the *Apologia* was directed, although shrewdly, Bernard sent it not to Cluny, where it risked suppression, but to his friend William, then abbot of St. Thierry, a Benedictine house in the diocese of Reims. Complicating the document's interpretation is the satiric literary form in which Bernard composed it and its partly composite character.[54] The brief sections that deal with architecture clearly refer to monastic churches; although Bernard names no specific abbey, his criticism was most likely directed to the large third church at Cluny, completed a decade earlier, and to other Cluniac churches. He writes "of the immense height of the churches, their immoderate length, their superfluous breadth, costly polishing and strange designs that, while they attract the eye of the worshiper, hinder his attention,"[55] and attacks the interiors in which he says are suspended "not coronae but wheels studded with gems and surrounded by lights . . . and instead of candlesticks . . . great trees of brass, fashioned with wonderful skill and glittering as much through their jewels as their lights." Whether these passages should be viewed as "straight" criticism or satire is open to question; if the former, it would be plausible to read them as implicitly advocating certain architectural values and, consequently, having

a direct programmatic content. It is significant that before they were written, the *Exordium* condemned the superfluous in architecture,[56] and that following their appearance, other Cistercian writers began to voice similar views. For instance, Ailred exhorts his novices at Rievaulx to avoid an architecture that is large or extravagantly vaulted and urges them to be happy "to say their prayers in a little chapel of rough unpolished stone where there is nothing carved or painted to distract the eye."[57] Bernard's words on architecture in the *Apologia* may thus be seen as representative of attitudes widely held within the order.

It is easy to forget that when Bernard formulated the *Apologia*'s sections on architecture, the Cistercians had no large-scale architecture of their own. In fact, it would be nearly a decade before they embarked on their own great building programs (around 1135 in the case of Clairvaux). Thus Bernard's strictures were made in the context of what the order's architecture was in the mid-1120s, namely, deliberately small-scale and austere, rather than what it would become in the mid-1130s.

The artistic sections of the *Apologia* were written by a monk for fellow monks and clearly imply the notion of a monastic style. Bernard concedes that in nonmonastic churches like cathedrals it is necessary to cater to the needs of the laity, to rouse their devotion through ornamentation, scale, and the like; for monks, however, such devices would be incompatible with the ideals of humility, with their spiritual education, as Bernard defined it. What had to be avoided was distraction, the *curiositas* that Bernard identified as leading to pride, "the restless intrusion of sensible images" mentioned in a number of his sermons. An ideal architecture for monks, then, would be an architecture in which these qual-

[54] For the *Apologia* and Leclercq's introduction, see M. Casey, trans., *The Works of Bernard of Clairvaux, Treatises I, Cistercian Fathers Series* 1 (Spencer, MA, 1970). For the date I depend on Constable, *Letters of Peter the Venerable* 2:272-73. For the circumstances of the *Apologia*, see A. H. Bredero, "Cluny et Cîteaux au XIIᵉ siècle: les origines de la controverse," *Studi Medievale* 12, 3rd ser. (1971), 135-75; and H.-B. de Warren, "Bernard et les premiers Cisterciens face au problème de l'art," in *Bernard de Clairvaux, Commission d'histoire de l'ordre de Cîteaux* 3 (Paris, 1953): 487-534.

[55] "Omitto oratoriorum immensas altitudines, immoderatas longitudines supervacuas latitudines, sumptuosas depolitiones,

curiosas depictiones: quae dum orantium in se retorquent aspectum, impediunt et affectum . . ." (*PL* 172, cap. 17, no. 28, col. 914). Many of the widely used English translations of the art sections of the *Apologia* are flawed, including that in the Cistercian Fathers Series.

[56] On the other legislation relating to art, and dating from 1119, see van Damme, "Genèse des Instituta Generalis Capituli," 36-41.

[57] *PL* 195, cols. 572-74. The translation of the *Speculum caritatis* is from G. Webb and A. Walker, *The Mirror of Charity* (London, 1962), 75.

ities had been expunged, an architecture that was neutral and simple. Unlike the interior of secular churches, therefore, the Cistercian interior was to be devoid of color—in glass, on wall surfaces, as highlights on sculpture, or as part of the sumptuary arts.

From the perspective of such Cistercian ideals, it is easy to see why the architecture, wall painting, and sculpture of the older orders was viewed as confusing, intrusive, or "superfluous." The absence of color for the Cistercian, or more accurately the predominance of white, evident in the habits worn by the monks, in the clear window glass, in the color of doors, suggests a distinct iconography of light. The relationship of light to architecture, specifically the way it conditioned a new luminous and spatial quality in the buildings, became in fact one of the most prominent features of the Cistercians' churches. Clear, white light complemented the simple forms and fine proportions of the buildings to produce interiors of coolness, quiet, and serenity. Ideals of peacefulness occur frequently in Cistercian writing, suggesting the ambiance toward which art and architecture should aim. The English-born Isaac, abbot of L'Etoile (Vienne), for instance, wrote: "How ever many we are, brought together in the one, at one in the one, made simple by that which is simple, let us, whenever we may, be still with that which is still, sleeping in stillness and resting in it, resting in peace."[58]

Translating purist ideals into physical form was a complicated matter, however. As the years passed, criticism of inappropriate forms turned out to be easier than the creation of appropriate ones. What little is known about the earliest churches, like Cîteaux and Clairvaux, indicates that a wide variety of buildings was used, though they all appear to have been small and severely plain.[59] Such an architecture was possible, however, only while communities remained small, perhaps a maximum of fifty or so men. But around 1130 the pressure of increasing numbers wishing to join the order became so great that an alternative to the endless establishment of small communities had to be found. So the size of existing houses was expanded instead.

With this decision began the second generation of the order's architecture. The change did not occur lightly, however. At Clairvaux, for instance, while Bernard was away in Rome in 1135, Prior Godefroid worked out a more spacious plan for the monastery on a nearby site; when Bernard returned, so the *Vita Prima* relates, he objected to the change, and it was only after long discussion that he was reluctantly won around to the idea (appendix B).

The increase in the size of the communities and the scale of the buildings was accompanied by more rigorous control of architectural design. In place of the loosely defined and often quite idiosyncratic form of the early buildings, standardization emerged in the 1130s, at least in the most influential and dominant filiation, that of Clairvaux. Esser in the early 1950s coined the term "Bernardine" to describe this new style in Cistercian architecture. Although some aspects of this new organizing concept need qualification—such as the degree to which practice was uniform, the precise role of Clairvaux in the development of the type, and the suitability of using Bernard's name to describe it in the light of his grudging support for the changes—there can be no question that the ideas were influential. With or without Bernard's direct backing, the formation of this new, impressive architecture coincided with the height of the saint's ambitions to build the order into a position of authority in European affairs; and it undoubtedly reflected this vision. Like the Franciscans a century later, however, the corporate ambitions and sense of identity of the Cistercians may have surpassed the personal views of its most powerful single figure.

Not surprisingly, the decision to expand severely strained the architectural ideals of the order. How was one to form an architecture that was both large-scale and at the same time devoid of strong expressive qualities? The Cistercians solved this problem by radically simplifying large-scale contemporary architecture, and because it was in Burgundy that the order originated, it was Burgundian Romanesque that was simplified. In many ways the process paralleled that employed earlier to free the liturgy from its accretions. Beginning with the typ-

[58] For sermon 21, see A. Hoste, G. Raciti, and G. Salet, *Isaac de l'Étoile, Sermons*, in *Sources chrétiennes*, vol. 130 (Paris, 1967); and vol. 207 (Paris, 1974).

[59] See J. O. Schaefer, "The Earliest Churches of the Cistercian Order," *Studies in Cistercian Art and Architecture* 1 (1982): 1-12.

ical Romanesque plan, the order eliminated as superfluous features that failed to reflect its simplified liturgy. Accordingly, the most radical changes occurred in the east end of the church. Cistercian planners, freed from the need to incorporate processional paths, relic space or the architectural iconography associated with them, clustered chapels around the transepts rather than the chevet as in traditional monastic architecture. The extent of Cistercian reductionism is indicated by the contrast between a developed Cluniac east end—multileveled, richly articulated, elaborately lighted, many towered—and a Cistercian one—rectangular, confined, small, plain. The Cistercian elevation shows a similar reduction to the simplest components of arcade and vault. Sparely lit from clear, unpainted windows in the terminal walls and aisles, with the walls and piers left clean and bare, the church stood in stark opposition to Cluniac interiors with their architectonic sculpture, figural decoration, mural painting, stained glass, rich fittings and furnishings—the "resplendence" denounced by Bernard.

But particularly in these early buildings there existed the roots of a conflict, which like the one surrounding material possessions, was ultimately to resist resolution. Decoration could be purged, furnishings minimized, figured sculpture and painted glass forbidden; but the problem remained of finding a suitably neutral, nonobtrusive architecture. Even an architecture employing minimal elements was still an architecture of wide range; it could essay to an elegance of proportion, a dignity in the shaping of space, a strength and lucidity in the manipulation of mass, all of which produced powerfully expressive effects and endowed a building with distinct individuality. The dilemma was sensed by Martène, the eighteenth-century antiquary, on a visit to Clairvaux, when he wrote of the church: "Elle est grande, spacieuse et belle, mais simple et sans beaucoup d'ornaments. . . . La nef est suivie du choeur des infirmes, et celui-ci du choeur des

religieux qui n'a rien que de simple, mais c'est un simplicité qui a quelque chose de grand."[60] But if individualism cannot be overlooked, neither should it be overemphasized. These churches, particularly the "Bernardine" group, bore distinguishable qualities of plan, structure, and effects that appeared in buildings over a vast region of Europe where architecture was marked by tenacious local traditions. Conformity to a Cistercian form was of course present from the order's early years, though then it was primarily a matter of small scale and humble materials. Now, as part of an important shift in identity, the dictates became more elaborate.

This architecture was not static, however, any more than was the identity that it reflected. A new architectural style appeared in the years following Bernard's death in 1153, with Early Gothic replacing Romanesque. Monasteries located in the most advanced architectural centers of France were the first affected.

The decades of the 1150s and 1160s are among the most critical in the Cistercians' history. All periods of transition invariably give rise to factions either championing innovation or defending tradition, and for the Cistercians the spate of statutes addressed to decoration and architecture in these years seem witness to such conflict and debate, despite the dry language of their formulation. In 1152 the establishment of new foundations was checked by a temporary moratorium; in the same year statutes on furnishings were repeated, but in a fuller and more augmented form, as if it were necessary to justify them; in 1157 the General Chapter regulated towers, doors, and bells; and in 1159 decrees were issued on stained glass.[61]

The transformation of Cistercian architecture after mid-century can be accounted for by factors aside from style, however, among them, changes in liturgical practice and the composition of the monk population.[62] In the early communities the proportion of monk priests was smaller than it became

---

[60] E. Martène and U. Durand, *Voyage littéraire de deux religieux bénédictins de la Congregation de Saint-Maur*, vol. 1, pt. 1 (Paris, 1717): 99.

[61] For the moratorium, see *Statuta* 1 (1152:1): 45; for the other statutes, see text above. For the augmentation, see J. A. Lefèvre, "Pour une nouvelle datation," 241-66.

[62] For the increase in priest monks, see B. Lucet, "Les Or-

dinations chez les cisterciens," *ASOC* 10 (1954): 268-301. The situation is unclear, however. At Fountains, of the thirteen original monks, twelve were priests and one a subdeacon. Moreover, the year following the foundation, the community was joined by seven more clerics. At Pontigny in 1157, fifty of the one hundred monks recorded there were priests (see Aubert, *L'Architecture cistercienne en France* 1:54).

later when their growing needs for altars led to the gradual redesign of the east parts of the church.[63] A firm correlation of monk priests to the number of altars is not yet possible for the statutes are vague on the point; late in the twelfth century choir monks were to receive Holy Communion on Sunday if they had not said Mass during the week or on feast days.[64] Daily Masses for monk priests do not seem to have been customary, though this was the practice of Bernard until his last illness. In 1202 the General Chapter reprimanded the abbots of Aberconway, Valle Crucis, and Llantarnam for very seldom celebrating Mass, which probably meant less often than once weekly; the *Chronicon* of Louth Park records the granting of a license in 1209 to all conventual clergy in England to celebrate once a week.[65] Yet the shortage of altars was acute, and it is specified as one of the reasons for the construction of the new choir at Fountains beginning in 1204.

The reiteration of earlier proscriptive statutes and the enactment of new ones during the last third of the twelfth century suggests a persistent unease concerning architecture as the Cistercians attempted to reconcile the founders' intentions with the developments coincident with Early Gothic. In 1182 a statute directed that painted windows had to be removed within two years.[66] In the same year abbeys with debts over fifty marks were prohibited from buying land or erecting new buildings, except where necessity obliged and then only with the consent of the mother house; the statute was reaffirmed in 1188, and in 1190, and again in 1191.[67] Opposition to this statute can be detected, however, in attempts to weaken it in decrees of 1191 and 1192.[68] In 1199 the statute condemning altar decoration and elaborate liturgical vestments was repeated.[69] Statutes against sumptuous decoration were reaffirmed in the early years of the thirteenth century. And later in 1263 the abbot and prior at Royaumont were punished for allowing in the church "picturas, imagines, et sculpturas, cortinas, columnas cum angelis circa maius altare" and were ordered to return the interior to the "humilitatem et simplicitatem antiquam ordinis."[70]

By the early 1190s then, violations of accepted building practice were increasing. In 1192 the General Chapter ordered modification of the dormitory at Longpont within three years because it violated "the form" of the order.[71] The same year no less a figure than the abbot of Clairvaux, Garnier de Rochefort, was called to task for neglecting his responsibility as the visitor to Vaucelles (Nord), and allowing, in the words of the General Chapter, "certain extravagancies there he did not correct, in particular the building of a church that is too costly and superfluous and shocked many."[72] For this omission Rochfort was punished and ordered to

[63] *Statuta* 1 (1134:12): 33. It is not clear what sources Martène used when he recorded the tradition at Clairvaux that an altar could be used only once a day (Martène and Durand, *Voyage littéraire*, vol. 1, pt. 1, p. 86).

[64] *Vita Prima*, lib. 5, cap. 1. In the order's early years there was apparently no rule that a priest monk must celebrate Mass daily (see *Consuetudines*, cap. 66, J.-M. Canivez, "Le Rite cistercien," *Ephermerides Liturgicae* 63 [1949]: 276-311).

[65] *Statuta* 1 (1202:35): 281. For Louth Park see *Chron. LP*, 10-11. Later in the fourteenth century a statute required priests to celebrate once a week as a minimum, *Statuta* 3 (1328:9): 379.

[66] *Statuta* 1 (1182:11): 91.

[67] Ibid. (1182:9): 90-91; (1188:10), 109; (1190:1), 117-18; (1192:4), 147. On the General Chapter's activities in the late twelfth century, see Knowles, *Monastic Order*, 654-61.

[68] A. Dimier, *Recueil de plans d'églises cisterciennes*, 2 vols. (Paris, 1949), 40. For the statutes, see *Statuta* 1 (1191:90): 14; (1192:4), 147. The latter is worth quoting: "The opinion that it should be built in this style was qualified by the evidence of their officials and of the father abbot or visitor as to how

they could settle the debt and by which means it would be possible to raise for one the funds required to build all, and so build without disregarding the opinion expressed in favor of not building. In the same way abbots to whom the freehold of any piece of land is adjudged by law to belong, may without penalty collect the revenues of the property in respect of non-purchase."

[69] *Statuta* 1 (1199:5): 233.

[70] For Royaumont, see ibid. 3 (1263:9): 11. An earlier statute, dated 1231, talks of infringements, ". . . quae deformant antiquam Ordinis honestatem . . ." (ibid. 2 [1231:8]: 93).

[71] Ibid. 1 (1192:23): 150.

[72] Ibid. (1192:31), 151-52: ". . . quosdam excessus ibi non correxit et praecipue aedificium ecclesiae quod sumptuosum nimis est et superfluum, et multos scandalizavit. . . ." Little is known about Vaucelles, but as the church had only been started two years earlier, objection probably centered on its size; at 132 meters it was the order's largest twelfth-century church (see F. Baron, "Histoire architecturale de l'abbaye de Vaucelles," *CN* 9 [1958]: 276-88).

return to Vaucelles accompanied by the abbots of Foigny and Ourscamp to suppress all "that did not conform to the simplicity of the order." Similar abuses occurred in England. An 1197 statute suggests certain architectural irregularities in three English houses: "Concerning the abbey that the abbot of Revesby wants to build, on account of the trouble with the abbeys of Netley and Forde, it is entrusted to the abbots from Rufford and Byland, so that they can go to the place and learn if it can and ought to stand according to what they hear from either side."[73] Somewhat earlier another abuse can be assumed, although it did not reach the General Chapter; at Meaux the first stone church, built *circa* 1165-1185, was torn down by abbot Thomas (1182-1197), the reason given in the *Chronicle* being that "it had been arranged and constructed less appropriately than was proper."[74]

Cases like these raise issues about the actual process of monitoring, about how violations came to the notice of the General Chapter, and about the role of the abbot of the house vis-à-vis that of the abbot charged with visitation. Presumably, denunciation at the General Chapter occurred when an abbot other than the regular visitor heard about architectural violations or witnessed them in the course of a visit. It is unclear, however, why at Vaucelles it was the visitor who was held responsible for the violations and at Longpont, the resident abbot.

Because architecture makes such a public declaration of institutional identity it is not difficult to grasp why the Cistercians were anxious about their buildings as the twelfth century drew to a close. Some, such as Pierre le Chantre in 1191, saw a solution in a return to Bernard's views on architecture.[75] Others resorted to the occult for answers. In one bizarre episode the abbot of Cîteaux traveled

to consult a famous female mystic, possibly Hildegarde of Bingen, to learn what in the order was most opposed to the purity of religious life. After much delay and prayer, she replied that three things particularly offended God: the immense extent of the order's estates, the vanity of their buildings, and the mannered chant.[76] That it was necessary to go outside the order to have this pointed out would have shaken the Cistercians' founders. But by the late twelfth century, under the pressure of adjusting to new forms and styles, confusion and uncertainty existed at the top levels of the order. What had been for Stephen Harding, or Bernard, or Ailred the ready object of attack and ridicule, now became the anxious subject of introspective questioning and statutory assertion.

While the Cistercian monks in England adhered to the legislative changes and shared the general shifts of attitude within the order, they were nonetheless exposed to a number of distinctive historical conditions that exercised an important influence on their architecture. A survey of these conditions throws light on the sequence of foundation, the location of houses, patronage, and ties of filiation.

Cistercian colonization in England followed a chronology unlike that in other countries. Of the fifty twelfth-century monasteries (out of an eventual sixty-four established in England), all but five were founded by 1154 (fig. 1).[77] From the first settlement at Waverley in 1128 until the death of Henry I in 1135, only five houses were established. Then a dramatic expansion in the nineteen years of Stephen's reign (1135-1154) brought the number of Cistercian abbeys from five to thirty-two, or forty-five when the monasteries belonging to the Congregation of Savigny, which joined the Cistercians in 1147/1148, are included. By contrast, in the

---

[73] "De abbatia quam aedificare vult abbas de Revesbi, in gravamen abbatiarum de Net et de Fordis, committitur abbatibus de Ruffort, et de Bealanda, ut ad locum accedant et cognoscant si stare possit et debeat secundum quod audierint ex utraque parte" (*Statuta* 1 [1197:35]: 217). The inclusion of Netley is puzzling since the date of foundation is usually given as 1239 (see D. Knowles and R. N. Hadcock, *Medieval Religious Houses: England and Wales*, 2d ed. [London, 1971], 122).

[74] See catalog under Meaux.

[75] Mortet, *Recueil de textes* 2:157. Pierre was an important

theologian and cantor at Notre Dame. In 1197 he joined the Cistercians at Longpont.

[76] Quoted by Dimier, *Recueil*, 40 and n. 59, on the identity of the saint.

[77] On the details of the foundations, see Knowles and Hadcock, *Medieval Religious Houses*. Seen in the context of the order's total development, the English houses accounted for 9.4 percent of the twelfth-century foundations (fifty of 525), but 13 percent of the expansion to Bernard's death in 1153 (forty-five of 345).

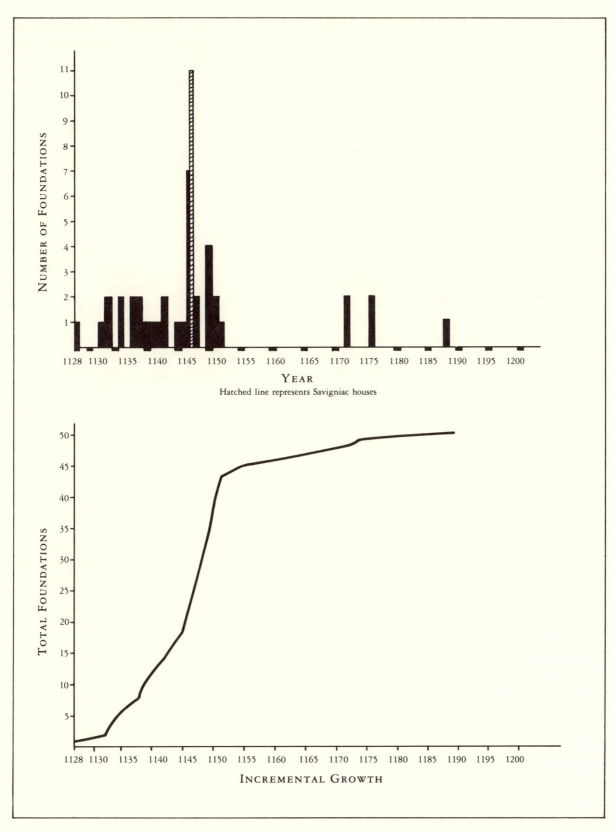

1. Charts of growth for twelfth-century Cistercian houses in England.

next thirty-five years, those of Henry II's reign (1154-1189), only four new foundations were established, and under Richard I (1189-1199), only one. Estimates of the order's manpower in this period suggest an expansion from around four hundred monks and lay brothers in 1135 to around six thousand by the century's end.[78]

The spectacular growth of the Cistercians under Stephen had little to do with support from the king himself, who patronized the Norman-based Savigniacs, but much to do with the political and social chaos of his reign. To strengthen his erratic authority, Stephen was forced to devolve power through the creation of new earldoms, the number growing from six at the start of his reign to twenty-two at its end.[79] In a sequence characteristic of the loss of central authority, these earls set about increasing their personal power at the expense of the crown's: in military matters they embarked on the construction of private castles; in religious ones, for reasons that were only partly spiritual, they patronized the new reform orders.

The new earls were connected by family ties that often meant a tradition of support for certain orders over others. B. Hill has shown how two families played the major role in the establishment of the Cistercians' largest geographical group in England, the abbeys in the Midlands. Dominating the first of these families was Ranulf de Gernons, earl of Chester, who controlled more land than anyone in England except the king. Ranulf was the Cistercians' most prolific patron, founding five monasteries and helping endow six others. With his brother's two foundations and four endowments, the family had a hand in promoting seventeen Cistercian monasteries. Bordering their lands were those of the second great family to patronize the White Monks, the de Beaumonts, whose sons, the earl of Leicester and the earl of Worcester, promoted another eight houses. These two families thus played a direct role in the patronage of twenty-five of the thirty-two Cistercian houses founded by 1154.

It was patronage rather than the availability of land that determined the settlement of monasteries, although the latter controlled a new monastery's growth. Viewed in retrospect, there were relatively few geographical areas of England where the Cistercians could not have settled, but without patrons to sponsor them, they were unable to do so. Southwest England, for instance, was well suited to the order's needs as thirteenth-century foundations show, but patrons here in the twelfth century were lacking, for reasons that are still unclear, and except for Buckfast and Cleeve, the area remained closed to the White Monks.

Patrons were motivated to establish monastic communities in part by piety, of course, although as already mentioned, other factors played their part. Politically, the relationship established between the feudal earls and the monks resulted in alliances that owed nothing to the king. As an order with an overtly international character, the Cistercians provided patrons with a direct line to the center of European power, at Rome or Clairvaux. The monks, for their part, when they needed support or more rarely defense in local disputes, naturally turned to their patron or his family. This interdependent character can still be grasped in its architectural guise at Rievaulx. The first Cistercian outpost in the north, Rievaulx had been established by a prominent border baron, Walter Espec. Secluded in its deep valley, the abbey nevertheless lay only two miles from the protection of Espec's great stone castle at Helmsley. Similarly, at Newminster the new abbey was built close to the castle of the monks' patron, Ranulph de Merlay; at Vaudey, near Bytham Castle; and at Sawley, near Clitheroe Castle. For a baron, then, a local foundation brought prestige and good connections, for the monastery, a strong patron assured protection against local disturbances.

Other benefits to the patron in having the White Monks as neighbors were more constant and more tangible. With the superior agricultural skills, knowledge of sheep and cattle rearing, experience in land clearance and drainage, the Cistercians offered patrons the chance to learn new techniques at little or no cost. Underscoring these advantages was the cheapness of establishing a Cistercian foundation, at least compared with other orders.[80] Since

---

[78] See J. C. Russell, "The Clerical Population of Medieval England," *Traditio* 2 (1944): 177-212, esp. 194-96.

[79] For the sections that follow on patronage I have drawn heavily on Hills' *English Cistercian Monasteries.*

[80] Knowles, *Monastic Order*, 246-47.

the General Chapter statutes required that houses be located in secluded areas, a patron rarely had to part with rich, developed estates. Moreover, the monks were forbidden to accept endowments of manors, tithes, and the like, and they were bound to a life of self-sufficiency, both of which absolved a patron from providing income-producing assets. Compared with a founder's responsibilities for a Benedictine or Cluniac house, which included land near populated centers, a running economy with endowed properties, and a physical establishment complete with buildings, the Cistercians' needs were extraordinarily modest. Yet even so, founders of the order's monasteries in England more often than not disposed of land parsimoniously; the monks got only the least productive or least valuable land, and in tightfisted amounts.

On occasion it is possible to follow this process in some detail. The most colorful example concerns Meaux in southeast Yorkshire, although there, ironically, the patron's grudging intention was turned against him.[81] The benefactor of Meaux was William "le Gros," count of Aumale and earl of York. As a young man he had vowed to go on pilgrimage to the Holy Land, but as the years passed and he grew increasingly fat, he sought release from his vow. Earlier he had founded St. Martin near Aumale (Cluniac), Thornton on the Humber (Augustinian), and Vaudey in Lincolnshire (Cistercian). William established Vaudey with a modest gift that soon left the community in straightened circumstances. To construct its buildings, the count employed Adam, a monk at Fountains, who already had experience in the layout and design of Cistercian abbeys at Kirkstead and Woburn. On a visit to his new foundation in 1149 the count's unease about the unfulfilled vow was detected by Adam, who shrewdly suggested a new Cistercian monastery as a means of securing its release. Bernard's aid at Clairvaux was sought, and through him the pope, Eugenius III, who had started his religious life at Clairvaux, agreed to the dispensation. The count was delighted by the news and invited Adam to select a site from his holdings for the new abbey. Coming to land a few miles east of Beverley, Adam noticed a location described later in the Meaux

Chronicle as "well planted with woods and orchards, surrounded with rivers and waters and favored with rich soil." This hardly matched the Exordium's site requirements that a new house be established in "locus horroris," but Adam struck his staff into the ground and declared: "Let this place be called a palace of the eternal king, a vineyard of heaven, and a gate of life." The count on learning of Adam's choice became greatly agitated, for only a few days earlier he had acquired the land at large expense as a hunting park for himself and had already begun to enclose its west side with a bank and ditch. Despite pressures and pleadings to find another location, Adam remained unmoved, and the count, realizing he had been outwitted, handed over the land.

In the years after the mid-twelfth century a significant shift in the patronage of the Cistercian houses occurred, with important implications for the architectural scale of new foundations. With Henry II's accession, the authority of the crown was forcibly reasserted. To weaken the power of the earls, Henry formed a bureaucracy from the knight class that was loyal to him, and it was from this class that the new patrons came.[82] Less wealthy than the earls and possessed of smaller landholdings, the knights could not afford outright gifts and required financial compensation for land donations. Sometimes this took the form of a straight cash payment; in other cases, rents were charged or service demanded. A specific example is recorded at Vaudey. As already mentioned, its founder, the count of Aumale, provided the first monks with land at Bytham, but it was insufficient to sustain the house; and it fell to a knight of the earl of Lincoln, Geoffrey de Brachecourt, to rescue the community. He provided a new site at Vaudey. Yet Geoffrey's resources were limited, as the agreement drawn up between him and the monks makes clear. In return for the gift of his whole residence with garden, the monks undertook to provide him and his wife with food and clothing (both linen and woolen) and to supply their two servants with food, all for so long as they lived. Geoffrey and his wife were to receive the same food as the monks, their servants the same as the lay brothers.[83] Arrangements such as these not

---

[81] The account is contained in *Chron. M.* 1:76-77.
[82] See Hills, *English Cistercian Monasteries*, 64ff.

[83] *Mon. Angl.* 5:490.

only violated the spirit of the order's statutes and dragged the monks into the world of law and finance but they meant smaller endowments and smaller-scale monasteries.

More serious compromises accompanied the absorption in 1147/1148 of the thirteen English houses of the Congregation of Savigny. Although this union brought to the Cistercians a number of large and wealthy foundations, such as Furness and Byland, it quickly proved problematic. Raised under a different discipline with different attitudes to wealth, economy, and even to the concept of monasticism, the Savigniac houses insisted on and won for themselves a number of concessions, which established a double standard. Their engagement in business, the failure of their abbots to attend regularly the General Chapters at Cîteaux (thereby avoiding censure), and their holding of income-producing property, accelerated a movement away from the idealistic simplicity and poverty insisted upon by the Cistercians. Men were not blind to the problems. In 1169 the pope, Alexander III, addressed a circular letter to the English Cistercians ordering them to adhere to their constitutions and warning: "the entire way of life has undergone injury and change, a decline from established customs, a leaving behind of the original manner of life of the institution."[84] Clearly the situation was worse in England than elsewhere, and it is not without interest that the major innovations in architecture occurred in houses that were formerly Savigniac, such as Furness, Byland, Jervaulx.

The degree to which involvement with the outside world affected other Cistercian houses in England is illustrated by the transition of monastic economies from land to monetary ones, and from self-sufficiency to profit making. At first this probably stimulated building, because in accordance with the custom mentioned in the *Exordium*, one-quarter of all income could be used for building; but the temptation to raise money to continue such

enterprises, or to extend estates (and thereby income) through the purchase of additional land, led the monks into such dubious schemes as selling their wool on forward contracts (a practice outlawed by the General Chapter in 1181), or simply to borrowing money outright. In 1189 ten Cistercian monasteries in the north, including Rievaulx, received permission from the king, Richard I, to compound with a creditor named Aaron of Lincoln for debts of 6,500 marks upon payment of a thousand marks down.[85] In all likelihood it was their difficulty that determined passage of the statute in the General Chapter the following year forbidding indebtedness and specifying building as one of its causes.

A further aspect of patronage was the network of filiation that resulted from it. Figure 2 reveals the tight-knit nature of the Cistercians' expansion in England. Excepting the Savigniac houses, virtually the entire White Monk establishment was controlled up to 1154 by three houses: Waverley, Rievaulx, and Fountains. Because Rievaulx and Fountains had Clairvaux as a common mother house, Bernard's abbey controlled the large majority of English Cistercian foundations in this period—eighteen out of thirty-two abbeys. Moreover, it was to Clairvaux that the Congregation of Savigny was submitted in 1147, adding thirteen more houses in England to the Clairvaux family.[86] Clairvaux's dominance over the English houses inevitably left its mark on their architecture, for filiation, although only one of several factors influencing architecture, provided, due to the order's centralized government and its custom of visitation, an important means of transmitting ideas as well as checking abuses or punishing violations.

Changes in patronage and filiation in the thirteenth century set into clearer focus conditions in the twelfth. The principal patron of the new foundations was now no longer the knight class but the crown. The first monastery of the new century, at

[84] The letter was probably written between 1162 and 1175 (see J. Leclercq, "Epitres d'Alexandre III sur les cisterciens," *Revue Bénédictine* 64 [1954]: 68-82).

[85] J. Jacobs, "Aaron of Lincoln," *Jewish Quarterly Review* 10 (1898): 629-48, esp. 635.

[86] On Clairvaux's dependencies, see A. Dimier, "Le Monde Claravallien à la mort de Saint Bernard," *Mélanges Saint Ber-*

nard, XXIVᵉ congrès de l'association bourguignonne des sociétés savantes (Dijon, 1953), 248-53. By the time of Saint Bernard's death the Clairvaux family numbered 167 (sixty-nine direct foundations, ninety-six more founded by them) out of total of 345; by the century's end Clairvaux counted 263 dependencies out of 525.

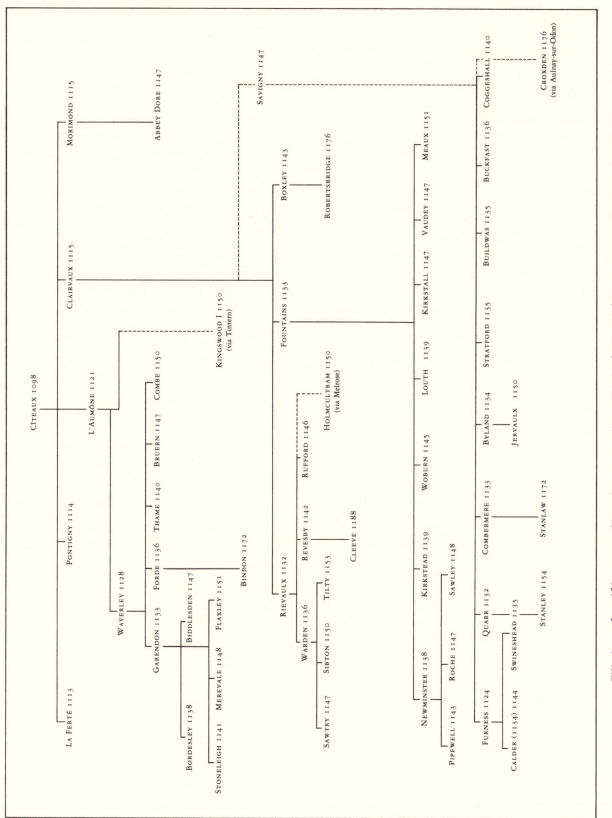

2. Filiations of twelfth-century Cistercian monasteries in England. Hatched line represents Savigniac houses.

Beaulieu in Hampshire, was established in 1204 by King John. No earlier monarch had acted as patron to a Cistercian house. Moreover, the founding monks came from Cîteaux, which hitherto had made no direct settlements in England. And just as the circumstances of Beaulieu's foundation differed from those of earlier houses, so did its architecture. A church of unprecedented size was constructed, using an elaborate ambulatory and radiating chapel plan never before seen in the order's abbeys in England. Under Henry III royal involvement increased, and on 17 January 1225 the young king was solemnly admitted as an associate in the order, the ceremony taking place at Waverley, the oldest and senior abbey.[87] Henry's subsequent generosity to the Cistercians was continued by his son, Edward I, whose building program at Vale Royal proved to be so grandiose it could not be finished.[88]

Throughout the thirteenth century the number of new monasteries established was much smaller, a slowing down the Cistercians shared with the other monastic orders. In part this can be explained by the arrival of the Friars, whose patrons were not the local barons either, but mainly townspeople, bishops, or the crown. What is significant is the great curtailment in the role of the baronage. The most likely explanation is that the major landed families already held some interest in an established religious house by 1200; instead of founding a new one, they were content to add to the endowments of an existing house started by their ancestors.[89] With some exceptions the new patrons had different intentions and goals, which from the very start gave the thirteenth century foundations a character that bore only small relation to that of foundations from the twelfth.

[87] See *Ann. W.*, 301.

[88] See R. A. Brown, *The History of the King's Works* (London, 1963), 1:248-57.

[89] H. Colvin, *The White Canons* (Oxford, 1951), 38.

2

The Earliest Architecture

THE FIRST community of Cistercian monks to enter England came from Normandy, from the abbey of L'Aumône, in late October 1128 and arrived under the sponsorship of William Giffard, bishop of Winchester. Giffard had earlier patronized the Augustinians; he had come in touch with the Cistercians in Normandy during his tenure as dean of Rouen. He provided land for the new foundation at Waverley in Surrey, where the monks built their monastery at the southern end of a broad valley closed by low hills and abundantly watered by the River Wey. The early stone church and parts of the claustral buildings at Waverley are known through Brakspear's excavation, and although the date is not fixed with precision, work on them probably started a year or two after settlement.[1] Before this the buildings occupied by the monks were temporary ones raised prior to the colonization of the site. Nothing is known of these structures, but some information on this aspect of the order's architecture can be assembled.

As already seen, the General Chapter exercised considerable care in establishing foundation procedures. Ten years before the settlement of Waverley, the *Summa cartae Caritatis* mandated: "No abbot shall be sent to a new place without at least twelve monks and . . . without the prior construction of such places as an oratory, a refectory, a dormitory, a guest house, and a gatekeeper's cell so that the monks may immediately serve God and live in religious discipline. No living quarters, only animal shelters, shall be constructed outside the gate of the monastery."[2] Because the great majority of Cistercian foundations were located in isolated areas where there had been no previous buildings, the first structures of a new monastery were probably built from timber, which was relatively cheap and easy to work and which could be obtained readily in the woodland or valley sites favored by the Cistercians.

Practical considerations were not the only ones for building wooden structures, however. The order's commitment to poverty was expressed, in the early years at least, in modest buildings. The authors of the *Vita Prima* recall Bernard's identification of stone buildings as the mark of those with riches—and riches that had gone to their heads. And Pierre le Chantre recounts how Bernard wept when he passed some small, straw-covered huts because they reminded him of the shelters that the Cistercians had used in their first years.[3] But the wish to emulate the founding conditions of the order's pioneer monks seems also to have been an important consideration. In 1075 when Molesme was settled, poverty forced the monks to build a wooden church of interlaced branches, and twenty-three years later when monks from Molesme established Cîteaux, they repeated the procedure.[4] Although the experience of living in temporary wooden buildings in the early years matched that at Molesme and Cîteaux, one important difference separated subsequent foundations; the first buildings were to be in place before the founding community set out to colonize the new site.

[1] See H. Brakspear, *Waverley Abbey* (London, 1905); also *VCH: Surrey* (London, 1905): 77-89.

[2] J. de la Croix Bouton and J.-B. Van Damme, *Les Plus Anciens Textes de Cîteaux* (Achel, 1974), 121. The translation is B. K. Lackner's in L. J. Lekai, *The Cistercians: Ideals and Reality* (Kent, OH, 1977), 448.

[3] For the *Vita Prima*, see appendix B to this study; for Pierre le Chantre, see A. Dimier, *Recueil de plans d'églises Cisterciennes* (Paris, 1949), 39.

[4] V. Mortet, *Recueil de textes relatifs à l'histoire de l'architecture en France au moyen âge, XIᵉ-XIIᵉ siècles* (Paris, 1911), 1:296.

It is not known if the first timber buildings at Waverley were erected by the monks' patron, William Giffard, or by lay brothers from the mother house of L'Aumône ahead of the arrival of the monks. Practice at other abbeys varied and throws some light on the problem. In two recorded cases the mother abbey undertook this responsibility. At Louth Park in Lincolnshire, a foundation established by Bishop Alexander of Lincoln in 1139, monks from Fountains were invited to settle what turned out to be an unsatisfactory site at Haverholm. According to the *Narratio* of Fountains, its abbot received the bishop's gift and "taking God for his help started the work. He sent brothers to the several places, constructed buildings and set up workshops (*edificia construit, erigit officinas*)."[5] When these were finished, the founding monks were dispatched to begin the life of the new house. Similarly, at Kirkstall, which was first sited at Barnoldswick as a dependency of Fountains, the abbot of Fountains dispatched lay brothers "to build humble buildings according to the form of the order (*missis fratribus officinas humiles erexit secundum formam ordinis*)" (see appendix B).

More usually the construction of these first wooden structures was undertaken by the patron. Robert Gait settled the monastery at Thame in Oxfordshire in 1138 with a gift of land at Otteley and built an abbey there (*construit ibi abbatiam*),[6] having first obtained from Waverley a promise to furnish monks. These were forthcoming, but the Otteley site proved unsuitable due to flooding and the community moved to Thame, its permanent location, two years later. Similarly, the founding charter of Sawley in west Yorkshire states that William de Percy, scion of the great northern family, constructed the monastery before summoning monks from Newminster to establish the community.[7]

On occasion a patron raised the timber buildings for a new monastic community without a clear agreement with a founding house, as is shown by events that preceded the settlement of Pipewell in Northamptonshire. William Batevileyn donated lands and prepared a site there before concluding negotiations to provide the founding monks.[8] He

had in fact approached two abbeys—Garendon in Leicestershire, which belonged to the filiation of Waverley, and Newminster in Northumberland, which belonged to that of Fountains—but his inquiries were sufficiently ambiguous as to foster false assumptions. Indeed, an abbot and founding monks from both Garendon and Newminster converged on the new site more or less together. Argument ensued and the monks from Garendon eventually withdrew, leaving Pipewell to be joined to the family of Newminster.

By far the fullest account of a patron's work is that contained in the *Chronicle* of Meaux. The circumstances that led to the foundation of this Yorkshire house by William "le Gros," count of Aumale and earl of York, have already been detailed. Despite his initial reluctance to surrender one of his prize estates to the Cistercians, Count William accepted his responsibility as patron, providing the first buildings for the new community as soon as the charters of foundation had been completed. In the words of the *Chronicle*, "he had a certain great house (*magnam domum*) built with common mud and wattle (*ex vili cemate*) . . . in which the arriving lay brothers would dwell until better arrangements were made for them. He also built a certain chapel next to the aforementioned house . . . where all the monks used the lower story as a dormitory and the upper to perform the divine service devoutly (*ubi monachi omnes in inferiori solario postea decubabant, et in superiori divina officia devotius persolvebant*)."[9] Only after the work was finished were the monks introduced to form the first community.

The arrangement of the Meaux building is decidedly unusual and might be dismissed as another of the count's eccentricities but for the fact that Adam, who had suggested the establishment of the new monastery and was now its abbot later copied it. As men joined Meaux, a larger building became necessary, and Adam, instead of adding onto the original structure, began a new, more spacious one that repeated the disposition of the first, namely, with dormitory below and oratory above. It was built of timber and was sufficiently large to hold about forty monks.

---

[5] *Chron. LP*, xxii.
[6] *Chart. T.*, 83.
[7] *Chart. S.*, 1-3.

[8] H. Brakspear, "Pipewell Abbey," *Associated Architectural Societies Reports and Papers* 30 (1909-1910): 299-313, esp. 300.
[9] See *Chron. M.*, 82; and catalog entry under Meaux.

The interest of the monks' building at Meaux is the unusual combination of the two building types, oratory and dormitory, in one structure. This cannot be explained away by Meaux's isolation or its poverty during the first decade or so of its existence. Abbot Adam was the most widely experienced builder known in the order's early history.[10] He had joined Fountains shortly after its foundation in 1132 and had probably been trained directly by Geoffroi of Ainai, the master jointly responsible for the rebuilding of the second stone church at Clairvaux begun in 1135. During his seventeen years as a monk at Fountains (where he would have been active in building) Adam had been sent to oversee the building of Kirkstead, established in 1139, of Woburn in 1145, and of Vaudey in 1147. He had been at work on Vaudey in 1149 when he met Count William and convinced him to found Meaux. Thus Adam had been entrusted by Fountains with the architectural development of all three daughter houses and would have known well the order's requirements for the initial buildings of a new monastery as well as for the first generation of permanent buildings. Moreover, like every Cistercian house, Kirkstead, Woburn, Vaudey, and Meaux would have been subject to annual visitation by the abbot of their mother house, Fountains in this case, which would have included keen scrutiny of the buildings. It is therefore most unlikely that Adam could have used unorthodox forms for his building at Meaux.

The buildings raised at Meaux, with a large upper chamber surmounting an undercroft, were in fact standard for domestic structures. In the 1150s the type was used for the guest houses at Fountains and Kirkstall, and it was also well known for secular buildings outside the order.[11] But the translation of the type from domestic into ecclesiastical is unusual. This is confirmed by the recovery through excavation of the plan of the wooden church and first cloister at Fountains dating to *circa* 1133, which are the only verifiable remains known of the order's

timber building.[12] Located where the south transept of the present building now stands (built twenty years after the first structures), the wooden church was small, rectangular, with at least six, perhaps eight, bays as defined by the square-sectioned principal posts of the outer wall. It had no transepts or apse. Traces of the cloister to the south show that the church was separate from the adjoining dormitory and thus adheres to accepted traditions of claustral layout.

Conclusions about the earliest wooden buildings raised for newly established monastic communities, based on the documentary evidence at Meaux and the physical remains at Fountains, must necessarily be tentative. It seems likely that the order permitted considerable latitude in the form of these buildings, despite the injunction of the *Carta Caritatis* that all Cistercian houses follow the same customs in all things. Probably what really mattered was that a patron provide certain functional spaces, leaving their use open to local interpretation. The odds on a new English monastic community's successfully colonizing a site on its first try were less than two to one, as Donkin has shown. Therefore, early visitations to a new house were most likely geared toward ensuring the survival of the community. If the buildings met the basic requirements, the order was prepared to accept a fair range of forms.

Returning to Waverley, it was at sometime between 1129 and 1131/1132 that the work of replacing the first wooden buildings with permanent stone ones would have begun. The monastery had attracted attention quickly and soon became the principal source of the order's expansion in southern England; within a decade four houses belonged to its line, and by mid-century the number had expanded to ten, nearly one-third of the total directly established in England by then.[13] Such growth is remarkable and demonstrates the abbey's

[10] P. J. Fergusson, "The First Architecture of the Cistercians in England and the Work of Abbot Adam of Meaux," *Jnl. BAA* 136 (1983), 74-86.

[11] See P. A. Faulkner, "Domestic Planning from the Twelfth to the Fourteenth Centuries," *Archaeological Journal* 115 (1958): 150-83, esp. 152-60.

[12] G. Coppack, "Fountains Abbey," *Archaeological Journal*

(in press). I would like to thank Dr. Coppack for his generous sharing of this information prior to publication of his article.

[13] Until mid-century five of the ten were direct foundations and five were daughter houses founded from them; by the end of the century one more abbey had been added (see filiation chart, fig. 2).

success in attracting patrons to found new abbeys and, just as important, in drawing postulants to its gates. Both speak strongly of unusual spiritual vigor and sound leadership.

In addition to being the mother house of the Cistercian monasteries in England, Waverley occupies an exceptional position in any study of Cistercian architecture. It is among the very few churches dating from the beginning years of the order that have been archaeologically investigated in any country and thus one of the few to give us an idea of the early churches' form and appearance. The modest size, attenuated proportions, and aisleless form of the plan contrast vividly with the plans developed a few years later and used prominently by the order, including in the north of England at Rievaulx. Waverley reflects an older, and short-lived tradition for the Cistercians' churches, but one whose influence was wider than is usually recognized. Equally notable, Waverley was not altered as the years passed as were most successful Cistercian abbeys.[14] In fact, it was not until a hundred years after its foundation that the community abandoned the eastern parts of its first church and took possession of a vastly larger choir.[15] So strong an attachment to the earliest forms of Cistercian architecture over so long a period by an abbey as powerful as Waverley and in the face of widespread acceptance within the order of larger and more modern buildings is without parallel in the English abbeys.

The only visible remains of the first church at Waverley are some traces from the south wall of the south transept. Now partly encased by the walls of the thirteenth-century church, they are intelligible thanks to Brakspear's excavation of 1899-1905 and the Department of the Environment's consolidation of the site between 1980 and 1981.

The plan of the church at Waverley (fig. 3) shows a small, nearly square east end (twenty-seven by twenty-four feet) with a straight terminal wall. The transepts, also terminating in straight walls, each

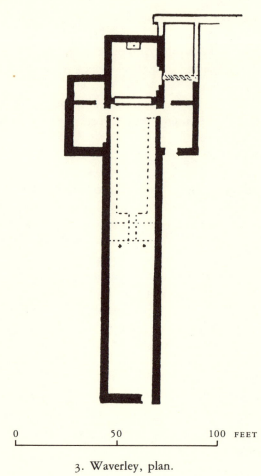

0   50   100 FEET

3. Waverley, plan.

had a single chapel that was virtually enclosed by a masonry wall on its west side, except for a door next to the choir. At the crossing flat responds faced the choir and transepts, indicating that arches were turned over the north, east, and south sides only. On the west where the responds were omitted there was no arch and so the nave continued unbroken through to the east arch of the presbytery. The crossing was unsegregated, therefore. Given this disposition, it is likely that the transepts were lower in height than the nave. A similar treatment of the crossing and transepts occurs at Tintern and Fountains in the first churches.[16] The nave at Waverley

---

[14] At Clairvaux for instance, the first church, built in 1115, remained in use for twenty years. A second, begun in 1135, replaced it, and was in turn replaced, beginning in 1153, by a third.

[15] The move occurred in 1231, and it is not inconceivable that it coincided with the centennial of the first church. Work on the second church began in 1203 a small distance to the north and east of the first church and was built as an envelope

around it (see catalog under Waverley). The whole building was finished in 1278.

[16] For the plan of Tintern, see A. W. Clapham, *English Romanesque Architecture after the Conquest* (Oxford, 1934), 76. In the rebuilding of Fountains after the 1147 fire, the church was designed initially without a segregated crossing (see Coppack, "Fountains Abbey").

was exceptionally narrow in its proportions (124 by 24 feet), and lacked aisles.

That this plan came to Waverley with the founding monks is confirmed by the plan of Tintern, a second abbey established by L'Aumône two years after Waverley, and by those of the recently discovered first and second stone churches at Fountains (*circa* 1135 and 1148). Similar plans appear at Sawley (*circa* 1150) and, farther afield, at Lysa in Norway, the first Cistercian foundation in that country, established by Fountains in 1146 with one of the original monks of Fountains as the first abbot. All these plans show similar long, aisleless naves, square-ended choir and transepts, and unsegregated crossings. At Fountains a further similarity is the closure of the transept chapels on their west sides.

The omission of aisles in all four abbey churches is curious. Aisles become standard in later plans—for large-scale churches after the mid-1130s, and for smaller-scale churches after the mid-1150s. But aisles in monastic churches (unlike in secular churches) did not serve primarily as corridors of communication (the monks entered and left the choir via the central vessel; see fig. 8, p. 45); rather they served as chapel space. And in the early churches the need for chapel space was not great. In France, for instance, where several of the first churches were also aisleless, three chapels was a normal number. The intended size of the community at Waverley when the church was con-

structed is not known, although a figure of around sixty to seventy men may be assumed. Fifty years later the numbers had grown considerably; by 1187, at the time of the election of Abbot Christopher, mention is made of seventy monks and 120 lay brothers.[17] How the church functioned with a community of this size is difficult to understand, particularly because by then altars were needed for an increased number of priest monks to celebrate Mass. Apart from an extension to the south transept chapel as part of the lengthening of the chapter house around 1180, no other changes were made.[18]

The plans of these early English churches resemble those of French churches from the same period, and their distinctive form when set against the next generation of buildings, those of the mid-1130s, needs to be emphasized. At Cîteaux, the first stone churches were still standing in the early eighteenth century when they were visited and described by Martène.[19] Cîteaux I, consecrated in 1106, was vaulted and had a choir that was approximately square (thirty feet to a side), with three windows in the straight east end, and a nave, also square (fifteen feet to a side), with two windows. It presumably had no aisle or transepts; for neither are mentioned by Martène. Pontigny was probably similar.[20] At Clairvaux the church took the form of a small, square, aisled building with a tall center space, resembling a stave church.[21] Closest to Waverley was Ourscamp (Oise), founded a year after

---

[17] For the population figures, see *Ann. W.*, 244. It is difficult to work out the placement of the stalls in the choir to accommodate this many monks. Assuming thirty-five monks to a side and a minimum of thirty inches for each stall, nearly twice as much space would have been needed. The change in altar requirements resulting from the higher proportion of priest monks after mid-century can be illustrated at Clairvaux. From three altars during the period from 1115 to 1135, the numbers expanded to twenty-two by 1174, and subsequently to thirty-two. In addition to chapels, altars were placed against the nave piers (see H. P. Eydoux, *B. Mon.* 133 [1975]: 185; also H. Michelant, "Un Grand Monastère au XVIe siècle," *Annales archéologiques* 3 [1845]: 223-59, esp. 226). In the sixteenth century at Clairvaux there were 128 stalls for the choir monks, thirty-four for infirm monks, and 328 for the lay brothers and novices. In the thirteenth century at Waverley there were eleven chapels. In the first church the existence of altars outside the east end is indicated by the mention that in 1214, after lifting the Interdict, Albin, bishop of Ferns, touched all the crosses in the first church with holy oil and blessed

them at the same time that the eastern chapels were hallowed (see *Ann. W.*, 282).

[18] The chapel's east wall was extended to form a continuous wall with that of the enlarged chapter house (see fig. 3). At the same time, the wall that enclosed the chapel on the west side was removed and an arch built, of which Brakspear found the north respond, which consisted of a molded base carrying a triple shaft (see Brakspear, *Waverley Abbey*, 19, and plate 1).

[19] See E. Martène and U. Durand, *Voyage littéraire de deux religieux bénédictins de la Congrégation de Saint-Maur*, vol. 1, pt. 1 (Paris, 1717): 223-24. The best recent discussion of the early churches is J. O. Schaefer, "The Earliest Churches of the Cistercian Order," *Studies in Cistercian Art and Architecture* 1 (1982): 1-12.

[20] See T. N. Kinder, "Some Observations on the Origins of Pontigny and its First Church," *Cîteaux—Commentarii cistercienses* 31 (1980): 9-19.

[21] Schaefer, "The Earliest Churches of the Cistercian Order," 4-8.

the English house. The first church here, consecrated in 1134, had a long, aisleless nave and transepts each with a single chapel; the east termination, however, was apsidal.[22]

Buildings that were influenced by the Cistercians shed additional light on these early monastic church plans. Other contemporary reform movements, notably two orders of regular canons—the Premonstratensians, founded by Saint Norbert in 1121, and the Augustinian or Austin canons, established in their post-Gregorian form around 1100—modeled their institutions of government closely on those of the Cistercians. In 1142 the Premonstratensians also entrusted visitation of their churches to the Cistercians. The following year the first Premonstratensian house was founded in England, at Newsham in Lincolnshire, and additional foundations were established rapidly thereafter. Early Premonstratensian abbeys resemble those of the Cistercians in their aisleless naves and square terminations for the transepts and choir, as for instance, at Torre (Devon), Cockersand (Lancashire), Egglestone (Yorkshire), or Bayham (Sussex).[23] Likewise, at the houses of the Austin canons, such as Kirkham (Yorkshire) and Haughmond (Yorkshire), similar plans were used, including at Kirkham the same detail of the walled-off transept chapels used at Waverley and Fountains. The buildings of the Premonstratensian and Austin canons provide a wider context, then, for regarding the early Cistercian plans as *exempla* of the new monastic architecture. This architecture appeared in England first at Waverley and continued in use for smaller foundations past mid-century.

Although nothing survives of the church at Waverley beyond a few wall fragments, its elevation can be partly reconstructed from this meager physical evidence and from what is known about the derivation of the type. The transept chapels were barrel vaulted, with the vault turning north-south,

as Brakspear has shown from the extant fragment of the south transept chapel.[24] The main spaces of the building, however, seem to have been wooden roofed. This combination of vaulted and wooden roofs is drawn from earlier traditions; it occurred in Norman architecture, for instance in the Caen churches, although it was not limited to this region. Barrel vaulting was less favored in Normandy in the later 1120s, as it was in England also, being displaced by rib or lighter groin vaults. Thus the barrel vaults at Waverley appear somewhat *retardataire*. On the other hand, this form remained popular in Burgundy until *circa* 1150 and was widely used in Cistercian architecture there as well as in other regions. On the basis of Cistercian practice it is plausible to posit the use of barrel vaults at L'Aumône in Normandy and to assume that it was from there that the vaulting form migrated to Waverley.

The interior of the church at Waverley must have had a highly distinctive character. Spatial effects would have been tight and attenuated, given the building's narrow proportions. And there can have been little to alleviate the plainness of surfaces, for architectural detail was limited to a sloping plinth on the crossing piers, a bell profile on the bases flanking the *sedilia*, and scrolled stops on the wall arches in the southwest angle of the south transept.

Scholarship on the first churches of the Cistercians in France has revealed the strong influence of small-scale architecture in Burgundy where the order had been founded. A number of surviving village churches, such as those at Uchizy, Malay, or Farges (St. Barthélemy), predate any standing Cistercian building and show the use of similar features: square-ended choirs, barrel vaults, and spare detailing.[25] In adopting this regional tradition, the Cistercians initially favored no uniform plan or elevation, however. For instance, Cîteaux and Pon-

[22] See A. Peigné-Delacourt, *Histoire de l'abbaye de Notre Dame d'Ourscamp* (Amiens, 1876). The building stood to the north of the much larger second church, which replaced it beginning around 1150.

[23] See A. W. Clapham, "The Architecture of the Premonstratensians, with Special Reference to their Buildings in England," *Arch.*, 73 (1923): 117-46.

[24] See Brakspear, *Waverley Abbey*, 19. The vault sprang from

a string course that is still visible although the ground level has risen considerably. The evidence for the vault and for the entrance respond is not completely clear, however. The eastern portion of the standing wall shows that the extension was wooden-roofed.

[25] See C. Oursel, "L'Abbatiale de Fontenay," *CN* 5 (1954): 125-27.

tigny were aisleless and longitudinal in plan, but Clairvaux was aisled and square in plan; Ourscamp ended in an apse, but the other churches had square ends; Cîteaux was vaulted, but Clairvaux was wooden roofed. Yet the differences are more marked in the earlier than in the later buildings. Significantly, the buildings constructed in the decade that separates Clairvaux or Pontigny from the first foundations outside Burgundy or in England share a number of common ideas. By the late 1120s, then, an architectural identity had begun to emerge that was easily transmitted over long distances, and it was this identity that was expressed in the buildings at Waverley,[26] Tintern, Fountains, and Sawley. Their characteristics—aisleless naves, square terminations, unsegregated "crossings" with the transepts lower than the nave and the nave carried through to the east arch framing the high altar, barrel-vaulted chapels, modest scaling, minimal detail—bear the unmistakable mark of French Cistercian architecture.

Although the first foundation in England, Waverley was the thirty-sixth Cistercian monastery to have been established since the settlement of Cî-

teaux in 1098. The rapid growth this represents suggests why the order was prompted to develop an architecture with readily understood and easily transmitted forms. From their early days the Cistercians instituted a system of government and discipline based on standardized practice, a notion that received explicit formulation in the *Summa cartae Caritatis* in 1119. This did not at first include architecture, however, and it is not until the late 1120s that a clear concern with standardization can be demonstrated. The time lag is hard to explain. Perhaps concepts of small-scale or bareness fulfilled the order's requirements sufficiently; only subsequently was formal variety deemed problematic. When the formation of a distinctive Cistercian architecture began, it was based on the components and vocabulary of Burgundian Romanesque. But the composition of these components and what may be termed the voice given to the vocabulary remained unique to the Cistercians and gave their architecture a recognizable identity. This process mirrored that employed a few years earlier for the restructuring of the order's liturgy and government institutions.

---

[26] Another distinctive feature at Waverley with parallels in the early French houses is the arrangement of buildings in the east range of the cloister. The monks' dorter did not sit over the chapter house (as became customary after *circa* 1140-1150) but lay at ground level in the southeast corner of the cloister.

3

The Colonization of the North

WILLIAM's conquest of the north of England followed very different lines from his conquest of the south; successive revolts in 1067, 1068, and 1069 drew the invading forces into the territory between the Humber and the Tees and culminated in the winter of 1069-1070 in its systematic devastation.[1] Resistance was fiercest in the North and East Ridings of Yorkshire, which became the special focus of William's forces as they hunted down the rebels in the hills and dales. William's vengeance was also directed at the peasant population; villages were burned, farms razed, families killed or driven from their homes, livestock slaughtered, seed corn destroyed. The effects of this brutal harrying can be judged twenty years later at Domesday (1086). Most of the once productive land still lay waste, and the recorded population of the Vale of York barely reached two men per square mile. Even in the early twelfth century William of Malmesbury reported that around York land remained waste for a breadth of sixty miles.[2] The Cistercians turned these conditions brilliantly to their advantage beginning in the 1130s.

Taken as a whole, the order's northern colonization was remarkable less for the number of houses established—considerably more were founded in the Midlands, for instance—than for their size and early date. Only twelve of the seventy-five abbeys (17 percent) founded by the Cistercians in England and Wales in the twelfth century were located in the north, but in wealth and influence they dominated all others. Most prominent were the eight foundations established in Yorkshire, in areas where William's devastation had been most severe.[3]

Northeast England was ideal Cistercian country. It was lightly settled by other religious orders making for thin competition for lay benefactors and thereby offering the chance to assemble large estates. Moreover, much of the land had been cleared and worked before the Conquest, and as Donkin has shown, the grange holdings of the Cistercians included a large percentage of such land.[4] This meant that the monks were not called upon to perform the back-breaking, pioneer roles endured by their colleagues in eastern Europe or northern Spain. Not least, the topography of the northeast, with its mixture of fertile valleys and high grassed moors, was well suited to Cistercian farming and grange organization (fig. 4). All things considered, the situation was tailor-made for an order whose constitution enjoined establishment "not in cities . . . nor in villages, but in places far from the concourse of men."[5]

To these material advantages were joined more personal ones. Yorkshire, in particular, was the

[1] See W. E. Kapelle, *The Norman Conquest of the North* (Chapel Hill, 1979).

[2] For population, see H. C. Darby and I. S. Maxwell, *The Domesday Geography of Northern England* (Cambridge, 1962), 37, 195-99. For William of Malmesbury's comment, see W. Stubbs, ed., *Willelmi Malmeshiriensis de Gestis Regnum, Rolls Series* 90 (1889): 208-209.

[3] See J. S. Fletcher, *The Cistercians in Yorkshire* (London, 1919); F. A. Mullin, *A History of the Cistercians in Yorkshire, 1131-1300* (Washington, D. C., 1932); T.A.M. Bishop, "The Norman Settlement of Yorkshire," *Studies in Medieval History presented to F. M. Powicke*, ed. R. W. Hunt (Oxford, 1948),

1-14; B. Hill, *English Cistercian Monasteries and their Patrons in the Twelfth Century* (Urbana, 1968). For settlement and economy, see R. A. Donkin, "The Cistercian Order and the Settlement of Northern England," *Geographical Review* 59 (1969): 403-16; B. Waites, "The Monastic Settlement of Northeast Yorkshire," *YAJ* 40 (1959-1962): 478-95.

[4] R. A. Donkin, "Settlement and Depopulation on Cistercian Estates during the 12th and 13th centuries, especially in Yorkshire," *Bulletin of the Institute of Historical Research* 33 (1960), 141-65, esp. 151.

[5] *Statuta* 1 (1134:1): 13.

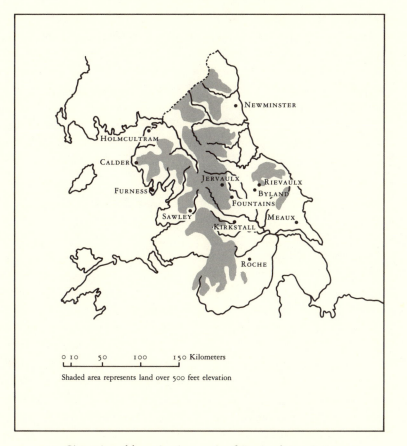

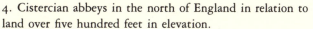

4. Cistercian abbeys in the north of England in relation to
land over five hundred feet in elevation.

homeland of men who early on had joined the Cistercians in France. A number of them had settled at Clairvaux and came to be included in Saint Bernard's inner circle. Their influence probably explains the dominance of Clairvaux in Cistercian settlement in the north: all eight Yorkshire abbeys belonged within its filiation, as did all but one of the four other northern houses. The success of the movement in the north stems largely from the energy, judgment, and opportunism shown by these first monks. By the second half of the twelfth century the northern Cistercian monasteries had eclipsed the order's other houses in England; some counted communities of hundreds of men, most controlled large cash revenues, and a few, like Fountains and Furness, amassed estates calculated at well over two hundred thousand acres a piece.

Much is known about the Cistercians' early architecture in the north.[6] In Yorkshire in particular the churches at Rievaulx, Fountains, and Kirkstall constitute a related group spanning a thirty-year period, unique in any country for the record they provide of the order's early architectural development. Adding to their interest, Rievaulx and Fountains are preserved in settings of spectacular beauty, with landscapes fashioned in contrasting modes in the eighteenth century; and Kirkstall, despite its location in industrial Leeds and its blackened appearance, offers some of the best preserved of the White Monks' early buildings in England.

In choosing to establish Rievaulx, twenty miles from York, as the first Cistercian abbey in the north, Bernard was influenced by a personal visit in 1131 from its lay founder, Walter Espec, one of the most

[6] The classic study is J. Bilson, "The Architecture of the Cistercians, with Special Reference to Some of their Earlier Churches in England," *Arch. Jnl.* 66 (1909): 185-280.

powerful barons in the north of England, a royal justiciar under Henry I, and a large landholder in Yorkshire and Northumberland.[7] The spring following Espec's visit to Clairvaux, the first monks crossed to England and settled in the deep, two-mile-long valley of the Rye. They were led by Abbot William, a native of York, who had risen to master of the schools there before offering himself as a postulant at Clairvaux, where his background qualified him to serve as private secretary to Bernard.[8]

Rievaulx was not established in a spirit of genteel piety but conceived like a military operation. Bernard's concept of the order as a spiritualized militia—the *Exordium* speaks of the monks as "novi milites Christi"—emerges clearly in his letter to Henry I introducing the men who, in accordance with Cistercian statute, were to survey the site before the party of monks was sent out to settle it:

In your land there is an outpost of my Lord and your Lord, an outpost which he has preferred to die for than to lose. I have proposed to occupy it and I am sending men from my army who will, if it is not displeasing to you, claim it, recover it, and restore it with a strong hand. For this purpose I have sent ahead these men who now stand before you to reconnoitre. They will investigate the situation carefully and report back to me faithfully. Help them as messengers of Your Lord and in their persons fulfill your duties as vassal of their Lord.[9]

In keeping with this attitude, elaborate efforts were made to ensure the new community's success. At Helmesley, two miles to the east, lay Espec's castle with its tall tower keep and stone gatehouses; Bernard, as just seen, enlisted the king's support and, further, solicited the help of the Scottish king, David; and Espec procured the backing of the reform-minded archbishop of York, Thurstan. When on 5 March 1132 the monks gathered on the site

for the official foundation ceremony, attended by Espec, his sisters Hawise, Albrea, and Odelina, his fellow justiciar in the north, Eustace FitzJohn, a group of clerics from Warter Priory, and a body of Espec's tenants and neighbors, the charter invoked the circles of power to which Rievaulx looked for support: "the foundation is made by the advice and permission of Thurstan, Archbishop of York, with the consent and counsel of Henry, King of the English, and confirmed by the Apostolic authority of the Lord Pope Innocent."[10]

The impact of Rievaulx was immediate, although its extent seems not to have been entirely expected. Espec's initial grant of land was in fact modest, particularly when compared with the endowments of Augustinian houses like Guisborough or Benedictine houses like Whitby. But the Cistercians clearly touched a responsive chord in the north; within months, monks at St. Cuthbert's Durham and St. Mary's York, the leading Benedictine houses in the region, called for reform along Cistercian lines, the chapter of the Minster Church at York was prompted to examine its practices, and nearer by the Augustinian canons at Kirkham agitated toward change. Something of the power exercised by the presence of the new monks is conveyed by the ancient chronicler Serlo writing around 1205: "there had come from a far country men of extraordinary holiness and perfect piety, who spoke on earth with the tongues of angels and by their virtues were most worthy of the name of monk."[11] Gifts poured in to Rievaulx, and postulants offered themselves in large numbers. In three years a colony could be sent to Warden (with Espec again as patron), indicating that the number of monks at Rievaulx had reached around sixty; within twenty years ten more colonies had been established, a total outlay of 143 monks and about two hundred lay brothers. By 1142, a decade after its foundation, Rievaulx housed three hundred men, a figure that had

---

[7] *Mon. Angl.* 5:280. For the early history of Rievaulx, see *Chart. R.*, lx-lxxxvii.

[8] William held this position by 1119 and was one of the five secretaries of Bernard's whose names are known (see J. Leclerq, "Saint Bernard et ses secrétaires," *Revue Bénédictine* 61 [1951]: 208-29). William's importance can be gauged by the fact that he was the scribe of the famous letter that Bernard wrote to his nephew, Robert of Châtillon, who had turned his

back on Cîteaux and returned to Cluny. William was also the central figure in the reform of the Cistercian chant (see C. H. Talbot, "The *Centum Sententiae* of Walter Daniel," *Sacris Erudiri* 11 [1960]: 269).

[9] B. S. James, trans., *The Letters of St. Bernard of Clairvaux* (London, 1953), letter no. 95.

[10] *Chart. R.*, 16-20.

[11] *Mem. F.*, 1:5.

doubled twenty years later.[12] The new community's appeal can be glimpsed in the *Vita Ailredi* where Walter Daniel quotes Ailred's promise that "strong and weak alike should find in Rievaulx a haven of peace, a spacious and calm home,"[13] words that carried a special resonance in the rough years of Stephen's reign.

Throughout the twelfth century Rievaulx remained the spiritual leader as well as the mother abbey of the Cistercians in the north; three of the order's four saints were monks there, and the flood of men attracted to it speak for the allure of its life. Happily, no site in England better preserves some of its original qualities of setting and landscape (plate 1); it is still worthy of Walter Daniel's description of the place eight hundred years ago:

the monks set up their huts near . . . a powerful stream called the Rie in a broad valley stretching on either side. The name of their little settlement and of the place where it lies was derived from the name of the stream and the valley, Rievaulx. High hills surround the valley, encircling it like a crown. These are clothed by trees of various sorts and maintain in pleasant retreats the privacy of the vale, providing for the monks a kind of second paradise of wooded delight. From the loftiest rocks the waters wind and tumble down to the valley below, and as they make their hasty way through the lesser passages and narrower beds and spread themselves in wider rills, they give out a gentle murmur of soft sound and join together in the sweet notes of a delicious melody. And when the branches of lovely trees rustle and sing together and the leaves flutter gently to the earth, the happy listener is filled increasingly with a glad jubilee of harmonious

sound, as so many various things conspire together in such a sweet consent, in music whose every diverse note is equal to the rest.[14]

Rievaulx quickly became much more than a mere outpost of Cistercian reform. Unlike even the mother houses of the order in France, Rievaulx seems to have experienced no gradual expansion of the community that gave rise to a series of larger churches as time passed, but rather, from the earliest years, had a clear idea of the community's intended scale. The first church at Rievaulx was three times larger than the church at Waverley and considerably bigger than even the second church at Fountains as conceived some eighteen years later. Still today it is hard to grasp the degree of self-confidence that prompted such ambitious building in what was lonely and wild country. Clearly, Rievaulx was soon considered the headquarters of the new reform impulse in the empty territory of the north.

When the monks arrived at Rievaulx in 1132, the wooden buildings required by statute would have been in place. Additions to them were soon made, including those to the guest house, which miraculously escaped destruction in 1134 when Ailred extinguished a fire there with a jug of English beer.[15] Work on the church could not have begun for a year or two after settlement, for extensive terracing of the sharply sloping site was necessary. But construction can be assumed to have started around 1134. Calculating a building period of about ten years, it seems likely the church was completed around 1145. A general confirmation of

---

[12] For the first figures, see *PL* 195:563; for the numbers at the time of Ailred's death, see F. M. Powicke, ed., *The Life of St. Ailred by Walter Daniel* (London, 1950), 38. Of the six hundred mentioned, only 140 were monks and the remainder are called *conuersos et laicos*. Not all were resident at Rievaulx, of course, and Walter Daniel says that the church was crowded with the brethren "like bees in a hive, unable to move because of the multitude . . . compacted into one angelic body" on feast days; in other words, only on those occasions when the lay brothers from the far granges would be back at the abbey. The numbers at Rievaulx have been questioned, as have those at other houses (see L. J. Lekai, *The Cistercians: Ideals and Reality* [Kent, OH, 1977], 44-46). Not all of them seem out of line, however. For instance, the seventy monks and 120 lay brothers mentioned at Waverley in 1189 (*Ann. W.*, 244) or the sixty-six monks and 150 lay brothers at Louth Park in the second quarter of the thirteenth century (*Chron. LP.*, 15)

do not seem unreasonable. Among the French abbeys comparable figures may be cited. The growth of Vaucelles is the best documented: in 1152, after twenty years of existence, there were 103 monks, three novices, 130 lay brothers; around 1200, 110 monks and 130 lay brothers; between 1204 and 1238, 111 monks and 180 lay brothers; and between 1238 and 1252, 140 monks and 300 lay brothers (see M. Aubert, *L'Architecture cistercienne en France* [1947], 1:10, 226). These figures are close to those mentioned in the 1231 visitation of the former Savigniac houses in England, which again seem plausible (see chapter 5 of this study, n. 64).

[13] Powicke, *Life of St. Ailred*, 37; the translation is from D. Knowles' *The Monastic Order in England*, 2d ed. (Cambridge, 1963), 258.

[14] Powicke, *Life of St. Ailred*, 12-13.

[15] Ibid., lv, lvi, and 73.

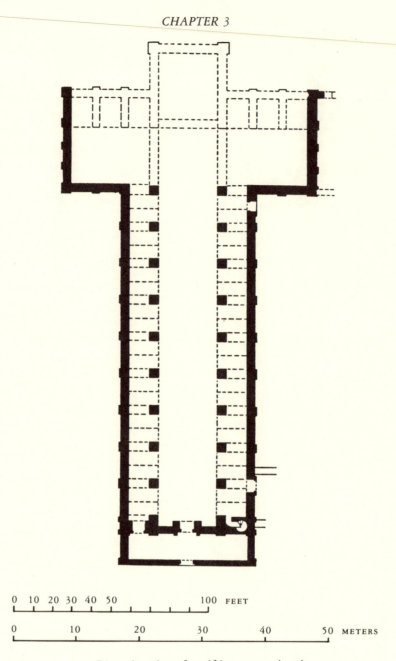

```
0  10 20 30 40 50              100  FEET
├──┼──┼──┼──┼──┼─────────────────┤

0          10        20        30        40        50  METERS
├──────────┼─────────┼─────────┼─────────┼─────────┤
```

5. Rievaulx, plan of twelfth-century church.

properties in that year accompanied by additional land grants may possibly signal the close of work.[16]

The plan of the church of Rievaulx (fig. 5) shows an aisleless, square-ended presbytery, transepts each with three chapels, an unsegregated crossing, and a nine-bay nave. In this form the church served the large community's needs for a century before a huge eastern extension transformed it. The plan resembled those of other Cistercian abbeys built between *circa* 1135 and 1160, especially those of sixty-eight

[16] *Mon. Angl.* 5:281-82. The date of 1145 for the finish of the church is also posited by Weatherill and by Peers (see J. Weatherill, "Rievaulx Abbey, The Stone Used in its Building," *YAJ* 38 [1954], 333-58; and Sir Charles Peers, *Rievaulx Abbey* [London: Department of Environment, 1967], 8). A papal confirmation by Alexander III, obtained in 1160 could coincide with the completion of the monastic buildings (*Mon. Angl.* 5:283). The literature on the architecture of Rievaulx is extraordinarily thin. There is still no comprehensive survey even, and virtually nothing on the first church.

direct descendants of Clairvaux, the Bernardine group, as they have been called.[17] Two features of Rievaulx emerge as distinctive, however, and they also come to mark the plans of other abbeys in the north, such as Fountains. First, the aisle walls lack articulation on their inner surface (plate 3), stretching east-west as an unbroken plane, whereas on the exterior the bays are divided regularly by wall buttresses. Second, the aisles are noticeably narrow in proportion to the nave and result in bays with a pronounced oblong plan, proportions that differ from those of the Bernardine group, or from those of numerous Romanesque churches, where the total width of the church is divided into four proportioned parts: two for the nave, one each for the aisles (the lines of division being fixed by the centers of the piers). The effect of both features at Rievaulx is to diminish the sharply defined character of the individual bay; and the same impulse, though expressed differently, may be discerned in other early Bernardine churches in Europe, such as the Swiss abbeys of Bonmont and Hauterive, or those in northern France, such as Vauclair I (Aisne), Clermont (Mayenne), and Boquen (Côtes-du-Nord).[18]

The distinctiveness of the church at Rievaulx is underlined by comparing its plan with that of the only other English house to be founded directly by Clairvaux, Boxley in Kent, founded in 1143. The proportions of the church at Boxley are the standard ones employed in the later Bernardine churches, like Fontenay, where the width of both aisles equals the width of the nave, and it is probably no coincidence that the second abbot, Thomas (1153-1162), came to Boxley from Fontenay.[19] Other Cistercian abbeys in England, like Bordesley and Kirk-

stall, both founded in the 1150s, follow these same proportions. Thus the plan at Rievaulx probably represents an early version of the Bernardine plan.

The plan of the church at Rievaulx is closely related to that of the French Cistercian abbey church at Vauclair, recently revealed by excavation.[20] Also founded by Clairvaux, two years after Rievaulx, Vauclair has similar proportions to the great English monastic church. The crossing, however, was segregated, unlike that at Rievaulx, where the west crossing piers are identical with those in the nave. Whether the segregated crossing at Vauclair represents a variant outside Burgundy, or whether Courtois' dating of the plan is too early is not certain. Interestingly, historical links connect Vauclair and the Yorkshire houses. Its first abbot, Henry Murdac, was a Yorkshireman and a celebrated schoolman noted for his scientific interests. Murdac had been the teacher of Abbot William of Rievaulx, and he later became his fellow monk at Clairvaux. In 1144 he was to become abbot of Fountains. Whether these links explain the similarities between the churches at Vauclair and Rievaulx or whether, more simply, they derive from a common source in Burgundy cannot yet be established. The plans confirm phases in the development of the Bernardine church, however.

The plans of all these churches indicate distinctive design and setting-out procedures which were effected through the use of modular systems derived from what has been aptly called "constructive geometry." The modular system cannot have been based on the crossing, or at least on the crossing square, as is often thought, because the crossings in these early Cistercian abbeys are rectangular.

[17] Karl-Heinz Esser was the first scholar to advance the idea of a "Bernardine" group, based on the study of the plans particularly of the filiation of Clairvaux (see bibliography). The term quickly entered the literature. Esser's thesis was extended by H. Hahn, *Die frühe Kirchenbaukunst der Zisterzienser* (Berlin, 1957). For other contributions, see J. A. Schmoll, "Zisterzienser-Romanik: Kritische Gedanken zur jüngsten Literatur," *Formositas Romanica* (Basel, 1958), 153-80; A. Dimier, "Eglises cisterciennes sur plan bernardin et sur plan bénédictin," *Mélanges offerts à René Crozet* (Poitiers, 1966), 2:697-704; W. Krönig, *Altenberg und die Baukunst der Zisterzienser* (Bergisch Gladbach, 1973), 31-64.

The only discussion of the plans of the English abbeys is H. V. Beuer, "Evolution du plan des églises cisterciennes en

France, dans les pays Germaniques et en Grande-Bretagne," *CN* 8 (1957): 268-89.

[18] See F. Bucher, *Notre Dame de Bonmont und die ersten Zisterzienser Abteien der Schweiz* (Bern, 1957); for Clermont and Boquen, see Aubert, *L'Architecture cistercienne en France* 1:232-33 and 172-73.

[19] P. J. Tester, "Excavations at Boxley Abbey," *Arch. Cant.* 88 (1973): 129-58, plan facing 130. For Thomas, see D. Knowles and C.N.L. Brooke, *The Heads of Religious Houses: England and Wales, 940-1216* (Cambridge, 1972), 128.

[20] See R. Courtois et le groupe sources, "La Première Eglise cistercienne (XIIᵉ siècle) de l'abbaye de Vauclair (Aisne)," *Archéologie médiévale* 2 (1972): 103-32.

Attempts to recover the module inductively have been made by Hanno Hahn and François Bucher for the German and Swiss abbeys, respectively, and recently, through precise measurement of a small number of churches, by David Walsh for the English houses.[21] Most probably it was based on a system of squares disposed sequentially or in a grid, or else turned diagonally. Setting-out practices based on the manipulation of squares are known from earlier buildings in Burgundy, including Cluny, and they continued into the thirteenth century; in Villard de Honnecourt's *Sketchbook* (circa 1230) the Picard master specifically identifies these practices with the Cistercians, inscribing a plan, "this is a church made of squares (*vesci une glize desquarie*) for the Cistercian Order."[22]

Studied together, the Bernardine plans reveal the attachment of the filiation of Clairvaux to a relatively standard layout for their churches. They also show the ease with which architectural ideas could be transmitted over long distances and the role exercised by a prototype design over subsequent copies. At Clairvaux, for instance, at least three masters were on hand to be dispatched as building needs arose within the filiation: Geoffroi of Ainai was sent to Fountains in 1133 and to Clairmarais in French Flanders in 1140, Archardus to Himmerod in 1138, Robert to Mellifont in Ireland in 1142.[23] Such a practice implies the use of standardized concepts that emerged in the mid-1130s to replace the much more varied architecture of the order's early years. Specific examples of this process also come from the family of Clairvaux in England. At Newminster, founded in 1138, Abbot Robert set out the monastery "after our manner" (*de more*), and the same phrase is used of the work of Adam of Meaux at Woburn, founded in 1145, and of

Abbot Alexander at Kirkstall in 1152 (see appendix B). In some cases monks were sent to the mother house to learn the correct form of buildings. At the Dutch abbey of Aduard, for instance, Abbot Wigbold ordered a member of the community to go to Clairvaux to copy its plan.[24] Although this dates from 1224, it could well reflect earlier practices, and it illustrates the commitment to specifically Cistercian forms.

The means by which fairly standardized ideas were transmitted can again be illustrated by the English houses. Present in Yorkshire in 1133, at the moment when plans for the church at Rievaulx were being formed, was one of the masters credited with the building of Clairvaux, Geoffroi of Ainai. He is documented at Fountains, only eighteen miles away, in the early summer of 1133, and his presence there raises the question of his possible activity at Rievaulx. Baker has argued on documentary grounds that Geoffroi was at Rievaulx and that Bernard sent him from there to get the Fountains' monks properly established.[25] In any event, the proximity of the two abbeys makes it likely that Geoffroi visited Rievaulx whose monks had been his colleagues at Clairvaux as recently as the year before. Interestingly, Robert, Alexander, and Adam were also at Fountains in 1133, and their later work in architecture makes it plausible that they were trained by Geoffroi, and that they in turn trained others (see appendix B).

Just as the plan of Rievaulx reveals a strong indebtedness to Burgundy, so too does its elevation, or the remains of it that provide the basis for a reconstruction (fig. 6). Organized in two storys and rising to a height of about fifty feet, the interior was both impressive and austere (plate 2). Bare wall separated the arcade from the clerestory, both of

---

[21] See Hahn, *Die frühe Kirchenbaukunst der Zisterzienser*; Bucher, *Notre Dame de Bonmont*, 184-90; D. Walsh, "Measurement and Proportion at Bordesley Abbey," *Gesta* 19 (1981): 109-13. In general, see B. Kossmann, *Einstens massgebende Gesetze bei der Grundrissgestaltung von Kirchenbauten* (Strasbourg, 1925). For the geometry used by the Cistercians, see W. Tschescher, "Die Andwendung der Quadratur und der Triangulatur bei der Grundrissgestaltung der Zisterzienserkirchen Ostlich der Elbe," *AC* 22 (1966): 96-140.

[22] H. R. Hahnloser, *Villard de Honnecourt*, 2d ed. (Vienna, 1972), 65-67, plate 28.

[23] See Hahn, *Die frühe Kirchenbaukunst der Zisterzienser*, 80,

253; for Mellifont, see A. Schneider et al., *Die Cistercienser: Geschichte, Geist, Kunst* (Cologne, 1974), 58; on Geoffroi's role at Clairmarais, see Aubert, *L'Architecture cistercienne en France* 1:97.

[24] See N. Uitterdijk, "Etude sur l'abbaye d'Aduard," *B. Mon.* 2 (1874): 216-24.

[25] D. Baker, "The Foundation of Fountains Abbey," *Northern History* 4 (1969): 29-43, esp. 38. Serlo, however, specifically mentions that the messengers returned from Clairvaux with a monk called Geoffroi "in their company" (see *Mem. F.*, 47.

6. Rievaulx, reconstruction of nave.

abbeys like Bonmont or Fontenay such vaults were part of a coherent structural system, which provided support at right angles for the barrel vault over the nave. But the argument for structural coherency can be overstressed; the Caen churches, for instance, mixed timber and vaulted roofs, as did Romanesque churches in England. Furthermore, the same arrangement used at Rievaulx is found in western France at Clermont (Mayenne) (*circa* 1155), and neither scheme implies an intention to vault the nave. In both cases (and also later at Fountains) the use of barrel vaults over the aisles probably stems from association with the architecture of the order's homeland in Burgundy.

Little is known of the east parts of the church at Rievaulx although excavation has recovered the plan of the original presbytery. The crossing was unsegregated; namely, the piers that framed it were the same size as those in the nave (and can still be discerned encased in thirteenth-century work). No tower, therefore, was planned.[28] Almost certainly the crossing took a similar form to the one at Clermont, being unsegregated and towerless and joining the nave, transepts and choir at equal height. There was thus no stepped arrangement for the east parts of the church (*hohenstaffelung*, in the more vivid German word) resulting from the choir's and transepts' being lower than the nave, a characteristic of the Bernardine church, like that at Fontenay.

One central question at Rievaulx, then, is its relationship to the larger family of Bernardine churches. In plan a distinction has already been made between an early phase, to which Rievaulx belonged, and a mature phase, best represented by Fontenay, and the same is suggested by the reconstruction of the elevation. The interior of the mature Bernardine church consisted of an arcade carrying a barrel vault, aisles with barrel vaults set perpendicular to the nave, and a choir and transepts

which were treated simply. Supports and openings, for instance, received minimal articulation or detail; the square piers lacked bases and only their front face was relieved by chamfered angles, a feature found also in the transepts at Pontigny (*circa* 1145) (plate 4).[26] A timber roof covered the nave,[27] but the aisles were vaulted (remains of the vault departures survive in the south aisle), each bay being barrel vaulted, with vaults turning transversely to the nave axis.

The barrel vaults are curious and seem redundant in the context of the wooden-roofed nave. In early

---

[26] Chamfering of piers occurs also at Sens, Chartres (St. Père), Etampes (St. Martin), Avallon (St. Lazare), Montréal, and Château Landon (see K. W. Severens, "The Early Campaign at Sens, 1140-1145," *JSAH* 29 [1970]: 97-107, esp. 102-103).

[27] It is mentioned in the sixteenth-century Dissolution inventory (see *Chart. R.*, 337): ". . . in the body of the church . . . the seling of the rofe payntyd . . . the clerestory of the body of XVIII lights of square stone." Hahn's claim that a barrel vault was intended (*Die frühe Kirchenbaukunst der Zister-*

zienser, 203) is not supportable by the wall thickness.

[28] I have not been able to follow on site Hope's statement in *VCH: Yorkshire, North Riding* (vol. 1 [London, 1914]: 497) that "parts of the Norman steeple" are actually in their original place on the south wall. Twelfth-century masonry is discernible in the thirteenth-century north crossing arch, but it has been recut with a thirteenth-century molding (that is, reused) and is too high to have been part of a twelfth-century crossing supporting a tower.

lower than the nave. Only one of these features appears at Rievaulx, the barrel-vaulted aisles. But Rievaulx predates the mature churches, and evidence suggests that it was based on a different model. Just which model is obscure still, though a possibility is Cîteaux II, begun around 1130. Few details are known about this building, but it is probably best reflected in a small surviving group of two-story structures with timber roofs and clerestories such as Clermont (plate 5) and Boquen in France, and Amelunxborn and Altenberg I in Germany.[29] As part of this family, then, Rievaulx emerges as in no way exceptional. Certainly, the timber roof and clerestory may not be accounted for, as they often are, in terms of climate and location in the far north of England. Most likely, Rievaulx adhered to an earlier prototype of the second-generation churches, based not on Bernard's later building, begaun in 1135, but on Cîteaux.

The reconstruction of Rievaulx reveals much about the earliest large-scale Cistercian architecture. The interior presented an apprearance of stripped austerity and mural flatness. Detailing was minimal, surfaces bare and devoid of articulation, ashlar rough in its composition and irregular in its coursing. Quotations abounded from the Romanesque architecture of Burgundy, asserting the foreign sources of Cistercian reform as well as declaring the architecture appropriate to it. Although the architecture's main effects would have resulted from the proportional interplay of the components of the elevation, and of this only guesses can be made, there is enough to indicate that within the broad spectrum of Romanesque architecture the large-scale Cistercian church, with its spare formal vocabulary and rejection of decorative detail, stood in opposition to the penetrated and often richly ornamented architecture in use elsewhere in England.

Set down in twelfth-century Yorkshire, then, a large-scale architecture of such calculated simplicity offered startling contrasts to the prevailing style of both Anglo-Norman cathedrals and of smaller-scale monastic churches like Lindisfarne. This was absolutely intentional. The Cistercians saw themselves as set apart, a transplanted vanguard of the new monasticism, and their fierce sense of identity was expressed with complete consistency in their architecture. It is no coincidence that when Ailred, writing during the years of construction of the church, warned of the "concupiscence of the eyes," he used architecture to illustrate his ideas. A monk, he said, learns to shun "any sort of habitation that is too large or extravagantly vaulted. . . . He is happy enough to say his prayers in a little chapel of rough, unpolished stone where there is nothing carved to distract the eye; no fine hangings, no marble paintings, no murals that depict ancient history or even scenes from Holy Scripture; no blaze of candles, no glittering of golden vessels."[30] What Ailred meant by "too large" is unclear, particularly considering the size of Rievaulx, but his words echo the deep convictions of the early Cistercians about the form and expression of their churches. Themes of avoiding distraction and emphasizing the interior life run throughout much of the *Speculum Caritatis*, and it may be argued that the architecture of Rievaulx was designed not just to illustrate these ideals but to promote them.

Within a year of the foundation of Rievaulx, work began on Fountains, the second Cistercian monastery in the north. The new monastery was established under highly irregular conditions, however, and lacked the intimate connections with the order's homeland in France that marked Rievaulx. It also never achieved the spiritual renown of the earlier abbey, despite the fame and dazzling reputation it enjoyed. The subtle differences of character are reflected in the architecture and, even more remarkably, still characterize the sites right up to the present. After a hesitant beginning Fountains grew at prodigious speed; at the height of its power in the thirteenth century the monastic buildings covered twelve acres, and the area within its precinct wall, fifty-five acres, was fitting testament to the wealthiest Cistercian abbey in the country (plate 6). Fronted since 1716 by the majestic landscape conceived by William Aislabie, the former chan-

[29] On Cîteaux and its successors, see Aubert, *L'Architecture cistercienne en France* 1:191-93; and Hahn, *Die frühe Kirchenbaukunst der Zisterzienser*, 238.

[30] *PL* 195, cols. 572-74. The translation comes from G. Webb and A. Walker, *The Mirror of Charity* (London, 1962), 74-75.

cellor of the Exchequer disgraced in the South Sea Bubble scandal, and surrounded now by swards of emerald-green grass, Fountains is the most often visited monastic ruin in Britain and unquestionably one of the most beautiful.

The early history of Fountains is richly documented thanks to a partly eyewitness account, Serlo's *Narratio.*[31] Although not one of the original monks, Serlo tells us he joined Fountains within two or three years of its foundation. Sent as one of the pioneer monks to establish Kirkstall in 1147, where he passed the rest of his life, Serlo dictated his history of Fountains to another monk around 1205. By then he was nearly one hundred years old. As an historical document, the *Narratio* has its share of problems, beginning with the advanced age of Serlo and the intentions of his scribe. Particularly suspect are attempts to draw self-promoting parallels between the histories of Fountains and Cîteaux. Although this makes it necessary to treat the account with caution, the *Narratio* nevertheless throws much light on the abbey's early years, particularly until 1147, the year Serlo left Fountains for Kirkstall, and on the sequence of construction of the buildings.

The founding monks were Benedictines from St. Mary's York who had been prompted to reexamine their approach to monasticism after learning of the new reform at Rievaulx. Their calls for change went largely unheeded, however, and they separated in early October 1132 amid scenes of physical violence in which the archbishop of York, Thurstan, came bodily to their aid. Settled at Skeldale shortly after Christmas of that year, on land given them by the archbishop, the monks lived for the first weeks in

caves, then in a structure built around a giant elm tree, and after some months in wattle huts. They also constructed a wattle chapel.[32] Only in the following spring (1133) did the community apply for affiliation with the Cistercians via Clairvaux. To instruct them on the Cistercian reform, Bernard dispatched Geoffroi of Ainai, a monk from Clairvaux who "had set in order and established many monasteries, especially those whose members by the counsel of the holy man [Saint Bernard] changed their habit for the greater perfection of their life and submitted themselves to the monastery of Clairvaux."[33] Serlo tells us how he saw Geoffroi in person and describes him as "of great age and modest gravity," but he adds that Geoffroi was "vir industrium" in matters human and divine. Under Geoffroi's direction the monks "built houses and set out workshops,"[34] their activity prompted by the need for more orthodox arrangements than existed before his arrival. Serlo omits any reference to Geoffroi's role in the construction of a church, implying that the wattle chapel already erected by the monks before his arrival met the order's requirements. On the other hand, the size and care with which the timber principal posts for the church were cut, as was revealed in Coppack's excavation, suggest a building demanding more time to erect than that mentioned by Serlo.[35]

Geoffroi's other architectural activities at Fountains are not detailed by Serlo. Despite his age Geoffroi was at the height of his career as one of the order's leading architectural masters; two years later, in 1135, he began work on the widely influential second church at Clairvaux (with Archardus). Considering the unfamiliarity of the Fountains monks

[31] Published in *Mem. F.* 1:1-129; see also D. Baker, "The Genesis of Cistercian Chronicles in England: The Foundation History of Fountains Abbey," *AC* 25 (1969): 14-41; and pt. 2, see vol. 31 (1975): 179-212.

[32] *Mem. F.* 1:34-35. The best account of the first buildings is R. Gilyard-Beer, "Fountains Abbey: The Early Buildings, 1132-1150," *Arch. Jnl.* 125 (1968): 313-19. Baker has drawn attention to the parallel between the story of the elm tree at Fountains with the same at Cîteaux, which, in view of similar attempts to match the histories of the two houses, casts some doubt on the authenticity of the Fountains' version (see "The Foundation of Fountains Abbey," 32 n. 20). Not surprisingly, the story has proved durable; in the mid-sixteenth century Leland recorded that the elm was still growing in the cloister

(T. Hearne, ed., *Lelandi Joannis De Rebus Britannicis Collectanea* [Oxford, 1713], 4:105). Gilyard-Beer believes the likely location was further down the valley (see "Fountains Abbey," 314).

On the rupture at St. Mary's, see D. Nicholl, *Thurstan, Archbishop of York, 1114-1140* (York, 1964), 151ff.

[33] *Mem. F.* 1:47.

[34] ". . . ad ejus consilium casas erigunt, ordinant officinas . . ." (ibid. 1:47).

[35] See chapter 2 of this study for description of the remains. Dr. Coppack believes the remains date from the church built following Geoffroi's arrival. I wish to thank Dr. Coppack for discussing the matter at length with me prior to the publication of the results of his excavation.

with Cistercian practice and given Geoffroi's experience and talents, it is highly probable that he left plans for the future development of the monastery as money and men permitted. And as already seen above, it is likely that he instructed three of the monks, Robert of Newminster, Dan Alexander of Kirkstall, and Adam of Meaux, in the order's architectural customs and methods.

A modest enlargement of the community in the year following Geoffroi's visit (1134) can be inferred from Serlo's distinction, in an account of a gift of bread, between the monks and the *carpentarii*, and the *operarii*, whose requirements of food came before those of the community.[36] The latter were most likely outside labor brought in to help with building.[37]

Throughout this period, however, the economy of Fountains was perilous; as a result of its unusual foundation history, the abbey lacked sufficient endowments of land or lay benefactors. By 1135 conditions had deteriorated to the point that hope of a permanent settlement was abandoned. Accordingly, the house sent a formal request for transfer to Clairvaux with the proposal that the monks move en masse to Burgundy. Bernard assented and assigned a grange at La Longué (Haut Marne) as their new home. With the arrangements for transfer already made, however, the fortunes of Fountains changed dramatically. The monks were joined by one of the most learned and prominent churchmen in the north, Hugh, dean of the Minster church of York (1093-1135), and a few months later he was followed by two other members of the York chapter. Together they brought money, land, and in the case of the dean, a considerable private library. In a matter of weeks, then, the whole economy of the abbey was transformed and the conditions of its future growth established.

In accordance with the *Exordium Parvum* (chap. 15), the new money was divided into four parts,

one quarter of which was set aside for building. Work must have started quickly on a stone church and cloister. The century-old debate over whether the present standing church is the original church, however, has at last been settled by Coppack's discovery in 1980 of an earlier stone church.[38] It was a small building (fig. 7), of a dimension, in fact, that would be plausible for a community numbering thirty.[39] Land and gifts to help in its construction and in the establishment of the monastery now arrived quickly. Those that specify the church date from between 1135 and 1146 and indicate a five- to ten-year construction period.[40] In these years new men joined the monastery in considerable numbers. Between 1135 and 1138, for instance, three new colonies were founded by Fountains—Newminster, Kirkstead, and Louth Park—entailing a total departure of thirty-nine monks and about fifty lay brothers.

Serlo's next mention of the buildings concerns the year 1147. The third abbot of Fountains, Henry Murdac, had been annointed archbishop of York in a disputed election. Controversy developed and passions became so intense in the locality that a mob assembled and descended on Fountains in search of Murdac. Serlo tells us that armed men scaled the abbey's outer walls and then

broke down the doors, insolently entered the sanctuary, rushed through the buildings, seized spoil, and as they did not find the abbot whom they sought, they set fire to that sacred building which had been erected with great labor, and reduced it to ashes. They had no respect for the order, they had no respect for the altar. The holy brotherhood stood by and saw with sorrow in their heart the building they had raised by the sweat of their brow wrapped in flames, soon to be ashes. The church alone, with the buildings close to it, was saved, reserved as they believed for prayer, and even the church was half-consumed, like a brand plucked from the burning.[41]

[36] *Mem. F.* 1:50.

[37] The practice was not unusual. Hired labor is mentioned four times in the *Exordium* and *Carta caritatis* (see appendix B) and later statutes regulated the food and clothing that the hired labor was allowed and specified the offices they should attend in the church.

[38] G. Coppack, "Fountains Abbey," *Arch. Jnl.* (in preparation).

[39] The figure is mentioned by Serlo, *Mem. F.* 1:53.

[40] For instance, see *Chart. F.* 1, no. 6, 705; and *Mem. F.* 1:57.

[41] "Veniunt Fontes in manu armata, et, effractis foribus, ingrediuntur sanctuarium cum superbia, irruunt per officinas, diripiunt spolia, et non invento quam quaerebant abbate, sancta illa aedificia, grandi labore constructa, subjectis . . . ignibus, redigunt in favillam. Non defertur ordini; non defertur altari. Stant prope, sacer ille conventus; et edificia, in sua sudore constructa, non sine cordis dolore, vident flammis involvi,

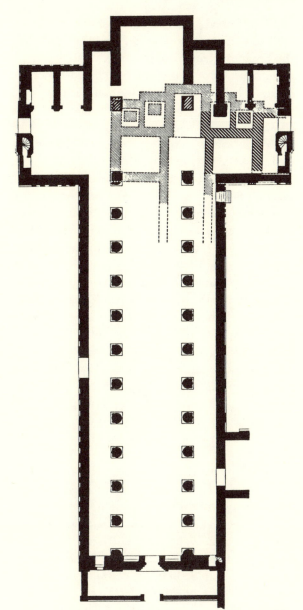

7. Fountains, plan showing first and second church.

The buildings to which Serlo refers can now be sorted out thanks to recent excavation. As already seen, the earlier wooden church had been replaced

by a stone building, Fountains I, constructed between 1135 and 1146. Part of the wooden structure may have still been standing, however, perhaps the west bays, projecting beyond the transept of Fountains I, and it was this that Serlo refers to as "the sacred building reduced to ashes." The masonry building was saved from the fire, although it was "half-consumed (*semiustum*)." Coppack uncovered floor levels strewn with debris consisting of burned plaster, melted glass, and charred wood that came from the fire damage to Fountains I. The fire must also have damaged much else, including parts of the east range, and presumably, the south and west ranges, of the cloister.

Reconstruction began immediately. Serlo says the monks "repaired the fallen places, rebuilt the ruins, and as it is written, the walls fell down, but with hewn stones was built again. They were helped by the faithful of the neighborhood; a new building rose up far more gorgeous than its predecessor."[42] Serlo seems here to compress matters. Evidence of renovation work on Fountains I was found, including new floors and it can be assumed that the church was reroofed and refinished internally. But shortly thereafter, perhaps as early as 1148, work began on a new building, Fountains II, which was much larger in scale. Started a little to the north of Fountains I (see fig. 7), it was raised initially as an envelope around the earlier church, which was then demolished. It is Fountains II that Serlo refers to as both new and "far more gorgeous" than its predecessor. In 1154, seven years after the fire, rebuilding was still in progress; Serlo mentions a conciliatory visit by the new archbishop of York (Murdac had died the year before) in which he viewed the new work and promised financial assistance.[43] By 1170 at the latest the east claustral range, two storys high, was finished; in that year Abbot Richard III was buried in the chapter house.[44] Building continued into the 1170s, however; Serlo says of the rule of Abbot Robert of Pipewell (1170-1178),

cineres mox futura. Solum illis, in tanto discrimine, salvatur oratorium cum officinis contiguis, orationis, ut creditur, usibus reservatum, ipsumque semiustum, sicut torris raptus de incendio . . ." (*Mem. F.* 1:101).

[42] ". . . lapsa reparant, ruinosa reformant, et sicut scriptum est, 'Lateres ceciderunt, sed quadris lapidibus reedificatur.' Adjuvabent eos de vicinia viri fideles; et consurgit fabrica longe festivior quam ante fuit." (Ibid., 102.)

[43] Ibid., 109-10; see also *Chron. M.* 1:116-17. Papal confirmations were obtained by the monks from Hadrian IV in 1156 and from Alexander III in 1162, perhaps to coincide with the completion of stages in the reconstruction (see W. Farrer, *Early Yorkshire Charters* [Edinburgh, 1914] 1:78-80, charter no. 80; 1:80-81, charter no. 81).

[44] *Mem. F.* 1:132.

"he recommenced work on the church and erected splendid buildings."[45] Since the remains of the church indicate completion around 1160, this important reference is difficult to interpret. Possibly it means the building of masonry screening such as a pulpitum or the provision of permanent choir stalls. The "splendid buildings" included the spacious refectory and parts of the west range.

Fountains II (fig. 7), the present standing church, was developed in two programs, as Coppack has shown.[46] The first, around 1150 saw the construction of an enlarged east end with the transept chapels expanded from two to three in each arm, an unsegregated crossing, probably without a tower, and an aisleless nave of five "bays." By any standard, the plan of the church was decidedly conservative, despite the size and growing importance of the abbey; aisles and a lengthened nave were established features of Cistercian churches by the late 1140s. Yet Fountains was not the only northern abbey around mid-century to adhere to the older pattern of aisleless, small-scale plans (discussed in chapter 2). At Sawley on the western slopes of the Pennines in Yorkshire, established in 1148, and related to Fountains at one remove (it was a daughter of Newminster, sent out by Fountains in 1138), the plan of the church was virtually identical in form and dimensions (see catalog). Building started at Sawley around mid-century. In the 1140s and 1150s reform orders like the Premonstratensians and Augustinians (see chapter 2) also copied the plan at Fountains. The plan's currency provides a context for understanding the wish of the community at Fountains to adhere to it after the fire, despite the scant room for altars.

By the early 1150s, however, halfway through the construction of the transepts, an important change was made in the plan at Fountains. Aisles were added to the nave (necessitating a shift of the cloister to the south), the west crossing piers were strengthened to provide support for a low tower, and the nave was lengthened westward for a total of eleven bays. In its final form Fountains II resembled Clairvaux II, the church laid out by Archardus

and Geoffroi of Ainai, the latter of whom had been at Fountains twenty years earlier. The reasons for the program change are lost. But clearly, enlargement reflected a more powerful identity for the abbey. The plan undoubtedly resulted from decisions made by the new abbot, Richard III (1150-1170), a Yorkshireman by birth, who had joined Clairvaux in the mid-1130s where he rose to the rank of precentor. In 1144 Bernard appointed him abbot of Vauclair, succeeding Henry Murdac, a position he held for the six years before coming to Fountains. Richard's appointment as abbot of Fountains was a critical one. The controversial Murdac had been followed at Fountains by two ineffective figures, both of whom ruled only briefly, and firmness and stability must have been essential qualities for the new abbot. When Richard left Vauclair, the church was still under construction; the plan was very similar to the one adopted at Fountains including the feature of a segregated crossing. Yet wholescale importation of the plan from France is unlikely; the layout procedures and proportions copy those at Rievaulx, and it is quite possible that monastic labor came from there to assist with work, a practice well known within the order (see appendix B).

Although the choir at Fountains disappeared in the early thirteenth century when it was replaced by the beautiful eastern extension, excavation has revealed the plan. This shows a small, aisleless choir with a straight-ended east wall and the transept chapels in a stepped arrangement. More information comes from Serlo in the *Narratio*, where, talking of the rule of Abbot John (1203-1211), he explains that the church then "flourished like a vine," with many flocking to it, and that "the congregation of monks was greater than usual, so that there were not enough altars to celebrate on, and the choir was too humble and dark and small for so great a multitude."[47] These words unintentionally reveal the first ideals of the order for architecture as well as documenting an expanded priest population among the monks with their needs for additional altars.

---

[45] ". . . instauravit ecclesiae fabricam, edificia construxit sumptuosa" (*Mem. F.* 1:114).

[46] Coppack, "Fountains Abbey."

[47] The critical parts read: "et facta est congregatio mona-

chorum numerosior quam solebat, nam altaria pauciora ad celebrandum, et chorus humilior et obscurior, et minus capax tantae multitudinis" (*Mem. F.* 127-28).

The plans of both Fountains I (*circa* 1135-1147) and Fountains II (1147-1152 and *circa* 1152-1160) show an unusual stepped arrangement for the transept chapels. Apart from Melrose (begun 1136), a daughter house of Furness, no further example is known in the British houses, and in France it is equally rare.[48] Liturgical practice required dual entrances to the monastic choir, one at the west end, the *inferior introitus*, and the second at the east, the *superior introitus*.[49] In churches with an aisleless presbytery, the *superior introitus* was gained by stopping the monks' stalls a few feet short of the east crossing piers. At Fountains a doorway may be deduced east of the crossing (see fig. 7), which would then explain the added length of the inner chapels.

The transepts at Fountains are preserved in relatively unaltered form. The elevation (plate 7) is carried on flat-faced piers with chamfered angles enclosing an inner arch of rectangular section. Capitals, moldings, and bases are omitted. Over the arcade the bare wall is punctuated with small, deeply splayed windows framed by string courses. This scheme probably resembled that at Rievaulx, completed a few years earlier, and is close to that at Clermont, also of the early 1150s (plate 8), or at Ourscamp II, *circa* 1155 (plate 9), similarly intended to be wooden roofed.[50] It is, in fact, the transepts at Fountains rather than the frequently illustrated nave that best show the architecture imported by the order into northern England.

In the nave of a little later this scheme is modified as befits the new program of work (plate 10). No disjuncture of style is apparent; the language is accepted, as it were, but the vocabulary is distinctly enlarged. Piers are now cylindrical with attached angle shafts to the aisles; bases have bell profiles; scalloped capitals support the arcade, which is enlivened with angle rolls; arch openings reach high into the plain wall surface; clerestory windows are lengthened. The changes constitute an elaboration of the style of the transepts, one characterized by greater relief, greater mural penetration, and a more monumental massing. Underlying these changes is a certain assimilation of English influence; many of the above-mentioned components derive from the architecture of mid-twelfth-century England in the north.

Yet as English as the components are, they are combined with others that can be explained only in terms of the order's origins in France. The barrel vaults covering each bay of the aisles (plate 11), for instance, are imported Burgundian features, as are, most likely, the pointed profiles of the arcade, the circular windows in the south transept gable and in the chapel end walls (plate 12), the corbeled supports of the transverse arch of the aisle vaults, and at the west façade, the lean-to porch with small arcades like a cloister on the outer face. There is, then, an unmistakable impression of English elements and French elements being brought together. The union is one of assembly more than synthesis, however—a quality seen, for instance, in the awkward "fit" of some parts of the system, such as the transverse arch of the aisle that joins the pier on a corbel that has "slipped" below the capital.

The modification of the architectural idiom of the Cistercians represented by the nave at Fountains contrasts with Rievaulx of the 1130s or even more with Fontenay of the 1140s. The change is important, and it is not limited to Fountains. At Rievaulx the chapter house of *circa* 1150 derives from a Durham source,[51] and at Kirkstall the church begun in the mid-1150s also shows a strong an-

[48] For the discussion of this *staffelchor* arrangement, see Krönig, *Altenberg*, 24-30. The same arrangement was used in the church the monks left in 1132, St. Mary's York.

[49] The churches of the Hirsau reform also used the same east plan (see W. Hoffman, "Hirsau und die 'Hirsauer Bauschule,'" *L'Architecture monastique—Die Klosterbaukunst, Numéro spéciale du Bulletin des relations artistiques Franco-Allemagne* [Mainz, 1951], no page numbers), and it was the arrangement for the presbytery at St. Mary's York whence the monks had come.

[50] See C. A. Bruzelius, "The Twelfth-Century Church at Ourscamp," *Speculum* 56 (1981): 28-40.

[51] This can be justified by the shafts from the interior, fragments of which are now in the store house on the site. They show a horizontal chevron design with petal flowers that relates to work at Durham Cathedral. Connections between Durham and Rievaulx probably came through the second abbot, Maurice (1145-1147), who had formerly been subprior at Durham. He subsequently left Rievaulx to become abbot of Fountains (1147-1148), although the appointment was not a success and he returned to Rievaulx where he died in 1167. (See F. M. Powicke, "Maurice of Rievaulx," *English Historical Review* 36 [1921]: 17-25.) The connection was kindly pointed out to me by Miss Katherine Galbraith.

glicizing trend. How should this break with architectural tradition be interpreted? One explanation is that it resulted from the gradual assimilation of local traditions that entered piecemeal via masons trained in local or regional workshops. This gradualist theory is far less plausible, however, than one holding that the change was conscious and intended. Political and historical writing of the 1150s suggest a climate open to deliberate adaptation. In Saint Ailred's *Genealogia regum Anglorum* (1153-1154) the abbot of Rievaulx interprets the recently ended Anarchy as a division between races and sees the new king, Henry II, as providing unity. To illustrate his point, Ailred employs an architectural metaphor: Henry is the cornerstone uniting the two walls of the English and the Normans.[52] Some of the same spirit pervades this phase of the order's architecture in the middle to late 1150s.

The arrangement of the interior of the church at Fountains (fig. 8) cannot be surmised from the uninterrupted space of the present-day structure, with its open vistas stretching west to east. A schematic reconstruction based on Hope's study of the cuts and holes in the piers from long-vanished screens and altars as well as traces of foundation walls shows that the church was formerly divided into four main parts.[53] In the east was the monks' choir, which extended through the crossing to include the first bay of the nave. Occupying the second bay was the pulpitum, a high masonry screen. Next followed the antechoir, occupying two bays, for infirm and sick monks, with a chapel on either side in the east bay and chapels in the flanking aisles of the next bay. A second screen across the nave divided the antechoir from the lay brothers' choir, which occupied the last seven bays of the building. Chapels were placed in the aisles of the fifth bay on the north

and south, and altars, in the sixth bay, north and south, and in the seventh bay on the south. In addition to the three chapels in each transept, therefore the nave contained eight more and an additional five altars, for a total of nineteen altars. Such a count is plausible; there were twenty-two altars at Clairvaux in 1174.[54]

The last work on the nave was carried out in the late 1150s and included the west bays and west façade. The latter was treated like a transept terminal and, as was also customary, was preceded by a one-story porch, of *circa* 1160, which opened to the west through arcading. The façade was at one time intended to have three entrances (as seen from the interior); but only the center and north doorway were built (the latter blocked), and coursing irregularities suggest the center doorway dates after the façade, though not by many years. The doorway is decorated with intricate moldings, with thin rolls and hollows and capitals with trumpet scallop and foliate designs (plate 13). The capitals are unlike any others in the church. The moldings resemble those in the east claustral range, however, and their appearance, marked by a lightness and linearity in direct contrast with the thickness and rectangularity of those in the transepts or nave. Such a change signals a stylistic watershed in the architecture of the monastery. Significantly, the doorway moldings do not resemble contemporary English work, but rather that from eastern France. Particularly striking are parallels with moldings from the Fontenay chapter house, dating to *circa* 1155 (plate 14).[55] Similarly, the west façade at Fountains was derived from France. Composed of a lower zone of three round-headed windows topped by a rose window, it resembles those at Silvacane and Trois Fontaines (plate 15).[56]

[52] See the *Vita S. Edwardi Regis*, in *PL* 195, col. 738-39.

[53] See W. H. St. John Hope, "Fountains Abbey," *YAJ* 15 (1898-1899): 36-44. Dating the various changes is tricky, but the arrangement seems characteristic.

[54] For Clairvaux, see chapter 2 of this study, fn. 17. At Mellifont in Ireland, to take another example, which was a smaller foundation than Fountains, ten altars are recorded in 1157, the year in which Devorgilla, wife of Tighernan O'Rourke, gave a chalice of gold for the high altar and costly furnishings for nine other altars (see M. Archdall, *Monasticon Hibernicum* [London, 1786], 479).

[55] Apart from Cistercian ties, a further connection may come

from the fact that the patron of Fontenay was Everard, bishop of Norwich. For the date, see R. Branner, *Burgundian Gothic Architecture* (London, 1960), 163.

[56] Sharpe's reconstruction was based on molding fragments surrounding the traceried fifteenth-century window (see E. Sharpe, *The Conventual Churches of the Cistercian Abbeys of St. Mary at Fountains and Kirkstall* [London, n.d. (1870)], plate 4). For Cistercian west façades, see Schneider et al., *Die Cistercienser*, 204-30. Rose windows were an archetypal Cistercian motif by the 1150s. They appeared in transept ends (Pontigny [1150], Preuilly [1155]), west ends (Bonmont [1145], Hauterive [1150]), east ends (Noirlac [1155-1160], Kirkstall [1155-

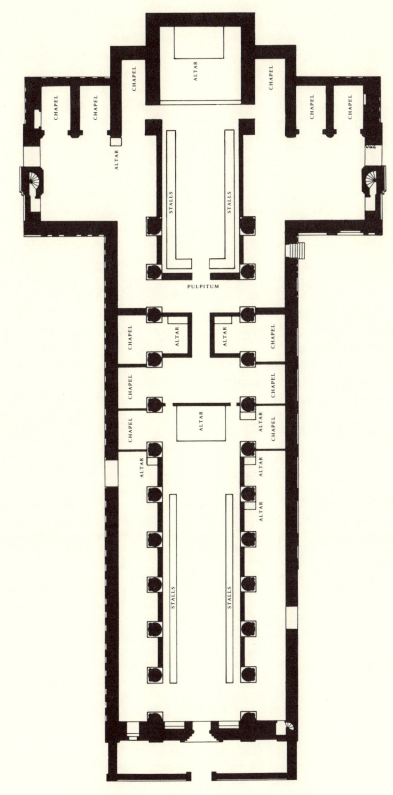

CHAPEL CHAPEL CHAPEL ALTAR CHAPEL CHAPEL CHAPEL

ALTAR

STALLS STALLS

PULPITUM

CHAPEL ALTAR ALTAR CHAPEL

CHAPEL ALTAR CHAPEL

ALTAR ALTAR

STALLS STALLS

8. Fountains, schematic divisions in church.

In addition to chronology and style, there is the issue of the segregated crossing and low stone tower at Fountains. Coppack's excavation has shown that the segregated crossing was not part of the first program of Fountains II but belonged to the modification dating from around 1152.[57] Assuming that plans for the tower were made at the same time, the tower was one of the earliest raised by the Cistercians. At other abbeys in England crossings and towers were also adopted from the late 1150s onward, for instance, at Kirkstall, Buildwas, Furness, Abbey Dore, Louth Park, Bordesley, Holmcultram, and Dundrennan (Scotland).[58] Outside England, in France and other countries, towers were also introduced after mid-century.

A crossing tower was not a mere ornamental addition to the Cistercian church. On the contrary, it fundamentally modified the eastern parts of the building. In the Bernardine church, like Fontenay (plate 16), the transept and presbytery were lower in height than the nave, which with its barrel vault continued as a unified, uninterrupted space through the "crossing" to terminate with an arch framing the east end. A tower required the support of a true crossing, marked off by projecting shafts carrying equal height arches on each of its sides and thus segregated from the nave, transepts, and chevet. Following from this, then, the transepts and chevet became the same height as the nave. On the exterior, the whole massing of the eastern end of the building was transformed.

Given the implications of these changes, it is not surprising that the General Chapter of the order addressed a statute to towers. Passed in 1157, it states tersely: "Let stone towers with bells not be built."[59] Another statute in the same year regulated the bells in a monastery; it permitted two bells, but they had to be rung singly, and their weight was restricted to five-hundred pounds so that one person might ring them.[60] In compliance with these statutes, churches such as Fontenay and Silvanes did not build towers and hung their two bells from a small bellcot. In other abbeys crossing towers were raised, but without bells.

Among the several possible interpretations of the tower statute, the most likely is a literal one: stone

---

1160]). Historical links connect Fountains and Trois-Fontaines; for instance, Theodald, after resigning as abbot of Fountains in 1151, was appointed abbot of the French house. For Trois-Fontaines, see A. Dimier, "Trois-Fontaines, abbaye cistercienne," *Mémoires de la société d'agriculture, commerce, sciences, et arts du département de la Marne* 80 (1965): 38-51. For Silvacane, see Aubert, *L'Architecture cistercienne en France* 1, fig. 254.

[57] Coppack, "Fountains Abbey." Two crossing piers remain, the southeast and northwest. The east piers, which belong to the first program, were square in section and plain, like the piers at Rievaulx. The west piers, however, were much larger (plate 10), enriched by angle shafts and decorated with an artichoke leaf capital, a motif that occurs in early form on some aisle responds (east bays, south aisle) and in developed form, like those on the crossing, in the west bays. The upper part of the southeast pier carries scalloped capitals surmounted by molded springers to the crossing arches, which frame a colonnette between. The molding profiles of the arches date to around 1155 (and compare with the parlor doorway) as does the capital, which shows artichoke leaves with a central decorative motif (similar to the capitals of the galilee [plate 39]). Equally telling, the crossing was not laid out in a square; it is eighteen inches shorter from east to west than from north to south.

[58] P. J. Fergusson, "Early Cistercian Churches in Yorkshire and the Problem of the Cistercian Crossing Tower," *JSAH* 29 (1970): 211-21. This article did not mention Newminster, which provides a similar example to Rievaulx, namely, of an early square pier used for the crossing of identical size to those in the nave, which were subsequently encased in later masonry (see B. Harbottle and P. Salway, "Excavations at Newminster Abbey, Northumberland, 1961-1963," *Arch. Ael.*, 4th ser. 62 [1964]: 95-171, esp. 109-10 and fig. 9). For Bordesley, see P. Rahtz and S. Hirst, *Bordesley Abbey, Reddich*, British Archaeological Association Reports, no. 23 (Oxford, 1976), 89ff.; for Dundrennan, see P. J. Fergusson, "The Late Twelfth Century Rebuilding at Dundrennan Abbey," *Ant. Jnl.* 53 (1973): 232-43.

[59] "Turres lapideae ad campanas non fiant" (*Statuta* 1 [1157:16]: 61). The statute was apparently reaffirmed in 1182; see the version of the General Statutes originating at Vauclair (J. Leclercq, "Épitres d'Alexandre III sur les cisterciens," *Revue Bénédictine* 64 [1954]: 68-82, esp. 77).

[60] "Campanae nostri Ordinis non excedant pondus quingentarum librarum: ita pulset, et numquam duo pulsent simul" (*Statuta* 1 [1157:21]: 62). It was not unusual to find even prominent monasteries with only one bell. At Waverley, for instance, the *Annales* record under the year 1219 that up until that date the monastery had possessed only one bell but that, thanks to the help of Abbot Adam I, the greater bell was obtained (*Ann. W.*, 110). By the late thirteenth and fourteenth centuries, however, bells were installed in crossing towers, which then had to be heightened beyond one story. This often led to severe difficulties due to insufficient foundations—as at Fountains, Furness, or Bordesley. Sherbrook mentions nine bells in the crossing tower at Roche in the sixteenth century (see app. A).

towers with bells were forbidden, but towers without them were allowed. The statute must have resulted from debate over the admissibility of towers raised in all likelihood by a test case. Such a case could have involved Clairvaux, where reconstruction of the church begun in 1153 included a crossing topped by a spire on the exterior. It had reached the initial stage of completion by 1157, the year of the decree.[61] Whether or not Clairvaux provided the impetus for enacting the statute, it is clear that arrangements like the one Israel Sylvestre shows there (plate 17), or like the low stone tower at Cadouin, lay within the limits defined subsequently by the statute. These towers were not higher than one story, and they barely projected above the roof line. In part, they were simple extensions of the crossing arches and must have served as structural braces.

The size and form of towers was a matter of considerable sensitivity, however, and later statutes show that the order's unyielding attitude continued well into the thirteenth century. At Boheries (Aisne), for instance, the abbot watched his tower demolished in 1217 because it was "contra formam Ordinis."[62] On the other hand, a tower for the new church at Waverley (begun in 1203) was mentioned in the *Annales* in 1248, when a workman fell from its top during construction but escaped injury.[63] The tower must have been a later addition, for the monks occupied the eastern parts of the building in 1231. Waverley's tower is close in date to the one at Meaux, where Abbot William of Driffield (1249-1269) built a belfry on the church (begun in 1207) and hung in it the great bell called "Benedict" (see catalog under Meaux). These references indicate a change in the use and size of the Cistercian's towers after the mid-thirteenth century. Even so, the general intentions of the order remained clear; an exemption issued in the General Chapter in 1274 granted the abbot of Valloires "his request concerning the making of the tower . . . because on account of the force of the winds it would

be dangerous in that abbey to build a wooden tower, provided that it not exceed the quantity and obligatory shape in conflict with the order's simplicity."[64] In other words, towers of the right "quantity and obligatory shape," in either wood or stone, were admissible, as is revealed by an expanded version of the 1157 statute issued in 1240: "Let stone towers with bells not be built nor wooden [towers] of extravagant height that would mar the simplicity of the order."[65] This statute, then, may be regarded as clarifying the order's position on the issue of towers, which can be summarized as: tall towers (i.e., those of more than one story) were taboo; towers could not house bells; and towers had to adhere to a certain form.

That the early English abbeys kept to these standards is shown at Fountains and in two abbeys that retain parts of their twelfth-century towers, Kirkstall and Buildwas (plate 106). At the latter abbeys the towers were low and the two windows in each face were placed near the angles on each side of the abutting roof, and the tower in consequence rose only slightly over the roof ridges. Their intended effect is probably best seen today at Brinkburn (Northumberland) (plate 18), an Augustinian house of *circa* 1180-1200, heavily influenced by the Cistercians.

So widespread are low towers and so various their forms that their appearance in the order's architecture has to be explained by reasons other than structural necessity, or regional preference. One clue to the adoption of towers may be the coincidence of legislation on burial with that on towers. Traditionally, one meaning carried by towers (one among several) was as a marker of burial places. Cistercian statutes on burial appear first in 1152 when the early prohibition on burial in the church was lifted to permit the interment of kings and queens, archbishops and bishops. This was probably the year when the tower at Fountains was adopted. Then in 1157, the same year the first statute on towers appeared, legislation on burial was expanded to

[61] The best summary of Clairvaux III is in W. Schlink, *Zwischen Cluny und Clairvaux* (Berlin, 1970), 91, 108-16, 138-41. See also, A. Dimier, "En Marge du centenaire bernardin, l'église de Clairvaux," *CCC* 25 (1974): 309-14.

[62] *Statuta* 1 (1217:27): 471.

[63] See *Ann. W.*, 340; also cf. n. 60 above.

[64] ". . . dummodo quantitatem et formam debitam contra simplicitatem Ordinis non excedat" (*Statuta* 3 [1274:39]: 135).

[65] "Turres lapideae ad campanas non fiant, nec ligneae altitudinis immoderatae que ordinis dedeceant simplicitatem" (A.R.P.H. Séjalon, *Nomasticon Cisterciense* [Solemnes, 1892], 287, no. 2).

permit the burial of lay benefactors in the church.[66] One likely explanation for the reconstruction of Clairvaux, with its new crossing and flèche, was the desire to provide a suitable architectural setting for the burial place of Saint Bernard (see below), and similar reasons may underline the appearance of towers, or their addition to existing buildings, in other abbeys of the order.

The church that stands today at Fountains, then, results from the rebuilding following the fire of 1147 and subsequent changes of program in the early 1150s. Completion of the whole fabric including the west porch, may be fixed around 1160. Serlo's characterization of this building as "far more gorgeous than its predecessor" was doubtless accurate in the context of the earlier church, although to us, perhaps, its severe grandeur makes such a judgment seem extravagant. By the general standards of the 1150s the architecture achieves an ingenious dualism: it combines up-to-date detailing that makes references to both England and France with what can only be described as a conservative expressive effect. The same cannot be said, however, of the other monastic buildings under construction at Fountains at the same time. For the chapter house, parlor, and guest houses, Early Gothic was employed, and the lightness and crisp richness of the new style contrasts strikingly with the gravity and simplicity of the church. The distinction in style between church and claustral buildings will be discussed in the next chapter, but it should be pointed out that this distinction was by no means limited to England; in France—for instance, at Fontenay—similar contrasts separate these two areas of the monastery.

The third monument of early Cistercian church architecture in the north of which substantial remains survive is Kirkstall (plate 19), a daughter house of Fountains settled in 1152. Although Kirkstall was dependent on Fountains, it is clear that the master at Kirkstall—possibly the abbot, Dan Alexander, formerly prior at Fountains—set out deliberately, even competitively, to refine and im-

prove his building on the basis of the other. Thus while the constituent elements of the two churches are similar, changes in proportion and massing produce very different effects. Remarkably for related houses the architectural detailing is fundamentally distinct. And further differences mark the layout of the claustral buildings at each house. Since no more than five years separate the church at Fountains from that at Kirkstall, clearly the order tolerated greater freedom in the interpretation of architectural standards in the mid-1150s than in the late 1140s.

An earlier settlement at Barnoldswick had had to be abandoned because it was hard to protect and subject to flooding. Abbot Alexander selected the new site, and the *Fundacio* tells us that his first task was to erect a church (*basilica*) and arrange humble offices according to order (*dispositis ex ordine humilibus officinis*) (see appendix B). These were probably the first wooden buildings, although they document Alexander's involvement in the work. Permanent stone buildings were begun shortly after occupation. Resources were plentiful; the monks' patron, Henry de Lacy, "stood by [Abbot Alexander], now providing the fruits of harvests, now supplying money as the needs of the establishment required. He had part in providing the buildings, laid with his own hands the foundations of the church, and himself completed the whole fabric at his cost."[67] Given this support, it is safe to assume that construction of the church began within a year or two of settlement. By 1159 a gift is recorded of one mark for clothing for the abbot and a half mark for the purchase of oil for the sanctuary lamp,[68] implying the monks' occupation of the choir and transepts. Certainly by the time Henry de Lacy died in 1177,[69] the church was finished (see the above quotation). Indeed, the history records that by the death of Abbot Alexander in 1182 all "the buildings of Kirkstall were erected of stone and wood brought there, that is, the church and either dormitory of the monks to wit, and of the lay brethren, and either refectory, the cloister, and the chapter and other offices necessary within the abbey, and

[66] *Statuta* 1 (1152:10): 47; and (1157:63), 68. On the general question of towers as markers of burial, see G. H. Forsyth, "St. Martin's at Angers and the Evolution of Early Medieval Church Towers," *AB* 32 (1950): 208-18.

[67] The passage reads: ". . . ipse edificijs prouidendis inter-

fuit ipse manu sua ecclesie fundamenta iecit, ipse totam ecclesie fabricam impensis proprijs consummauit" (*Fund. K.*, 180).

[68] Farrer, *Early Yorkshire Charters* 3: 192-93, charter no. 1500.

[69] Ibid., p. 199.

all these covered excellently with tiles."[70] Assuming that the eastern parts of the church were finished in 1159 and knowing that financial help was constant, completion of the church around 1165 is plausible.[71]

Beginning with the plan, different setting-out techniques were employed at Kirkstall than at Fountains. Instead of a sequence of squares arranged in additive form, Walsh has shown that the procedure was based on diagonally turned squares.[72] As at Fountains, the eastern end shows two programs of work. To the first belong most of the choir and the lower courses of the east walls of the transept; to the second belong the crossing, the upper and west parts of the transepts, and the east bays of the nave.

The choir at Kirkstall, the only one to survive from the early churches in the north, has evidence of an important modification in the upper walls and vaulting. Outside, the flanking walls are divided into three equal bays by wall buttresses (plate 20), whereas inside they show two bays and are bare. It seems the alteration was made once the outer walls had been constructed. The unusual thickness of the lateral walls suggests that a barrel vault was originally intended, but rib vaults eventually replaced it. These are quadripartite (plate 21) and must be later insertions to judge from extensive scarring in the masonry. The vaults cover the choir except for a four-foot gap preceding the crossing, which is filled by a narrow barrel vault.[73]

Comparison of the two programs shows changes to the crossing. On the west side the nave was set out about three feet wider than the choir, and this

meant that an adjustment had to be made to the east side. Accordingly, shafts were applied to the earlier scheme, projecting out on either side of the choir and leaving a strip of bare wall immediately flanking the choir.[74] Refinements in the capitals, abaci, and arcade moldings bear witness to the program changes; all take on slimmer proportions than those of the choir arch (plate 23). A low tower was raised over the new crossing, and if, as seems likely, this change occurred around 1155, it follows by a year or two the adoption of the same feature at Fountains.

In the transepts (plate 24), the chapels are separated by solid walls and covered by barrel vaults, as at Fountains, but the piers, by contrast, are flat-faced, accentuating the continuity of the wall surface. The chapel entrances are flanked by an attached shaft to carry the outer moldings, and the jambs have triple shafts to support roll moldings in the arch soffit. Capitals are mostly scalloped, but in some cases an unusual interlace design is used.[75] Equally unexpected are the appearance of chevron ornament in some moldings and the carving of corbels on the exterior under the chapel roof. Such motifs are unique to Kirkstall in the Cistercians' architecture. Their singularity indicates a decorative exuberance and an association with nonmonastic architecture that was frowned upon at other abbeys. It also points to a connection with English sources that is confirmed by other un-Continental features like the soffit rolls.

In the nave (plate 25) the influence of Fountains is unmistakable in the form and proportions of the elevation. And yet the Kirkstall master mason's

---

[70] *Fund. K.*, 181.

[71] This is also the date suggested by Bilson in his classic study of the building: "The Architecture of Kirkstall Abbey Church," *T. Soc.* 16 (1907): 84; also *Arch. Jnl.* (1909): 199 and n. 2. In addition, confirmations were obtained from Pope Hadrian in 1156 and from Henry II between 1156 and 1162 and again between 1170 and 1173, possibly to coincide with the completion of stages in construction (see Farrer, *Early Yorkshire Charters* 3:152-53, charter no. 1452; 3:157-58, charter no. 1461).

[72] Walsh, "Measurement and Proportion at Bordesley Abbey," 111-12, established a close connection between the transepts at Kirkstall and Bordesley. Bilson drew attention to the nearly identical dimensions of Kirkstall and Fontenay ("Architecture of Kirkstall Abbey Church," 88).

[73] In the first program one or two details derive from Fountains, like the abbreviated clasps attached to the base molding

on the exterior (center bay, east wall), but they were omitted thereafter. According to Hope, the east wall originally contained a circular window over three round-headed windows; the circular window was in turn surrounded in the spandrels by four small, round windows, see "Kirkstall Abbey," *T. Soc.* 16 (1907): 1-72, esp. fig. 18. The design may be compared with that of the façade of Les Vaux-de-Cernay.

[74] Fergusson, "Early Cistercian Churches in Yorkshire," 217-18.

[75] See J. T. Irvine, "Notes on Specimens of Interlacing Ornament which Occur at Kirkstall Abbey," *JBAA* 48 (1892): 26-30. The closest parallels to the Kirkstall interlace occur in contemporary manuscripts and on the capitals at Southwell. I wish to thank Katherine Galbraith for pointing out the connection to me. Even more eccentric are the base moldings of some of the nave piers, which unwind into interlace patterns on the plinths (see plate 22).

different conception of architecture emerges clearly. Most noticeably, he shows an aversion to the inert massing of Fountains and a marked preference for articulation and subdivision. In the five eastern nave bays, for instance, the piers swell gently outward into eight incipient shafts from the core of the pier, with each shaft separated by rolls or fillets; the arch moldings are forceful and larger in scale than those at Fountains, and enriched and softened with soffit rolls; the capitals, bigger and flared in profile, show variants of the scallop motif; the bays are slightly longer; and the arcade rises higher than at Fountains. On the exterior, the clerestory is framed by shafts. Altogether, the elevation is tighter, more lively, and shaped more insistently than the stout, bare forms at Fountains.

The aisles at Kirkstall (plate 26) carry rib vaults, the master abandoning the transverse barrel vaults that had created difficulties for his counterpart at Fountains. The vaults lack wall ribs, but their crown line is uniform in height, and the aisle reads as a unified whole, trends that were implicit in the unarticulated aisle walls at Rievaulx and Fountains. These vaults are English in their form and construction, descending from those of Durham and Lincoln.[76] Equally English is the triforium in the south wall of the south transept, which provided access to the outer corners of the transept and thence to the transept chapel roofs. The same feature is known at Hereford Cathedral (*circa* 1110) and at St. Cross Winchester (*circa* 1165).

It is against this background of increasing Anglo-Norman influence that the appearance of new work in the three west nave bays and in the west façade needs to be seen. Even though the overall scheme of the earlier work was respected in the later construction, detailing and structural elements were changed. The piers, for instance, were worked in fasciculated form (twelve shafted with shafts of three different diameters), the abaci carry triple grooves, and on the outside, artichoke leaf designs decorate

the capitals in the clerestory. The fasciculated pier, is of particular interest because it marks the appearance of a form that was subsequently to enjoy a long popularity in Cistercian and non-Cistercian architecture in the north of England. Although piers of generally similar form had been used in the eleventh century in both England and France (for instance, at Great Paxton, Huntingdonshire, or at St. Remi, Reims), they fell out of use, and their reappearance in the twelfth century seems an unrelated development. Around 1140 fasciculated piers appear in northeast France—for instance, at Berteaucourt-les-Dames (Somme) (plate 27), Heuchin (Pas-de-Calais), Pogny (Aube), and Selincourt (Somme).[77] The Cistercians picked up the form around 1150-1155, virtually simultaneously in France in Burgundy (Fontenay, chapter house, plate 28) and in England in Yorkshire (Fountains, east guest house, plate 29). Within fifteen years fasciculated piers appeared at Furness, Kirkstall, Byland, and Roche, and in secular churches such as York Minster (crypt) and Ripon.

Unlike the Romanesque compound pier, the new pier had the virtue of offering a more compact and unified appearance. As a free-standing support it diagramed the converging linear accents of the rib vaults, which it carried with much more coherence than was possible using the separated, additive vocabulary of the compound pier. The process leading to its adoption can be followed at Fountains, in the east guest house, where the ground story was divided by a row of columns down the center, each of which supported rib vaults. In the north bays the ribs were received on a smooth, round column that had corbels attached under the capital and (inverted) above the base. This looked piecemeal, however, and in the south bays the corbels were connected top and bottom, as it were, to form shafts. At Kirkstall the same desire to clarify relationships can be inferred from the different diameters in the twelve shafts used in the west nave

[76] Bilson, "Architecture of Kirkstall Abbey Church," 123. On early rib vaults in England, see also J. Bony, "Diagonality and Centrality in Early Rib-Vaulted Architecture," *Gesta* 15 (1976): 14-25. It should be noted that in Burgundy the Cistercians had also largely abandoned the barrel vault for the rib by *circa* 1155—for instance, at Clairvaux III, Pontigny, Ourscamp, and Fontenay (chapter house) (see Branner, *Burgundian*

Gothic Architecture 16-19, 127-28, 141-42.

[77] See P. Héliot, "La Nef de l'église de Pogny et les piles fasciculées dans l'architecture romane," *Mémoires de la société d'agriculture, commerce, sciences, et arts du département de la Marne* 83 (1968): 80-92. Héliot omits Cistercian examples of the piers' use.

piers. Shafts of varying diameters also convey a more dynamic appearance, and the standard solution employed after *circa* 1170 thus divided the shafts into majors and minors, thereby imputing to them qualities of dominance and subordination.

The change in architecture noted in the west bays of the nave at Kirkstall is made even more palpable in the west façade (plate 30), whose composition differs markedly from façades at Fountains and other Cistercian abbeys in France. The porch and rose windows were eliminated in favor of a two-windowed arrangement (framed by shafts) over an imposing gabled doorway. Design and detailing—such as chevron moldings, keeling,[78] artichoke leaf and early volute capitals, and a pediment with intersecting arcades—recall northeastern France, for instance, the façade of the Collegiale St. Omer, in Lillers (Pas-de-Calais) (plate 31).[79]

The chapter house was contemporary with the western nave bays and façade at Kirkstall and equally north French in form and feeling. Here vaults with keeled ribs rest on two free-standing piers, the west one with a cylindrical core and grouped, detached shafts *en délit*, the east one a squat version of the west nave piers with keeled major shafts.[80] Detailing here and in the now ruined cloister arcade (plate 44) may be compared with that of Fountains and at the infirmary cloister at Rievaulx.

The churches at Rievaulx, Fountains, and Kirkstall are related in an architectural development spanning thirty years. That they were part of a still wider group is suggested by fragmentary remains at two other Cistercian abbeys: Sawley in Yorkshire and Louth Park in Lincolnshire.

The plan at Sawley is strikingly similar in dimensions to that at Fountains II before its enlargement (see catalog under Sawley). The elevation is more severe and closer to Rievaulx in such details as the chamfered angles with ball terminals of the transept openings. Yet, more importantly, the elevation was divided vertically by projecting shafts (plate 32), a prominent feature that occurs at neither Rievaulx, Fountains, nor Kirkstall but is close to French examples like Ourscamp or Pontigny (see plates 9 and 4). Nothing is known about how the building was covered. Adherance to French models at Sawley needs to be contrasted with the deliberate absorption of English ideas at Fountains and Kirkstall. If the date of Sawley is early 1150s, as seems likely, then the English impulse in the order's architecture in the north can be narrowed more precisely to the period between about 1153 to 1160.

Louth Park was established by Fountains in 1139 after one false start. Laid out on an ambitious scale the church measured just a few feet shorter than Fountains. Only the east end was finished however, perhaps in the 1150s, and it was eighty years before Abbot Richard Dunham (1227-1246) "completed the [other] half of the body of the church at great cost and labor, as may be estimated from the timber work, likewise also the cloister of the *conversi* ad-

---

[78] The earliest example of keeling in the north of England appears to be in the Durham chapter house rib vaults and door (*circa* 1135). It can also be found in the west door at Lincoln (*circa* 1150). In France, keeling was in use in the 1130s (see C. Enlart, *Manuel d'archéologie française* [Paris, 1902], 1:459). The Cistercians in England used it at Louth Park (see text below) around 1155, at Fountains in the east guest house piers and rib vaults around 1155, and at Kirkstall on the west façade door and in the chapter house rib vaults and supporting triplet shafts around 1165. Thereafter, it becomes nearly universal. The earliest example of its use by the Cistercians in France is at Ourscamp, in the west end south door molding in about 1155.

[79] On Lillers, see C. Enlart, *Monuments religieux de l'architecture romane et de transition dans la région Picarde* (Paris, 1895), 228-34; P. Héliot, *Les Eglises du Moyen-âge dans le Pas-de-Calais* (Arras, 1951), 400ff. The collegial was not of exceptional importance, but with so much else destroyed, it survives as the only major work in northeastern France more or less entire.

The motif of the pedimented gable placed over the outer moldings is also found in this area (see L. Devliegher, "L'Architecture romane de la Flandre française au nord de la Lys," *Mélanges offerts à René Crozet* [Poitiers, 1966], 499-506, examples at Bourbourg St. Jean and Renescure). Likewise, the crenelation in the outer order of the north door of the nave at Kirkstall may also be compared with examples in northeast France (see M. Anfray, *L'Architecture normande, son influence dans le nord de la France aux XIᵉ et XIIᵉ siècles* [Paris, 1939], 348), although it also occurs widely in England—for instance, at Lincoln in the west façade.

[80] The entrance from the cloister mixes coursed-in shafts with shafts *en délit*. On the latter, see J. Bony, "Origines des piles gothiques anglaises à fut en délit," *Gedenkschrift Ernst Gall* (Berlin, 1965), 95-122. Apart from the piers at Furness, Bony does not consider Cistercian examples in the north. In addition to the Kirkstall piers, those in the chapter house and day room at Rievaulx should be mentioned, the latter being almost certainly older than Bony's other examples.

joining the said church" (see catalog under Louth Park).

The plan at Louth Park shows an east end arrangement like the early Yorkshire churches. The presbytery was formed by massive walls and was narrower by three feet than the nave, both features that recall Kirkstall. Solid walls separated the transept chapels, the original crossing appears to have been unstressed, and rib vaults covered the aisles, again like Kirkstall. The nave piers were cylindrical with four attached shafts on the cardinal points, a form used, though with the shafts detached, in the Rievaulx chapter house and day room and later in the crypt at York Minster.[81] Architectural detailing included rib vaults with a mixture of rounded, chamfered, and keeled profiles.[82] The evidence at Louth Park is so fragmentary that it is hard to be precise about its relationship to Fountains and Kirkstall, but on detailing alone a date around 1160 is plausible, with a suggestion of closer contact with French sources than either of the Yorkshire churches.

The relationship of the early English abbeys—Rievaulx, Fountains, Sawley, Kirkstall, and Louth Park—to their French counterparts has never been satisfactorily explained. Sir Alfred Clapham emphasized the English qualities of the houses, and Hanno Hahn went so far as to suggest that they sprang from a purely local school.[83] If anything, recent emphasis on the Bernardine churches has intensified the difference between the French and English styles; the barrel vaults, windowless naves, towerless exteriors, and stepped east ends of the French houses stand in apparent contrast to the English with their clerestories, timber roofs, and towers. Yet strict definitions of the Bernardine elevation are to some extent suspect. As has been seen, the abbey church of Clermont, a direct de-

scendent of Clairvaux's, shows an elevation with striking parallels to Cistercian churches in England. And Sawley shows strong resemblances to eastern French models. Clermont indicates the existence of forms different from those at Fontenay or other mature Bernardine churches.

The destruction of both Cîteaux II and Clairvaux II has hindered the assessment of this entire second-generation architecture. The loss of Clairvaux is particularly unfortunate since all five English abbeys discussed above were affiliated with it. From Clairvaux came monks, architectural advice in the person of Geoffroi of Ainai, support, and visitation, and there, of course, lived the order's greatest figure, Saint Bernard, in whose lifetime all five abbeys were begun.

Clairvaux I, a small aisleless building, had served the community for two decades (circa 1115-1135); Clairvaux II, the prototype Bernardine church, was begun in 1135 and consecrated in 1145; and Clairvaux III, begun 1153/1154 and consecrated in 1174, stood until the early nineteenth century.[84] Of particular interest is the surprising speed with which Clairvaux II, with barrel vaults and small straight-ended presbytery, was succeeded by the third church, with rib vaults, clerestory, and a fully developed ambulatory and radiating chapel scheme (best represented in the seventeenth-century painting at Ville-sous-la-Ferté, Aube, plate 33). What led to the rejection of the earlier architecture after less than a decade has never been established. Even more puzzling is why the third church was so rarely copied, when the second church was so widely influential. Not only has the singularity of Clairvaux III raised questions about Saint Bernard's role in the design, specifically his knowledge or ignorance of it, but it has also led to the speculation of possible "heresy" in a design that was subsequently used so rarely. Although the latter appears unlikely, the

[81] For the York piers, see J. Browne, *The History of the Metropolitan Church of York* (Oxford and York, 1847), vol. 2, plates 17-19.

[82] See E. Trollope, "The Architectural Remains of Louth Park Abbey," *AASRP* 12 (1873-1874): 22-25.

[83] A. W. Clapham, *English Romanesque Architecture after the Conquest* (Oxford, 1934), 2:79; Hahn, *Die frühe Kirchenbaukunst der Zisterzienser*, 203.

[84] Demolition started in 1808. The bibliography is exten-

sive; besides the work mentioned in n. 61 above, see P. Jeulin, "Les Transformations topographiques et architecturales de l'abbaye de Clairvaux," *Mélanges Saint Bernard* (Dijon, 1954), 325-41, with a valuable source bibliography, 340-41; also P. Jeulin, "Quelques Découvertes et constatations faites à Clairvaux depuis une vingtaine d'années," *Bulletin de la Société nationale des antiquaires de France* (1960), 94-118. The most recent treatment is Krönig, *Altenberg*, 65-98.

third plan poses serious problems. In England it was adopted only at Beaulieu. Elsewhere a total of about ten examples are recorded, of which Alcobaça in Portugal and Pontigny III are the best known. Most were raised around the year 1200.[85]

Discussion of the third church at Clairvaux has thus far focused almost exclusively on purely architectural considerations. The circumstances of Bernard's death and burial, which bear on the program of the building, have been largely ignored. Long before his last illness Bernard was regarded as the order's spiritual father and as a saint in fact if not in name. Actual canonization occurred in 1174, but from the moment of his death at 9:00 A.M. on August 20, 1153, and his burial before the high altar two days later, Clairvaux actively pushed the process leading to it. Geoffrey of Auxerre was commissioned to complete Bernard's *Vita*, begun by William of St. Thierry and Arnaud of Bonneval.[86] By 1159 liturgical commemoration of Bernard had been authorized. Accounts tell of the many pilgrims who came to Clairvaux and particularly of the wish of the dying to find solace and burial near the body of the "saint." Indeed, before 1153 had closed, the zeal with which the movement for canonization was advanced led to a weakening of the program of poverty Bernard had insisted upon and to a modification of his texts with an eye to improving his credentials for sanctity.

It is in this atmosphere of emotion and belief that the program for the new church must have been formed. Clearly the overriding intention was to provide a fitting setting for Bernard's burial and, after canonization, for the elevation to the altars of the Cistercians' greatest figure. That this involved a break with the earlier architecture was probably a matter raised after the formation of the program. Work must have been undertaken in confident anticipation of canonization, possibly even as part of its promotion. Thus features appropriate to both burial and shrine space were employed: a lengthened choir, an ambulatory, a ring of chapels around a semicircular apse, and a crossing topped by a flèche.

The plan of the chevet was distinctive to the program, a feature that best explains the lack of immediate followers. Work was completed in stages: the east end was finished in the late 1150s; the nave, with its lead roof paid for by Henry II, not until 1178. The elevation of both chevet and nave was two story with a clerestory and covered by rib vaults; in appearance it probably resembled Ourscamp I, *circa* 1155 (plate 9), and Pontigny of a little earlier (plate 4). Except for the plan, the influence of the new architecture was widespread throughout the huge family of Clairvaux and beyond. To see these buildings of the 1150s and 1160s as departures from the orthodoxy of the Bernardine church exaggerates such orthodoxy and conceals the openness of the Cistercians' to new ideas in architectural style and construction.

In the light of these developments in France, the architecture of the order's abbeys in England can be better understood. The first buildings of the 1130s, typified by Rievaulx, adhered to a pre-Bernardine prototype now lost, but perhaps identifiable as Cîteaux II. The similarity of Rievaulx to Clermont shows that far from their being exceptional or products of a local school, both buildings reflect close contact with Burgundy and embody the order's prescribed expressive qualities. French contacts show a distinct weakening in the early 1150s, however. The second program at Fountains, the early work at Kirkstall, and the chapter house at Rievaulx all reveal a strong awareness of English architecture. But this awareness did not develop and was quickly displaced by renewed influence from France. This emerges around 1160, at Fountains in the cloister east range, and at Kirkstall in the west nave bays and west façade. Underlying the redirection of interest was the introduction of a new model, that of the mother house of all these abbeys, Clairvaux III. With rib vaults, Early Gothic detailing, a new spatial character, and a freshly conceived luminosity Clairvaux presented its entire family of monasteries with a line of contact to the latest developments in eastern France from the late 1150s onward.

---

[85] See A. Dimier, "Origine des déambulatoires à chapelles rayonnantes non saillantes," *B. Mon.* 115 (1957): 23-34.

[86] J. Leclercq, *Bernard of Clairvaux* (Kalamazoo, 1976), 95-101.

4

The Advent of Early Gothic

THE LAST HALF of the twelfth century was marked by prodigious building in the north of England. Stimulated by an increased population, a revived economy, expanding cities, and the settlement of the open lands of the northeast by the monastic orders, this building activity included virtually all types of architecture: cathedrals, abbeys, priories, parish churches, castles, civic and domestic structures. The result transformed the architectural map of this large area in England.[1]

How much of the new work was Early Gothic and where the new style appeared first are issues of central importance in understanding this great phase of building. Complicating the matter, however, are the less than convincing definitions of what constituted Gothic. Clearly it was more than the isolated use of single structural members such as the pointed arch or the rib vault, both of which had been employed at Durham Cathedral before 1130, for Durham remained Romanesque despite these two features, while the rib and pointed arch combined with other components to become part of the vocabulary of Early Gothic after mid-century. The distinction lay in the way the structural elements or details were employed in the larger categories of architecture, for instance in redefining and articulating space, in changing boundaries, in rethinking openings and hence the values of light, or in altering the expressive language of form.

Early Gothic was not created in England but in France around 1140. Thus the questions surrounding its appearance in England are the means and

points of entry, the particular sequence by which it was assimilated, and the resulting adaptation with indigenous architectural traditions. Since the issue is not one of invention, the new style may as easily have appeared in a number of small buildings as in one of large scale from whence its influence trickled down. Thus even though Early Gothic was used in the second program in the large new choir at York Minster (*circa* 1160s), the most important single building in the north of these years, the new style was already familiar a decade earlier in the conventual buildings of the Cistercians. At Fountains after the fire of 1147, for instance, the chapter house and guest houses were rebuilt using Early Gothic architectural detailing—waterleaf and volute capitals (plate 98), keeling, fasciculated piers, moldings with gorged crowns—and just as important, using them to give an enlarged sense of space, to lighten mass, and to sharpen the accents of architecture. Drawn from sources in eastern France, particularly from around Laon, the most dynamic area in the formation of the Early Gothic style, these ideas entered during the rule of Abbot Richard III (1150-1170), who, as already seen in the preceding chapter, had come to Fountains from Vauclair (Aisne), twelve miles to the south of Laon. At Rievaulx, likewise, Early Gothic was used in conventual buildings like the day room and the infirmary (*circa* 1150).[2] Why the new style appeared initially in these secondary structures rather than in the churches is unclear; perhaps it could be justified there on technical grounds alone.[3] In any

---

[1] The scale and intensity of architectural activity in the south was less than that between the Humber and the Tees, although the single major monument of these years, north and south, remains Canterbury Cathedral. The history of Early Gothic in the north of England has yet to be written, but for the main outlines, see G. Webb, *Architecture in Britain: The Middle Ages* (Harmondsworth, 1956), 72-95; and T.S.R. Boase,

English Art, 1100-1216 (Oxford, 1953), 126-55.

[2] The conventual buildings at Rievaulx have not been convincingly analyzed. The only useful discussion is Sir Nikolaus Pevsner, *BoE: Yorkshire, North Riding* (London, 1966), 303-306. For a plan see Sir Charles Peers, *Rievaulx Abbey* (London: Department of the Environment, 1934).

[3] The same is true of the French abbeys; for instance, at

event, an innate conservatism dominated the churches of the Cistercians well into the 1160s, and with the possible exception of Louth Park in Lincolnshire they remained resolutely Romanesque in style.

By the middle to late 1160s, however, Early Gothic was permitted in church architecture, and it rapidly transformed the buildings. Four churches first showed the new style: Furness in Lancashire, Roche in Yorkshire, Byland in Yorkshire (to be discussed in chapter 5), and Abbey Dore in Herefordshire (to be discussed in chapter 6).[4] Each developed independently of the others, and each employed a distinct version of the Early Gothic style that may be traced to prototypes existing in separate areas of France.[5] The architectural ideas embodied in these buildings dominated Cistercian architecture until the end of the century. In the assimilation of Early Gothic, however, a clear regionalism emerges that differentiates this phase of architecture from the earlier ones of the Cistercians.

The first Cistercian church in the new style was not in Yorkshire but on the other side of England, at Furness (plate 47), two miles from the Irish Sea.[6] Three-storied, spacious, with modern detailing, it introduced a fully developed version of French Early Gothic architecture into a region that until then had seen very little twelfth-century religious building.

The area's slow development resulted from climatic and geographical factors that made the northwest less attractive than the northeast to monastic pioneers. The land was not as fertile, and a high annual rainfall made it harder to grow the cereal crops that formed the basis of the monks' vegetarian diet. Moreover, mountains to the south and east hampered communications with the rest of England. Only to the north did the mountains subside into rolling hills, and this facilitated swift raids by Scottish border tribes. Thus struggles for territorial control troubled abbeys in the northwest for much of the twelfth and thirteenth centuries, and monastic chronicles are filled with accounts of invasion and harrying raids. This explains why buildings at Furness, Calder, and elsewhere are a patchwork of repairs and also why the architecture tended to develop along fairly self-contained lines.

For its first quarter-century Furness was not Cistercian but part of the Congregation of Savigny. Founded in 1124 at Tulketh and transferred to Furness in 1127, five years before the Cistercians came north to Rievaulx, it headed the thirteen abbeys established in rapid succession in the following years. As a Norman reform movement, the Congregation received Norman dynastic backing; its founder, Stephen, count of Mortain and Boulogne, was soon to become king of England. The foundation charter says proudly of Stephen: "hanc hac valle domum Stephanus comes aedificavit."[7] Included in Stephen's gift was his large forest of Furness, and to this were soon added other sizable estates. Within a short time the abbots enjoyed the status of great border barons with feudal independence over a huge territory. Men joined the founding monks in such numbers that by 1135 colonies could be sent to Calder, Rushden (Isle of Man), and Swineshead. The Savigniac dominance of the area probably explains the absence of early Cistercian settlements.

Work on the first church at Furness (Furness I) began *circa* 1130-1135, but all that remains of this building are some traces in the west walls of the transepts and south aisle. Hope's excavation in 1900, however, has shown that the east end followed the

---

Fontenay the chapter house is full-blown Early Gothic (plate 28), while the church is Romanesque (plate 14).

[4] To these examples can be added the last work at Kirkstall, namely, the west bays and west façade (see chapter 3 of this study).

[5] The influence of France in these decades was not, of course, limited to architecture; it included manuscript painting and enamel work as well (see C. M. Kauffmann, *Romanesque Manuscripts, 1066-1190* [London, 1975], 27). It is not clear exactly how or why these contacts operated. For the Cistercians, the order's French origins and ties were obviously fundamental, although other factors were involved. One that can only have contributed to the closeness was the use made by Becket and his entourage of the order's French abbeys. Becket spent 1164-1168 at the newly completed abbey of Pontigny, for instance, and was recorded at Clairmarais in 1164 and at Clairvaux in 1169.

[6] For the bibliography on Furness, see catalog.

[7] T. J. Beck, *Annales Furnesienses. History and Antiquities of the Abbey of Furness* (London, 1844), 284. In addition to the support of Stephen, the Congregation had the backing of the king, Henry I, who was a personal friend of the founder of Savigny, Vitalis de Mortain, and of his successor, Geoffrey de Bayeux.

characteristic Benedictine *en échelon* plan, with two apsed chapels in each transept, except that the presbytery was apparently aisleless and square-ended. Since the same features appear at Les Vaux-de-Cernay (Seine-et-Oise), a Savigniac house begun in 1135, they suggest that in architectural matters the Congregation kept to older, more conventional forms.[8]

In 1147, during a visit to Bernard at Clairvaux, Abbot Serlo of Savigny requested that the entire Congregation be joined to the Cistercians. His action seems to have been largely impulsive; certainly his consultation with the other Savigniac houses on the merger had been sketchy at best, and objections quickly surfaced, particularly from the houses in England led by Furness. After months of acrimony the dispute was finally settled by papal fiat in favor of the union, although in Eugenius III, a former Cistercian monk from Clairvaux, the opponents cannot have found the most impartial adjudicator. When news of the decision reached Furness, the monks rose in rebellion, and it was only in 1149, with the replacement of the abbot, that peace was restored. When building resumed at Furness, in the lay brothers' quarters, Burgundian influence had replaced Norman.[9]

It was some years after the two orders were joined that work began on far-reaching changes to the church. A specifically Cistercian plan was substituted for the earlier Benedictine one (fig. 9) and this involved the destruction of Furness I.[10] The wish for a larger building played a part in the decision, but the adoption of the new plan is also proof of the unacceptability of the old forms. In a further sense, too, when viewed from the context of the rebellious history of Furness, the new plan affirmed Cistercian orthodoxy.

Of the major Cistercian buildings surviving from the Dissolution, Furness remains the least studied. Not only has the building sequence of the new church (Furness II) not yet been determined but, more seriously, there has been no attempt to place the architecture in any wider context. It is true, however, that extensive changes to the fabric of the building carried out in the fifteenth century, as well as destruction at the Dissolution and after, have made analysis of the architecture difficult. Even so, certain aspects of the original form of the church can be discerned in the fragmentary remains.

Discussion should begin with the parts of Furness I that were most likely finished at the time the abbey became Cistercian in 1148, among them the presbytery, transepts, and monks' choir, extending a bay or so west of the crossing, and the monks' quarters, forming the east side of the cloister. Such buildings would make sense in an abbey of Furness' resources with twenty years of prosperous existence, and it also helps us understand the first building done after the merger, now the earliest standing remains on the site, the lay brothers' range to the west. In all likelihood these quarters would have been the next to be built anyway.

Changes began around 1160,[11] first with work on the south aisle and on the nave extending to the

[8] For Vaux-de-Cernay, see M. Aubert, *L'Abbaye des Vaux-de-Cernay* (Paris, 1934).

[9] See J. Bony, "Origines des piles gothiques anglaises à futs en délit," in M. Kühn, ed., *Gedenkschrift Ernst Gall* (Munich, 1965), 95-122, esp. 110-11. Similar changes occurred at the other Savigniac abbeys. At Coggeshall in Essex, for instance, the *Chronicle* mentions that in 1168, a year after the consecration of the church, Abbot Simon de Toni "returned to his own house of Melrose," suggesting that his stay at Coggeshall was connected with a reform program, possibly including building.

[10] A few rare examples of Cistercian churches with Benedictine plans are known in France and Germany, and one in Scotland. None are known in England. In France the examples are Gimont and Reigny (see A. Dimier, *Recueil de plans d'églises cisterciennes* [Paris, 1949], plate 242; and in the same author's *Supplément* 1967, plate 108). In Germany, examples are Bildhausen, Altzella, and Bronnbach (see W. Krönig, *Altenberg*

und die Baukunst der Zisterzienser [Bergisch Gladbach, 1973], 29). Melrose was founded from Furness in 1136 (see J. S. Richardson and M. Wood, *Melrose Abbey* [Edinburgh, Department of Environment, 1962].

[11] The chronology of work at Furness is complex, and to make a confusing situation worse, the two principal scholars who have worked on the building, Hope and Brakspear, differ in their interpretation of the archaeological evidence and posit opposed construction sequences. In brief, their positions are: for Brakspear, building proceeded from east to west in the customary manner (meaning that the Savigniac presbytery and transepts were demolished first); for Hope, construction proceeded in a counter-clockwise direction, beginning in the south aisle (see H. Brakspear, "On the First Church at Furness," *Trans. LCAS* 18 [1900]: 70-87, esp. 85; and W. H. St. John Hope, *The Abbey of St. Mary in Furness* [Kendal, 1902]: 229). Bilson apparently accepted Hope's view, (see app. 1 in J. C. Dickinson, "Furness Abbey: An Archaeological Reconsidera-

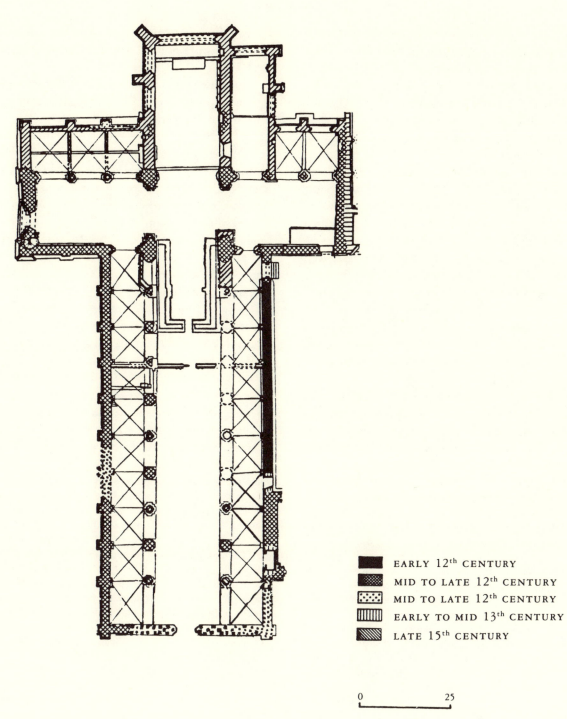

EARLY 12th CENTURY
MID TO LATE 12th CENTURY
MID TO LATE 12th CENTURY
EARLY TO MID 13th CENTURY
LATE 15th CENTURY

0   25

FEET

9. Furness, plan of remains.

eighth bay west, a decidedly odd place unless the east end of the first church continued in use. When finished, the aisle and nave were presumably closed with temporary wooden screening and served for the next few years as the monks' choir.[12] The east parts, dating from the Savigniac period, were then demolished. To increase the number of chapels in the south transept, the former slype was absorbed, a procedure that involved cutting back the wall surface there and in the monks' dormitory above. Next followed the rebuilding of the presbytery and north transept, and lastly, the north aisle and final two west bays.

It is unfortunate that the nave is the least well preserved portion of the church, because the later transepts offer only a heavily scarred impression of the Furness master's original design. But despite the losses, certain features of the three-storied nave can be reconstructed. The piers alternated, round and fasciculated, the latter with eight colonnettes separated into major and minor shafts. The aisles were covered by rib vaults (plate 48), though unlike the Yorkshire abbeys, they were supported by single shafts in the south aisle and triple shafts in the north, and the vaults included a wall rib.[13] Overall,

the interior was taller and broader than that of the early Yorkshire abbeys, rising to about sixty-five feet.

With these parts complete, work then moved to the east crossing piers.[14] For some reason the piers were raised independently of the east walls of the transepts, which were constructed a little to the east (plates 49 and 50). The crossing piers were dressed with shafts in massed groups of fours and fives on a rectangular core. On the inner face the shafts were supported on consoles decorated with a beaded ribbon-scallop and flat pattern-iron motif (plate 51), features unique in a Cistercian church but familiar in the northeast of England, for instance at the Bishop's Hall of Durham Castle (plate 55) and at Bridlington.[15]

The north and south transepts show extensive reworking but retain enough original masonry for a reliable reconstruction (fig. 10). They were three-storied with a clerestory, as was the nave, but the arcade was supported now on uniform fasciculated piers. Over each bay opened a small gallery covered by a recessed, round-headed arch enclosing twin, tri-lobed arches with a blind roundel sunk in the spandrel. String courses divided the elevation, clearly

---

tion," *Trans. CWASS* 67 [1976], 77-79). Bilson also dated the work: ". . . scarcely earlier than 1160, or more likely 1170" (p. 78).

More specific points of disagreement can be illustrated by the two authors' discussions of the east wall of the presbytery. Hope interpreted it as square-ended in the first church, apsidal in the second (pp. 227-28, 244-45). Brakspear favored the reverse (pp. 80-81). Both interpretations depend on a reading of the footings, but the critical feature in this—the relationship of the footings to the east crossing piers—is not clarified in Curwen's drawing (see Hope, *St. Mary in Furness*, facing 244), which omits anything more than a purely schematic rendering of the coursing. A reexamination of the juncture of the presbytery and east crossing piers is needed to determine the progression from one form to another.

In my view, except for Hope's interpretation of the presbytery end, his sequence of building matches the material remains. Hope does not give dates for the chronology, however, nor does he trace the source of the architecture.

[12] Dickinson links this to the unusual jointing of the piers on this side of the church, which he suggests were built as half cylinders ("Furness Abbey," 56). This is hard to credit; the elevation they carried would be full height. The piers at Jervaulx are constructed similarly.

[13] Shafts were omitted only in the two west bays, the last work on the church. There the ribs rest on corbels, the east

one a reversed palmette, the west an early volute form with the angle leaves pinched together into the center of the capital (plate 102). Rib profiles also differ between the north and south aisles: on the north they are triple rolls; on the south they show a chamfered center section flanked by a keeled roll.

[14] The crossing piers are very puzzling. The shaft bases have bell profiles, the only place in the building where this early profile occurs (plate 50). For this reason, presumably, Hope placed them with the first work on the building (i.e., from Furness I). But as the parts above all belong to Furness II, the bases must be either reused or be the profile adopted by an earlier master. Similar base profiles appear at Fountains II (1150s), Kirkstall (late 1150s), but must have been regarded as old-fashioned by around 1165-1170.

It could be argued that some work was in fact carried out on the model of the Yorkshire houses. The west bay of the chevet can still be traced in the masonry, and it shows that the monks' *superior introitus* was placed east of the crossing, like that at Fountains and Melrose (see chapter 3 of this study). Excavations indicate that the presbytery was one-half bay deeper than usual to accommodate this arrangement. The entrance was round-headed with unmolded arches; it was blocked in the fifteenth century (plate 49) in an attempt to stabilize the crossing.

[15] For Bridlington, see Boase, *English Art, 1100-1216*, plate 47a.

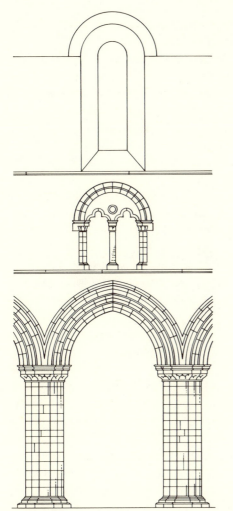

10. Furness, reconstruction of north transept.

11. Val Chrétien, nave.

defining the three-story scheme, and a wooden roof covered the space. Construction progressed from the south to the north transepts to judge by the progressively more elaborate moldings.

The use of a middle story at Furness for the first time in the Cistercian architecture of England was unconnected with liturgical practice. Although defined by twin openings, the story was not treated as a true gallery; behind the openings, the pent roof covering the rib-vaulted chapels was pitched at an angle that made the space unusable. The

purpose of the openings was principally to permit access for maintenance of the vaults over the chapels. Reflecting this, the openings occupy barely half the bay leaving large areas of plain wall surface to either side; they are in effect only piercings in a wall that is continuous, an impression accentuated by the absence of any vertical articulation within the bay. This element should thus more properly be called a contracted gallery or pseudo-gallery, as distinct from a genuine gallery, which spans the full bay, as for instance at Selby.[16] The size of the

<hr />

[16] See P. O. Rave, *Der Emporenbau in Romanischer und Frühgotischer Zeit* (Bonn, 1924). For the resulting appearance of the pseudo-gallery, I use the formulation made by J. Bony, "French Influences on the Origin of English Architecture," *JWCI* 12 (1949): 14, n. 1, though Bony uses it not in the context of

these buildings. For a similar and contemporary example of the tri-lobed design in the Furness gallery, see the arcading in Archbishop Roger Pont L'Evêque's palace cloister at York, illustrated in J. Browne, *A History of the Metropolitan Church of York*, vol. 2 (Oxford and York, 1847), plate 32.

opening is only one aspect of the difference; the master at Furness thinks of his wall as a surface through which openings are cut, whereas in a true gallery scheme the opening is primary and the wall contracts into a framework of shafts and piers.

Changes in the transept chapels were related to the addition of this middle story. Rib vaults were added to cover the chapels, for instance, and the solid dividing walls customary in the early churches were omitted (plate 52). Both of these features transformed the spatial effects of the chapels; expansiveness and luminosity replaced the dark, enclosed, mural character of the earlier chapels. The rib vault accounts structurally for the change, but aesthetic considerations determined its choice. Masonry evidence suggests that the changes were made piecemeal; in the vaults and arcades it is clear that modifications were made during the course of work. The rib profiles show rolls with a gorged center, as do the arch moldings where fillets are added. Such motifs give a thin, sharply linear accent to these parts and differ markedly from the forthright plasticity of the roll moldings used earlier in the nave and crossing.[17]

The architecture at Furness cannot be explained by any sequential development within English Romanesque but results from the importation of new forms. Comparable treatment of both elevation and detail can be found in churches in France, particularly in the northeast. Similar three-storied elevations, for instance, with pseudo-galleries in wooden-roofed structures are present in the collegiale church at Lillers (Pas-de-Calais) from *circa* 1140 (plate 53) and are known in the Premonstratensian abbey of Val-Chrétien (Aisne) of 1150-1170 (fig. 11).[18] Both represented somewhat conservative, if not old-fashioned designs, particularly the latter, which lacks

vertical articulation and has a wall system closely resembling that at Furness.

Architectural detailing and individual components confirm that France was the origin of the ideas expressed at Furness, and these, additionally, permit a more specific identification of source. For instance, alternating supports just like those in the nave at Furness can be found in the nave at Berteaucourt-les-Dames (Somme) near Amiens, dating to *circa* 1150-1160 (plate 27); capitals and similar rib and arcade moldings occur frequently in churches in the Aisne valley (for instance, Glennes, Val-Chrétien, Nouvion-le-Vineux, plate 54); massed shafts like those at the crossing can be found at Vailly (Aisne) and Nouvion-le-Vineux.[19] Such comparisons suggest the likelihood that the master mason at Furness came from or received his training in this area of France.

Although these parallels establish the fundamentally French character of the building, there are one or two features at Furness that stand out as completely English. So prominent is the change in vocabulary that the statement had to be deliberate. The exterior doorway of the north transept (plate 56), is an insertion (the plinth is cut back), although one that cannot be more than a year or two later than the rest of the building. The doorway's most noticeable feature is the elaborate billet molding with dog-tooth beading that covers the outer orders. This motif can be associated with northeast England, especially the area around Durham; a contemporary example is the doorway to Bishop Pudsey's Hall at Durham Castle, dating to *circa* 1160-1173 (plate 55). As already seen, the same area provided parallels for the decoration of the corbels in the choir.

The north transept doorway at Furness presents

---

[17] From the back (plate 52) it can be seen that the vaults rose higher than the arcade. In addition to the profiles of the arcade moldings, surrounding masonry suggests a change or substitution, probably during the actual course of construction. The nave carried similar moldings to the crossing, as may be seen in the fragment in the east bay on the south side.

[18] For Lillers, see H. Bernard and P. Héliot, "Les Fouilles de la Collégiale de Lillers," *Les Monuments historiques de la France* (1955), 182-86. In general, the middle stories of both buildings are essentially archaizing versions of Anglo-Norman architecture (see M. Anfray, *L'Architecture normande: Son Influence dans le nord de la France aux XIᵉ et XIIᵉ siècles* [Paris, 1939],

164-75). For a similar treatment of the recessed gallery in a vaulted building, see Acey (plate 67).

[19] For Berteaucourt, see C. Enlart, *Monuments religieux de l'architecture romane et de transition dans la région picarde* (Paris, 1895), 72-87. For Glennes, Val-Chrétien, and Vailly, see E. Lefèvre-Pontalis, *L'Architecture religieuse dans l'ancien diocèse de Soissons au XIᵉ et au XIIᵉ siècles* (Paris, 1894), plates 66-69, 91, and 86-90. To these could be added similar molding profiles found at the Cistercian abbey of Foigny (Aisne), A. Dimier, "L'Eglise de l'abbaye de Foigny," *B. Mon.* 118 (1960): 191-205.

two questions: Why was a substitution made? And why were forms used that diverged so noticeably from the architectural vocabulary of the rest of the building? The issue becomes more pertinent when the doorway's context is considered. It was not just a secondary entrance to the building, as were those of most north transepts. Due to the compressed site, the church was laid out across the narrow valley, and the north transept thus became the principal entrance. Moreover, it faced the abbey's gatehouse, which, in turn, was situated toward Dalton, then the only significant center of population in the vicinity. The emphasis given the doorway may have been further justified by the apparent use of the north transept as the *capella extra portas*, that is, accessible to laymen, a function it retained into the late thirteenth century.[20] These uses gave the doorway, then, an unusual prominence, accentuating the visibility of the deliberately substituted motifs drawn from the area around Durham.

Historical links between Furness and Durham during these years may well explain the architectural tie. Reginald of Durham records a legal dispute involving Furness and Henry II, which was resolved by the miraculous intervention of Saint Cuthbert.[21] It centered on rival claims to a sizable tract of land (thirty-four miles long and four miles wide) and pitted Furness against a favorite of the king's. The abbot, John, had lost the first round of this legal battle, and his appeal to secular judges had been turned down. But he persisted, finally taking the case to Rome. There, however, he found the abbey outmaneuvered by the king, who successfully prolonged litigation year after year. Worldly means failing him, therefore, the abbot erected an altar to Saint Cuthbert in the church at Furness and prayed for the saint's aid. Cuthbert heard his prayers, and when Abbot John traveled to Henry's court to personally vindicate his claim before the king, he found his former enemies miraculously become his friends. Cordially they ceded the disputed land to Furness. In thanksgiving the abbot vowed to make a pilgrimage to Durham, where he testified to Cuthbert's thaumaturgic powers. Unfortunately, the written account is undated, and Reginald omits details of Abbot John's visit to Durham. Furthermore, the dates of John's abbacy are vague; he is mentioned in 1152, 1155, and 1158, and the name of his successor, Walter, occurs first in 1175.[22] Since Reginald notes that litigation was protracted, the earliest date for the altar's placement would seem to be *circa* 1160-1165.

Given the amount of land at stake in this legal battle and its importance to Furness as a source of revenue, it would not be surprising to find some tangible commemoration of Cuthbert's help. It can be argued, then, that the reworked principal entrance to the abbey and the consoles flanking the entry to the sanctuary were intended to serve as physical testimony to this critical episode in the history of the house.

Even before the completion of the church at Furness, its influence could be felt at other Cistercian abbeys in the northwest. Calder, a daughter house first established in 1134 but abandoned after a Scottish raid and later refounded in the early 1140s, suffered a second raid in 1216 that seems to have left most of the twelfth-century stone church in ruins.[23] Reconstruction was prompt, however; a general confirmation of the abbey's rights by Henry III in 1231 may mark its completion, and this date can be reconciled to the statement of Denton (in 1610) that Thomas de Multon of Egremont Castle (d. 1240) "finished the works and established a greater convent of monks" at Calder.[24]

As it stands today in a peaceful valley (plate 57), the abbey's troubled early history is hard to imagine, though the scarred and muddled architecture

---

[20] See "Furness Abbey," 62. Dickinson also notes that the church served as a local center of pilgrimage and that the populace heard sermons in the chapter house. Both practices violated Cistercian statutes and further underline the independence of Furness.

[21] For the account, see J. Raine, ed., *Reginaldi monachi dunelmensis admirandis Beati Cuthberti, S. Soc.* 1 (1835): 112-14, cap. 55. Miss Katherine Galbraith kindly drew my attention to this episode.

[22] See D. Knowles and C.N.L. Brooke, *The Heads of Religious Houses: England and Wales, 940-1216* (Cambridge, 1972), 134.

[23] See *VCH: Cumberland* 2 (London, 1905): 174-78. The best account of its architecture is Sir Nikolaus Pevsner, *BoE: Cumberland and Westmorland* (London, 1967), 84-87.

[24] See *Mon. Angl.* 5:340-41; R. S. Ferguson, ed., "John Denton's Account of Cumberland," *Cumberland and Westmorland Antiquarian and Archaeological Society Tract Series*, no. 2 (1887), 22.

bears witness to it. Of the twelfth-century church, all that remains is the west door, some masonry courses in the north transept, and parts of the east wall of the south transept. Detailing on the doorway (plate 58) resembles that on the crossing at Furness and suggests a date around 1175. Little else is known about Calder I, although it is possible that a memory of its pier arrangement survives in the alternating plain and fasciculated piers that still stand from the thirteenth-century reconstruction.

Much more is to be seen at Holmcultram, now Abbey Town. At the Dissolution the townspeople petitioned Thomas Cromwell to spare the church, which was a "grete ayde, socor and defence for us ayenst the Scotts. . . ."[25] Saved then, it fell later in ruin. Around 1730 the six western nave arches with the original elevation above removed were walled in to make the present boxy building, which is still in use by the parish (plate 60).

Under its able and long-lived first abbot, Everard (1150-1192), Holmcultram enjoyed considerable prosperity. The region is poor in stone, which had to be shipped over a considerable distance to the site, but construction seems to have proceeded without breaks. The standing parts of the church, namely, the last parts to be built, date to around 1175-1180. A start in the early 1160s can therefore be assumed. Completion of the east parts is confirmed by the burial in 1186 of Christian, bishop of Whitehorn.[26] The burial must be taken to mean in the church, since this is the place sanctioned for the burial of a person of his rank in the order's statutes.

The eighteenth-century engravings by Stevens and the remains *in situ* indicate that the elevation at Holmcultram was three-storied.[27] As at Furness, no vertical articulation of the bays was used, and string courses alone divided the elevation, giving the stories a firm, layered quality. Detailing such as the capitals, bases, and fasciculated piers is similar to that at Furness, though the piers are uniform as in the transepts at Furness. A bulky compound pier marks the juncture of the monks' and lay broth-

ers' zones of the church, a rare Cistercian example of this division receiving architectural definition. The plain, rectangular moldings of the arcade contrast to the moldings at Furness with their rolls and hollows. This severe note is abandoned at the west doorway, however, which survives protected by Abbot Chambers' sixteenth-century porch. Detailing here (plate 59) is richer even than at Calder and recalls that in the crossing at Furness.

Seen together, Furness and Holmcultram (and possibly Calder) form a distinct regional version of the Early Gothic architecture of the Cistercians. None of the other Cistercian abbeys treated the elevation in precisely the same manner. The master who began work on Furness II in the 1160s did so under the influence of French architecture from the Laonnois and Soissonnais, and this gave these buildings an indelible Continental imprint. That Furness was the leader in this importation is not surprising considering its prominence, wealth, and history of assertiveness. The group's lack of influence outside the northwest is probably explained by its choice of somewhat conservative prototypes. Not everything is explained by the sources, however, and the group's relative geographical isolation also ensured a minimum of outside contact.

While work on the northwestern churches was underway, a start was made on Roche in southwest Yorkshire (plate 61). As at Furness, the architecture at Roche was based on ideas from France, but the prototype derived from a different center, thus the church bears no architectural relationship to Furness. With a fully vaulted interior and strong, dynamic massing, Roche provides evidence of contact with a more advanced version of Early Gothic. Considering the nascent state of Gothic in the north of England, this architecture might well have played a pioneer role in the introduction of the new style. Yet the most prominent feature—four-part rib vaults covering all parts of the building—was not exploited in the north for another thirty years.[28] One puzzle concerning Roche, then, lies in its failure

[25] H. Ellis, ed., *Original Letters, Illustrative of English History*, 1st ser., 2 (London, 1825): 90.

[26] F. Grainger and W. C. Collingwood, "The Register and Records of Holmcultram," *Cumberland and Westmorland Antiquarian and Archaeological Record Series* 7 (1929): 54, no. 141.

[27] J. Stevens, *The History of Ancient Abbeys* (London, 1723), plates facing 55 and 56.

[28] A comparison of interests in vaulting between the north and west country gives evidence of the regional character that Early Gothic quickly took in England. In the west country

to inspire followers. Either the architecture represented qualities so removed from prevailing regional interests that it was ignored, or it appeared too late after other ideas had got established.

Roche was never a large abbey. Founded in 1147, her limited resources and comparatively modest size stemmed from a small endowment. Expansion was hampered by the abbey's situation on crown lands and by the unwillingness of Henry II to alienate property to it. Early abbots like Dionysius (1159-1171), Hugh de Wadworth (1179-1184), and Osmund (1184-1223) made strenuous efforts to overcome this drawback by purchasing land at some distance from the abbey. Under Hugh these included an estate at Roxby in north Lincolnshire secured with £1,300 borrowed from the Jews of York, a transaction that soon placed the abbey "obligata in magnis debtis in Judaismo."[29] The purchases must have generated new income, however, and it is partly from this that construction would have been financed.

Building of some kind clearly preceded this. An undated charter from one of the two founders, Richard de Buili, allowed the monks to take sufficient timber from his forest at Maltby "for the completion of their buildings" and made them an unusual grant of timber for fencing;[30] the gifts were to be supervised by de Buili's forester, unless he was uncooperative, in which case the monks could take their wood without him. From the second founder, Richard, son of Turgis, came fifty loads of wood from his forest at Wikersley, although again no date for the gift survives.[31] Work on the church began around 1170 and continued actively for about fifteen years. In 1186 Pope Urban III issued a general confirmation of properties and gifts to the house.[32] In 1241 a gift in connection with a dedication is recorded, but building had been completed long before. The dedication may refer to a renovation or addition to the interior of which details are lost or may simply be a delayed dedication, not an infrequent occurrence.[33]

The remains at Roche, with much of the eastern walls still standing, are the most complete from the order's northern buildings of this period. The presbytery retains the lateral walls, which were treated in three stories, the upper two similar to the transepts, the lowest left bare. At the east of the lateral walls, lancets provided additional light to that from the terminal wall (plate 62); they were rebated externally with a glazing groove, a new technique for setting the glass, which in France can be dated to around 1180.[34] The end wall is largely ruined, but it may well have resembled that at Cistercian Preuilly (Seine-et-Marne) (plate 63), based on other analogies between the two houses.

In the transepts the three-story elevation shows the middle story decorated with paired blind arches. The bays were prominently framed by a single, thick, attached shaft which ran from the floor to the vault springer. The introduction of this new organizing feature into the elevation is connected with the use of rib vaults throughout the building. These also account for the heavy massing in the elevation. No external buttressing was used, in contrast to contemporary Canterbury Cathedral or St. Remi, Reims, and the walls thus needed to be sufficiently bulky to absorb the full load of the upper vaults. The transverse arch of the vault was supported by the single shaft, but the diagonals were received on tiny tapering corbeled out capitals bonded in with the ashlar (plate 75). No wall ribs were used. In composition the vaults reveal the French technique of construction, which used thinly

---

after the choir of Malmesbury was built in *circa* 1160, all buildings of any importance were vaulted. In the north the issue is the loss of interest in vaulting after about 1180 for a period of nearly thirty years. Of course, Roche was not the only building in the north to use vaults during the years between about 1165 and 1180; York, Ripon, Kirkstead and Bardney were all vaulted.

[29] See *Mon. Angl.* 1:839.

[30] ". . . in silva mea de Maltbye ad ea aedificia construenda dam totaliter perfaciantur . . ." (S. O. Addy, *Cartae XVI ad Abbatiam Rupensem Spectantes* [Sheffield, 1878], 19-20).

[31] J. Burton, *Monasticon Eboracense* (York, 1758), 323.

[32] *Mon. Angl.* 5, no. 12, p. 505.

[33] For the dedication, see ibid., 5:504, no. 10. Dedications were often arranged simply to take advantage of the presence of a high ecclesiastical dignitary in the area. Delay in dedications was a problem in the twelfth and thirteenth centuries; see the letter read by the Papal legate, Otto, to the clergy of England, which Matthew Paris includes in his *English History*, trans. and ed., J. A. Giles (London, 1852), 1:75-6.

[34] At earlier abbeys a wooden armature for the glass is simply attached to the window opening. Mr. John James kindly drew my attention to this detail.

cut, long, wedge-shaped stones coursed parallel with the ridge, rather than the English, which used rubble fill coursed oblique with the ridge.

Small but important variations in architectural detailing distinguish north from south transepts. In the south transept the arches leading into the chapels are treated as three distinct setbacks, each of which is supported by its own order of shafts. On the north, however, the outer order unaccountably lacks its shafts, suggesting a loosening of architectonic "logic"; in addition, the setting out of the arch openings on the north is irregular (plate 61).[35] The capitals also vary; on the north the vault springers have subdued versions of the waterleaf pattern (plate 75) like those at Kirkstall (cloister) (plate 44), Selby (nave), or Byland (nave); but on the crossing piers waterleaf and molded capitals are mixed, and in the south transept all the capitals are molded. Such an evolution from waterleaf to molded is characteristic of the mid-1170s, occurring, for instance, in the chapel of the castle at Newcastle upon Tyne (1172-1177) and at Byland.[36] In general, severe decorative restraint distinguishes the capitals at Roche—a striking contrast to the robustness and variety of capitals at Byland.

Enough remains of the rest of the transepts to permit a fairly complete reconstruction of their walls. The west walls were bare, without any attempt to divide them into bays reflecting the facing elevation. Quite possibly the outer bay had a window in each story as at Kirkstead (see below). The elevation of the north transept's terminal wall is more certain; it was composed in three tiers, each with three windows. In the lower two tiers the openings were flanked by shafts with waterleaf capitals, and

the second tier was a double-wall construction, allowing a wall passage. The boldness at Roche in piercing the wall with multiple openings surpassed anything attempted earlier in the abbeys in France or England (at Kirkstall, for instance, there were two tiers[37]), although it resembles the wall organization of unvaulted buildings like Peterborough.

Taken together, the numerous windows in the transepts, crossing, and east end brought a new quality of light into the interior of the building. Since only grisaille glass was permitted, its effect would have been of a dominant, clear, slightly green luminosity set off by lively geometrical patterns established by the varied designs of the leads. The absence of color in the glass gave Cistercian interiors like Roche a clarity and atmosphere distinct from those of other orders. Because of the difficulty of its manufacture, clear glass was the most expensive of all glass. The intense interest in light, and the recurrence of clear light as an image in Bernard's *Sermons* underlie this new luminousness.[38]

In the nave a number of design changes from the transepts may be noted. Uniform fasciculated piers replace the compound piers used for the transept chapels.[39] Since they have a regular geometry, this means that the front shaft from the vaults overhead would not have been connected to the piers as was possible with the compound form. Instead, it is likely that vertical articulation began above the pier in the spandrels of the arcade. In the presbytery the vault springers have stiff-leaf capitals with a semioctagonal abacus (plate 76) that is later than anything else in the church and suggests a date in the 1180s.[40]

Compared with earlier Cistercian architecture in

[35] The masonry of the north wall does not bond in with the east wall, and the north wall clearly belongs to a subsequent building campaign.

[36] The castle provides a rare example of a precisely dated building in the north in this decade (see W. H. Knowles, "The Castle, Newcastle upon Tyne," *Arch. Ael.*, 4th ser., 2 [1926]: 1-39, esp. 31-34).

[37] At Kirkstall, a triforium passage was also used in the south transept. The use of a triforium in a transept terminal wall has a long history going back in England to St. Albans (1077). For French examples, see M. Aubert, *L'Architecture cistercienne en France* (Paris, 1947), 1:294.

[38] In the *Sermons for the Seasons*, for instance, Bernard says: "The brightness of the true and living light shall occupy all things . . . expelling the shadows and the darkness" (1:331).

On light and its importance for the Cistercians, see L. Grodecki, "Fonctions spirituelles," in M. Aubert et al., *Le vitrail français* (Paris, 1958), 39-54; H. J. Zakin, "French Cistercian Grisaille Glass," *Gesta* 13 (1974): 17-28; C. Brisac, "Grisailles romanes des anciennes abbatiales d'Obazine et de Bonlieu," *102ᵉ Congrès national des sociétés savantes* (Limoges, 1977), 129-43; E Melczer and E. Soldwedel, "Monastic Goals in the Aesthetics of Saint Bernard," *Studies in Cistercian Art and Architecture* 1 (1982): 31-44.

[39] The bases of the nave piers are hard to interpret. On the south, the profiles are similar to those in the transepts, but on the north they have steep bell forms (i.e., without scotia or lower torus). The latter look distinctly out of date for a building of the 1170s.

[40] The earliest dated stiff-leaf known to me occurs at St.

England, a number of important changes appear at Roche, including the fully vaulted interior, the system of articulation, and the middle story. Overall, the architecture has a stacked and massive quality, which is complemented by detailing that is notable for its sturdy and heavily scaled proportions. Even so, there is nothing hesitant or eclectic about Roche; the architecture suggests a single idea worked through from start to finish.

The appearance of a middle story used in conjunction with vaults marks a decisive change in the Cistercian elevation. The first vaulted Early Gothic elevations in the French abbeys were two-storied, as at Ourscamp (plate 9), Pontigny (plate 4), and Clairvaux III, all dating from the 1150s.[41] The third story is not known before about 1180 when it appears in churches like Mortemer (Eure) (plate 66), Acey (Jura) (plate 67), and slightly later at Ste. Marie d'Aulps (Haute-Savoie). These all show contracted gallery schemes and may be compared with churches outside the order like Creil, St. Evremond (plate 68); Gournay-en-Bray, Ste. Hildevert (plate 69); and Nouvion-le-Vineux (plate 54).[42] The contracted gallery may have been connected with attempts to lighten the wall as well as to provide access to the aisles vaults. None of the arrangements resembles that at Roche, however, where there are twin blind arches that extend the full width of the bay. Such an arrangement raises questions: Was the middle story conceived of as decoration, like the blind arcading in the choir of the Cathedral of Noyon? Or was it thought of as a simulated triforium? Neither seems likely. More plausibly, the form was determined by structural needs resulting from the vaulted interior. It may even reflect a specifically Cistercian solution to the problem; at the abbey of Fontainejean, *circa* 1200, for instance, two blind arches per bay in the middle story appear at the back of the elevation, and a little later the same feature was used at the abbeys of Longpont and Vauclair.[43] In these cases the twin arches were designed as relieving arches and were invisible to the interior. The same idea probably determined the arches at Roche. Although these French buildings postdate Roche, it is likely that earlier instances existed in France that have since been demolished.

The architecture at Roche can be traced specifically to the churches on the southern and eastern borders of the Ile-de-France. Close parallels to surviving Cistercian abbeys in this area can be seen at Preuilly (plate 65), begun between 1165 and 1170 and already mentioned in connection with the choir at Roche.[44] The south transept has a three-story elevation with a small pseudo-gallery consisting of a single opening. The proportions and bay divisions are similar to those at Roche, and four-part rib vaults without wall ribs covered each bay.

Yet these features are shared by other churches in the areas bordering the Ile-de-France in the 1160s and 1170s as well. And architectural detailing allows a more precise identification of source. Similarities between Preuilly and Roche are in this respect less close than those between Roche and churches lying to the north in the Aisne valley. At Bellefontaine (Oise) (plate 70), Creil, and Nouvion-

---

Frideswide, Oxford, in the west bays of the chevet of 1178-1180. Stiff-leaf appears in the Corona Chapel at Canterbury, 1182-1184, and in the chapel of Dover Castle, 1181-1187. Abaci with a chamfered profile appear in the west bay of Byland, between 1185-1190.

The precise chronology of Roche is still unclear. I would argue for a date in the 1170s for the nave and transepts, and the early 1180s for the east end and vault. D. Parsons, "A Note on the East End of Roche Abbey Church," *Jnl. BAA*, 3d ser., 37 (1974): 123, corrects my statement in *Jnl. BAA* 34 (1971): 33 about the base molding in the presbytery without, however, advancing an understanding of the building. His comment about the arcading should wait assessment until the campaigns of work have been fully worked out. If anything, recent visits have strengthened my view that the transept east walls were raised first, before either the north transept north wall or the presbytery walls.

[41] These in turn may be related to such buildings outside the order as Poissy and St. Martin at Laon. For Poissy, see A. Saint-Paul, "Poissy et Morienval," *Mémoires de la société historique de Pointoise et du Véxin*, vol. 16 (1894); for St. Martin, see, E. Lefèvre-Pontalis, "Saint Martin de Laon," *Congrès archéologique* 1 (1911): 225-39.

[42] For Creil, see R. J. Johnson, *Specimens of Early French Architecture* (London, 1864); for Nouvion-le-Vineux, see Lefèvre-Pontalis, "Saint Martin de Laon," 388-98.

[43] See C. A. Bruzelius, "Cistercian High Gothic: The Abbey Church of Longpont and the Architecture of the Cistercians in the Early Thirteenth Century," *An. Cist.* 35 (1979): 73.

[44] For illustrations, see M. De Maille, "L'Eglise de Preuilly," *B. Mon.* 89 (1930): 257-306, esp. 286-90. Bilson suggested Mortemer as the source for Roche (*Arch. Jnl.* 66 [1909]: 227), but the detailing indicates a date after Roche.

le-Vineux setback moldings with thin angle rolls similar to those in the transepts at Roche can be found, along with similar steeply profiled bases and waterleaf capitals. These churches, particularly Nouvion, also provide parallels for the austere treatment of the upper stories; and the same region has examples of the unusual corbelled vault departures for the rib diagonals and for the keeling of the piers.[45]

It is worth emphasizing that Roche, despite the massiveness of its architecture, would have appeared unmistakably French to contemporaries. Within the context of architecture in England of the 1170s and 1180s, Roche was as different and modern as Archbishop Roger Pont L'Evêque's vaulted choirs at York Minster (*circa* 1165-1175) and Ripon (*circa* 1175-1180) (to be discussed in chapter 5). Even the materials of the abbey and especially the exceptional regularity and precise cutting of the ashlar blocks would have looked French; later this feature of the building still stood out and elicited praise as "magnificentiam" from the earl of Surrey in 1345 and was hailed again by Michael Sherbrook at the Dissolution.[46]

Three other Cistercian abbeys in the north can be generally associated with Roche. The most interesting is Kirkstead in Lincolnshire, forty miles to the southeast (plate 71). The elevation is quite similar, and like Roche, the church was fully vaulted. The anteriority of one building over the other has not been established, however.

Founded in 1139 from Fountains, Kirkstead was first settled on a different site, but probably close to the present one. Formal permission for a move was granted in 1187,[47] a date that seems likely to mark the end rather than the beginning of work on the church. Unfortunately, only one visible fragment remains, the southeast angle of the south transept, but it can be supplemented by a 1716 engraving by W. Stukeley (plate 72). The elevation was three-storied, with a pointed arcade, a false gallery with paired, round-headed openings, and a single clerestory window with flanking colonnettes inside and out. Four-part rib vaults covered each bay. The engraving by Stukeley also shows the west wall of the transept, with a triple tier of windows, all of which were flanked by shafts inside and out, a slightly richer version of the same arrangement on the terminal wall of the north transept at Roche.[48]

Kirkstead remains an enigma. No record of a clearance survives, and this suggests that important material may be awaiting excavation.[49] At present, however, interpretation rests on minimal evidence. The major difference between the two buildings—the open middle story at Kirkstead rather than the closed one at Roche—can be argued either as the conservatism of Roche discarded by the Kirkstead master, or as the boldness of Kirkstead cautioning the Roche master. Judged by this and the different detailing (plate 77), it is most unlikely that Kirkstead is the work of the same master. Probably the buildings depended on a common source in France, which each master interpreted differently, although on balance, Roche appears the earlier of the two and the more consistently French.

Other Cistercian abbeys suggest further connections with Roche. At Dundrennan in southwest Scotland, a remodeling of the transepts was begun in the 1180s. Work started in the south transept

---

[45] Other examples of corbeled vault departures for rib diagonals occur at Cheux (Calvados), Arcy-Sainte-Restitute (Aisne), and Provins, and in England, at Rievaulx (in the chapter house). Pevsner mistakenly took the corbeled vault departures as evidence of a late decision to vault (*BoE: Yorkshire, West Riding* [London, 1959], 415). For keeling, see chapter 3, n. 78.

[46] *Mon. Angl.* 5:502 n.g. His words were ". . . magnificentiam operis lapidei. . . ." For Sherbrook, see app. A.

[47] *VCH: Lincolnshire* 2 (London, 1906): 135.

[48] Despite its inaccuracies, Stukeley's print suggests the form of these openings. Over each window he drew masonry turning toward the interior rather than toward the viewer (as on the east wall). This implies a wall passage, although no indication

of it is shown at the juncture with the south wall.

Surviving detail at Kirkstead is limited to two capitals and does little to clarify relationships between the two houses. On the exterior the clerestory was shafted, and the remaining shaft carries a scalloped capital. Inside, the capital that served as the springer for the diagonal rib shows artichoke leaves around a hollowed bell (plate 77). The first suggests a date before Roche; the latter, after. Rib moldings are a single roll with flanking hollow, a profile that differs from the principal ribs at Roche but is the same as those in the transept chapels. Another feature that separates the two abbeys is the ashlar work, which is well below the quality at Roche.

[49] The site is presently owned by the University of Nottingham, which plans an excavation at some date in the future.

(plate 73) where, despite the absence of vertical shafts to divide the bays and the omission of vaults over the major space,[50] the influence of Roche and Kirkstead emerges in the general proportions of the elevation and in the form of the middle story. Connections are confirmed by such details as the fasciculated piers (these suggesting the influence of the nave at Roche rather than the transepts), and by the treatment of the west crossing piers.

At Newminster in Northumberland, the mother house of Roche, the plan has been recovered by excavation and shows the typical early form and dimensions of a large house such as Rievaulx.[51] This implies a building campaign before 1150, a date supported by the square, unstressed crossing piers and plain nave piers, which resemble those at Rievaulx. In the transept chapels, however, there were no lateral walls, a feature the plan shares with Roche, and the only above-ground remains, the reerected shaft fragments of the innermost pier in the south transept, have the same form as the nave piers at Roche.[52] The transepts at Newminster thus follow the disposition of those at Roche and date to the late 1170s. Further work from this campaign probably included the rebuilding of the cloister, judging by the many cloister arcades and capitals (plate 45) reerected on the site.[53] Most likely, a remodeling of the transept chapels in connection with the elimination of lateral walls in the chapels and the insertion of rib vaults explains this sequence of work.

Despite the differences that distinguish Roche and Kirkstead, the two churches, with Dundrennan and the transepts at Newminster, are still related. Roche and Kirkstead show that the Cistercians in this part of England had mastered fully vaulted interiors over three-story elevations. (They were not alone in this; the remains of Bardney Abbey, a Benedictine house close to Lincoln, show similar detailing to that in the south transept to Roche.[54]) Establishing precise relationships among these buildings is difficult, however, for the antecedents of Early Gothic in this area are not clear. Enough is known of Lincoln Cathedral, which was rib vaulted by Bishop Alexander in the 1140s and which in the west façade shows an awareness of St. Denis and, further north, of the new choir at York Minster of the 1160s, to suggest that both buildings played an important role in the Early Gothic movement.[55] Unfortunately, little is known about the other four Cistercian abbeys in Lincolnshire, all of which had been established by 1150 and were large houses in command of extensive resources. Only archaeology could establish if Early Gothic was used in these buildings ahead of those discussed above and if priority in the introduction of the new style belongs to the Cistercians.

In summary, then, both groups of Cistercian buildings—the one in the northwest of England dominated by Furness, the other in the northeast associated with Roche and Kirkstead—can be shown to have drawn heavily on prototypes in the areas along the eastern border of the Ile-de-France, and specifically in the Aisne valley. During the years 1145-1170 this was one of the Gothic style's most advanced regions in France.[56] At the center of these architectural experiments lay the city of Laon, the old capital of Carolingian France. There and in surrounding areas extensive church building was underway at the parochial, monastic, and cathedral level. Bishop Barthélemy of Laon, according to an

---

[50] See D. MacGibbon and T. Ross, "Dundrennan Abbey," *Archaeological Association Collections, Ayrshire and Galloway* 10 (1899): 57-97; P. J. Fergusson, "The Late Twelfth Century Rebuilding at Dundrennan Abbey," *Ant. Jnl.* 53 (1973): 232-43. An additional parallel to Roche, omitted in this article, is the form of the west crossing piers and their plinths.

[51] See B. Harbottle and P. Salway, "Excavations at Newminster Abbey, Northumberland, 1961-1963," *Arch. Ael.*, 4th ser., 42 (1964): 95-171.

[52] The shafting is identical to Roche, namely, fasciculated with eight shafts separated into majors and minors, all with keeled profiles. The high plinth is different, however, as is the waterholding base molding.

[53] For the Roche capitals that have disappeared, see illustration in F. R. Fairbank, "Roche Abbey and the Cistercian Order," *AASRP* 18 (1884), facing 50.

[54] H. Brakspear, "Bardney Abbey," *Arch. Jnl.* 79 (1922): 1-92, esp. 13-33.

[55] For the west façade, see G. Zarnecki, *Romanesque Sculpture at Lincoln Cathedral, Lincoln Minster Pamphlets*, 2d ser., no. 2 (London, 1963): 13.

[56] For the architectural context, see E. Gall, *Die Gotische Baukunst in Frankreich und Deutschland: Die Vorstufen in Nordfrankreich von der Mitte des elften bis gegen Ende des zwölften Jahrhunderts* (Leipzig, 1925).

inscription on his tomb, built four Cistercian and five Premonstratensian abbeys before retiring in 1150 to spend his last eight years as a Cistercian monk at Foigny; Bishop Joscelin of Soissons surpassed even this total. Historical connections between the Laonnois and the Cistercians in the north of England were close. As already seen, two successive abbots of Vauclair, twelve miles south of Laon, took charge of Fountains during the critical years of its history and building—Murdac (1144-1147) and Richard (1150-1170). Other more general connections between the two regions may be mentioned: in 1151 Abbot Theodald of Fountains was appointed abbot of Trois-Fontaines (Marne); Raoul and Isaac, both English born, became the first abbots, respectively, of Vaucelles (Nord) and L'Etoile (Vienne); and Gilbert, also English, was abbot of Cîteaux from 1163 to 1166.[57] Apart from these links, Laon stood on the major north-south road through eastern France, the one used by the English abbots as they traveled to the General Chapter at Cîteaux.

Cistercian churches in the Laonnois have not survived, but an inkling of their relationship to the abbeys in northern England can be gained from the buildings of the Premonstratensians, an order of canons founded by Saint Norbert in 1121, who modeled their statutes and architecture closely on the Cistercians.[58] In fact, so close were the two orders that in 1142 the Premonstratensians entrusted the Cistercians with the visitation of their abbeys. Three buildings of the Premonstratensians can be singled out as representative, and each can be associated with a contemporary Cistercian building. The first is Saint Norbert's church, the *prima filia* of the order, St. Martin at Laon.[59] Square-ended in the presbytery and transepts, sober in decoration, strongly massed, and vaulted at the east end with four-part vaults without wall ribs (plate 74), it resembles Ourscamp of a decade or so earlier and thus can be related to Roche and Kirkstead in general terms. Dommartin, on the region's northern boundaries, had a radiating chapel plan, a three-story elevation, and fully vaulted interior, all features that probably influenced Clairvaux III.[60] And Val-Chrétien was close in plan to St. Martin at Laon, although wooden-roofed like Furness. The buildings of the Premonstratensians supply, then, a missing link in the chain of connections tying the architecture of the Cistercians in England to that of the Cistercians in this area of France in the decades of the 1150s and 1160s. Although somewhat greater variety marks the Premonstratensians' buildings, this quality may have served as a means of "laundering" up-to-date ideas before their subsequent adoption by the Cistercians.

[57] To these may be added English patrons who helped the Cistercians in eastern France, such as Everard, bishop of Norwich, who financed Fontenay, or Henry II, who paid for the roofing of Clairvaux III in 1179.

[58] See N. Backmund, *Monasticon Praemonstratense*, 3 vols. (Staubing, 1949-1956). For the architecture, see A. W. Clapham, "The Architecture of the Premonstratensians, with Special Reference to their Buildings in England," *Arch.* 73 (1923): 117-46; I. Hardick, "Praemonstratenserbauten des 12 und 13 Jahrhunderts im Rheinland. Ihr Verhältnis zu den französischen und belgischen Vorstufen," *Analecta praemonstratensia* 11 (1935): 3-64.

[59] The building dates to the third quarter of the twelfth century (see Lefèvre-Pontalis, "Saint Martin de Laon," 225-39).

[60] The east parts of Dommartin were consecrated in 1163 (see P. Pontroué, "Quatre ans des recherches archéologiques a l'abbaye de Dommartin," *Bulletin de la commission départementale des monuments au Pas-de-Calais* 9 [1973], 266-80). For Clairvaux III's plan, see W. Schlink, *Zwischen Cluny und Clairvaux* (Berlin, 1970), 108-16, 138-41. Previously it was thought that the Cathedral of Thérouanne provided the model for Dommartin, but this idea now has to be abandoned (see H. Bernard, "Les Fouilles de la cathédrale de Thérouanne," *Bulletin de la commission départementale des monuments historiques du Pas-de-Calais* 9 [1973]: 245-56).

5

The Cistercian Church
Transformed

NOTHING the Cistercians had previously built anticipated the architecture of Byland. The changes went well beyond what could be called a development or elaboration of the order's building in England and constitute instead a new departure. Three features in particular set Byland apart: the adoption of a new, highly articulated chevet, the dramatic enlargement of the scale of the church, and the elaboration of all its parts. Such qualities were not lost on contemporaries: Roger, abbot during the construction of the church, described it as "pulchram et magnam" and it was doubtless in the mind of William of Newburgh when he listed Byland as one of the three "luminaries" of the north. Such judgments reflect the shift in values embodied by the architecture of the church. They also offer a dramatic contrast to the ideals of architectural poverty and modesty enunciated by Saint Ailred of Rievaulx at mid-century.

In addition to its central position in Cistercian architecture, the church at Byland should be seen in a wider context. It is not possible to evaluate York Minster and Ripon Cathedral, both of which are accepted as seminal structures for Gothic architecture in the north, without considering By-land.[1] The relationship of Byland to both churches remains unresolved, however. Was Byland the means through which the simplicity and restraint of Cistercian architecture influenced the development of Early Gothic in the north, as Bilson implied? Or did it, as Hearn suggests, merely absorb and reflect trends already established by the two Minster churches raised by the ambitious archbishop of York, Roger Pont L'Evêque?[2]

The early history of Byland was very troubled. It originated in 1135 as a daughter house to Furness and, therefore, belonged in its early years to the Congregation of Savigny. First established thirty-five miles north along the west coast, at Calder in Cumberland, this settlement survived only three years before it was devastated by the Scots, and the community fled back to Furness. Arriving outside the abbey gates, however, the monks found it barred against them. The reasons for this extraordinary action are unclear. The pretext seems a patent legalism; by Savigniac laws it was impossible for two abbots and two communities to live within one house, and the new abbot, Gerald, declined to resign his office or to release his monks from obedience to him. Rebuffed thus and closed out of the

[1] There is no detailed treatment of Gothic in northern England, but it is touched on in the authoritative account of Early Gothic in England as a whole by J. Bony, "French Influences on the Origin of English Architecture," *JWCI* 12 (1949): 1-15, and is surveyed in G. Webb, *Architecture in Britain: The Middle Ages* (Harmondsworth, 1956), 82-86. For France, see R. Branner, "Gothic Architecture 1160-1180 and its Romanesque Sources," *Acts of the XX International Congress of the History of Art* (Princeton, 1963), 1:92-104; also P. Héliot, "Les Oeuvres capitales du gothique français primitif et l'influence de l'architecture anglaise," *Wallraf-Richartz Jahrbuch* 20 (1958): 85-114; and P. Héliot "La Diversité de l'architecture gothique à ses débuts en France," *Gazette des Beaux-Arts* 69 (1967): 269-306.

The literature on the architecture at Byland bears no relation to the importance of the abbey. For general treatments, see Sir Charles Peers, *Byland Abbey* (London: Department of Environment, 1934); Sir Nikolaus Pevsner, *BoE: Yorkshire, North Riding* (London, 1966), 94-101. See also P. J. Fergusson, "The South Transept Elevation of Byland Abbey," *JBAA*, 3d ser., 38 (1975): 155-76.

[2] J. Bilson, "The Architecture of the Cistercians, with Special Reference to Some of their Earlier Churches in England," *Arch. Jnl.* 66 (1909): 185-280, esp. 279; M. F. Hearn, "On the Original Nave of Ripon Cathedral," *JBAA*, 3d ser., 35 (1972): 29-45, esp. 39.

protecting walls of Furness, Gerald turned on the parent house, renounced it, and severed ties with the now ruined Calder. Followed by his monks, he struck inland over the Pennines, their possessions piled in a single wagon pulled by eight oxen. They headed for York, where Archbishop Thurstan's support of Fountains six years earlier was already part of monastic legend; clearly, the monks saw a parallel between their own experience and that of the monks at Fountains driven out of St. Mary's York.

On the road traveling eastward, the monks encountered the steward of Lady Gundreda, mother of Roger de Mowbray. He heard their story and advised them to seek his patron's help at Thirsk Castle. As they approached the castle, they were observed by Gundreda from an upper window, and the poverty of their appearance deeply moved her. Through these unusual circumstances, then, the community found as their patron one of the most prominent families in the north. But plans for a new foundation were complicated by the fact that Gundreda's son was still a ward, which restricted her right to cede away land. As a temporary measure, therefore, she sent the monks to a relative, Robert de Alneto, who was living as a hermit at Hood, a mile or so east of Thirsk. He welcomed them with reverence and shortly thereafter joined their ranks.

The Mowbrays' piety and support of the new foundation quickened the devotion of family retainers, among them certain older knights who now joined the community as lay brothers. They included Henry Bugge who, the Byland *Chronicle* tells us, had charge of building the small settlement

that now rose at Hood; he is described as "custos operis abbaciae."[3] New recruits presented themselves, but the site seems to have been too restricted to permit proper expansion;[4] only one novice is mentioned in 1142 when Abbot Gerald died and the novice master, Roger, was elected abbot. Under Roger a move was made the following year to Old Byland, but this site proved just as short-lived. Three years later another transfer was made to Stocking. There the monks built a stone church—the *Chronicle* calls it a "parvam ecclesiam"—along with a cloister and other buildings and offices. Their patron, Roger de Mowbray, provided building material for the monks' quarters.[5] At this stage in the history of Byland, then, everything points to the site at Stocking being considered permanent. But it did not turn out to be so. In 1177 the monks moved once more, this time for good, to Byland.

Looking back over forty-three years and four false starts, some of the failures might have seemed avoidable: Calder lay in disputed territory, Hood lacked room for expansion, Old Byland was too close to Rievaulx (a mile upstream) and its bells bothered the older community, Stocking offered an insufficient water supply. But hindsight obscures the piecemeal character of the community's growth from utter poverty to considerable size under Mowbray patronage. And random as the sites sound, Hood, Old Byland, and Stocking were all within five miles of Byland, so the monks would have had a long familiarity with the area that was to become their eventual home.

The steady accumulation of Byland's lands can be followed in a number of donations that included

---

[3] See *Mon. Angl.* 5:349-54, esp. 350. The history that supplies the account of Byland's early years, detailed in the text above, dates to about 1197. It is the earliest foundation history of a Cistercian abbey in England (see A. Gransden, *Historical Writing in England c. 550-1307* [Ithaca, 1974], 290-91). It was dictated by Abbot Roger to his successor, Abbot Philip, although Philip tells us he did not rely solely on Roger's memory but consulted "many others." The substantial accuracy of the history can be accepted, even if some passages contain traces of revisionism. No critical edition of the history or of the abbey's cartulary, now in the British Museum Egerton (MS. 2823), has been published. For the history of Byland, see *VCH: Yorkshire* 3 (London, 1913): 131-34; and D. Knowles, *The Monastic Order in England*, 2d ed. (Cambridge, 1963), 249-51.

[4] The phrase Abbot Roger used was ". . . locus de Hode

nimis arctus fuit ad abbaciam construendam" (*Mon. Angl.* 5:350).

[5] For the Mowbray gift, see D. E. Greenway, ed., *The Charters of the Honour of Mowbray, 1107-1191* (London, 1972), 32, charter no. 40. The account in the *Chronicle* reads: ". . . ubi ipsimet diligenter construxerunt ibi et aedificaverunt unam parvam ecclesiam lapideam, claustrum, et caeteras domos et officinas" (*Mon. Angl.* 5:350). As late as 1197 these were still "plainly to be seen in the same place," but they have subsequently disappeared. The site probably lay at Oldstead Hall (see J. McDonnell, "A Gazetteer of Local Place Names in the Vicinity of Byland Abbey and Newburgh Priory," *Ryedale Historian* 5 [1970]: 41-63, esp. 46-47). Medieval tile and architectural fragments found in the grounds there seem to confirm the location.

in 1147 the site of the future monastery.[6] At the time of gift the land was virtual wasteland, typical of what patrons frequently gave the Cistercians. This much can be inferred from Abbot Roger's description of how the monks "began manfully to root out the woods and by long and wide ditches to draw off the abundance of water from the marshes; and when dry land appeared they prepared for themselves an ample and worthy site."[7] Yet construction seems not to have begun at once. The earliest buildings at the site of Byland proper, those of the lay brothers, can be dated by their architectural detailing and masonry to about 1155.

The gap between possession of the site in 1147 and its development in the mid-1150s is puzzling, although the turmoil of the abbey's history in the early 1150s reveals a possible explanation. The year after Byland acquired the land, the Congregation of Savigny was joined to the Cistercians, although for Byland the merger did little to solve one major problem: as early as 1138 legal claims and lawsuits had been filed by Furness and Calder over the right of maternity to the foundation that was now at Stocking.[8] The dispute went back to the incident outside the gate at Furness. So persistently were the claims pressed that Cîteaux appointed a commission in 1154 to adjudicate the matter, consisting of thirteen English Cistercian abbots presided over by Saint Ailred. In due course, they found in favor of the community at Stocking. To seal the verdict, the monks immediately had their charters confirmed by the archbishop of York, Roger Pont L'Evêque, and placed themselves under his protection. The dispute and the uncertainties surrounding

its resolution must have preoccupied the community while they were at Stocking and consumed a fair proportion of their resources—and it would have allowed little thought of a move. With their legal troubles behind them and their numbers growing, however, the idea of a large-scale community and of an ambitious building program now became possible.

Papal confirmations of the abbey's rights and privileges were obtained under Hadrian IV (1154-1159), and again under Alexander III in 1163, 1171, and 1175.[9] All of these confirmations were issued to the monks of "Bellalanda" rather than Stocking, suggesting that even before the formal move in 1177, the community had been identified with the location of the Mowbray land at Byland.

Unfortunately, documentation of the building programs is scanty, though some details survive from two sources. The first lists a gift of land from Richard Malebisse "for the purpose of unconditional and continuous money toward the construction of the church. Therefore the church having been brought to completion, I grant and concede and confirm by means of this present charter of confirmation, the aforementioned intended two bovates [thirty acres] of land with all the appurtenances to God and St. Mary and the aforementioned monks of Bellalanda and for the purpose of buying wine to celebrate Mass for ever after."[10] The charter can be dated between 1175/1176 when Malebisse succeeded to his lands, and about 1192, a date indicated by comparison of the witness lists with a charter in the *Pontefract Cartulary*.[11] The Malebisse gift helps little in fixing the date for the start of

---

[6] See Greenway, ed., *Charters of the Honour of Mowbray*, 34-35, charter no. 44. J. McDonnell and Dom E. Everest draw attention to the date of the acquisition of the site in "The Waterworks of Byland Abbey," *Ryedale Historian* 1 (1965): 32-39.

[7] ". . . viriliter extirpare coeperunt de nemore, et per fossas longas et latas magnas acquas de paludibus extrahere: ac postquam apparuit solida terra paraverunt sibi locum latum, ydoneum, et honestum" (*Mon. Angl.* 5:353).

[8] On the dispute see B. Hill, *English Cistercian Monasteries and their Patrons in the Twelfth Century* (Urbana, 1968), 100ff.

[9] *Mon. Angl.* 5:343.

[10] ". . . in puram et perpetuam elemosinam ad ecclesiam construendam. Peracta ideo ecclesia, tunc dono et concedo et presenti carta confirmo predictas suas bovatas cum pertinentiis

Deo et Sancte Maria et monachis antedictis de Bellalanda ad vinum emendum ad missas celebrandas imperpetuum." (W. Farrer, ed., *Early Yorkshire Charters* [Edinburgh, 1916] 3:460-61, charter no. 1850.)

[11] Farrer dated the charter to 1176-1200. In his note he compares the witness list with one in the *Pontefract Cartulary* (no. 271) where Richard Malebisse appears with four of the seven witnesses of the Byland charter. The latest possible date of the Pontefract charter is given by the appearance on the list of William de NovoMercato, who died between 1197 and 1198, and the charter probably dates to before 1192 when one of the witnesses occurs as dean of Pontefract (*Pontefract Cartulary*, no. 278). I would like to thank Dr. Greenway for this information.

building, but it is important for establishing completion by *circa* 1192 at the latest.

A second document, dated by Farrer to 1170-1190, is a grant of land for cattle at the abbey's grange at Murton, which includes among the witnesses the name of "magister Godwyno cementario."[12] Godwyn may be identified as the master mason at Byland, although with qualification due to the somewhat complex nature of witness lists (see appendix B). Godwyn's title—*magister cementarius*—is notable because it would not have been used by a member of the monastic community, who instead would add his appropriate rank, such as *monachus, cellerarius, conversus,* etc., and thus it signifies secular standing. Construction using outside labor is recorded in many cases, for instance at Clairvaux and Fountains, and it can be assumed at Byland from the numerous masons' marks found there, but these were ordinary masons, not the *magister cementarius*.[13] In France the only confirmed case of a secular master mason assisting at a Cistercian site before 1200 occurs at Bonnecombe (Aveyron) in 1162.[14] The reasons why the community at Byland might have engaged the services of a secular master will become more obvious below in the light of the building's new conception and structural complexity.

Writing his history of the foundation of Byland twenty years after the final move from Stocking in 1177, Abbot Roger recalled that once the site had been drained and prepared, the monks "built from

new their own church, beautiful and large, as it is plain to see, which may the All Highest perfect (*consummet*) and keep for evermore. And they removed thither from Stocking on the eve of All Saints, in the year of our Lord's Incarnation, in 1177, and where with God willing, they shall prosperously remain forever."[15] Roger's pious hope for the perfection of the church was clearly meant to indicate spiritual perfection rather than physical completion. As such, the conclusion of work can be inferred, and this would complement the Malebisse document of the early 1190s, which suggests the same.[16]

While it is accepted in the literature that Byland was occupied by the monks in 1177, it is far from clear what parts of the church were finished at that time. The situation is complicated by three distinct building campaigns that may be discerned in the present shattered remains and the lack of agreement on their dates. Sir Charles Peers, who cleared the site for the British Ministry of Works between 1922 and 1924, dated the first campaign to pre-1177, the second to 1180-1200, the third to 1200-1225. This would mean a sixty-year building period. Others date the church more generally, although opinion is divided between those who argue that 1177 is the date of completion (for the east parts at least), and those who see it as the start of work.[17] Based on the following analysis of the building, I hope to establish that the most likely dates for the cam-

[12] Farrer, *Early Yorkshire Charters* 3:449, charter no. 1839; see also J. Harvey, *English Medieval Architects: A Biographical Dictionary down to 1550* (London, 1954), 116.

[13] For the Byland masons, see P. Svengard, "Byland Abbey: The Builders and their Marks," *Ryedale Historian* 3 (1967): 26-29.

[14] M. Aubert, *L'Architecture cistercienne en France* (Paris, 1947), 1-99; and M. Aubert, "La Construction au moyen-âge," *B. Mon.* 119 (1961): 18.

[15] ". . . ubi de novo ecclesiam suam pulchram et magnam construxerunt, dicut patet praesenti, quam consummet altissimus et conservet in secula seculorum. Et sic de Stockying se illuc transtulerunt in virgilia Omnium Sanctorum anno Incarnationis Dominicae mc. septuagesimo septimo, ubi, Domino annuente, foeliciter manebunt in aeternum." (*Mon. Angl.* 5:353.)

[16] Burials that might provide additional evidence for the church's completion are unverifiable. R. A. Cram, *The Ruined Abbeys of Great Britain* (Boston, 1927), 157, records the dis-

covery in 1819 of the tombs of Gundreda and Roger de Mowbray in the church and the removal of their remains to Myton, but their identities are open to question. Gundreda died in 1154, and Roger de Mowbray died in 1188 while on crusade in the Holy Land where his burial is documented (see Greenway, ed., *Charters of the Honour of Mowbray*, xxix, xxxii).

[17] Peers does not give reasons for his dating, and there is no record of the location of his excavation notebooks. For those holding that work had finished (for the east end at least) *before* 1177, see E. Sharpe, *The Architecture of the Cistercians* (London, 1874), 54; J. Bilson, "The Architecture of the Cistercians," *Arch. Jnl.* 66 (1909): 200 n. 2; A. Hamilton Thompson, *Roche Abbey* (London: Department of Environment, 1954), 7; and P. Kidson and P. Murray, *A History of English Architecture* (London, 1962), 65. For those holding that work began *after* transfer in 1177, see T.S.R. Boase, *English Art, 1100-1216* (Oxford, 1953), 139; Webb, *Architecture in Britain*, 83; and Pevsner, *BoE: Yorkshire, North Riding*, 94.

paigns are: the first, *circa* 1160 to 1170; the second, including the choir, transepts, and east bays of the nave, *circa* 1170 to 1177; the third, including the remaining bays of the nave and west facade, 1177 to *circa* 1190.

The only visible remains of the first campaign are the lower ashlar courses of the south aisle of the nave and the south transept to a point level with the east range of the claustral buildings (fig. 12). The ashlar is coarse and irregular, identical to that in the claustral buildings to the south and remarkably similar, in fact, to that at nearby Rievaulx, which was largely finished by about 1160.[18] Since the claustral buildings were completed to a height of at least one story in this technique, it can be assumed that the church was raised before or at least along with them. This would mean that the present church was preceded by an earlier one. That such a church was at least started is suggested by two features in the south transept. The first is a different arrangement of the night stair that led from the adjacent monks' dormitory into the church. Originally the stair lay within the south wall of the transept in the manner customary in early churches such as Rievaulx, Fountains, and Newminster. At some time in the 1170s the stair was blocked and replaced by a ramp stair located in the newly inserted western aisle of the transept. A second feature is the coincidence of a masonry break on the exterior of the south transept chapel with the east range of the claustral buildings. East of this break is new work, identifiable by higher quality masonry. This suggests a termination of an original chapel range at this juncture in line with the claustral buildings. A smaller church with a standard Cistercian plan is suggested, probably with three chapels in each transept but without a western aisle. This seems the only possible explanation for the earlier date of the chapter house and other domestic structures to the south and for the change in masonry in the south transept. Based on the similarities of the ashlar work with that of the claustral

buildings, such a church would date to the 1160s.

For reasons that are now lost, this plan was abandoned and a wholly new scheme introduced. The change was far-reaching, and the plan was to have widespread implications for the architecture of the Cistercians. The new work is recognizable immediately by fine, regularly coursed, precisely jointed ashlar in place of the broken and irregular earlier masonry set in wide mortar beds. At the same time, radical changes were made concerning virtually the entire concept of the church. A much bigger and more ambitious plan for the choir replaced the presumed early form. When the new choir was laid out, the axis of the building was corrected and aligned more accurately eastward, an example of a new geometrical precision that occurs elsewhere in the building.[19] The night stair from the monks' dormitory was reworked, as already mentioned, to an arrangement common in the French abbeys. This campaign terminated in the fifth bay of the nave, that is, at the western limit of the monks' choir, although the lower courses of the remaining bays to the west façade seem also to have been set out at the same time. As conceived the church at Byland now measured 327 feet from east to west, larger by a third than the original dimensions of either Rievaulx or Fountains and rivaling even twelfth-century cathedrals in its scale.

Important innovations were made in the new plan at Byland. An aisle surrounded the two-bay, square-ended presbytery, and thus instead of the spatially contained and heavily surfaced walls that bounded the presbyteries of the earlier abbeys, the high altar was now flanked by arcades through which space and light flowed freely. Immediately east of the presbytery lay the aisle, which was within the full-height elevation of the building. From this aisle opened a range of five chapels, one story high, that formed a straight-ended closure to the building. The transepts also saw changes, among them the construction of aisles on the west sides; thus in consequence, the elevation repeated that on the east

---

[18] Architectural detail in the claustral buildings can be compared with that at other houses. In the lay brothers' range, the vault springers have scallop and artichoke leaf capitals (plate 35), and the bases of the center piers are attic in form. These, and the severely chamfered rib profiles, are very similar to

corresponding elements in the warming room at Fountains (*circa* 1160) and to detailing in the west claustral range at Kirkstall (*circa* 1155-1160).

[19] P. J. Fergusson, "Notes on Two Cistercian Engraved Designs," *Speculum* 54 (1979): 1-17.

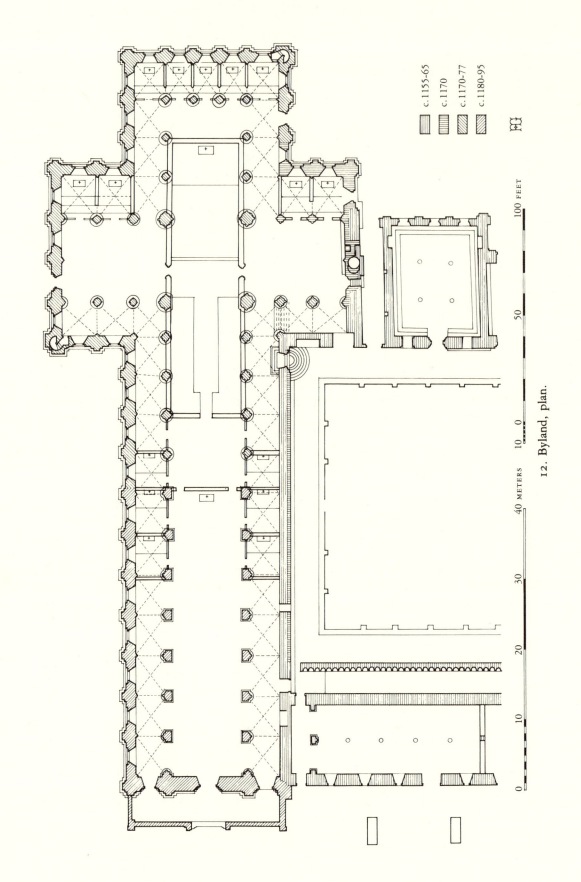

100 FEET

50

40 METERS

10   0

30

20

10

0

12. Byland, plan.

walls, unifying the transepts with the choir and nave.

The reasons for adopting the new plan can be inferred from building programs in the other larger churches of the order in the 1150s and 1160s. In the French and German abbeys, for instance, chapels were often added to the transept arm opposite the cloister. Such an arrangement had a makeshift quality, however, and posed particular problems for the placement of east-facing altars. Abbeys in England had the same need for more chapel and altar space, but they met it in a different way. Altars were not added to the transept ends or western aisles, nor, after the abandonment of the aisleless choir, to the north and south sides of choir extensions as in the Continental houses. Instead, altars were placed east-facing at the east end of the choir only. Such a preoccupation with eastern orientation characterized other twelfth-century planning in England and could well be the source of this concern at Byland.[20] Later Cistercian houses in England that adopted the rectangular ambulatory plan—such as Abbey Dore, Jervaulx, Revesby, Waverley, Netley, Sawley, Tintern, and Rievaulx—omit a western aisle in the transepts,[21] although this feature marked the plans of thirteenth-century houses in France such as Longpont and Royaumont as well as High Gothic cathedrals like Amiens and St. Omer.

In addition to its extensive use by the Cistercians in England, the rectangular ambulatory plan appears in Continental houses and in non-Cistercian churches in England. It was adopted, most prominently, at Cîteaux in the remodeling completed in 1193 and at another of the five great mother houses,

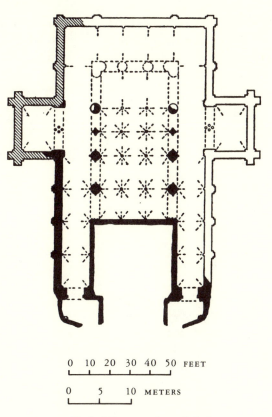

0 10 20 30 40 50 FEET

0   5   10 METERS

13. York Minster, plan of choir.

Morimond (see below); it was also used at Fontainejean (Loiret) in the early thirteenth century and in a number of the German abbeys. Among non-Cistercian churches it appears in such large-scale buildings as York Minster (*circa* 1165-1180) (fig. 13), Ripon (1170s), Glastonbury (*circa* 1185), and Litchfield (*circa* 1215).[22] The sources for this plan have important implications for Byland. It would be one thing if the plan reflected regional

[20] See H. Benson, "Church Orientations and Patronal Festivals," *Ant. Jnl.* 16 (1956): 205-13.

[21] At Byland the west aisle of the south transept was taken up by the night stair. On the north, significantly, Peers found no remains of altars in his clearance. The purpose of the western aisle there is a mystery; there are no cuts in the piers or holes in the west wall that might indicate screens either for chapels or sacristies. In Continental abbeys, by contrast, west aisles were used as chapels: for instance, at Pontigny, Le Cour-Dieu, Vauluisant, Barbeau, Clairvaux; or at Villers in Belgium; or Casamari in Italy.

The omission of this feature of the plan at Byland in the later Cistercian abbeys in England has been overlooked. For Jervaulx, see text below; for Waverley, see H. Brakspear, *Waverley Abbey* (London, 1905); for Revesby, T. Baker, "Re-

cent Excavations on the Site of Revesby Abbey," *AASRP* 10 (1869): 22-26; for Netley, G. Guillaume, *Architectural Views and Details of Netley Abbey* (Southampton, 1848); for Tintern, O. E. Craster, *Tintern Abbey* (London: Department of Environment, 1956); and for Rievaulx, Sir Charles Peers, *Rievaulx Abbey* (London: Department of Environment, 1967). A western aisle does appear at Pipewell, however, although it probably dates from a fourteenth-century rebuilding (see catalog).

[22] For York, see R. Willis, *The Architectural History of York Cathedral* (London, 1874); for Glastonbury, W. H. St. John Hope, "Notes on the Abbey Church of Glastonbury," *Arch. Jnl.* 61 (1904): 185-96; for Litchfield, R. Willis, "On Foundations of Early Buildings Recently Discovered in Litchfield Cathedral," *Arch. Jnl.* 18 (1861): 20; for Ripon, see text below.

trends in England, or in France, another if it evolved within Cistercian architecture, and another again if it were copied from one specific building. These alternatives define the problem of the plan at Byland.

One possibility is that the plan at Byland derived from a prototype in the north of England—specifically, York Minster. The large, new chevet at York was started by Archbishop Roger Pont L'Evêque probably in the early 1160s. A gift was confirmed in the crypt in 1166, and donations to the fabric are recorded in the early 1170s.[23] Work was most likely completed by August 1175 when William I of Scotland placed his spear, saddle, and breastplate on the altar of St. Peter, presumably the main altar of the new choir; it was certainly finished by 1181 when the archbishop was buried in the middle of the newly constructed choir.[24]

Excavations carried out at York after the 1829 fire revealed the plan of the northeast corner of the chevet, but it has proved difficult to establish important details. A major problem is determining whether the full-height, three-story elevation continued to the terminal wall, or stopped one bay west of the terminal wall to step down to a one-story chapel range. Willis has suggested the latter, reasoning that the terminal wall was not thick enough to support a full-height elevation and that the eastern bay was slightly longer than the others.[25] But Browne in fact shows that the east wall was thicker than the side walls and, further contradicting Willis, that the outer buttress in the last but one bay is not strengthened, whereas the final east buttress is.[26] More likely is that the building terminated

with a high east gable. It was this arrangement that Pont L'Evêque used at the other great undertaking of his rule, Ripon Cathedral, begun circa 1170.

The plan at York can be related to other, older traditions in England. The general components of a square-ended presbytery surrounded by aisles with an east chapel range is known at Evesham (1044-1054), Old Sarum (circa 1110-1120), Romsey (circa 1120-1125), and Chertsey (circa 1110).[27] In all these the east chapels were probably one story and lower than the rest of the building. The earliest examples of an east termination with the chapels within the full-height elevation are Rochester (circa 1115) and St. Cross Winchester (circa 1160).[28] Although located in the south, these buildings could well have been known to Pont L'Evêque who before his appointment as archbishop of York had held the office of treasurer at Canterbury. Connections to Canterbury even are suggested at York by the unusual projecting spaces north and south of the chevet aisles, which have been interpreted variously as tower bases or eastern transepts, and which recall the same features in Archbishop Anselm's famous Romanesque choir at Canterbury (1090s-1114).

A second possibility is that the plan at Byland derived not from an English prototype but from a Cistercian house in eastern France—that is, Morimond (Haute-Marne). Excavation at Morimond undertaken by Henri Paul Eydoux in the early 1950s revealed a rectangular ambulatory and chapel scheme (fig. 14) that he dated to about 1155-1170.[29] Thus a possible prototype existed within the order independent of anything in England. The plan at

[23] It is not impossible that Thomas of Bayeux's eleventh-century choir had a crypt and that the signing took place there. For the most recent treatments of these parts of York, see H. M. Taylor and J. Taylor, Anglo-Saxon Architecture (Cambridge, 1956), 2:700-709; E. Gee, "Architectural History until 1290," in G. E. Alymer and R. Cant, A History of York Minster (Oxford, 1977), 122.

[24] Aylmer and Cant, A History of York Minster, 122.

[25] See Willis, York Cathedral, 11; also J. Browne, A History of the Metropolitan Church of York, vol. 2 (Oxford and York, 1847). Complicating the whole problem of York is the absence of an accurate plan. The published ones vary widely. Unfortunately, no additional light on this problem comes from the recent decade of work on the crossing.

[26] See Browne, A History of the Metropolitan Church of York,

vol. 2, plates 12-31.

[27] See M. F. Hearn, "The Rectangular Ambulatory in English Medieval Architecture," JSAH 30 (1971): 187-208, esp. 195ff.

[28] W. H. St. John Hope, "The Architectural History of the Cathedral Church and Monastery of St. Andrew at Rochester," Arch. Cant. 23 (1898): 204-209; for Holy Cross, see Sir Charles Peers and H. Brakspear, "Winchester Hospital of St. Cross," VCH: Hampshire and the Isle of Wight 5 (London, 1912): 59-66.

[29] H. P. Eydoux, "L'Eglise abbatiale de Morimond," B. Mon. 114 (1956): 253-66; H. P. Eydoux, "L'Eglise abbatiale de Morimond," ASOC 14 (1953): 2-116; H. P. Eydoux, L'Eglise abbatiale de Morimond (Rome, 1958).

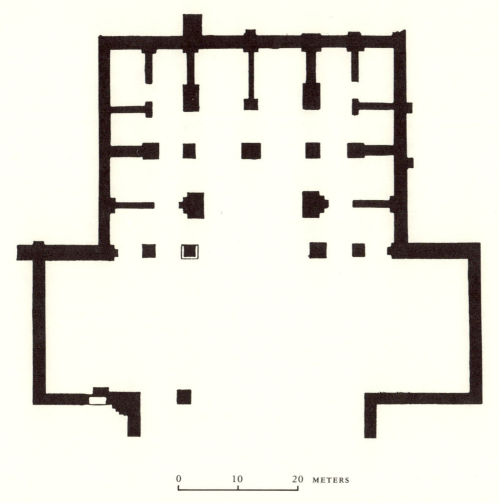

0   10   20 METERS

14. Morimond, plan of the church.

Morimond has a number of features not found at Byland, however: chapels lined both the north and south aisles of the presbytery; the east end terminated in a range of six chapels; and the full-height elevation was closed by two arches the same width as those in the flanking walls, meaning that the axial feature was a pier. An axial pier became, in fact, the customary arrangement in the Continental houses of the Cistercians using this plan—at Cîteaux, for instance, or in Germany, Schönau or Heisterbach.[30] In England, on the other hand—as at Byland, for instance—the prescribed solution was for an arcade arrangement using three arches, with the axial element now an open arch rather

than a pier, but with the openings narrower than those in the flanking elevation.

There are a number of unsettled questions about the chevet at Morimond, including the date. In new excavations in 1963 Leopold Grill found evidence of an earlier chevet, thereby casting doubt on an important argument in Eydoux's dating— that none had previously existed.[31] The Eydoux plan also poses other problems of interpretation, such as the unexplained size of the second pier in the presbytery and its nonalignment with adjacent piers. Since the plan was used at other, earlier buildings in the north of France such as St. Etienne, Beauvais (*circa* 1140), revealed by excavation, St.

[30] See W. Krönig, *Altenberg und die Baukunst der Zisterzienser* (Bergisch Gladbach, 1973), 67-75.

[31] Grill's excavation has also not been published. See dis-

cussion in W. Schlink, *Zwischen Cluny und Clairvaux* (Berlin, 1970), 92-94.

Bertin at St. Omer (*circa* 1100), and Ste. Hildevert at Gournay-en-Bray (*circa* 1150), its appearance at Morimond should be seen as reflecting influence from this region.[32]

Morimond was one of the five mother houses of the order with a filiation of dependent houses that numbered over two hundred. It was thus extremely influential. But firm evidence that the plan of its church provided the model for Byland is lacking. There are no precedents for influence in Yorkshire from this part of France and no other trace of it at Byland, either in the elevation or in the detailing. Filiation would also argue against it. Even at Abbey Dore (about 1185), the only foundation in England to spring from Morimond, the plan repeats the disposition of space at Byland rather than that at Morimond. Furthermore, abbeys in which the influence of Morimond has been demonstrated, such as those in Germany differ from Byland and Abbey Dore.[33] Morimond thus seems a less than primary source for the plan at Byland.

A third alternative is that the plan of Byland reflected regional trends in northeastern France, Lorraine, and French Flanders. These areas, unlike Normandy, had a long tradition of rectangular ambulatory plans, which can be traced back to Carolingian and Ottonian outer crypts.[34] In the eleventh century St. Feuillen at Fosses and in the twelfth century St. Bavo in Ghent and St. Bartholomew in Liège had rectangular chevet schemes with eastern chapel ranges, although the chapels were organized in stepped or *en échelon* plans. The region also provides examples of western aisles in transepts, a feature that Robert Branner has shown derived from earlier English and French sources. It was adopted again by a number of large Early Gothic churches in northeastern France, such as the cathedrals of Arras and Laon, and at Lillers, St. Lomer at Blois, St. Bertin at St. Omer, and Ste. Hildevert at Gournay-en-Bray.[35]

The absence of an exact prototype from this region for the church at Byland does not eliminate it as a possible source. Destruction of medieval monuments is greater there than elsewhere. Furthermore, a case can be made for the currency of the plan on the basis of the drawing by Villard de Honnecourt from about 1230. Villard, who came from the vicinity of Cambrai in the county of Hainault—namely, in the heart of this region—drew a rectangular ambulatory plan (fig. 15) with the title: "This is a church made of squares for the Cistercian order."[36] It is interesting that Villard's plan was only a design; the walls are drawn with single lines, unlike the other plans in his *Album*, which he shows with wall thickness. As such, then, the plan exists as an ideal—this is likewise suggested by the absence of any identification on the inscription—but an ideal based on Villard's familiarity with standing examples.

In addition to the three possible sources for the Byland plan discussed above, a more recent theory claims an evolution for the plan within the order, involving only minimal outside contact.[37] It can be argued that once the Bernardine east end was abandoned, the notion of taking the familiar square-ended plan and surrounding it with chapels does not entail a dramatic architectural development, particularly in regions where a tradition of such straight-ended plans already existed, as, for instance, in England and northeastern France. The idea that the rectangular ambulatory plan "evolved" in an English or French context would be an evolution in keeping with Cistercian ideals.[38]

Examination of these alternatives reveals, then,

---

[32] The excavations at St. Etienne came too late to be considered by Eydoux but are not mentioned by Krönig (see *Altenberg*, 68; and see J.-P. Pacquet, "Les Traces Directeurs des plans de quelques édifices du domaine royal au moyen âge," *Les Monuments historiques de la France*, n.s. 9 [1963], 68-71, figs. 10 and 12). For St. Bertin, see P. Héliot, "Le Chevet roman de Saint-Bertin à Saint-Omer et l'architecture franco-lotharingienne," *Revue Belge d'archéologie et d'histoire de l'art* 22 (1953): 73-96; for Ste. Hildevert, see L. Régnier, "Gournay-en-Bray," *Congrès archéologique de France, Beauvais* 76 (1905): 75.

[33] Krönig, *Altenberg*, 67-75.

[34] See R. Maere, "Cryptes au chevet du choeur dans les anciens Pays-Bas," *B. Mon.* 91 (1932): 81-119; and A. Verbeek, "Die Aussenkrypta werden einer Bauform des frühen Mittelalters," *Zeitschrift für Kunstgeschichte* 12 (1950): 7-38.

[35] See Branner, "Gothic Architecture 1160-1180," 98.

[36] H. R. Hahnloser, *Villard de Honnecourt*, 2d ed. (Vienna, 1972), 65-67, fol. 28b.

[37] See Krönig, *Altenberg*, 68. Hearn discounts such an evolution, however, at least within an English context (see "The Rectangular Ambulatory in English Medieval Architecture," 205-206).

[38] England as the place of origin is suggested by J. A.

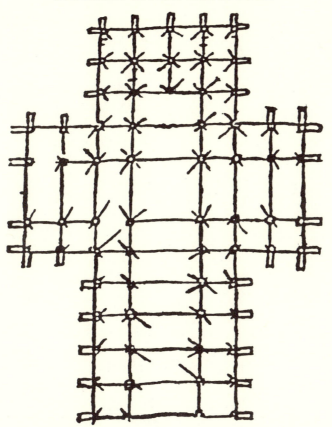

15. Villard de Honnecourt, "Album," MS FR. 19093,
fol. 28b, Paris, Bibliothèque Nationale.

that the rectangular ambulatory plan had a history of recent use in England before Byland as well as in northeastern France and French Flanders, that the closure of the eastern elevation with three arches and the omission of chapels on the lateral sides were identifiably English solutions, that the use of western aisles in the transepts was probably not, and that in general the plan was eminently adaptable to Cistercian needs and fitted the order's traditions of straight-ended plans. Whether once adopted at Byland the plan then became the source for its later use by the order awaits further evidence, but more cautiously, it seems that the plan at Byland exemplified a tendency in Cistercian planning in the 1170s to experiment with chevet schemes and that its form was based on traditions of planning well established in both England and northeastern France.

The elevation adopted at Byland (plate 78) was much more complex than that at Furness and Roche and much richer in its effects. A reconstruction (fig. 16) based on the remaining parts shows a three-story composition: an arcade carried by fasciculated piers with multi-molded pointed arches; a middle story conceived as a contracted gallery with a center opening indented from the plane of the wall, divided by two pointed arches, and surmounted by a relieving arch with single flanking blind arches; and a double-wall clerestory with a single window in the outer wall and triple arcades facing the interior (plate 79).[39] In the transept terminal walls a band triforium was topped by a double-wall clerestory; thus two levels of passages penetrate the upper elevation.[40]

The elevation at Byland, like that at Roche, was

Schmoll, "Zisterzienser-Romanik: Kritische Gedanken zur jüngsten Literatur," Formositas Romanica (Basel, 1958), 153-80, esp. 172.

[39] Fergusson, "South Transept Elevation of Byland Abbey," 156-58; an earlier reconstruction used by Bilson is faulty.
[40] Parts are visible in plate 78 of this volume. The window

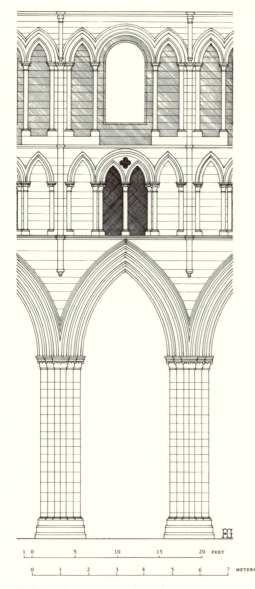

16. Byland, reconstruction of south transept.

in comparison with the bulky proportions at Roche), and its singularity indicates the absence of an intention to link it to a system of vaults or transverse arches. Unconnected to either pier or vault, then, the single shafts reveal a concept of bay division that may be defined as one of vertical punctuation rather than as a system of wall shafts related to and carrying rib vaults.

The architecture of Byland shows a different handling of elements from that at Roche in other ways as well. For instance, the arch moldings at Roche are composed of setbacks conceived as a series, each of which is separately supported by columns and setbacks corresponding to a compound pier. At Byland this serial character of moldings and piers is eliminated and with it any sense of connection between the moldings and the fasciculated piers. Instead the parts fuse, the multiplicity of thinner lines breaking down the separate nature of the earlier forms.

Similarly, the aisles at Byland were rib vaulted with sharply pointed four-part ribs, but with moldings and supports noticeably thinner and lighter than those used at either Roche or Kirkstall. The vault over the central vessel was of wood rather than of stone, as can be inferred from the articulation of the walls described above, as well as the surviving remains and early drawings. On the south wall of the south transept is a fragment of curved wall rib that originally extended the full span of the space; as such it can be seen in two drawings (plates 80 and 81) made before the collapse of the upper parts of the wall in the early nineteenth century. A pedimented gable rose above the wall rib. The remains indicate, therefore, a double shell: an outer pitched roof over an inner vault. Since the walls were not thick enough to support a masonry vault, and since a flat, timber ceiling would obscure much of the wheel window at the west end and would be inconsistent with the wall rib, the most plausible cover would be a wooden barrel vault of semi-circular or slightly pointed form.[41]

articulated by marked vertical accents, but the systems differ. There was no attempt at Byland to link the fasciculated piers to the upper stories as in the transept at Roche; instead the single shafts that frame the bay extend only to the spandrel of the arcade. Moreover the shaft is relatively thin (at least

arrangement in the transept end is established in Thomas Atkinson's 1806 print (plate 11 in ibid.), and also by descriptions in *Gentleman's Magazine* 81, pt. 2 (1811): 107-109; and in *A Description of Duncombe Park, Rivalx Abbey, and Helmsley Castle, with Notices of Byland Abbey, Kirkdale Church, etc.* (Kirby Moorside, 1821), 40.

[41] Remaining parts of the west façade (plate 84) confirm this idea. The upper half is dominated by a large wheel window, which rises above the top of the clerestory. Had an open timber roof closed the space, it would have cut the rose in two. Only a barrel-vaulted timber construction would permit an unimpeded view.

Compared with the features of the order's earlier churches, these establish a dramatically new character for the architecture of Byland. The elevation is richer and more open, with mural boundaries cut into and hollowed out. The upper stories in particular are composed with a new freedom, using double-walled construction for the clerestory instead of a monolithic wall mass through which openings were "cut." In addition, the articulating elements of the system take on a different linear character: profiles are tighter, moldings thinner and more delicate, shafting slimmer in form and sharper in outline. And unlike the other abbeys, the whole composition is enlivened by large capitals carved with verve and conviction. The whole expression of the interior assumes, then, a quality that is much less severe and stern than Fountains or even Roche, one that Geoffrey Webb aptly characterizes as "humane and at times almost romantic."[42]

The sources of this architecture require careful consideration. The middle story belongs, of course, to the same family of contracted galleries found at Furness. Unlike the Lancashire house, however, where bare walls flank the opening and the impression is of a continuous wall pierced serially by small openings, the Byland system is one of divisions and enframements within each bay. Such blind or purely decorative arcading in the upper stories is particularly characteristic of the architecture of northeastern France and can be seen at Ste. Marguerite-sur-Mer (Seine-Maritime) (plate 82), Pogny (Aube) (plate 83), St. Evremond, Creil (Oise) (plate 68), and in the chevet at St. Omer in Lillers (Pas-de-Calais).[43] It also occurs in French Flanders, at Cappellebrouck, and in the area in and around Tournai, for example, at St. Brice in the city.[44] Except for Lillers and Creil, all these churches have wooden barrel vaults, a form of vault nearly universal in the 1170s and 1180s in this region and also in the area to the north of Tournai. The double-walled clerestory, although part of an old tradition of architecture in England, was also widely used in northern France (for instance at the Cathedral of Arras) and Flanders. The way the wall passage was constructed in this region, however, differs from the Anglo-Norman tradition where arches or even narrow barrel vaults were used. Instead, and this is the technique used at Byland also, the wall passage was covered by lintels extending the thickness of the wall and thus linking the inner and outer planes of the wall (plate 79). The technique is found at Verdun (1144 forward) and in the transepts at Tournai Cathedral (1160s).[45]

Architectural detailing also connects the abbey to northeastern France. Two types of pier, both fasciculated, were used: a twelve-shaft pier in the chevet and north transept and an eight-shaft pier in the south transept and first four nave bays.[46] In both the principal shafts were keeled. The moldings were equally French; they included rolls with a gorged profile, a form used in the Soissonnais.

Study of the capitals at Byland confirms the decidedly French character of the architecture. The capitals include a wide range of waterleaf (plate 94), volute (plate 100), and molded types.[47] In quality of carving and freshness of modeling they

[42] Webb, *Architecture in Britain*, 83.

[43] For Ste. Marguerite, see F. Deshoulières, "L'Eglise de Ste. Marguerite-sur-Mer," *Congrès archéologique de France* (Rouen, 1926), 319; for Pogny, P. Héliot, "La Nef de l'église de Pogny, et les piles fasciculées dans l'architecture romane," *Mémoires de la société d'agriculture, commerce, sciences, et arts du département de la Marne* 83 (1968): 80-92; for Creil, R. J. Johnson, *Specimens of Early French Architecture* (London, 1864), plates 5-6; for Lillers, H. Benard and P. Héliot, "Les Fouilles de la Collégiale de Lillers," *Les Monuments historiques de la France* 3 (1955), 182-86.

[44] For Cappellebrouck, see R. Rodière, "Notes archéologiques sur quelques églises de la Flandre Maritime," *Société d'études de la province de Cambrai* (1936), 5-75; for the Tournai churches, see P. Rolland, *Les Eglises paroissiales de Tournai* (Brussels, 1936).

[45] See Branner, "Gothic Architecture 1160-1180," 96; for the use of wooden barrel vaults in this area, see R. Branner, "The Transept of Cambrai Cathedral," in M. Kühn, ed., *Gedenkschrift Ernst Gall* (Munich, 1965), 69-86, esp. 72.

[46] L. Serbat stressed the French quality of these piers more than seventy years ago (see "L'Architecture des cisterciens dans leur plus anciennes églises en Angleterre," *B. Mon.* 74 [1910]: 434-46, esp. 442). For examples, see P. J. Fergusson, "The Late Twelfth Century Rebuilding at Dundrennan Abbey," *Ant. Jnl.* 53 (1973): 232-43, esp. 238.

[47] The volute capitals were originally painted with red highlights (see Webb, *Architecture in Britain*, 84). Similar use of color emerged at Roche (see F. R. Fairbank, "Roche Abbey and the Cistercian Order," *AASRP* 18 [1884]: 47). In addition to the capitals still in place at Byland or in the abbey museum or the stone dump, further ones from the main arcades may

far surpass those at Roche and Furness. French influence and possibly even French workmanship is suggested when they are compared to capitals in churches along the northeast French coast or to capitals in Picardy and the Laonnois.[48] The change from one style to another in capitals can be fairly precisely dated. In the south of England, at Canterbury, volute capitals replaced waterleaf around 1175-1176, namely, in the west bays of William of Sens' choir, and molded capitals appeared first in 1179 in the Trinity Chapel crypt, the work of the English William. In the north of England approximately the same chronology can be demonstrated. The chapel of the castle at Newcastle upon Tyne, constructed by Master Maurice between 1172 and 1177, has capitals that mix waterleaf and molded types.[49] Changes in the *in situ* capitals at Byland from waterleaf to volute and then to molded are, therefore, entirely consistent with trends in the middle-to-late 1170s.

The date of the eastern parts of the church at Byland becomes more certain in the light of the preceding comparisons. All construction on the church accords more plausibly with the choir's being completed in the 1170s rather than in the 1180s. Only if the architecture were deliberately *retardataire* would the latter date be appropriate, and there is nothing to suggest that this was the case. Rather, the freshness of the style argues strongly for the vitality of the building's conception. As already mentioned, the first claustral buildings on the site, those of the lay brothers, date from 1155 to 1160, and the other claustral buildings and the first church program from the 1160s. The years separating these dates from the date for the construction of the second, enlarged church in the

1170s and from that for the community's documented move in 1177 are probably best explained by a delay in completing the eastern end of the church following the decision to scrap the first program in favor of the more ambitious second one. Practical considerations also support this. The move from nearby Stocking (just over a mile to the southwest) would imply a completed choir; it seems most unlikely that the monks abandoned the church and cloister that had served them for the previous thirty years for unfinished temporary quarters. If work had begun only in 1177, the monks would have spent about ten years in a temporary church at the new site, an improbability with Stocking so near.

The third and final campaign saw the seven west nave bays and west façade finished (plate 84). Completion by the early 1190s is suggested by documents and confirmed by the remains. The three-story elevation established in the eastern parts was continued to the west wall, though the detailing became severely plain. A square pier replaced the fasciculated pier, aisle responds were topped by plain molded capitals, and the lancet windows lacked the keeled surrounds of those in the east end. Only in the upper portions of the west façade was this severity moderated. The façade itself (plate 85) repeated a type of composition used in the French and English abbeys since mid-century—at Trois-Fontaines (plate 15), for instance, or at Fountains—but its enlarged scale and its propensity toward tightened profiles and decorative elaboration gave it a clearly Early Gothic appearance.

Three portals, with rich and dense moldings, led from a porch to the interior, the center portal with a trefoil head as was used earlier in the refectory at

---

be found in the grounds of Myton Hall, Myton-on-Swale (North Yorkshire), where Mr. and Mrs. Thomas kindly permitted me to examine them.

[48] Similar examples of waterleaf survive at Berzé-le-Sec (Aisne) (plate 95) and at the abbey of Vaucelles (Nord) (plate 97). Comparable volute capitals occur at Licques (Pas-de-Calais), at Laon in the cathedral and in the Episcopal Palace Chapel, and at Dommartin (Pas-de-Calais). At Dommartin—where work began in the 1150s, and the east end was consecrated in 1163—the similarities are particularly striking (plates 96 and 101). Close connections between Dommartin and England came about in 1171 when one of its monks, Guillaume, brought to the abbey two relics of Thomas à Becket, martyred the year

before. Shortly thereafter, these relics were visited by the grand prior of Canterbury, who verified their authenticity. By this time an impressive pilgrimage to the monastery had begun, which was promoted vigorously under Abbot Hugues de Aleste (1176-1179). Relations with Canterbury continued, extending to an annual exchange of monks. In 1179 Henry II intervened on Dommartin's behalf to force the submission of the abbey's chief enemy, Jean, count of Ponthieu.

[49] See W. H. Knowles, "The Castle, Newcastle upon Tyne," *Arch. Ael.*, 4th ser., 2 (1926): 1-39. The molded capital may be regarded as another importation from France; it appears there a good two decades before it appears at Canterbury—for instance, at Berteaucourt-les-Dames (see plate 27).

Rievaulx. The façade was dominated by three large lancets surmounted by a giant rose window, twenty-six feet in diameter—the first of such size in England. Recessed on the interior by about four feet and surmounted by a wide relieving arch, the window was fringed by arcading supported on four colonnettes, perhaps following the model of the north transept rose at Canterbury.[50] Dogtooth moldings decorated the interior faces of both arch and window, and the capitals supporting the arch were stiff-leaf (plate 105), in contrast to the molded capitals of the west aisle bays. Outside, slender blind arcades flank the lancets in a 1 : 2 : 2 : 1 composition with a dogtooth pattern in the hood moldings and shafts with ring moldings. Similar details are found in the Rievaulx refectory (*circa* 1185-1200), the south transept at Arbroath about 1190, the presbytery at Tynemouth Priory (*circa* 1200) (plate 86), and on the south nave doorway at Jervaulx (*circa* 1190) (plate 87).

Shortly after the completion of the eastern end of the church at Byland, its influence appears in other buildings, mainly in the north. At Dundrennan in southwest Scotland (fig. 17) the remodeling of the north transept around 1185 reveals its debt to the Yorkshire abbey in the twelve-shaft fasciculated piers, the types of moldings, the vertical framing of the bays by a single shaft rising from the spandrels of the arcade, and to a lesser extent, in the composition of the second-story arcading. Connections between the houses may explain these links; the abbot of Dundrennan, Sylvanus, succeeded Ailred as abbot of Rievaulx (four miles from Byland) in 1167 and retired to Byland in 1187.[51] At Abbey Dore in Herefordshire the

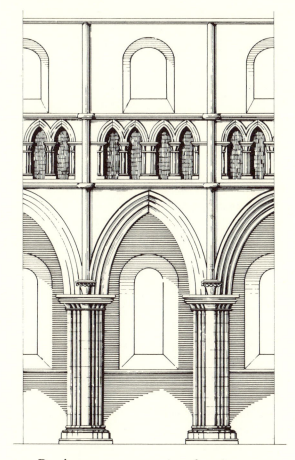

17. Dundrennan, reconstruction of north transept.

plan of the church (*circa* 1185) (see fig. 20, p. 97), followed the Byland model, as did that at Waverley II begun in 1203.[52] Less certain on account of schematic evidence is the influence of Byland at Revesby (Lincolnshire) in the plan and at Vaudey (Lincolnshire) and Meaux (Yorkshire) in architectural detailing such as the piers.[53] There is a hint that the use of the wooden vault at Byland influenced Meaux,

[50] For evidence of the colonnettes, see C. H. Fowler, "Byland Abbey," *YAJ* 9 (1886): 395-96. In general, the chronology of the west façade is confused. The south door is older than the others and courses through with the outer wall of the south aisle. The center and north doors do not course through with the inner face of the west end, although on the interior, the lower courses, at least, appear to have been laid out with the west bays of the nave. On the exterior, capitals are strangely mixed, some foliate with square abaci, others waterleaf, and others molded. The double waterleaf capital on the main portal may be a case of deliberate reuse, perhaps from Stocking.

[51] Another link may have come via Walter, perhaps Espec's former chaplain. He witnessed a land confirmation by the bishop of Durham 1153-1155 and later became prior at Dun-

drennan (see F. M. Powicke, *Ailred of Rievaulx and his Biographer Walter Daniel* [London, 1972], 10).

[52] For Abbey Dore, see chapter 6 of this study; for Waverley, see catalog entry.

[53] For Revesby, the evidence is undated but came to light in an exploratory dig by the local clergyman (see T. Barker, "Recent Excavations on the Site of Revesby Abbey," *AASRP* 10 [1869]: 22-25). A sixteen-shaft pier (from the crossing?) and other "clustered piers" at Vaudey are mentioned in *The Gentleman's Magazine* 122 (1851): 155, although no trace of them survives; for the sixteen-shaft pier, compare with examples in France mentioned by Branner, "Gothic Architecture 1160-1180," 94 n. 6. For Meaux, see catalog.

where a "testudine caelata" was raised in the mid-thirteenth century, and Louth Park (Lincolnshire), where an extensive timber "fabricatione" completed the church around 1240 (see catalog entries).

The architecture at Jervaulx was also influenced by the developments at Byland. Jervaulx, affiliated with Byland in 1147 when it was struggling into existence, received as abbot John of Kinstan, one of Byland's founding monks. Under his long rule (1149 to *circa* 1185-1190) Jervaulx was established and its buildings begun. A transfer from an earlier site at Fors took place in 1156, and the first buildings at Jervaulx, the lay brothers' range, date from around 1160, to judge by the masonry work and artichoke leaf capitals (plate 36; cf. Byland, plate 35). Thus Jervaulx followed the same sequence of building and used detailing similar to that at Byland in the early programs of work. Thereafter, the building chronologies of each abbey diverge. The nave of the church at Jervaulx, dating to about 1185, preceded the east end, for reasons that are unclear; the chevet was begun a decade or so later. Such a sequence suggests an earlier church, perhaps of timber, though no signs of it emerged in Hope's and Brakspear's excavation.[54]

The chevet at Jervaulx (fig. 18) terminated at full-height at the east end, the east chapels being within the elevation rather than outside it as at Byland. The full-height termination was the same as that used at Rochester (1115-1125), Holy Cross, Winchester (*circa* 1160-1175), probably York Minster (*circa* 1165), Bardney (*circa* 1175), Ripon (*circa* 1170s), St. Frideswide, Oxford (*circa* 1175), Waltham (*circa* 1170-1190), and Brinkburn (*circa* 1190-1200).[55] Thus the plan at Jervaulx relates to a different tradition than that at Byland, one that is explicitly English.

Of the elevation at Jervaulx the only sizable fragment remaining is the southwest corner of the south aisle (plate 88), which shows that the aisles were rib vaulted, the vaults rising from springers formed of molded capitals and abaci that were cut from one block, the same technique employed at Byland. Pier bases show that the piers were fasciculated with eight shafts and keeled profiles. The doorway into the west bay of the aisle had a finely worked dog-tooth pattern (plate 87), and this detailing can be compared to the west façade at Byland (*circa* 1190), although the doorway at Jervaulx did not bond in with the flanking masonry. In the eastern nave bays, transepts, and chevet, the piers were given fillets, and the shafts, alternately keeled and semicircular, were separated by hollows, all features that can be dated to about 1190-1200. In the chevet's south aisle, the master designed responds for the vaults, but they were left unfinished, even though the vaults themselves were completed—a persistent effort to avoid aisle articulation in the Cistercian churches of Yorkshire, which extends back to Rievaulx.

But did the influence of Byland remain a strictly Cistercian phenomenon, something localized among the order's churches and other monastic buildings? A wider impact may be claimed among a group of buildings that lay in varying degrees outside the orbit of the Cistercians. The most compelling case is Old Malton Priory, founded in 1150, a house belonging to the Gilbertines who were strongly influenced by the Cistercians. Work on a new church began around 1175 to judge by fragmentary remains of the south transept.[56] The west bays of the nave of the 1190s survive in large part (plate 89), and there the influence of Byland emerges in the pier design, the composition of the middle story,

[54] See W. H. St. John Hope and H. Brakspear, "Jervaulx Abbey," *YAJ* 21 (1911): 303-44. The publication on Jervaulx is uncharacteristically general, and the remains have never been systematically examined. The west responds have bases with earlier profiles than those of the west door, which are waterholding. Likewise, the piers change as work on the nave moved eastward. The south door and the exterior buttresses do not course through; they look like later work of about 1185-1190.

[55] For Rochester and Winchester, see n. 28 above; for St. Frideswide, see *RCHM: Oxford* (London, 1939), 35-46; for Bardney, see H. Brakspear, "Bardney Abbey," *Arch. Jnl.* 79 (1922): 1-92; for Brinkburn, *Brinkburn Priory* (London: De-

partment of Environment, 1967); for Waltham, see *RCHM: Essex* 5 (London, 1966): 172. This solution probably derives from France, as Hearn has argued in "The Rectangular Ambulatory in English Medieval Architecture," 202.

[56] At Old Malton the present church preserves only part of the former nave. In the eighteenth century the aisles were removed, the arcades blocked, and the clerestory dismantled. For the building's former appearance, see S. Buck, *Buck's Antiquities; Venerable Remains of Castles, Monasteries, Palaces in England and Wales* (London, 1774), plate 332. The plate, made in 1728, shows a single clerestory window over each bay. For the priory's history, see *VCH: Yorkshire* 3 (London, 1913):

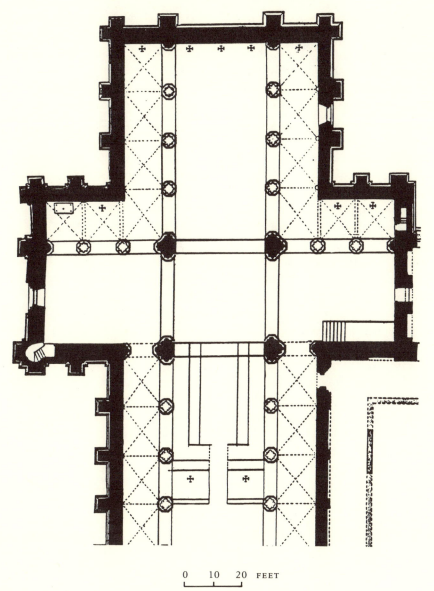

0   10   20 FEET

18. Jervaulx, plan of east end.

and the system of shaft articulation that frames the bays.

More puzzling, and one of the central problems of Early Gothic architecture in the north of England, is the relationship between Byland and Ripon, then one of four Minster churches of the archdiocese of York, but a cathedral since 1836.[57] As already seen, the plans of these two contemporary buildings are different and unrelated versions of the rectangular ambulatory plan, with termination of the east

253-54; Pevsner, *BoE: Yorkshire, North Riding*, 232-33. In addition to the similarity of the second story to that at Byland, the bays were also framed by single shafts, which drop just below the string course supporting the gallery. In the two west bays fasciculated piers similar to those at Byland were substituted for the plain columnar pier used before. In the earlier but now ruined south transept, capitals on the outer

door (plate 103) show a nearly identical foliate design to those now in the museum at Byland.

[57] Documents state only that the church was begun *de novo* by Archbishop Roger Pont L'Evêque (1154-1181), who gave £1,000 for the work (see J. Raine, ed., *Historians of the Church of York and its Archbishops* [London, 1894], 3:82, no. 63). The date of the gift is not known. Although large, the sum rep-

wall at Ripon at full-height, that is to say, with the chapels within the main elevation (rather then outside it as at Byland), a scheme that probably reflects the archbishop Pont L'Evêque's chevet at York. But if Byland and Ripon differ in this respect, there is, on the other hand, a powerful similarity between the transepts of the two buildings. They resemble each other so closely and are, in fact, only eighteen miles apart, that questions of priority, prototypes, and relationship have to be addressed.

At Ripon matters are complicated by the difference between the elevation of the choir (plate 90) and that of the east walls of the transepts (plate 91). In the former the piers are eight-shaft versions of the fasciculated pier without keeling (namely, like those at Furness) and rest on round plinths. By contrast, the piers in the transepts are compound piers with triple shafts on the front face that rise from floor to ceiling. The arrangement of compound pier and continuous shaft recalls older Norman ideas, but it is given up-to-date profiling like that at Fécamp. In the choir, above the pier capitals, five wall shafts that are bonded in with the wall rise to the clerestory. The shafts differ in size and are combined in an arrangement that indicates the intention to vault with four-part rib vaults complete with wall ribs. Evidence that vaulting was actually begun survives on the east wall where the masonry is scarred following the line of a vaulting web. But in the west bays of the choir the idea of vaulting was abandoned by the time the clerestory was reached; the shafts stop abruptly, and above, the number and diameters of the colonnettes are reduced and the shafts worked as detached, *en délit* shafts. A double wall clerestory and timber roof completed the elevation. No such revision is evident in the transepts, however, where a wooden roof was clearly decided on early in the program. This can be seen in the terminal walls and west walls, which are articulated differently from the east walls.

For buildings in such close proximity to each other, Byland and Ripon share remarkably few similarities in architectural detailing, indicating that the masons' yards were not in touch with each other. For instance, the capitals in the choir aisles, in the transept chapels, and on the exterior of the lower, outer walls at Ripon (namely, on the parts that would correspond to a procedure of building in which the new work was raised as an envelope around the old), are a mix of dull, rubbery waterleaf and volute types that date to the 1170s. Only after the change in program at Ripon that led to the abandonment of the vault does detailing become close to that at Byland.

Taken together, the evidence at Ripon indicates that the choir precedes the transepts and reflects the original vaulted prototype, and that the later transepts show an amalgam of ideas, including a number from nearby Byland. What occasioned these changes in program at Ripon is not known. It may have had to do with the death of Pont L'Evêque in 1181, which could well have interrupted funding and led to a pause in work of some years.

The obvious relationship between the transepts at Byland and Ripon result, then, from modifications in the original program at Ripon. What began as a fully vaulted building with connections to eastern France and to such buildings as Acey (plate 67), Roche (plate 61), or the transepts at Laon Cathedral was modified into a timber-ceilinged building with a double-wall clerestory along the lines of Byland. Most likely, the original design at Ripon did not come directly from France but was based on the choir at York of a decade earlier. Both buildings shared the same patron, their plans are similar, and architectural detailing has points in common. But if York can be extrapolated from Ripon, was York the source for Byland? This is unlikely. In the first place, it would mean that the Cistercian abbey adapted a plan developed for a secular cathedral and modified it for monastic purposes, then adjusted a wall system designed for vaulting to a wooden barrel vault. Yet to read the architecture at Byland in terms of assembly of parts gathered from here and

---

resented only part of the archbishop's considerable resources; in 1170 he boasted a treasury of £10,000, which he pledged to Becket's downfall (see J. Shirley, trans., *Garnier's Becket* [London, 1975], 133).

For analysis of the whole building, see C. Hallet, *The Ca-*

thedral Church of Ripon (London, 1901); Sir Nikolaus Pevsner, *BoE: Yorkshire, West Riding* (London, 1967), 403-14. For the nave, see Hearn, "On the Original Nave of Ripon Cathedral," *JBAA*, 3d ser., 35 (1972): 39-45; and 39 (1976): 93-94.

there is unconvincing. The architecture carries the hallmarks of freshness and consistency, with none of the abrupt juxtapositions associated with piece-meal compositions. Ripon, on the other hand, has a distinctly eclectic quality. Even where the two buildings are closest, as in the transepts, Ripon seems to be an anglicized version of the Cistercian house.

The most convincing source for Ripon, and York, as vaulted three-story structures using cautious openings of the middle story, is in the general area of the Champenois and Laonnois. For Byland, by contrast, the source lay to the northeast of this area. Centers around Valenciennes and northeast into French Flanders provide the most likely models for the design. The tradition there of wooden barrel vaulting, of rectangular ambulatory plans, of arcading of interior and exterior wall surfaces, of separate techniques of wall passage construction, and of architectural detailing like the capitals offers an unmistakable source for the architecture of Byland.

Although both Byland and Ripon in the 1170s and early 1180s show the close contact of the north of England with the mainstream of Early Gothic architecture in France, this was not maintained in the last two decades of the century. The nature of the new interests can be seen at St. Andrews Cathedral in Fife, an Augustinian foundation established in 1162. Originally a church of about the same size as Byland, St. Andrews was enlarged in the early thirteenth century to a building of nearly four hundred feet in length, a scale explained by the cathedral's role as the national shrine and mother church of Scotland. Uncertainty surrounds the date of construction; Eric Cambridge has argued on mainly documentary grounds for work in the 1160s and 1170s for the choir and east nave bays, while R. G. Cant favors the 1190s on stylistic grounds.[58] At the east end, which was raised first, the surviving

parts of the projecting, aisleless, square-ended axial chapel permit a reconstruction of the elevation. It rose in four stories, with three stories of windows over an arcaded dado, the upper two with wall passages. Rib vaults covered the space. The east gable wall as reconstructed by MacGibbon had three tiers of windows, each with three windows, a composition resembling the north transept terminal at Roche.[59] Architectural detailing in the choir and south transept at St. Andrews—for instance, in the nibbed profile given to the keeled, eight-shaft, fasciculated piers in the choir, the nook shafts with ring moldings, and the gorged rolls and intricacy of the moldings of the nave aisle into the south transept—resembles that at Byland and Jervaulx and would support a date around 1190.

On the other hand, the plan of the cathedral, the gallery used in the main elevation, and the likely proportions of the elevation with the height of the arcade and gallery similar to each other relate more to the traditions of Anglo-Norman Romanesque. The hybrid character of the architecture precludes the likelihood of direct transmission of the design from France; it is plausible that a number of the components reached St. Andrews via a Cistercian prototype, as Cambridge suggests.[60] But the question is: which prototype? The later dating of the building to *circa* 1190 makes it probable that it was Byland.

Buildings related to St. Andrews bring into clearer focus the role that the design at Byland played in the architecture of the 1190s. At Jedburgh, another Augustinian house, resemblances to St. Andrews appear in the use of a full gallery, the double-wall clerestory, and the proportions of the three-story nave elevation.[61] Yet the piers and capitals show the influence of Byland (plate 104). A similar amalgam of ideas—some from St. Andrews, some from Byland—can be discerned at Arbroath, as Webb has shown.[62] On the other hand, buildings in the

[58] See E. Cambridge, "The Early Building History of St. Andrews Cathedral, Fife, and its Context in Northern Transitional Architecture," *Ant. Jnl.* 57 (1977): 277-88; and R. G. Cant, "The Building of St. Andrews Cathedral," *Innes Review* 25 (1974): 77-94.

[59] D. MacGibbon and T. Ross, *The Ecclesiastical Architecture of Scotland* (Edinburgh, 1896-1897), vol. 2, fig. 444.

[60] Cambridge, "Early Building History of St. Andrews," 284.

[61] For Jedburgh, see *RCHM Scotland: Roxburghshire* (Edinburgh, 1956); 194-204. The main similarities to Byland are the eight-shaft fasciculated piers (with keeled principals and rounded minors, the same pattern as Byland), the waterleaf capitals (plate 104), and the arcade moldings with gorged crowns. Connections with Byland are limited to the arcade story, however.

[62] Webb, *Architecture in Britain: the Middle Ages*, 85-86.

early thirteenth century like Hexham, Whitby, and Rievaulx show a richness of effect and pursue an openness in the walls that differ from Byland; they belong more clearly to a line of descent from St. Andrews. For these earlier buildings outside the order, then, the importance of Byland lay not so much in the development of its system as in regarding it as a showcase of new components. Selections could be made, and when combined with components from other traditions, an architecture was formed that constituted a north of England version of Gothic architecture.

Finally, it is necessary to consider the architecture at Byland in the broader context of the changing ideals of Cistercian architecture. It is clear that the Yorkshire abbey goes well beyond what might be called modernization. Byland represents instead a fundamental shift in the appearance and values of Cistercian architecture. Given the order's sensitivity on artistic matters and its control of art and architecture, the new qualities of the church at Byland are intriguing.

As already stated, Byland was one of the richest and most powerful abbeys in the north. The size of its community is difficult to fix with precision, but the thirty-five monks and one hundred lay brothers proposed by Knowles and Hadcock almost certainly represent too small a number.[63] With this manpower Byland would have been smaller than Waverley, which does not seem in keeping with the scale of the abbey's buildings and the cathedral size of its church. More plausible are the numbers mentioned in the 1231 visitation conducted by Abbot Stephen of Lexington, which resulted in the issuance of a series of statutes regulating discipline and administration. He ruled that the community not exceed 80 monks and 160 lay brothers and prohibited the reception of new lay brothers until their numbers had been reduced to 160.[64] Funding for the work during the active decades of construction—from about 1155 to 1185—appears, from the small amount known, to have caused no difficulties. Expanded landholdings would have pro-

vided resources to sustain the ambitious building campaigns, and it is significant that Byland was not listed for accumulated building debts as were most other Cistercian houses in the north in 1189. Commerce in wool from the abbey's extensive sheep farming undoubtedly linked Byland to northeastern France and French Flanders during these years.[65] But these ties do not explain the architecture, for other Cistercian abbeys were similarly connected to this region without those connections leading to new or even similar architectural influence.

The distinctive characteristics of Byland's architecture need to be seen first in the context of developments in France. Modifications of the order's simpler architecture there can be documented in the last quarter of the twelfth century, though none of the known instances predates Byland. One important example is Vaucelles (Nord) built between about 1175 and 1192 and thus exactly contemporary with the Yorkshire abbey. The church has been destroyed, but the remains of the chapter house and cloister furnish analogous architectural detailing to Byland's; and whatever form the church took, it elicited condemnation in the General Chapter of 1192 as being "too costly, and superfluous," and was described as "shocking many."[66] Vaucelles indicates a broader geographic context, then, for the architectural innovation at Byland that ran counter to the order's earlier traditions.

What explains this shift in the architectural character of the church at Byland? The notion of its being an isolated aberration can be dismissed since more than one building was involved. Feelings about the change ran high, as the fierce language used to condemn Vaucelles indicates, yet the effect on other buildings within a generation or so indicates a not inconsiderable acceptance and enthusiasm for the point of view that the new architecture embodied. Unfortunately, the deeper motivations underlying the change still remain obscure, although their recovery may well result from renewed research into this critical moment of crisis in the identity and aims of the order.

Another question is how Byland managed to get

[63] D. Knowles and R. N. Hadcock, *Medieval Religious Houses: England and Wales*, 2d ed. (London, 1971), 117.

[64] See B. Griesser, "Registrum Epistolarum Stephani de Lexinton," *ASOC* 8 (1952): 181-378, esp. 205, no. 15.

[65] See Fergusson,, "South Transept Elevation of Byland Abbey," 174 n. 1.

[66] *Statuta* I (1192:31): 151-52.

away with these fundamental changes in architecture, given the order's system of annual inspection and its passion for standardization. How did a church like Vaucelles elicit censure when the one at Byland did not?[67] Adding to the mystery is the case of Revesby in Lincolnshire, where the architecture was apparently related to that at Byland and where the General Chapter ordered it checked in 1197, thereby implying specific violations of some kind.[68] If Revesby attracted attention, or other abbeys in the 1190s where the statutes reveal that architecture was deemed out of line, how did Byland escape notice?[69]

An important clue to these questions may lie in the particular situation at Byland and, specifically, the role of its leader, Abbot Roger. By any standard, his career was extraordinary. It had begun around 1130 at Furness, where he professed as a monk of the Congregation of Savigny. In 1135 he went as one of the founding monks to Calder, where he held the office of subcellarer, and he was present during the troubled days when the monks separated themselves from Furness and trekked across the Pennines to Yorkshire in search of a home and patron. By the early 1140s, and now Cistercian at Hood in Yorkshire, Roger had risen to master of the novices, and it was there in 1142 that he was elected abbot. For the next fifty-four years, until his retirement in 1196, Roger guided Byland's affairs. During this vast tenure, he settled three sites, won the abbey's independence by legal means, assembled its estates by the acquisition of massive landholdings, both local and farther afield, and built

nearly all the buildings at Byland. By the late twelfth century Byland rivaled Fountains and Rievaulx as the richest in the land. All this indicates a man of exceptional ability, force, and leadership—the kind, indeed, who would know how to get what he wanted and who by about 1170 (after more than a quarter-century in office as abbot) had the seniority and, doubtless, the astuteness to steer such matters as architectural preference past the critical eyes of the order's visitors to Byland. One of these visitors, for at least the first decade of construction (though the monks remained a mile away at Stocking), was none other than Saint Ailred, and it is hard to imagine his assenting to the building whose remains we now see. By Ailred's death in 1167, however, and still ten years before the community's removal to the new site, only the first campaign of building was accomplished, and the work then in hand, as far as can be judged, was entirely in keeping with the order's orthodox early style.[70] In fact, the work was remarkably similar to that of Rievaulx in detailing, probably in plan, and in masonry construction. But in the years following Ailred's death the tastes of Abbot Roger underwent a dramatic liberation. Just as important, he seems to have found in Ailred's successor, Sylvanus, not just a sympathetic visitor to his house but an enthusiastic supporter for his new architecture.[71] As much can be assumed from two observations: at Sylvanus' former abbey of Dundrennan, the influence of Byland surfaces in the reworked north transept; and much closer, at Rievaulx, the ambitious refectory (plate 92), the most notable architectural undertaking of

---

[67] There is a hint it may not have. In 1190 the General Chapter reprimanded the abbey, disciplining Abbot Roger and also the abbot of Jervaulx. The pretext is unknown, and it may have had no connection with architecture. It reads: "The abbot of Byland with John the former abbot of Jervaulx taken with him, let him come to Savigny at Christmas, and there let them both obey the ruling of the head abbot of Savigny and his co-abbots. The head abbot of Savigny will announce it to them." (Ibid. [1190:72], 131.)

[68] Ibid. (1197:35), 217. The abbots of Byland and Rufford are named as visitors. The visitation occurred after Roger's retirement, in the first year of Philip's rule. One wonders whether the similarity of the plan of Revesby to that of Byland results from this monitoring visit or precedes it. There was, of course, no question of the plan's being unorthodox; it had already appeared at Cîteaux consecrated three years earlier.

[69] See chapter 1 of this study, 15-16.

[70] Roger's friendship with Ailred is attested to, and it was he who anointed Ailred on his deathbed (see C. H. Talbot, "A Letter of Roger, Abbot of Byland," ASOC 7 [1951]: 218-31).

[71] Another example of a visitor who colluded in "un-Cistercian" building without encountering trouble was Abbot Guido of Clairvaux (1195-1214). Before his appointment there and while abbot of Ourscamp (1170-1195), Guido had overlooked the construction of an un-Cistercian chevet at one of his daughter houses, Mortemer. Then, while abbot of Clairvaux, he countenanced the construction at Longpont of a large-scale Gothic church. (See C. A. Bruzelius, "Cistercian High Gothic: The Abbey Church of Longpont and the Architecture of the Cistercians in the Early Thirteenth Century," An. Cist. 35 [1979]: 58-59.)

Sylvanus' abbacy, shows striking similarities of style to the west parts of Byland.[72] Firm evidence for Sylvanus' attachment to Byland comes from his last years, when after resigning as abbot of Rievaulx, he moved to Byland to place himself under the guidance of Abbot Roger. And it was at Byland that he died in 1189.[73]

Throughout the years of their association then—1167 through 1189—Roger as abbot of Byland and patron of its new church and Sylvanus as the senior visitor to the house would have watched the new church rise from the ground and pass through all phases of its construction. Although Roger's star-

tling characterization of his monumental building as "pulchram et magnam" appears on first reading to be out of character for a Cistercian, affirming the "concupiscence of the eyes" explicitly condemned by Saint Ailred, the half-century that separates Ailred in his prime from Abbot Roger in his retirement saw a transformation across the whole spectrum of Cistercian affairs. Seen in the light of the order's established status, Abbot Roger's church and his prideful description of it exemplify a new identity as accurately as they define a new architecture.

---

[72] Sir Charles Peers dates the refectory to 1200 (*Rievaulx Abbey*, 15; see plan legend). Comparison of the capitals and moldings with those from the west parts of the church at Byland, however, show that a date from about 1180 forward is likely, at least for the parts nearest the cloister.

[73] His obit appears in the Melrose Chronicle: ". . . obiit

pie memorie Siluanus quondam abbas Rievallis, vij idus Octobris apud Belelande, ibique honorifice supultus est" (J. Stevenson, ed., "Chronica de Mailros," *Bannatyne Club* 49 [1835]: 81 and 149; see also, D. Knowles and C.N.L. Brooke, *The Heads of Religious Houses: England and Wales*, 940-1216 [Cambridge, 1972], 129).

6

Cistercian Architecture
in the West Country

ALTHOUGH the most dramatic expansion of the Cistercians took place in the north of England, their presence south of the Humber was nonetheless impressive. The larger number of smaller houses here may be explained in part by the scarcity of land and the greater population, which made amassing extensive estates considerably more complicated than it was in the north.[1] In addition, many regions, particularly in the west country and midlands, had already been settled by earlier monastic movements; thus the Cistercians had to compete for patrons, recruits, and benefactors. These circumstances inevitably affected the architecture of the order; it is no coincidence that building programs in general assumed a more modest scale.

Our understanding of the order's architecture in this large area of England is hindered by the almost complete destruction of most of the monuments. There are substantial above-ground remains of only two of the thirty-eight twelfth-century churches—Buildwas and Abbey Dore—and some scanty parts of five others—Bindon, Cleeve, Kirkstead, Louth Park, Stoneleigh. But the situation is not as hopeless as these figures imply. A surprising number of sites have fragments that provide useful comparative material; and some notable claustral buildings still stand, such as the entire monks' dormitory at Cleeve, large parts of the east range at Stoneleigh, portions of the monks' undercroft and abbot's lodging at Coggeshall, the lay brothers' range at Rufford and Flaxley, nearly complete chapter houses at Forde,

Combe, and Buildwas, and parts of chapter houses at Bindon, Warden, and Stoneleigh. Furthermore, the plans of a number of vanished churches are known. In the south and southwest, for instance, archaeology has retrieved the plans of Quarr (founded 1132), Forde (1141), Rufford (1146), Buckfast (1148), Flaxley (1151), Bindon (1172), and Cleeve (1198). Except at Forde, where a thirteenth-century extension is likely, these show the traditional early forms, suggesting both a relative conservatism and small size compared with abbeys in the north of England.

Losses in the east, southeast, and midlands are particularly acute; minimal remains at Sibton, Boxley, Flaxley, and Rufford hint at the extent of Cistercian building activity. Much new information has come, however, from the thirteen seasons (and continuing) of excavation at Bordesley in Worcestershire, which is the most complete to have been undertaken at any Cistercian site. Evidence again suggests an architecture that was less pioneering than that in the north.

The oldest certain remains are at Buildwas in Shropshire (plate 106).[2] Settled in 1135 as a daughter house to Furness, Buildwas belonged to the Congregation of Savigny for its first thirteen years. The abbey never grew to a large size, even after union with the Cistercians in 1148; it sent out no colonies, and its revenues remained modest. Documentary records are silent about the buildings, most of which were raised during the long and

---

[1] Sibton in Suffolk and Buckfast in Devon managed to assemble sizable holdings, however; for Sibton, see A. H. Denning, ed., *The Sibton Estates, Suffolk Record Society* 2 (1960); for Buckfast, see J. Stephan, *A History of Buckfast Abbey* (Bristol, 1970).

[2] See J. Potter, *Remains of Ancient Monastic Architecture* (Lon-

don, n.d. [1846]); M. E. Walcott, *The Four Minsters Round the Wrekin* (London, 1877), 334-44; Sir Nikolaus Pevsner, *BoE: Shropshire* (London, 1958), 88-90. The plates in Potter's publication are the earliest measured drawings of a Cistercian house published in England.

distinguished rule of Abbot Ranulf (1155-1187), but a general confirmation obtained in 1192 from Bishop Hugh de Novant and signed in the company of a gathering of abbots may well have coincided with the completion of work on the church.[3]

The sequence of construction at Buildwas is relatively straightforward, although work took an unusually long time by the standards of the order. Four main campaigns may be discerned, extending over a forty-year period. Work began only after Buildwas became Cistercian in 1148, and a plan characteristic of the order's early churches was adopted, with a two-bay rectangular presbytery and two straight-ended chapels in each transept (fig. 19).[4] Compared with the big abbey churches in the north, the building's size was modest: 163 feet east to west, which was eighty feet shorter than Fountains.

The first building campaign (circa 1150-1160) saw the completion of transepts and presbytery. The transept chapels were entered through low, narrow unarticulated arches with three rectangular setbacks devoid of either capitals or bases (plate 107). This gave the openings the effect of being cut back through a solid mass. A string course separated the chapel entrances from the plain clerestory, but otherwise the walls were completely bare. Unbroken lateral walls separated the small chapels, which were vaulted with rib rather than barrel vaults. The vaults sprang from angled corbels, and the ribs had chamfered profiles similar to those in the warming house at Fountains from about 1160.[5] Similarly, the crossing was rectangular in plan with piers at this stage of work of simple rectangular form; both features suggest the absence of a crossing tower. The architecture of this first program, then, was one of uncompromising formal austerity and mural bareness with parallels to the contemporary Yorkshire abbeys, most particularly with Rievaulx and the transepts at Fountains (plate 7).

Around 1160, however, this severity gave way

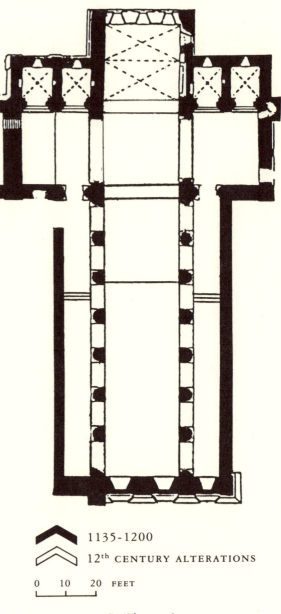

1135-1200

12th CENTURY ALTERATIONS

0   10   20   FEET

19. Buildwas, plan.

to Early Gothic tendencies, just as occurred in the north. At Buildwas these appeared first in the chapter house (plate 108), and the new style contrasted with the old one used in the church. Whereas the

---

[3] *Mon. Angl.* 5:359.

[4] There is some question as to whether any parts of the church date from the Savigniac years. Almost certainly the crypt under the north transept does, crypts otherwise being unknown in Cistercian architecture. But the relation of the crypt masonry to the first work is unclear. An early phase of work on the presbytery may be recognized by distinctive cours-

ing in the lower walls; the ashlar consists of nearly square shaped stones with wide mortar joints containing stone infilling.

[5] Nearly all the ribs of the vaults are gone except for some fragments in the south chapel of the south transept. In appearance, then, the vaults give the appearance of groins and are so mistaken by Pevsner in *BoE: Shropshire*, 89.

transepts were massive, squat, and articulated by rectangular setbacks—Romanesque in style—the chapter house was defined by forms notable for their slimness and by detailing distinguished by a crisp, precise linearism. As a conseqence, space appeared enlarged and a sense of lightness dominated, both Early Gothic qualities. The interior was fully vaulted, and the vaults were carried on alternating octagonal and rounded shafts and supported on the walls by semioctagonal responds. Capitals included artichoke leaf designs typical of the 1150s and 1160s (plate 126). The transverse arches of the rib vaults were pointed and the diagonals semicircular, just as in the aisles at Kirkstall, in the slype at Fountains, and in the west country, in the chapter house at Forde (plate 109).[6] Compared with the rib vaults at Forde, those at Buildwas were characteristic of Early Gothic; even the vault construction showed differences, the vault webs being of cut ashlar rather than rubble fill, namely, in the French rather than the English manner.[7]

This new stylistic impulse was permitted only partial expression in the church at Buildwas, however. Around 1165 a second campaign was started that saw the addition of a tower over the crossing (as in the northern abbeys in the late 1150s and 1160s) and the articulation of the supporting crossing piers, formerly plain, with attached shafts (plate 111). The shafts carried capitals of similar design

to those in the chapter house (plate 127). At the same time, the first two bays of the nave were begun with alternating supports, and the piers were provided with waterholding bases and angle spurs.[8] These motifs continued the French vocabulary already seen in the chapter house. But the new scheme was abruptly rejected between the second and third bay, and the architecture reverted to a conservative mode. Alternation in the piers was dropped, arcade moldings became plain, proportions once again were low. In the detailing, too, older motifs were preferred, such as the scalloped capitals, many of trumpet shape with ribbon and beading motifs, features popular in the west country in the 1170s and 1180s, which occurred again in other Cistercian houses such as Stoneleigh (plate 129).

Work on the nave progressed slowly, however, implying difficulties with funding. By the time the clerestory was reached, the disposition once again had become more elaborate; shafts with capitals of crocket type were employed, and these in turn carried moldings. At the west façade, the windows had dogtooth moldings, shafts were belted, and capitals acquired windblown foliate volutes in double tiers (plate 130) like those at Wells, Glastonbury, and St. Mary's Shrewsbury of about 1190.[9]

In a last campaign, dating to about 1190, the presbytery was modestly updated. The walls were raised by some eight to ten ashlar courses and rib

[6] This was the standard form used by the Cistercians for their early rib vaults. Its use in the nave aisles at Malmesbury in the 1160s led Bony to suggest Cistercian influence there ("French Influences on the Origin of English Architecture," *JWCI* 12 [1949]: 3).

In the chapter house at Forde, dating from about 1160, the vault spans the entire space, a bolder solution than at Buildwas. Profiling, though, is purely Romanesque. The chapter house at Bindon (plate 110), may have been similar to that at Forde, for the responds are clearly related.

[7] Bilson noted that the profiles of the ribs (two rolls separated by a fillet) were the same as those in the north aisle at Gloucester and the choir aisles at Peterborough, but he also related them to similar profiles in the north of France—for instance, at St. Denis and at St. Martin-des-Champs ("The Architecture of the Cistercians, with Special Reference to Some of their Earlier Churches in England," *Arch. Jnl.* 66 [1909]: 264).

In addition, L. Serbat pointed out the French technique in the cutting of the ribs at Buildwas and contrasted this with that at Kirkstall (see "L'Architecture des cisterciens dans leurs plus anciennes églises en Angleterre," *B. Mon.* 74 [1910]: 442).

[8] The bases are similar to those on the center door of the west façade at Roche, *circa* 1175-1180. The bases in the chapter house at Buildwas are attic (as are those on the crossing shafts), but waterholding bases were used in the Fountains chapter house before 1170, and in the transepts at Abbey Dore, *circa* 1175.

As can be seen in plate 111, the arches of the two bays are lower by eighteen inches than those to the west. The first pier on both the north and south is octagonal to the aisles but rounded to the nave, an unusual form. Alternation of octagonal and rounded piers must derive from the chapter house. An earlier Cistercian example may be found in the infirmary cloister at Rievaulx, *circa* 1160, and outside the order on a monumental scale in the choir at Canterbury, 1175-1179.

[9] For Wells, see L. Stone, *Sculpture in Britain: The Middle Ages* (Harmondsworth, 1955), plate 75A; for Glastonbury, see G. Webb, *Architecture in Britain: The Middle Ages* (Harmondsworth, 1956), 87-90; for Shrewsbury, see Pevsner, *BoE: Shropshire*, plate 11.

vaults, probably replacing an earlier barrel vault, were added, rising from springers flanked by thin, tapering corbels (plate 131), similar to those in the transepts at Abbey Dore (plate 114).[10] At the same time, the window on the south wall was lengthened, and the two tiers of round-headed windows in the east wall were modified into single, narrow lancets. A sedilia was inserted with nailhead in the arches and molded capitals and abaci. Work was probably finished by 1192 when the convocation of abbots mentioned in the confirmation of that year assembled at Buildwas.

These four campaigns thus extended from around 1150 to 1190. The first two may be compared with contemporary work at Kirkstall, Furness, and Roche, though by their standards, there is little question that Buildwas was old-fashioned. As mentioned above, the decisive moment occurred around 1160 when Early Gothic was used in the chapter house. But it stimulated relatively few changes in the church apart from the crossing. The subsequent reversion to older models and the adoption of detailing that carried local accents is particularly distinctive. This rejection of the up-to-date may be seen as a conservative reflex in the order's architecture.

In the modern literature it is usual to regard Buildwas as something of a poor relation to the big Yorkshire abbeys like Fountains and Kirkstall. Yet the obvious similarities that spring from a common architectural tradition within the order should not be allowed to obscure the individual qualities of the Shropshire house. In the nave at Buildwas (plate 112) the walls took on a noticeable play of depth with the inset and shafted clerestory, a feature reflected in the capitals with their indented angles.

More important, in contrast to Fountains and Kirkstall where the naves were tall and compactly massed, at Buildwas the proportions were broader and the arcade spacing was slow and easy. The interior thus combined a certain intimacy with an overall reticence in the formal vocabulary. There is, in fact, an unaffectedness about the Shropshire abbey that stands in subtle contrast to the calculated authority and intensity of the Yorkshire houses.

A second monastery in the west country that dates from about the same years is Abbey Dore in Herefordshire (plate 113).[11] The similarities end there, however, and the architecture of Abbey Dore underscores the conservative nature of Buildwas. A major monument, not only in its scale and the developed character of its architecture but also in its relation to Early Gothic in the west of England, Abbey Dore, like Byland in the north, served as one of the centers for the spread of the new style. Its role in the movement, however, has been given slight attention.[12]

What survives at Abbey Dore is nothing less than the entire chevet and transepts—and they constitute the most complete remains of a twelfth-century Cistercian church in Britain. At the Dissolution the church was adapted for the parish and thus was spared from destruction. Some time later, use lapsed and the condition of the fabric deteriorated to the point where cattle sheltered in the building.[13] In 1633, however, restoration was started by Viscount Scudamore, whose ancestors had been the original patrons. The intention was to save the east parts and to return them to parochial use, a purpose that, happily, they still serve.[14]

[10] The top six ashlar courses look as though they are of a later date. The tremendous thickness of the north and south walls, which measure over five and a half feet across, is unusual. The relative narrowness of the presbytery makes them clearly excessive and raises the possibility that a barrel vault was originally built.

[11] See R. W. Paul, "The Church and Monastery of Abbey Dore, Herefordshire," *Trans. BGAS* 27 (1904): 117-26; E. Sledmere, *Abbey Dore: Herefordshire* (1914); *RCHM: Herefordshire, South-West* (London, 1931), 1-9; Sir Nikolaus Pevsner, *BoE: Herefordshire* (London, 1963), 57-62. The most thorough and perceptive analysis is C. Malone, "*West Country Gothic Architecture, 1175-1250*" (Ph.D. diss., University of California at Berkeley), chap. 2. Dr. Malone kindly allowed me to read this chapter on the genesis of Gothic architecture in the west

of England. For the history of the abbey, see D. H. Williams, *White Monks in Gwent and the Border* (Pontypool, 1976), 1-58.

[12] For instance, Abbey Dore is ignored in the basic account of Early Gothic in the west country: H. Brakspear, "A West Country School of Masons," *Arch.* 81 (1931): 1-18. Jean Bony was the first to realize the importance of the abbey as a source for Early Gothic in the west, "French Influences on the Origin of English Architecture," 11. For a survey of Early Gothic in the west country see Webb, *Architecture in Britain: The Middle Ages*, 87-95.

[13] Williams, *White Monks in Gwent*, 5.

[14] The restoration took two years and was carried out by the famous west country carpenter, John Abel (see *RCHM: Herefordshire, South-West* 1:1-6).

The abbey was founded in 1147 by monks from Morimond, the sole daughter house established by this monastery across the channel. This filiation may account for the large scale of Abbey Dore in comparison with Buildwas; conceivably, it was thought of as a colonizing outpost in the border areas—the hilly site is only three miles from the Welsh border—analogous to Rievaulx in the north.

Nothing is known of the early decades of the abbey's history, unfortunately. The first document dates only to *circa* 1170 and records a gift of land from Baldwin Sitsylt. Around 1173 Abbey Dore appropriated the nearby temporary Cistercian foundation of Trawscoed with all its resources and donations.[15] Increased revenues from these sources doubtless provided money for building.

Three distinct building programs were carried out at Abbley Dore in the last thirty years of the twelfth century. The first extended from about 1170 to 1180 and comprised the transepts and eastern parts of the church. A second, dating to the early 1180s, saw work begun in the nave but in a very different style from that of the first. A third program, dating from around 1186 to around 1210, included a big eastern extension that necessitated the destruction of much of the presbytery from the first program. In its late twelfth century form the church measured 250 feet east to west, making it a little longer than Fountains and Kirkstall. The programs reveal three fundamentally different approaches to architecture and must be considered separately.

As originally laid out, the plan at Abbey Dore (fig. 20) followed a standard early Cistercian form similar to that at Furness and Roche, which were erected in the same years.[16] The transepts and the west bay of the presbytery survive from this church and can be recognized in part in the present building. This is because the changes involved in the eastern extension (that constitute the third program of work) saw the ends of the inner transept chapels

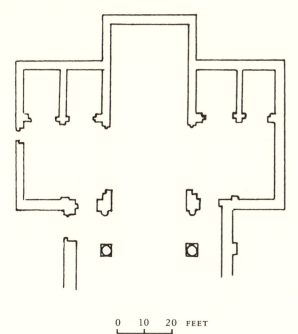

0   10   20   FEET

20. Abbey Dore, plan of first church.

broken through to form the first bay of the ambulatory of the new scheme and the piercing of the lateral walls of the old presbytery to provide for an arch and clerestory of the new chevet (plate 121).

The transepts (plates 114 and 115) provide an exceptional record of Cistercian architecture at the moment of its greatest influence in the twelfth century. The elevation was two-storied, with the bays framed by groups of five boldly projecting shafts coursed through with the wall. As at Roche and Byland, the architecture at Abbey Dore affirmed the principle of bay division and rejected the tendency toward unarticulated volumes that distinguished the order's earlier buildings (Rievaulx, for instance). The transepts were originally vaulted with four-part rib vaults with wall ribs.[17] The wall ribs received shafts that rose from the floor but were not given capitals, in contrast to the shafts carrying the transverse arch and rib diagonals. All five shafts rose from a common plinth and individual bases.

---

[15] Williams, *White Monks in Gwent*, 9.

[16] This came to light in Roland Paul's late nineteenth century excavation (see R. W. Paul, *Abbey Dore* [Hereford, 1898]). A scheme probably preceding Abbey Dore I may be discerned in the north transept, which adjoined the cloister. A changed roof line and a blocked oculus in the outer chapel are the

evidence for this.

[17] Just when the actual vaults over the transepts were built is uncertain. Although the springers and shafts are contemporary, Paul's excavation revealed fragments of rib with thirteenth-century profiles.

Taken together, the system of shafts in relation to the vaults resembled the classic French clarification of the vault system, which neither Roche nor Byland adopted. With the present timber roof, the interior volume has a tall and cubic effect; but the original vaulting would have given the space a lower, more rounded effect.

The lighting in the transepts was generous, entering from a single lancet in each bay of the east and west walls. In the south terminal wall (the cloister was on the opposite arm at Dore), two large lancets were topped by a small ovoid window (plate 115).[18] Since the original glass was grisaille, the light would have been similar to the constant but not brilliant light that animates the interior today. Compared with the light in the later twelfth century chevet, the light in the transepts was more diffused and clearer; it strongly resembled that of the transepts and nave of the French abbey of Pontigny of a decade earlier.

The chronology of construction at Abbey Dore is complex. Construction on one part of the abbey would continue to a certain height, and then attention would switch to another. The crossing piers were begun first, followed by the south transept, where the chapels are divided by solid walls, and then by the north where the chapels are undivided.[19] This progression can be followed also in the changes in rib, base, and arcade profiles. Capitals in the early parts were waterleaf, artichoke, and rich acanthus types (plate 132), but these were soon supplemented by trumpet scallop and thin, crossed-stemmed stiff-leaf (plate 133). Such a range of capitals is unusual for a Cistercian building. Arch moldings (less elaborate on the north) consisted of soffits with angle rolls, an outer molding that was chamfered and continuous, and a hood molding

with dogtooth fleurons. Difficulties in setting out, such as in the centering of the arch openings, and a lack of coordination in the vault springers point to a certain unfamiliarity with the full system.[20]

These early parts of Abbey Dore are characterized by a distinctly Cistercian variant of Early Gothic. Restraint in the decoration and an affirmed murality pervade, yet detailing is crisp, with thin, linear profiling, and the system of supports set out from the wall states a new structural clarity for the space. Such qualities are accentuated by window openings that create a luminous interior.

Nothing in the west of England prior to the transepts at Abbey Dore can be unambiguously identified as Early Gothic. The abbey of Malmesbury, dating from the 1160s, although vaulted, was Romanesque in its forms and expression. Sources in France underlay the design of the Dore master, though it did not originate in the area around Morimond, which supplied the founding monks, or in the Aisne, whence models for Furness and Roche had come, or in French Flanders, the source for Byland. Instead the transepts were inspired by the architecture in areas of eastern Normandy and the Vexin. There, as Jean Bony has shown, Abbey Dore's most pronounced characteristics—prominent bay articulation established by projecting piers with five shafts and the vaulted, two-story elevation covered by four-part rib vaults over each bay—could be found in the mid-1160s through 1170s—for example, at Mortemer (Eure), Chars (Val d'Oise), and Le Bourg-Dun (Seine Maritime) (plate 116).[21] Parallels between Abbey Dore and Le Bourg-Dun are striking, and although the shafting is more vigorous and the articulating system more broken down into component parts at the latter, the effects are close; indeed, even the detailings in the two

---

[18] The origins of long lancet windows are obscure. Certainly Dore was early in this use of them, although it was preceded by Romsey (south transept) and by Malmesbury. By the late 1170s examples are numerous, notably at Canterbury. The Dore lancets are heavily splayed and framed by a continuous roll molding. The splay has the effect of doubling the size of the actual opening and gives the illusion of increased scale as well as permitting greater amounts of light to enter the interior.

[19] The crossing shows one important change. All the bases have attic profiles and spurs except for the northeast pier where the latter are omitted. Waterholding bases with spurs first

appear in the north transept, then in the south, and then in the nave piers.

[20] The setting out of the openings in the north and in the south transepts are puzzling; in brief, on the south the arches are too narrow, leaving an awkward gap between the outer molding and the projecting shafts that divide the bays, whereas on the north the outer molding is flush with these shafts while the molding next to the crossing is not. The vaults spring from different heights at the crossing, between the chapels, and against the end walls.

[21] See Bony, "French Influences on the Origin of English Architecture," 11.

churches is similar (cf. plates 135 and 136). Further French qualities appear in the use of *congés* for the springers of the soffits or the semioctagonal responds that frame the chapel entrances.[22]

The new program, which saw the construction of the nave, was identifiable at once by a change in style. The marked French qualities of the transepts were replaced by English, and the first bay of the nine-bay nave was developed in a completely different idiom.[23] The change at Abbey Dore was much more insistent than that at Buildwas where a similar shift in style occurred. Although the circumstances that occasioned this change at Abbey Dore are lost, it is clear that the master mason formerly in charge of work was replaced by another man.

To analyze the nave, it is necessary to reconstruct it from the blocked and ruined parts of the east bay dating from Viscount Scudamore's restoration (plates 117 and 118). The elevation was carried on round piers of squat proportions similar in form and with similar waterholding bases to those at Buildwas. A string course separated the stories and the vertical framing of bays used in the transepts was dropped. The piers receive triple-corbeled supports to the aisles, attached to the capitals that served as springers for the rib vaults. The capitals were trumpet scallop, separated above by a flattened leaf motif, and early stiff-leaf with crossed stems of more organic form than those in the transepts (plate 134). Unfortunately, the upper parts of the elevation are uncertain. On the basis of the remains (plate 119), it is plausible to posit a false gallery, which in turn would have been "absorbed" into the clerestory, a single-arched opening enclosing both. The elevation would thus have looked two-storied even though it comprised three. This unusual composition occurs elsewhere in the west country and

[22] *Congés*, with respect to rib or arch moldings, refer to the springer immediately above the capital that is *not* cut to the shape of the molding. Popular in Burgundy in the mid-twelfth century, it is used there by the Cistercians in their first rib vaults, e.g., at Fontenay (plate 28).

[23] The Royal Commission plan and the plans in Roland Paul's 1898 and 1904 publications (see catalog) show the nave with nine bays. Paul later discovered a tenth bay, however, which had been added in the thirteenth century (see "Abbey Dore Church, Herefordshire," *Arch. Camb.* 82 [1927]: 270).

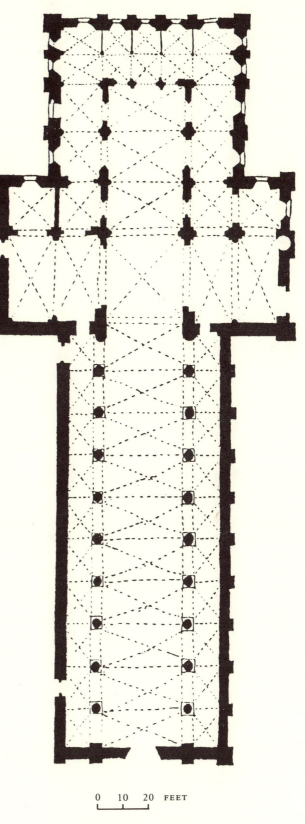

0   10   20   FEET

21. Abbey Dore, plan of church as finished.

is a marked regional feature of Early Gothic there. For instance, it survives at St. David's Cathedral (*circa* 1180), where it is richly decorated and robustly treated, and also at Llanthony Priory (*circa* 1190), a house of Austin canons only five miles away from Abbey Dore, where the handling is much more austere. Llanthony seems later than Abbey Dore, however, and most likely reflects its design.[24] The changed vocabulary between Llanthony and Abbey Dore, and St. David's is difficult to interpret in terms of a development. In all probability it had less to do with chronology or style than with different modes for a monastic church and a cathedral.

The decision to rebuild the presbytery of the first church within five to ten years of its completion and to replace it with a large-scale chevet was probably determined by the need for more altars. One may also suppose that as at Fountains the monks desired something more glorious than the dark, small, humble form of the early choir. A new grandiose scheme was begun, therefore, which was most likely inspired by the recently completed rectangular choir with ambulatory and chapels at Byland. This immensely costly work was probably initiated by Abbot Adam (1186-*circa* 1216) in the early years of his tenure. An aggressive and dynamic man, Adam shrewdly expanded Abbey Dore's properties, thereby providing additional resources out of which the new work could well have been funded.

The plan of the new chevet at Abbey Dore (fig. 21) was generally based on that of the chevet at Byland. As in the Yorkshire house, the choir was three bays deep with a flanking aisle on the north and south and was closed at the east by three arches, leaving an arch opening rather than a pier as the axial element. The high altar was in the third bay and thus the east aisle was placed outside the east gable in a lower one-story space the same height as the five chapels that formed the end wall (at Byland the east aisle lay within the elevation of the choir). To provide lateral aisles, the ends of the inner transept chapels of Abbey Dore I were opened, reducing the number of chapels to one in each transept. This decision saddled the master mason

with bays whose width and length differed from those of the rest of the chevet, but he resolved the difficulties skillfully. Work moved from west to east; a temporary screen at the east crossing piers was probably erected and the monks' choir transferred temporarily to the nave. The master was clearly unwilling to risk the axial misalignment that could result when a new chevet was constructed as an envelope around an old choir with demolition of the earlier choir delayed until the last possible moment.[25]

The differences between Abbey Dore and Byland were the result of refinements in the rectangular ambulatory plan. At Abbey Dore clearer architectural definition was given to the separate functions of the eastern parts: ambulatory, chapels, and choir. At the Cistercian mother house, Cîteaux, begun only a few years earlier and constructed in 1193, the east aisle was also outside the elevation, a solution that thereafter became standard;[26] and this idea at Dore was probably borrowed from the Burgundian abbey, whose architecture would have been familiar as a result of repeated visits by the abbot of Dore to the General Chapter. At Cîteaux, however, chapels were added to both the north and the south aisles, forming a continuous rectangular chapel range, and these in turn were roofed separately from the ambulatory. At Abbey Dore, such flanking chapels were omitted, just as they had been at Byland, perhaps also out of respect for the tradition in England for precise eastern orientation. As can be seen from the exterior, each aisle bay was originally covered with its own gabled roof, but in the restoration under Lord Scudamore these were replaced with a continuous sloping roof (plate 120).

Features are used in the elevation that derive from the regional architecture of the west country. As mentioned earlier, the first bay east of the crossing was adapted from the early arrangement and represents an initial phase of work, or possibly an attempt to ease the transition from the simpler style of the transepts to the new richness of the choir. A comparison between this bay and the adjacent bay to the east (plate 121) sets off the marked

---

[24] Malone, "West Country Gothic," suggest Llanthony as a source for Abbey Dore, however.

[25] There are, of course, numerous examples of this difficulty; for an analogous sighting difficulty in a Cistercian case, see

R. Gilyard-Beer, "Rufford Abbey, Nottinghamshire," *Med. Arch.* 9 (1965): 161-63.

[26] For Cîteaux, see M. Aubert, *L'Architecture cistercienne en France* (Paris, 1947), 1:109.

differences that distinguish the mature statement of this master's aims. The two-story elevation of the transepts was retained in the choir (and equally the height of the vaults), but it was handled in a profoundly different manner. Proportions became squat, with a delight in compact massing (plate 122), openings were decorated with continuous rolls, and flat wall surface was avoided—in the lower story by elaborately splayed and molded arcades carried by sixteen-shaft piers, and in the upper story by extending the window splays the full height of the story though the windows themselves remained relatively small. Rib vaults covered the space, but although wall ribs were used, they were not provided with supporting shafts. Thus the bays were divided by shafts in groups of threes, leaving the wall ribs to be carried by corbels flanking the capitals at the springing of the vaults. It is clear, then, that whereas restraint, murality, slender profiling, and the clear expression of supports predominated in the transepts, preference was given in the new choir to a ponderous richness, to openings with repeated framings, and to an interest in an overall linearism at the expense of logical articulation.

Most of this work may be dated between the late-1180s and the first decade of the thirteenth century. Bases were waterholding, moldings became thin and tense with applied fillets, and capitals mixed trumpet, scallop, acanthus, and molded types. The work concluded in the somewhat compressed ambulatory chapels at the east end (plate 124), where the piers were given a mannered slimness, arch and rib moldings were keeled, and abaci molded. Detailing on the north is the latest in date. As a whole, the chapel range conveys a sense of lightness that contrasts with the oppressively heavy effects of the choir, and it is more fastidious in its proportions.

The sources for the chevet at Abbey Dore lie in developed west country architecture of around 1190. One important influence was Hereford Cathedral, eleven miles to the east (plate 125), where a new rectangular retrochoir and lady chapel were begun

in the late 1180s. The early parts of this scheme have many parallels with the work at Abbey Dore.[27] In the retrochoir, for instance, shafts in groups of three carry the vaults, and the capitals resemble those at Abbey Dore. In the later lady chapel, openings were given multiple framings using continuous rolls and chamfers. As already discussed, the nave design at Abbey Dore derived from local regional architecture of the west country; now we see this tradition continued, with the architecture moving closer to that of nonmonastic structures.

For Abbey Dore's twelfth-century church, then, three separate styles defined the architecture. Whereas the last two—those seen in the nave and in the extended chevet—reflected an unequivocal assimilation of local west country influences, the first— seen in the transepts—was remarkable for the purity of the Early Gothic ideas imported directly from France. Only the transepts, therefore, influenced the spread of Early Gothic in this area of England. Although no other building copied Abbey Dore's system completely, its architecture influenced the master at Worcester Cathedral working around 1180.[28] There, in the west bays of the nave, the vaults and their supports employ the distinctive system of framing the bays with five shafts running the full height of the elevation, a feature that suggests knowledge of the Cistercian master's work. Other influences also affected the Worcester design, however, indicating the Worcester master's wide awareness of contemporary architecture. Yet ultimately the future of Early Gothic in this area of England lay in directions emphatically different from those enunciated in the first work at Abbey Dore. Even by about 1180-1185, the soberness and restraint at the abbey itself were firmly set aside in favor of robust, decorative interests that sprang from the workshops of the west country. Regional influences surface also in the monastic buildings; the chapter house, for instance, was raised on a polygonal plan, rather than the traditional rectangular one, that derives from the chapter house at Worcester Cathedral.

[27] As Pevsner recognized (see *BoE: Shropshire*, 29). See also G. Marshall, *Hereford Cathedral, its Evolution and Growth* (Worcester, 1951), 52-66.

[28] C. Wilson dismisses Abbey Dore as a source for Worcester, although he acknowledges the similarity of the vault shafts

in the two buildings ("The Sources of the Late Twelfth Century Work at Worcester Cathedral," *Medieval Art and Architecture at Worcester Cathedral, Trans. BAA* 1 [1978]: 80-90, esp. n. 40).

Completion of the entire church at Abbey Dore, including the west bays of the nave, was delayed another sixty years. Despite the gift of additional land from King John in 1216,[29] the death in the same year of Abbot Adam marked the start of a decline in the abbey's affairs. By 1260 the bishop of Hereford, Peter Acquablanca, was offering indulgences to anyone contributing to the completion of the church, even though in the same document he referred to it as "sumptuous."[30] Most likely, the reference applied only to the east end, and the nave lay unfinished. Excavations by Roland Paul revealed a rebuilt south aisle, lengthened nave, and new west façade from these years, as well as rib vaults.[31] Acquablanca's indulgences proved effective, however, and the church was finally consecrated during the episcopate of Thomas Cantelupe (1275-1282).[32]

[29] *Mon. Angl.* 5:553-54.
[30] See T. Blashill, "The Architectural History of Dore Abbey," *Jnl. BAA* 41 (1885): 367.

[31] Paul, "Abbey Dore Church, Herefordshire," 271.
[32] *RCHM: Herefordshire, South-West* 1:1.

7

Conclusion

A STUDY OF the twelfth-century architecture of the Cistercians in England reveals two distinct tendencies. The first was a conscious withdrawal from existing traditions. On occasion this produced old-fashioned and even archaizing solutions; more frequently, it resulted in a persistent simplification of Romanesque architecture. All areas of Cistercian architecture, from the churches to the workshops and grange structures, responded to this tendency in greater or lesser degree. In adopting an architecture of such calculated simplicity, the Cistercians transformed twelfth-century notions about monastic architecture and developed what can be plausibly called a monastic style. The concept of such a style was defined by the early leaders of the order like Saint Bernard and Saint Ailred and was to have a long history in the architecture of the reform movements that extended through the great buildings of the mendicants. Whereas the new architecture was witness to the order's commitment to poverty, it also gave expression to deep convictions about a purified monasticism distinct from that of the older orders. William of St. Thierry writing in the early 1140s aptly summed up this view: "Let those whose care for what is within . . . erect for their own use buildings conceived according to the form of poverty, taking holy simplicity as a model, and following the lines laid down by the restraint of their fathers."[1]

The second tendency saw a cautious return to contemporary movements. The expansions, rebuildings, and alterations that formed much of the history of the English houses after the mid-twelfth century reflected this new influence. They included the adoption of segregated crossings and low towers beginning in the 1150s, the modification of transept chapels in the 1160s and 1170s, and the far-reaching reorganization of east ends in the 1170s, 1180s, and 1190s. Such changes need to be seen in the context of shifting historical circumstances as well as new stylistic trends. They were the physical manifestations of institutional developments within the order as its customs and liturgy grew; and they reflected a receptivity to the developing Early Gothic style. The new style in particular posed problems for the Cistercians. Whereas it offered easier and quicker construction techniques with lighter, less massive walls and larger openings, its expressive and aesthetic qualities challenged the order's earlier views about the character of architecture. Not surprisingly, the version of Early Gothic chosen by the Cistercians was a singularly restrained one. Rarely did this return to contemporary movements involve outright modernization or overt experimentation, as it did later, by contrast, in the order's ambitious buildings of the first quarter of the thirteenth century.

In the long term these tendencies were successive, although at certain periods in the order's history they moved toward each other and ran as parallel and simultaneous. Under the latter circumstance, such as in the last third of the twelfth century, it is easy to mistake convergence for contradiction. In the case of a single region, such as the west country, two architectures might be pursued at the same time; for instance, Cleeve or Buildwas followed simplified traditional forms, while at Abbey Dore the architecture reflected several different but always contemporary styles. Above all else the emergence of both tendencies bears witness

[1] *The Golden Epistle of William of St. Thierry, Cistercian Fathers Series* 12 (Kalamazoo, 1971), 60. William, to whom Saint Bernard had sent his famous *Apologia*, remained a Benedictine until 1140 when he joined the Cistercians at Signy. A close friend of Bernard's, he wrote the first chapters of the saint's *Vita*.

to tensions, whether toward a retreat from current trends, or toward the maintenance of a position in the face of a rapidly changing world.

Part of the answer to the emergence of one tendency over another has to do with the particular conditions at each monastery. The attitude of the abbot was without doubt critical. As the formulator of the program, as the presiding on-site authority watching all developments, and as the most widely traveled and thus most knowledgeable person about developments elsewhere, the abbot exercised decisive control over the work. The rich documentary account of the buildings at Meaux (see catalog) where four churches were begun in the monastery's first sixty years makes it clear that three of them involved the destruction of earlier work, which in each case had proceeded some way, and resulted from different schemes instituted by new abbots. Of importance also was the attitude of the official visitor to the house; his strongly held views could check a too rapid acceptance of new ideas. Equally, grandiose building programs could be furthered by his uninvolvement, or overt collusion, in the work, as is suspect in at least the case of Byland.

Change and expansion were not inevitable, however. In fact, active resistance to change over lengthy periods is an interesting characteristic in its own right. And when it involves two of the order's greatest houses—Waverley and Rievaulx—it poses serious questions. Both communities had a clear need for additional space, for instance, and ample funds at hand for building operations. Practical and economic factors must therefore have been secondary to more elusive factors like the attitude toward the old buildings. Resistance to change may well

have had less to do with an entrenched conservatism than with veneration for the first buildings raised during the heroic early years of settlement.[2] Sentiment and maybe also a sense of tradition held change in check, whether or not the abbot viewed the buildings as inadequate or old-fashioned.

One emphasis of this study has been to highlight the separate nature of the architecture of the Cistercians from that of the rest of England during the twelfth century. When stylistic developments occurred they did so, with one or two exceptions, in a series of largely contained movements that had only minimal reference to what was happening in the rest of England. This hermetic character affirmed the strongly supranational nature of the Cistercians who imposed a pattern of life with little regard to national boundaries, and it reflected as well their studied aloofness and sense of superiority. In this context it is useful to distinguish, then, between English Cistercian architecture and Cistercian architecture in England, the former implying a national variant of the order's forms, the latter an imported architecture located in, but not essentially influenced by, trends in England. This view of the architecture of the Cistercians contradicts that of some scholars, including Bilson and Clapham, who stressed the Norman or Anglo-Norman character of the order's early architecture, and Hahn, who interpreted it as a simplified version of regional schools.[3] What is remarkable is the absence of these influences for the most part, and the closeness of the order's architecture to the mainstream of European architecture during at least two critical phases of Cistercian development in England.

Rather than seeing Cistercian architecture in terms

---

[2] Attachment to the early buildings extended to the first timber churches. For instance, Serlo refers to the earliest church at Fountains as "that sacred building" (*Mem. F.* 1:101), and at Bordesley the excavation by Rahtz has found evidence that the timbers from the first church were used to bury the founding monks. In France the *Chronicle* of Signy (Ardennes) records that materials from the early buildings that were not reused in the new were buried within the precincts of the monastery by Abbot Alard (1156-1174) (see M. Aubert, *L'Architecture cistercienne en France* [Paris, 1947], 1:102). In addition, many monasteries preserved their earliest structures long after others had rendered them redundant. The fullest information comes from Clairvaux (see J. O. Schaefer, "The Earliest Churches of the Cistercian Order," *Studies in Cistercian Art and Architecture*

1 [1982]: 1-12).

[3] See J. Bilson, "The Architecture of the Cistercians, with Special Reference to Some of their Earlier Churches in England," *Arch. Jnl.* 66 (1909): 277. Bilson qualified his statement, however, and made it clear that it was based only on Fountains and Kirkstall; see also A. W. Clapham, *English Romanesque Architecture After the Conquest* (Oxford, 1934), 2:74-83. For the proposal about regional schools, see H. Hahn, *Die frühe Kirchenbaukunst der Zisterzienser* (Berlin, 1957), 203. In more general terms the same argument is made by A. Dimier, *Les Moines bâtisseurs* (Paris, 1964), 106-108; and by M. Aubert, "Existe-t-il une architecture cistercienne?" *Cahiers de civilisation médiévale* 1 (1958): 153-58.

of an undeviating linear movement, I have argued for a series of phases that reveal variable interests and influences. These phases may best be grasped not by reference to what was happening in England, but by measuring the reactions in the abbeys to the stimulus of new ideas emanating from northeastern France. Such a method shows that four distinct phases may be distinguished.

The first of these phases extended from the Cistercians' initial foundation in England in 1128 to around mid-century. It was marked by the nearly complete dependence on the architecture of France and specifically that of Burgundy. Quite simply this was what those who traveled across the Channel to colonize the houses were familiar with. The phenomenon of the order and its architecture were imports to England. Such an architecture contrasted vividly with existing traditions and thus matched the Cistercians' sense of themselves as set apart, the vanguard of a new monasticism. Early buildings at Waverley, Tintern, and Fountains bear the unmistakable impress of Burgundy in their plans and elevations. Similarly, the first monumental architecture, at Rievaulx, and somewhat later at Fountains (in the second church), Sawley, Bordesley, and Boxley, borrowed forms from the order's homeland in Burgundy. Although Rievaulx, with its clerestory and timber roof, might seem to have departed dramatically from the now more widely known Bernardine church, with its single-story elevation and pointed barrel vault, it probably belongs to a family of buildings that predates the design of Clairvaux in 1135. Most plausibly it derived from the second church at Cîteaux, whose appearance may be traced in a group of abbeys now best represented by Clermont (Mayenne).

The second phase in the development of the Cistercians' architecture in England can be discerned in the early 1150s. Interestingly, there is little evidence that the English houses had been subject to the same architectural standardization claimed for the filiation of Bernard's abbey during the years from about 1135/1140 to 1155. This may be due to the lack of secure examples to demonstrate the argument one way or the other, or it may be due simply to the cycle of growth and expansion that was part of the English houses during these years. By the 1150s, however, while smaller foundations like Bordesley and Boxley remained relatively unaffected, a discernible shift marked the architecture of the larger houses in the north: at Fountains (second church), Kirkstall, and the chapter house at Rievaulx. These buildings show the emergence of English influences. The resulting mixture of French and English forms produced an architecture sharply different from that of the first generation buildings. The facts of the change are clearer than the reasons for it, however. External forces such as the widespread political and social turmoil of these years of the so-called Great Anarchy probably played a minor role in this lessened influence from France. At any rate, proof is lacking that the order's contact with the English houses was seriously weakened, and the late 1140s and 1150s far from seeing retreat saw the most self-confident expansion in the Cistercians' entire history. Possibly the architectural changes at Fountains and Kirkstall resulted from the assertion of an independent architectural identity, or perhaps they reflected a clear-minded and deliberate effort to fuse English and French forms that paralleled attitudes and hopes in the years immediately following the accession of Henry II in 1154.

These anglicizing trends were firmly set aside, however, in the third phase of the Cistercians' development, which extends from about 1160 to 1180 and ranks as the most remarkable in the architectural history of the order in England. It coincides with Henry II's reign and is marked by the strong renewal of French contacts. In style and technique the architecture is Early Gothic, and the new style had penetrated the north of England nearly two decades before the rebuilding of the Canterbury choir by William of Sens. Once again the Cistercians asserted in their architecture a powerful contrast with late Anglo-Norman Romanesque.

The source of this influence lay in the region where the Early Gothic style had developed first: northeastern France. The broad valleys descending to the Oise, Aisne, and Seine rivers, which were among the richest farming areas of medieval France and were traversed by the great trade routes, were also heavily settled by the Cistercians, particularly the houses of Clairvaux.[4] From its earliest years,

[4] R. A. Donkin, *The Cistercians: Studies in the Geography of Medieval England and Wales* (Toronto, 1978), 29.

Bernard's abbey had received support from the counts of Champagne in whose territory the monastery lay. Historically, Clairvaux's filiation and influence was centered not in Burgundy but in the Champenois and extended northeastward again from there. Assimilation of architectural traditions and innovations from this area of France was critical in the 1150s and 1160s. It appears in the new chevet at Clairvaux, begun in the years following Bernard's death, which was a highly visible and influential structure both on account of the abbey's prominence as the head of a vast empire of affiliated houses and for its focus as the goal of constant pilgrimage to the venerated body of Saint Bernard. The disappearance of Clairvaux and the destruction through wars of the abbeys in the Aisne and Oise belonging to the filiation of Clairvaux make it difficult to trace the exact steps by which Early Gothic was absorbed in the third quarter of the twelfth century. Only at Ourscamp (Oise) does enough remain to permit a reconstruction and to glimpse the importance of the development that occurred there.[5] Yet in these and other buildings there is sufficient evidence to suggest that the Clairvaux filiation, as distinct from the others, served as a pacesetter in the adoption of Early Gothic in the second half of the twelfth century. Documentary proof of the filiation's support of a more ambitious architecture comes in statutes directed against its abbeys' claustral buildings in the 1180s and in the punishment of the abbot of Clairvaux, Garnier de Rochefort, in the early 1190s for failing to stop construction of the church at Vaucelles whose architecture "shocked and scandalized many" in the words of the General Chapter.[6]

In more general terms, the dissemination of the new style throughout the entire order served as one of the great forces for change within twelfth-century architecture. In countries with strong traditions of local Romanesque, Early Gothic appeared in the buildings of the order as early as the 1150s.[7] In England Early Gothic was used first in conventual structures, where it seems a greater openness to modern ideas was permitted than in the church, and it was only a decade or so later, in the 1160s, that the new style was accepted for the church. No single source or region supplied the models for the Early Gothic of the Cistercians in England. Different versions of the new style, which had developed in the first decades of its use, were drawn on. At Furness and Roche, and in the chapter house and east range at Fountains, it was the architecture of the Aisne valley which served as the prototype; at Abbey Dore (transepts) it was the more northern axis of Early Gothic the area around Seine-Maritime; at Kirkstall (west parts) and at Byland it was Picardy and French Flanders, whence the new style had spread only a few years after its establishment further south. These major buildings were not a provincial reflection of this architecture, or an internally generated architecture. Rather, they mirror the contemporaneous phases of Early Gothic in France and show that the order's buildings in England were closely associated with it.

The nature and identification of Cistercian qualities in Early Gothic remain valid concerns for the abbeys in both France and England.[8] The central question is deciding whether or not the Cistercians succeeded in establishing an architecture with its own style, apart from the essentially cosmetic differences imposed by the general restraint in decoration or by the mandated use of colors like white for doors and windows.

Nowhere is the question more germane than in the most fertile area of the new architecture, northeastern France. In addition to style, however, a further distinction needs to be made in any study of these buildings. It has to do with different modes

---

[5] C. A. Bruzelius, "The Twelfth-Century Church at Ourscamp," *Speculum* 55 (1981): 28-40.

[6] *Statuta* 1 (1192:31): 151-52.

[7] Disputes over the definitions of Romanesque and Early Gothic in the mid-twelfth century are a conspicuous feature of the literature. For instance, Cistercian architecture during this period should be classified as "rib vaulted Romanesque" according to R. Branner, *Burgundian Gothic Architecture* (London, 1960), 14, and "half Gothic" according to K. J. Conant,

Carolingian and Romanesque Architecture, 800-1200 (Harmondsworth, 1959), 130.

[8] For specific interpretations of Cistercian qualities, see P. Frankl, *Gothic Architecture* (Harmondsworth, 1960), 62-69; W. Krönig, *Altenberg und die Baukunst der Zisterzienser* (Bergisch Gladbach, 1973); C. A. Bruzelius, "Cistercian High Gothic: The Abbey Church of Longpont and the Architecture of the Cistercians in the Early Thirteenth Century," *An. Cist.* 35 (1979): esp. 10ff.

in the handling of style, and two can be discerned. The better known is that used in the pioneering cathedral designs at Laon, Noyon, and elsewhere, which employed tall, diaphanous elevations with multiple openings.[9] Very different, however, was the architecture of the Cistercians as seen in buildings like Preuilly, Acey, and Mortemer, or like Roche and Abbey Dore in England, or at smaller scale in churches outside the order like Le Bourg-Dun or Nouvion-le-Vineux. In these buildings Early Gothic was a style predicated on the maintenance of the wall, although treating it with a new language of sharpened linear articulation, opening windows through its mass that were filled with grisaille glass to produce a new luminousness, and unifying and thinning down components of the elevation like the piers.[10] On occasion these two modes of Early Gothic may still be seen together in abrupt juxtaposition. At Laon, for instance, which lay at the center of Early Gothic experiments, the architecture of the cathedral at one end of the city epitomizes the penetrated walls and logically articulated interests of Early Gothic. At the western end of the city, however, the mural, monastic version of the same style is exemplified at the church of St. Martin, the headquarters of the reform order of Premonstratensian canons. Grasping the coexistence of these two architectural modes of Early Gothic is essential to an understanding of this phase of the architecture of the Cistercians. Such a contrast was, of course, as much a matter of typology as style. Beginning with Bernard, monastic architecture was intended for the first time to be recognizably separate and distinct from cathedral architecture. This concept of a monastic style is most clearly seen in cases where the same patron sponsored two contemporary but very different architectures, as occurred, for instance, with Bishop Simon de Vermandois at the Cathedral of Noyon and at Cistercian Ourscamp, which are only four miles apart.[11]

The actual process of assimilation of Early Gothic by the Cistercians was complex, however, and may perhaps be understood in terms of an analogy between vocabulary and syntax. Whereas all the elements of Cistercian architecture were drawn from the architectural vocabulary of northeastern France, the process of assembly, its syntax, differed. Several essential features separate Cistercian from non-Cistercian. One involved more restraint in the amount and prominence of architectural detailing used in relation to the scale of the building. Articulating elements became contracted, with the result that Cistercian buildings look barer and trimmer. Another, as has been seen, was a commitment to mural continuity with the consequent sense of closed boundaries, the counterpart of the order's effort to create an ambiance conducive to inward spiritual focus. A third was the formal simplification of the elements of architecture, both structural and decorative. And a fourth had to do with the use of distinctive proportions. Just as Cistercian plans frequently employed a two-to-one ratio of nave width to aisle width, the elevations often show the nave with a height twice its breadth, or equally, since each aisle was half the width of the nave, of a height equal to the total width of nave plus aisles.[12] Correspondences such as these were extolled by contemporaries. For instance, Baldwin, abbot of Forde, and later archbishop of Canterbury wrote: "Unity of dimension established on the principle of equality, appropriate arrangement, adaptation, and the commensurate concordance of parts is not the smallest factor of beauty. What falls short of proper measure, or exceeds it, does not possess the grace of beauty."[13]

Qualities like these ensured an identifiable similarity of form among the order's buildings. When

[9] On this phase of Early Gothic, see E. Gall, *Die Gotische Baukunst in Frankreich und Deutschland: Die Vorstufen in Nordfrankreich von der Mitte des elften bis gegen Ende des zwölften Jahrhunderts* (Leipzig, 1925); J. Bony, "French Influences on the Origin of English Architecture," *JWCI* 12 (1949): 1-15; R. Branner, "Gothic Architecture 1160-1180 and its Romanesque Sources," *Acts of the XX International Congress of the History of Art* 1 (Princeton, 1963): 92-104.

[10] In this sense it is plausible to see a building like Pontigny as transitional. The piers, for instance, give the appearance of

being extensions of the upper wall and the arches as having been cut through it. The impression is strengthened by the articulation of the bays with square sectioned responds.

[11] See Bruzelius, "Cistercian High Gothic," 13ff.

[12] On the proportions favored by the Cistercians, see F. Bucher, "Cistercian Architectural Purism," *Comparative Studies in Art and Literature* 3 (1960): 89-105; also O. von Simson, *The Gothic Cathedral* (Princeton, 1962), 54-55.

[13] See W. Tatarkiewicz, *History of Aesthetics* (The Hague, 1970), 2:89.

combined, they underlie the "cool reticence" noted so frequently of the interiors, which can still be sensed at Pontigny or Clermont, or in the transepts at Abbey Dore. For all its reserve, such an architecture is extremely expressive, a dualism noted by Martène in the eighteenth century when he recorded that Clairvaux had a "simplicité qui a quelque chose de grand."[14]

Although churches like those at Roche, Furness, Kirkstead, and Abbey Dore show the typical architecture of the order's Early Gothic period, they also provide a measure to assess the most remarkable of all the Cistercians' buildings in the twelfth century, Byland Abbey. Abbot Roger's great and influential undertaking changed the whole scale of the Cistercian church in England, substituting a building of cathedral size and splendor for the smaller earlier buildings and initiating a new chevet plan. Just as important, Byland enunciated a new tradition of roof cover in the use of lighter timber ceilings. That this occurred at the same time that vaulting was being used at Roche needs emphasizing; problems of complex wall abutment basic to any vaulted architecture were thus side-stepped and attention directed to the development of lighter and more elaborated wall systems. It was this interest rather than that of vaulting that dominated Early Gothic in the north of England for the next three decades.

These new mural values coincided with the appearance of a middle story between the arcade and clerestory. As a comparison of Byland with the transepts at Abbey Dore shows, it led to changes to the interior. Since the middle story was never used as a gallery, the usual explanation for its appearance is that it provided access from the nave for inspection of the rib vaults over the aisles. Plausible as this is, it is not wholly convincing for the obvious reason that there are other churches with rib vaulted aisles that lack a middle story. The use or omission of the middle story may result from regional practice, or the tradition of a particular

filiation, as in the case of Pontigny, for instance, where the middle story was assiduously avoided.[15] In England the way the middle story was used reveals a range of problems. In early cases like Furness it appears as a series of openings cut into a wall, which was in every other way regarded by the master mason as continuous. This was changed at Roche, a fully vaulted building, where the middle story was both part of a defined bay system and also served a structural purpose, with the blind arcades most likely representing a Cistercian attempt with important parallels in France to deal with structural demands of high vaults. The same thinking underlay the open, paired, but otherwise unadorned arches used at Kirkstead and perhaps in the south transept at Dundrennan and was reflected across Europe at the abbey of Aulps (Haute-Savoie). At Furness, by contrast, and at Byland, the middle story played no structural role, and decorative reasons determined its employment. A weakening of this interest can be discerned in the north transept at Dundrennan where the middle story was treated more soberly. In France a similar range of interests also characterizes the handling of the middle story.[16]

After about 1180, in what can be identified as the fourth phase in Cistercian architecture, a perceptible loss of interest in French models can be discerned and a turn toward English ones. The most striking example is Abbey Dore, where the unmistakable French influence apparent in the transepts was suddenly displaced first in the nave and then in the choir by features that were purely west English in origin. But the same occurred in the north: at Jervaulx the choir owed more to the model of York and Ripon than to any known example in France, and at Dundrennan the presbytery and transept terminals also indicate a greater distancing from French prototypes. Furthermore, the notable undertakings of the early thirteenth century, such as the enlarged chevet at Fountains or the new church at Waverley, fit unequivocally into the context of *English* Gothic architecture.[17]

[14] E. Martène and U. Durand, *Voyage littéraire de deux religieux bénédictins de la Congregation de Saint-Maur*, vol. 1, pt. 1 (Paris, 1717), 99.

[15] C. A. Bruzelius, "The Transept of the Abbey Church of Châalis and the Filiation of Pontigny," in B. Chauvin, ed., *Mélanges à la mémoire du Père Anselme Dimier* (Arbois, 1982), 3:447-54.

[16] See Aubert, *L'Architecture cistercienne en France* 1:287-90.

[17] Although English influences are important for these abbeys, they were not constant throughout the thirteenth century, and the order's architecture was marked by periods of closeness to France. For instance, at Beaulieu, Croxden, Hayles, and Vale Royal, the churches have plans with ambulatory and radiating chapel schemes that are related to abbeys like Long-

This reaction to Early Gothic on the part of the English abbeys marks a watershed in the architecture and decisively separates developments in England from those in France. From the beginning there existed the inescapable difference that Early Gothic was created in France as an indigenous style. The order had only to simplify it to match its reform ideals. In England, by contrast, the whole milieu differed. Early Gothic was an import. Once introduced, therefore, the major factors in its development turned around the interaction and assimilation with quite different older traditions. The resulting process saw Early Gothic in the 1180s in England take on a strongly accented regional character quite different from that in France.

At the same time, to explain the rejection of French influences and the turn toward English ones in terms of the inner workings of style alone is implausible. The change was too emphatic for that. External factors must also account for the switch, and three may be suggested. One involved the process of building. In the mid-1130s Ordericus Vitalis explicitly praised the Cistercians for their self-sufficiency in building, and the work of men such as Abbot Adam of Meaux, Abbot Robert of Newminster, later canonized, and Abbot Alexander of Kirkstall support his claim (see appendix B). Yet even before mid-century there is evidence that the monks were turning to outside labor, and by the last third of the century fairly extensive examples of this practice can be cited. The increasing size and complexity of their buildings was doubtless encouraging this. It was one thing for Abbot Adam to raise a two-story structure of mud and wattle at Meaux in the 1150s, quite another for Abbot Roger to use double-wall construction, high timber barrel vaulting, and intricate detailing at Byland. Everything, from overall design to exacting stereotomy, called for professionalism and demanding training, of a kind, in fact, much greater than might be expected within the monastic community.

A second factor behind this change in influence may have had to do with the role of the abbot, who was the principal figure behind any architectural undertaking. In the early years abbots had moved frequently back and forth between England and France. Men such as Saint William of Rievaulx, Henry Murdac and Richard both of Fountains, Thorold of Trois-Fontaines, Raoul of Vaucelles, Gilbert of Cîteaux, Robert of Newminster, Isaac of L'Etoile, Gilbert of Hoyland (at Swineshead), Alexander, Adam, and William all of Mortemer, and Thomas of Boxley had spent lengthy periods of their monastic lives in both countries.[18] But abbots assuming office in the last decades of the twelfth century lack this wider experience.

A third factor concerns the character of the Cistercian movement in England. There is unmistakable evidence that the General Chapter of the order tolerated, or more accurately, was powerless to change, a less rigorous observance of Cistercian practice in its Cistercian colleagues. A decline in rigor can be documented as early as about 1170 in the stern letter of remonstrance sent from Pope Alexander III to the English houses; a decade later it was explicitly remarked on by Walter Map; and in the late 1180s and 1190s it can be inferred from the statutes of the General Chapter.[19] Particularly injurious was the absorption of the former Savigniac houses. Efforts to "Cistercianize" them are documented at Furness and Stoneleigh and probably also occurred at Coggeshall, but a stronger degree of independence continued even so. Innovations in architecture at Furness, Byland, and Jervaulx—all Savigniac houses—could be related to this. By the late twelfth century it is clear that slippage from the standards of the order included architecture (as was also the case in France). Violations of accepted norms were explicitly recorded at Meaux, Revesby, Netley, and Forde, and in 1189 they were hinted at in ten other abbeys that were listed as heavily in debt for ambitious building operations.[20] To find

---

pont and Ourscamp (see Bruzelius, "Cistercian High Gothic," 136); for Vale Royal, see F. H. Thompson, "Excavations at the Cistercian Abbey of Vale Royal," *Ant. Jnl.* 42 (1962): 183-207.

[18] See D. Knowles and C.N.L. Brooke, *The Heads of Religious Houses: England and Wales, 940-1216* (Cambridge, 1972), 126-48.

[19] For Pope Alexander's letter, see J. Leclercq, "Epitres d'Al-

exandre III sur les cistercerciens," *Revue Bénédictine* 64 (1954): 68-82. For Walter Map's observation, see D. Knowles, *The Monastic Order in England*, 2d ed. (Cambridge, 1963), 656. For the statutes relating to the specific problems with the houses in England, see chapter 1 of this study.

[20] J. Jacobs, "Aaron of Lincoln," *Jewish Quarterly Review* 10 (1898): 629-48, esp. 635.

a lessening of contact with France under these circumstances is not surprising, nor is its consequence, an assertion of a more distinctly English idiom in the architecture of the order.

By the end of the century the Cistercians could look back on more than seventy-five years of remarkable activity. Although the self-contained quality of Cistercian architecture throughout this period has been emphasized in this study, the buildings of the White Monks nonetheless had a significant impact on England in the twelfth century. What was their mark on the complex development of Gothic architecture in England?

Much as the Cistercians craved isolation and stood aloof from contemporary life, their reform attracted attention and was widely admired. Within months of their arrival in the north of England, for instance, clamor for reform along Cistercian lines is documented in Benedictine communities at Durham, York, and Whitby: in Augustinian houses at Kirkham and Hexham; and even in the chapter of the Minster church of York.[21] Not surprisingly, Cistercian architectural influence surfaces first in those reform movements that modeled their constitutions and spirtual ideals most closely on the Cistercians. Particularly prominent were the regular canons—notably the Premonstratensians, Augustinians, and Gilbertines—whose foundations in England in the twelfth century well outnumbered those of the Cistercians.

Like the Cistercians, the canons enjoyed their greatest success in the north. Successive archbishops of York, beginning with Thurstan (1114-1140), deliberately fostered their foundations. Thurstan saw the canons as effecting the reform and resettlement of the northern province still recovering from the harrowing of William the Conqueror. A typical example of his policy was the creation of prebends served by the canons, some of whom, such as the Augustinian canons at Nostell and Hexham, were granted stalls in the Minster church; they assisted in singing Divine service, but they also played an important role in the administration of the province.[22] The canons' influence and their base of operation was broader than these examples suggest, however. Since their revenues came from churches granted to them that they then had the obligation to serve either directly or by providing for the support of a priest, the canons had within their hands or under their direct influence scores of churches in the York province. The Cistercian *Dialogus duorum monachorum* (*circa* 1155) speaks, for instance, of the Premonstratensians as those who "deny that they are monks because they wish to be called preachers and rulers of churches."[23]

Far from being in conflict or competition with the Cistercians, the canons' life was viewed as complementary in a number of ways. Their goals were similar, though their paths to them differed. While the Cistercians withdrew from the world, the canons were to some degree involved in it, as teachers and as brethren to their rural and urban neighbors, in a manner not far removed from the mendicants in the thirteenth century. Close friendships between the Cistercians and canons affirm these complementary roles; among the Augustinians, for instance, Waltheof of Kirkham was a friend of Ailred's of Rievaulx, and Robert the Scribe of Bridlington, of Gervase's of Fountains.[24] And like the Cistercians, the canons rose high in the church hierarchy of the twelfth century; the Augustinian canon Aethelwold, for example, became bishop of Carlisle, the major diocese in the northwest.

The impact of the Cistercians on the architecture of the canons first becomes evident around mid-century. The most prominent of the independent congregations of canons, the Premonstratensians, employed plans for their churches very similar to those of the Cistercians, both of the first generation without aisles to the nave and of the second with them, as for instance, at Torre (Devon), Bayham (Sussex), Easby (Yorkshire), Talley (Carmarthenshire), and elsewhere.[25] The layout of Augustinian churches was similarly influenced—for instance, at Kirkham (Yorkshire), Lannercost (Cumberland), and

[21] Knowles, *Monastic Order*, 231ff.

[22] D. Nicholl, *Thurstan, Archbishop of York, 1114-1140* (York, 1964), 117.

[23] J. C. Dickinson, *The Origins of the Austin Canons and their Introduction into England* (London, 1950), 199.

[24] Nicholl, *Thurstan*, 240.

[25] See A. W. Clapham, "The Architecture of the Premonstratensians, with Special Reference to their Buildings in England," *Arch.* 73 (1923): 117-46.

Bolton (Yorkshire). Most easily documented was the influence of the Cistercians on the Gilbertines, particularly in the late 1130s and 1140s. Under their founder, Gilbert of Sempringham, the Gilbertine canons fell heavily under the spell of the Cistercians. Cistercian practices were adopted and at one stage a merger was even discussed. Not surprisingly Cistercian architectural influence can be detected at Watton and Old Malton.

In addition to plans, the actual designs of elevations also reflect Cistercian architecture, although the massive destruction of most of the canons' buildings makes it difficult to document. At Kirkham, for instance, the peculiar early Cistercian practice of closing off the west sides of transept chapels was followed. The influence of Byland on the church of Old Malton is more substantial, with the latter adopting a similar three-story elevation with wooden roof in the late 1180s.

In most cases, however, the major surviving evidence of Cistercian influence is architectural detailing, usually in fragmentary condition and torn from its context in the fabric of the building. Firm attributions on this basis to Cistercian rather than to French influence from other sources are hazardous. In some instances, nevertheless, a strong argument can be made. After mid-century, to take one example, a new type of pier using fasciculated shafts different in geometry and form from Romanesque compound piers appears in church building in the north. Its use in Cistercian conventual structures, like the east guest house at Fountains of about 1150-1155, occurs a good decade before it appears in the upper choir of York Minster (*circa* 1165-1170), and its widespread dissemination in the architecture of the monastic orders—for instance, at the Benedictine abbey of Bardney (Lincolnshire) around 1165—probably derives from Cistercian rather than secular church sources. Likewise, the penchant for keeling the shafts of these piers (and of other architectural members), although not original to the Cistercians, was widely used by them and partly spread through their agency. More broadly, the commitment of the Cistercians to a simpler, barer architecture offered a compelling alternative to the rich relief and exuberant deco-

rative tendencies of late Anglo-Norman Romanesque.

To imply that influence went one way only—from the Cistercians to the canons—oversimplifies the situation, of course. A good case in point is offered by the Premonstratensians: in 1142 they entrusted the Cistercians with the official visitation of their houses, and the statute *De construendis abbatiis* laid down rules identical to the Cistercians about the number and type of buildings required prior to settlement.[26] Yet it is clear the Premonstratensians gave as well as took. A prominent source for Clairvaux III, for instance, was the now ruined Premonstratensian abbey of Dommartin (Pas-de-Calais); and in England the new church at Furness drew on a building very similar to the White Canons' priory at Val-Chrétien (Aisne); likewise, Byland drew on Dommartin. This process of exchange was nowhere more important than around Laon, the headquarters of the Premonstratensians and the most dynamic center of Early Gothic. Patrons like Bishop Barthélemy of Laon and his neighbor, Bishop Joscelin of Soissons, gave prodigious support to both the Cistercians and Premonstratensians, settling more than twenty of their foundations in the two dioceses. The mother church of the Premonstratensians, St. Martin at Laon, provides ample testament to Cistercian influence in both its plan and simplified elevation. As already mentioned, the building offers the starkest contrast to contemporary work at the cathedral, perfectly exemplifying Saint Bernard's distinction of forty years earlier between an architecture appropriate to the monastic church and that appropriate to a cathedral. In general, Premonstratensian abbeys like Dommartin used a less conservative architecture, however, and they suggest that the canons sanctioned a relatively greater variety of solutions. This may well have permitted the Cistercians to consider a wider range of models in the course of their visitations of Premonstratensian churches.

Most of the Premonstratensians' houses in England were part of the filiation of Licques (Pas-de-Calais), itself one of the three mother houses of the congregation. The interchange of ideas between the Premonstratensians and Cistercians during the pe-

[26] H. Colvin, *The White Canons in England* (Oxford, 1951), 50.

riod from around 1160 through 1190 in the arc extending from Laon and Soissons through the Pas-de-Calais and into England, was both an important factor in the development of Early Gothic and a powerful agent in the transmission of ideas into areas like the north of England. An understanding of this best explains the appearance of Early Gothic at Byland and separates its forms from those employed by Archbishop Roger Pont L'Evêque in his new choir at York and a little later at Ripon.

It was through the architecture of the canons, then, that the Cistercians exerted their widest influence on English architecture, and particularly in the north, in the last third of the twelfth century. There is an irony that in the very years when the Cistercians were struggling to define their own identity in architecture, the perception of that identity by others served as one of the main propagating influences extending over a wide range of buildings from priory churches to the parish level. Conclusions about the exact nature of Cistercian influence remain tentative, however. So much has been destroyed in both England and northeastern France that our knowledge of the exact steps by which ideas were transmitted is irremediably curtailed.

On the other hand, what survives of the architecture of the Cistercians shows their extraordinary achievements as builders in the first seventy-five of their four-hundred-year life in England that terminated with the Dissolution. From the smallest scale and most inauspicious beginnings on wild and uncleared sites, the expansion of the order proceeded with astonishing speed. Forty years after their arrival at Waverley in 1128, the Cistercians were a force to be reckoned with in almost every region of the country, and the greatest houses—Rievaulx, Fountains, and Byland—were communities of truly formidable size, backed by huge resources first of land alone and then of money, and influencing the spiritual, economic and political life of England. The physical remains of these achievements survive for us, eight centuries later, in a few imposing ruins, set off by clipped lawns and displayed in picturesque landscapes. Yet, plundered and shattered as they are, the remains bear powerful witness to the great energies and infectious ideals that motivated the Cistercians throughout these years, as well as with their passion for giving them tangible form in building.

CATALOG

In the catalog entries that follow I have tried to provide three kinds of information for each abbey: the principal documentary references to the buildings, their history from the Dissolution to the present, and the record of clearance and excavation where it has been carried out. In the bibliography at the end of each entry I cite only those references that I consider to be pertinent scholarly contributions.

The old names of counties have been used rather than the new ones resulting from the reorganization of local government in 1974. Since most of the scholarly material is organized under the old names, use of the new county groupings would have been unnecessarily complicating.

Unless otherwise stated, the dates of foundation are those given in D. Knowles and R. N. Hadcock, *Medieval Religious Houses England and Wales* (2nd ed. London, 1971).

ABBEY DORE (Shropshire)

Robert Fitz Harold of Ewyas established Abbey Dore in 1147, with the monks coming from Morimond in the Champagne, one of the five original mother houses of the Cistercian order. Dore remained Morimond's only daughter house in England.

For the architecture, see chapter 6 of this study, pp. 94-100. Little is known about the history of the buildings between the thirteenth century and the Dissolution. A report in 1540 mentions that the present bell tower was constructed over the inner chapel of the south transept around 1500 (*L. and P. Henry VIII* 15: 179, no. 89). The abbey was dissolved in 1536, and some of the monastic quarters and parts of the church fell into ruin. Enough of the east end of the church remained for it to be restored to use as the parish church of the village by Viscount Scudamore in 1633. Only a year was needed to complete the work, which was largely carried out by the famous west country architect and carpenter, John Abel (Morgan, 155ff.)

Between 1896 and 1907 Roland Paul sympathetically renovated the fabric and carried out a series of excavations on the church and adjoining buildings. The transepts and chevet of the former monks' church are still in use as the parish church of St. Mary.

T. Blashill, "The Architectural History of Dore Abbey," *Jnl. BAA* 41 (1885): 363-71.

R. W. Paul, *Dore Abbey: Herefordshire* (Hereford, 1898).

T. Blashill, "The Seventeenth-Century Restoration of Dore Abbey," *Trans. WNFC* 17 (1901); 184-89.

R. W. Paul, "The Church and Monastery of Abbey Dore, Herefordshire," *Trans. BGAS* 27 (1904), 117-26.

E. Sledmere, *Abbey Dore: Herefordshire* (Hereford, 1914).

R. W. Paul, "Abbey Dore Church, Herefordshire," *Arch. Camb.* 82 (1927): 269-75.

RCHM: Herefordshire, South West 1 (London, 1931): 1:9.

H. M. Colvin, "Abbey Dore," *Trans. WNFC* 32 (1948): 235-37.

F. C. Morgan, ed., "The Steward's Accounts of John, First Viscount Scudamore of Sligo (1601-1671) for the Year 1632," *Trans. WNFC* (1949-51), 155-84.

Sir Nikolaus Pevsner, *BoE: Herefordshire* (London, 1963).

D. H. Williams, "Abbey Dore," *Monmouthshire Antiquary* 2 (1966): 65-144.

D. H. Williams, *White Monks in Gwent and the Border* (Pontypool, 1976), 1-58.

BIDDLESDEN (Buckinghamshire)

Biddlesden was founded by Ernald de Bosco, steward of Robert de Beaumont, earl of Leicester, in

1147 with monks sent out from Garendon. The founding gift was disputed, however, and the monks were forced to engage in lengthy litigation before obtaining confirmation of their lands.

Little is known about the history of the abbey's buildings. Between 1157 and 1167 William de Dadford and his wife directed that their bodies be buried at the abbey (Roundell, 282). At some date in the late twelfth century Ralph Harenge and Walter de Westbury gave the monks leave, on completion of the monastic buildings, to cut timber in Westbury (ibid., 287, no. 11). Henry III granted the abbot wood for choir stalls in 1237 (*CR: Henry III, 1234-1237*, 470). In 1255 Mathew Paris records that Hernaldus de Bosco was buried in the conventual church before the high altar (*Chronica majora* 5:487).

The abbey was dissolved in 1538 and purchased by Sir Robert Peckham, who began dismantling the church. Parts of the claustral buildings were incorporated into a sixteenth-century mansion. When Browne Willis visited the site in 1712, he found ruins of the church and the abbey house in good part standing. In addition, there were then to be seen the walls of the east side of the cloister and a part of the tower, together with a small chapel and the chapter house, which was a handsome room, forty feet square, supported on four pillars (Willis, 152). On a return visit in 1735 he records that the proprietor, Henry Sayer, had "totally demolished everything" and leveled the ground (ibid., 155).

Today, the site of the former abbey is partly covered by Biddlesden Park, an eighteenth-century mansion with heavily wooded grounds. There is no record of any excavation, and no above-ground remains are recognizable.

B. Willis, *The History and Antiquities of the Town and Deanery of Buckingham* (London, 1755), 150-64.
W. H. Kelke, "The Destroyed and Desecrated Churches of Buckinghamshire," *Records of Buckinghamshire* 4 (1858): 81-84.
H. Roundell, "Biddlesden Abbey and its Lands," *Records of Buckinghamshire* 1 (1858): 275-87; 2 (1863): 33-38.
VCH: Buckinghamshire 1 (London, 1905): 365-69; and 4 (London, 1927): 153-57.
RCHM: Buckinghamshire 2 (London, 1913): 20.
Sir Nikolaus Pevsner, *BoE: Buckinghamshire* (London, 1960), 64.

BINDON (Dorset)

Bindon was founded by William de Glastonia and his wife on a site at West Lulworth in 1149. Monks from Forde provided the first community. For some reason, possibly shortage of water, West Lulworth proved unsuitable, and in 1172 the community moved northwest to new land at Bindon near the village of Wool. Unusually, new patrons are mentioned—Roger Newburgh and his wife, Maud—and they are credited with the construction of the church.

Details of Roger's twelfth-century building are not known. Some rebuilding occurred in the thirteenth century, however. In 1213 King John stayed at the abbey and gave fifty oaks and thirty cart loads of lead for roofing the monastery (*VCH: Dorset* 2:83). Twenty years later another royal visitor, Henry III, gave another sixty oaks *ad fabricam ecclesie sue* (*CR: Henry III 1231-1234*, 195) and the following year issued a charter of confirmation (*Mon. Angl.* 5:657-58).

Today only the lower courses of the church and chapter house survive on the overgrown, privately owned site. The four west bays of the north nave arcade still stood in 1733 when Buck engraved them (plate 139), and they were mentioned in 1770 (Hutchins, 352). At the beginning of the nineteenth century, however, the then owner, a Mr. Weld, carried out excavations and subsequently leveled much of the site (ibid., 352). No report of this work was printed.

The first plan of the monastery was published in 1872 (Hills, plate 20) and shows a standard early Cistercian form for the church, with two chapels without dividing walls in each transept. The overall length of the building (about 190 feet) suggests that there were more bays in the nave than the five shown (cf. Buildwas, which was 163 feet long and had seven bays).

The few remains of the church, principally the outer walls to a few courses in height and fragments of the west end, are difficult to date precisely. The two-story nave shown in Buck's print was supported on round piers with undecorated capitals. It was also vaulted, and the springers are visible in the engraving. Was the original church, then, simply vaulted in the thirteenth century, or was it built anew? The latter explanation seems more likely, at least to judge from the few correspondences between the ashlar from the remaining courses of the wall from the church and that from the chapter house (plate 110), which may be dated in the 1170s.

J. Hutchins, *The History and Antiquities of Dorset* 1 (London, 1861).

G. Hills, "Proceedings of the Weymouth Congress," *Jnl. BAA* 28 (1872): 298-301.

H. J. Moule, "On Bindon Abbey and Woolbridge," *Proceedings of the Dorset Natural History and Antiquarian Field Club* 7 (1886): 54-65.

VCH: Dorset 2 (London, 1908): 82-86.

J. M. Bohs, *Bindon Abbey* (Dorchester, 1949).

J. Newman and Sir Nikolaus Pevsner, *BoE: Dorset* (London, 1972), 93-94.

BORDESLEY (Worcestershire)

Bordesley was founded in 1138 by Waleran de Beaumont, count of Meulan and earl of Worcester. The monks came from Garendon, a foundation of Waleran's brother, which in turn had been established by Waverley.

Bordesley attracted gifts of land rapidly and eventually included twenty granges among its properties. Within thirteen years of its own foundation it had established three daughter houses: Stoneleigh (1141), Merevale (1148), and Flaxley (1151). By the early fourteenth century, however, the abbey's popularity had begun to wane; a visitation in 1332 recorded a community of thirty-four monks, one novice, eight lay brothers, and seventeen serving men (*VCH: Worcestershire* 2:153). Fifty years later these numbers had fallen to fifteen (fourteen monks and one lay brother), the "pestilence" being cited as partly responsible. Bordesley's wealth revived, however, and in 1535 it was listed in the *Valor Ecclesiasticus* as ninth wealthiest among the Cistercian houses (3 [1817]: 271-73).

The site chosen by the monks for building their church was low and subject to flooding, thus it seems that before work could start, draining operations were required, including some rerouting of the River Arrow. In the original endowment the monks were granted wood and material for building from Feckenham Forest. A gift of quarries at Combe, the source in all likelihood of Bordesley's oolitic limestone, was confirmed between 1147 and 1153, and a consecration (undated) is recorded as having been performed during the rule of Bishop Simon of Worcester (1125-1150) (Woodward, 18). Whatever the bishop consecrated, it seems unlikely from the archaeological evidence that it included more than the eastern parts of the church. Construction on the claustral buildings can be assumed in the third quarter of the twelfth century. Additions to these in the early thirteenth century were made with stone from quarries that the monks acquired at Hewell and Tardebigge (Rahtz and Hirst, 68ff.).

The monastery was dissolved in 1538, with surrender taking place on July 17. But disposal was not orderly and two months later in a letter to Cromwell it was noted that the buildings had been "defacid and plucked downe, and the substance therof solde to dyverse persons without proffitt or lucre paide or aunswerid to the kinges majestes use for the same" (T. Wright, *Letters Relating to the Suppression of Monasteries, Camden Society*, 1st ser. 26, no. 134 [1843]: 279-80; see also appendix A to this study). The remaining walls and foundations were soon buried; Nash's view of 1782, though purportedly showing the church, in fact confuses it with the *capella extra portas*.

The site was partly cleared by Woodward in 1864. Then in the early 1960s a series of excavations was begun by Pretty, Webb, and Rowley. In 1968 Rahtz and Hirst undertook their systematic excavation of the church, which continuing through fourteen seasons with exemplary rigor and patience, has recovered a greater body of reliable information than have excavations at any other Cistercian site.

Many periods of work on the church have been identified by Rahtz and Hirst (58ff.). Construction of the first permanent building was started in the 1150s, with the plan showing a two-bay, square-ended, aisleless presbytery, three chapels in each transept separated by unbroken walls, and a nave of eight bays. The proportions of the church were similar to those of the churches at Boxley and Kirkstall, and all three buildings were distinct from the earlier churches at Rievaulx and Fountains (see chapter 3 of this study, p. 46).

The crossing piers at Bordesley were composed on the inner faces of a flat rectangular respond flanked by an attached shaft. Base moldings were bell shaped, close in profile to those at Kirkstall. The crossing carried arches and, doubtless a low tower, an innovation of the 1150s comparable to that at Fountains, Kirkstall, and Louth Park. The first pair of nave piers has a rectangular face to the east, echoing the crossing piers, but a semicircular one to the west (cf. Buildwas). The next pair of piers is octagonal, and the one beyond, circular.

In a second program begun around 1200, the south side of the crossing was strengthened by building up the southwest pier, suggesting possible subsidence in that direction. New buttresses were also added to the eastern corners of the presbytery. The marshy ground on which the abbey was built seems to have caused the problems. At the same time, the east parts of the church were tiled, and a new set of choir stalls was constructed with the backs set against partially blocked arcades in the nave.

In the second half of the thirteenth century work was undertaken on both sides of the crossing for structural reasons. The choir stalls were also redesigned, most likely with two tiers of seats. Around 1330 or 1340 more radical work occurred at the crossing, this time possibly to restore it after a collapse. The responds for the western crossing arch were taken to the floor, which had the effect of making the crossing more distinct. In the fifteenth and sixteenth centuries the consequences of the shrinking monastic population are registered with the disuse of some of the south transept chapels, the entrances of which were blocked, and the reduction in the number of the choir stalls and their removal from the area west of the crossing, though around 1400 a new cloister was built and much of the nave reconstructed.

T. R. Nash, *Collections for the History of Worcestershire* 2 (London, 1782): 405-16.

J. M. Woodward, *The History of Bordesley Abbey* (London, 1866).

VCH: *Worcestershire* 2 (London, 1906): 151-54; 3 (London, 1913): 223-26.

Sir Nikolaus Pevsner, *BoE: Worcestershire* (London, 1968), 248.

R. T. Rowley, "Survey of Bordesley Abbey Earthworks—1967," *Trans. Worcestershire Archaeological Society* 3rd ser. 1 (1968): 62-64.

M. Aston, "The Earthworks of Bordesley Abbey, Redditch," *Medieval Archaeology* 16 (1972): 133-36.

P. Rahtz and S. Hirst, *Bordesley Abbey, Redditch*, British Archaeological Reports, no. 23 (Oxford, 1976).

D. Walsh, "A Rebuilt Cloister at Bordesley Abbey," *Jnl. BAA* 132 (1979): 42-49.

D. Walsh, "Measurement and Proportion at Bordesley Abbey," *Gesta* 19 (1980): 109-13.

D. Walsh, "The Changing Form of the Choir of the Cistercian Abbey of St. Mary, Bordesley," *Studies in Cistercian Art and Architecture* 1 (1981), 102-11.

S. M. Hirst, D. Walsh, and S. M. Wright, *Bordesley Abbey II. Second Report on Excavations at Bordesley Abbey, Redditch*, British Archaeological Reports (Oxford, 1983).

BOXLEY (Kent)

William of Ypres, son of the count of Flanders, founded Boxley in 1143, with the monks coming from Clairvaux; Boxley thus became only the second abbey in England to be filiated directly to the great Burgundian house (Rievaulx was the first). Boxley was situated near the main London-to-Canterbury road, and its abbots, due in part to this location, played a prominent role in English political affairs in the late twelfth century. It was Abbot Walter, in fact, away on business with Thomas à Becket in Canterbury, who buried the murdered archbishop in 1170.

No documents on the construction of the buildings at the abbey are known.

Dissolved in 1538, Boxley passed into private hands. The few fragments visible today are part of a garden scheme of the country house built over the southwest side of the former claustral buildings.

Excavations were carried out in 1897-1898 by George Payne and the then owner, Major Best, but no results were published. New investigations were then undertaken in 1953, 1959, and 1966, the last in the south transept. Tester's excavations of 1971-1972 retrieved the plan of the monastery. The church, which was medium-sized (194 feet from east to west, ninety-four feet across the transepts), shows a characteristic early Cistercian plan with a slightly deeper presbytery than usual (by a half bay), three chapels in each transept arm with unbroken separating walls, and a nave of eight bays. The lengthened presbytery occurs at Bordesley and Newminster, and also at Fountains III, although there with extended inner transept chapels. Compared to the aisles at the Yorkshire houses, those at Boxley were broader in proportion to the nave, and together approximate its width; a different setting out procedure was therefore used, one closer to the mature Bernardine plan (see chapter 3 of this study, p. 35).

The unbroken walls of the transept chapels suggest that barrel vaults covered them originally; but vaulting ribs with thirteenth-century profiles found in the north transept during excavations (Tester, figs. 4 and 6) may point to a later change. The nave was probably carried on cylindrical piers with scalloped capitals (one such, found in the south transept, is now in the Maidstone Museum). Fragments of architectural detailing unearthed in 1971-1972 are extremely simple. The only standing portion of the church is a plain round-headed doorway at the west end of the south aisle. All the evidence suggests a building campaign in the 1150s and 1160s. The sole addition to the church occurred in the fourteenth or fifteenth century when a tower was raised outside the church and abutting the west doorway; Tester discovered its foundations.

The cloister had an unusual rectangular form, with the west range set one bay east of the usual position. In addition, the refectory retained its east-west orientation rather than adopting the more usual north-south axis.

F. C. Elliston-Erwood, "Plans of, and Brief Architectural Notes on, Kent Churches," *Archaeologia Cantiana* 66 (1953): 45-51.

VCH: Kent 2 (London, 1962): 153-55.

J. Newman, *BoE: North East and East Kent* (London, 1969), 149.

P. J. Tester, "Excavations at Boxley Abbey," *Archaeologia Cantiana* 88 (1973): 129-58.

BRUERN (Oxfordshire)

Bruern was founded in 1147 by Nicolas Basset with monks from Waverley.

Very little is known about the abbey's buildings. The twelfth-century church was altered in the early thirteenth century; in 1232 Henry III gave the monks wood from the forest of Wuchewud: "ad rogum quendam faciendum ad operacionem ecclesie sue" (*CR: Henry III, 1231-1234,* 73). That the work involved an eastern extension is suggested by the consecration in 1250 of altars to the Virgin Mary and Saint Edmund the Confessor (*VCH: Oxfordshire* 2:80). The only other reference occurs in 1366 when Abbot John de Dunster petitioned for an indulgence for those who had contributed to the repair of the monastery.

The size and extent of the buildings at Bruern remain unknown. No clearance or excavation is recorded, and nothing survives above ground. An eighteenth-century country house covers the site.

VCH: Oxfordshire 2 (London, 1907): 79-81; 10 (London, 1972): 238-39.

J. Sherwood and Sir Nikolaus Pevsner. *BoE: Oxfordshire* (London, 1974), 499-500.

BUCKFAST (Devon)

Ethelward de Pomeroy founded Buckfast in 1136 on the site of an earlier Saxon monastery that had been depopulated in the eleventh century. At the time of foundation Buckfast belonged to the Congregation of Savigny, but it joined the Cistercian order in 1148. For more than two centuries Buckfast enjoyed considerable wealth deriving from large landholdings that made it the dominant monastic establishment in the southwest.

Little is known about the buildings. According to Stephens, the first Savigniac community built a church that was enlarged when the monks became Cistercian (Stephens, 20). Confirmations of the abbey's charters were obtained from Henry II in 1161 and Richard I in 1189 (Rowe, 58, 60-61). An eastern extension of the church in the late fourteenth century can be inferred from the mention that the arms of James and Thomas Audelay were placed in the window "of the west end of the Conventual Church and in the window of the gable end in the Lady Chapel there" (ibid., 95). Under the abbacy of William Slade (1413-1415) important additions were made to the claustral buildings (ibid., 96).

The abbey was dissolved in 1539, and the site passed into the hands of Sir Thomas Dennis. A brief inventory dating from 1555 mentions the lead from the roof and five bells in the tower of the church (ibid., 111). When Samuel Buck visited Buckfast in 1734, he depicted only parts of the claustral buildings as still standing (*Antiquities* 2, plate 15), but a report in *Gentleman's Magazine* (66, [1796]: 194-96) indicates more extensive remains: "on the north side appear the walls and foundations of this once splendid seat of superstition, the abbey church and remains of its tower all lying around in such massy fragments that it is scarcely to be conceived by what power so vast a fabrick could be joined." The ruins were estimated by the writer as being 250 feet in length with the tower situated on the south. In 1806 Westcote and Risdon spoke of "the skeleton of a huge body whereby may be conceived what bigness once it bore" (152). Shortly thereafter, however, the owner, S. Berry, leveled the site.

Cistercian monks returned to Buckfast in 1882, and a new church was built over the site of the medieval one (1907-1937).

The foundation walls of the twelfth-century church were exposed in 1882 and again in 1907 at the start of work on the new building. According to Rowe (591), the church measured 220 feet from east to west, the nave was thirty-one feet in width, with aisles of twelve feet, and the transepts were thirty feet square. Dimier published the first plan (*Recueil*, plate 54), which shows a deep, square-ended choir surrounded by aisles. That this was a late twelfth- or early thirteenth-century extension of an earlier church is suggested by the single chapel in each transept; most likely an inner pair existed that were sacrificed to form the aisles for the extension, as occurred at Abbey Dore and Coggeshall. The square chapel to the east is probably an addition dating from the fourteenth century.

In the same clearance fragments of purbeck marble shafts and "a small three-quarter base of a Norman pillar with a bead ornament" were discovered

around the crossing (Rowe, 593). Clear evidence of patching and restoration in the fifteenth century was also unearthed.

J. B. Rowe, *Contributions to a History of the Cistercian Houses of Devon* (Plymouth, 1878), 52-138.

J. B. Rowe, "On Recent Excavations at Buckfast Abbey," *Trans. Devonshire Association* 16 (1884): 590-94.

J. Stephens, "Buckfast Abbey," *Chimes* 2 (1922): 8-22.

C. Norris and D. Nicholl, *Buckfast Abbey* (London, 1939).

Sir Nikolaus Pevsner, *BoE: South Devon* (London, 1952), 68-69.

J. Stéphan, *Buckfast Abbey* (Buckfastleigh, 1962).

BUILDWAS (Shropshire)

Buildwas was founded in 1135 by Roger de Clinton, bishop of Chester, as part of the Congregation of Savigny. The monks came from Furness. In 1148, along with the Congregation's other houses, Buildwas became Cistercian. The major figure in the abbey's early history and the man responsible for establishing the house and constructing its buildings was Abbot Ranulf (1155-1187). Possessed of remarkable energy and intellect, Ranulf may have been appointed initially to effect the change from Savigniac to Cistercian ways. The same occurred earlier at Furness, Stoneleigh, and Coggeshall.

In 1152 Buildwas was entrusted with the care of Basingwerk, and in 1166, with St. Mary's Dublin. A general confirmation of the abbey's possessions was obtained from Richard I in 1189 (*Mon. Angl.* 5:359), and two years later another was obtained from Bishop Hugh de Novant at the abbey itself in the presence of a gathering of abbots (Eyton, 329-30). The latter may well have coincided with the completion of the church, including the modifications to the choir (see chapter 6 of this study, pp. 93-94). In 1220 Philip de Broseley gave the monks permission to quarry stone, although for what purpose is unknown. A visitation to Buildwas in 1231 by Stephen of Lexington limited the number of monks at the house to eighty and the number of lay brothers to 160 (B. Griesser, "Registrum Epistolarum Stephani de Lexinton," *ASOC* 8 [1952]: 181-378, esp. 205), but it is not certain that this number was ever reached. In 1232 Henry III gave thirty oaks from Shirlot forest *ad reparationem ecclesie sue* (*CR: Henry III, 1231-1234,* 66), and in 1255 more oaks for the work (*CR: Henry III, 1254-1256,* 109).

Buildwas' tradition of custodianship continued into the fourteenth century; in 1328 Edward III placed Strata Marcella under its care, referring to Buildwas as a place where "wholesome observance and regular institution flourishes" (*CR: Edward III, 1327-1330,* 410). Later the monastery was increasingly troubled by Welsh raids; after one such attack in 1406 Hugh Burnell added property to the abbey's holdings as compensation for losses when parts of the church were burned.

For the architecture, see chapter 6 of this study, 91-94.

Buildwas was classed as one of the smaller houses at the Dissolution and was surrendered to the commissioners in 1536. Subsequently, the site passed through several changes of private hands, until 1925 when the church and claustral buildings came into the guardianship of the government; the abbot's house and part of the infirmary court are still privately owned. From the plate made in 1731 by Buck (*Antiquities* 1, sec. 7, plate 3), it is clear that the abbey has sustained relatively few losses in the past 250 years. Apart from the clearance and consolidation of the remains by the Department of the Environment, no program of excavation has been undertaken.

J. Potter, *Remains of Ancient Monastic Architecture* (London, 1846).

R. W. Eyton, "The Monasteries of Shropshire: Their Origin and Founders, Buildwas Abbey," *Arch. Jnl.* 15 (1858): 318-33.

R. W. Eyton, "Buildwas Abbey," *Antiquities of Shropshire* 6 (London, 1858): 317-35.

J. L. Petit, "Architectural Notices of the Conventual Church of Buildwas Abbey, Shropshire," *Arch. Jnl.* 15 (1858): 334-44.

G. M. Hills, "Buildwas Abbey," *Collectanea Archaeologica* 1 (1862): 99-112.

R. W. Eyton, "The Monasteries of Shropshire," *Shropshire Archaeological Society Transactions* 11 (1887-1888): 101-30.

A. H. Thompson, *Buildwas Abbey* (London: Department of Environment, 1937).

Sir Nikolaus Pevsner, *BoE: Shropshire* (London, 1958), 88-90.

M. Chibnall, "Buildwas Abbey," *VCH: Shropshire* 2 (London, 1973): 50-59.

BYLAND (Yorkshire)

For the early history and architecture of Byland, see chapter 5 of this study.

The abbey was dissolved in 1539, and the site was granted to Sir William Pickering. Considerable dismantling occurred between then and 1721, when Buck depicted the remains from the south (*Antiquities* 1, sec. 1, plate 1). Subsequently, the principal loss has been the south wall of the south transept. This still remained in 1821 when it was described in an anonymous guide, but shortly thereafter it collapsed. An excavation is mentioned in 1855 (W. Grainge, *The Castles and Abbeys of Yorkshire* [York, 1855], 255), and a partial clearance was made by Fowler in 1886. The church remained under heavy debris, however, until 1921 when the ruin was gifted to the nation. An excavation by Sir Charles Peers cleared the site between 1922 and 1924, but apart from a brief guide no record has been published.

J. Burton, *Monasticon Eboracense* (York, 1785), 328-40.

Anonymous, *A Description of Duncombe Park, Rivalx Abbey and Helmsley Castle with notices of Byland Abbey, Kirkdale Church, etc.* (Kirby Moorside, 1821).

J. R. Walbran, "Some Observations on the History and Structure of the Abbey of the Blessed Mary of Byland," *AASRP* 7 (1863): 219-34.

E. Sharpe, "Byland Abbey," *YAJ* 33 (1876): 1-8.

C. H. Fowler, "Byland Abbey," *YAJ* 43 (1886): 395-96.

W. H. St. John Hope, "Byland Abbey," *The Builder* 71 (1896): 270-71.

J. W. Bloe, "Byland Abbey," *VCH: Yorkshire, North Riding* 2 (London, 1923): 10-13.

Sir Charles Peers, *Byland Abbey* (London: Department of Environment, 1934).

Sir Nikolaus Pevsner, *BoE: Yorkshire, North Riding* (London, 1966), 94-101.

P. Svendgaard, "Byland Abbey: The Builders and their Marks," *Ryedale Historian* 3 (1967): 26-29.

P. Fergusson, "The South Transept Elevation of Byland Abbey," *Jnl. BAA*, 3rd ser. 38 (1975): 155-76.

P. Fergusson, "Notes on Two Cistercian Engraved Designs," *Speculum* 54 (1979): 1-17.

CALDER (Cumberland)

Superbly situated in a low, wooded valley close to the sea, Calder was first settled by monks from Furness in 1134. A Scottish invasion four years later forced its abandonment, however, and the community eventually settled at Byland. A new colony from Furness was sent out to reoccupy the site around 1143. Ranulph de Meschin, earl of Chester, was the patron, as he had been for the first settlement. Until 1148 the monks were under the jurisdiction of the Congregation of Savigny.

The first permanent church was built by William FitzDuncan of Egrement Castle (Loftie [1886], 475). Most of this church has disappeared, and the remains that one sees today date from about 1225. What led to the rebuilding is unknown. A general confirmation of the abbey's rights was obtained from Henry III in 1231 (*Mon. Angl.* 5:340-41), perhaps to mark completion of the church since it agrees with Denton's statement (*History of Cumberland*, 1610) that Thomas de Multon of Egremont Castle (d. 1240) "finished the works, and established a greater convent of monks at Cauder, or Caldre" (Denton's source is unfortunately lost). An invasion by the Scots in 1322 severely damaged the church and monastery, and extensive repairs were needed before the buildings could be used again.

The monastery was dissolved in 1536, and the site fell into the hands of Thomas Leigh, the most notorious of the Dissolution commissioners in the north. From him it passed to a series of private owners down to the present day.

Buck's view of Calder in 1739 (*Antiquities* 2, plate 2) shows some of the south aisle still in place, but apart from loss of this section, the abbey's condition is little changed. Clearance of the ruins and some general excavations were conducted in 1880-1881 by A. G. Loftie. No trace of this work is visible.

Substantial portions of the church survive, though mostly from the thirteenth- and fourteenth-century rebuildings, and only the aisles of the nave and the south arcade cannot be traced. The plan published by Loftie (1892) shows the standard early Cistercian form. This was followed in the later rebuildings except for a deepening of the choir. The building was always small, measuring only 147 feet from east to west.

The only major part of the church to survive from the twelfth century is the doorway at the west end (plate 60 in this study). It has three orders in the jambs, supported by shafts that carry waterleaf capitals and intricate moldings. The latter are similar to those at Furness, with the exception of the outer molding, which carries a fringe of cusping, a motif quite common in the north. Stretches of wall in the north and south transept are original, and there are some details in the chapels (waterleaf capitals in the windows, for instance) that suggest reuse. Loftie published drawings of responds found in his clearance; these included scalloped and cross-stemmed foliate designs, all dating from the twelfth century, and presumably coming from the aisles.

Since the west doorway dates to *circa* 1180, and assuming that construction went from east to west (which the generally earlier date of the other details supports), the program of work at Calder may be placed in the 1160s and 1170s.

A. G. Loftie, "Exploration at Calder Abbey," *Trans. CWAAS* 6 (1883): 368-72.

A. G. Loftie, "Calder Abbey," *Trans. CWAAS* 8 (1886): 467-504.

A. G. Loftie "Calder Abbey," *Trans. CWAAS* 9 (1888): 206-39.

A. G. Loftie, *Calder Abbey, its ruins and history* (London, 1892).

VCH: Cumberland 2 (London, 1905): 174-78.

Sir Nikolaus Pevsner, *BoE: Cumberland and Westmorland* (London, 1967), 84-86.

CLEEVE (Somerset)

Cleeve was founded between 1186 and 1191, though the exact date is lost (Gilyard-Beer, 1). Colonization of the site, however, is given as 1198. The founder was William de Roumare, third earl of Lincoln, the grandson of one of the Cistercians' most consistent early patrons. His grandfather's foundation at Revesby supplied the monks. Cleeve was always one of the smaller houses of the order; in 1297 at a period when Cleeve was prosperous twenty-six monks are mentioned.

Building is specified as being underway in 1198, but no details are given. In 1232 Henry III granted the abbey oak for choir stalls (*CR: Henry III, 1231-1234*, 77). Since no indication of any enlargement can be distinguished in the eastern remains, the gift indicates the slow completion of a single program of work. In 1535 a valuation listed eleven bells; a tower existed, therefore, probably over the crossing.

Cleeve was dissolved in 1537, and parts of the claustral buildings were converted into residential quarters, with the cloister becoming a courtyard for the house. After several changes of ownership, the site came under the guardianship of the Department of the Environment in 1951. T. Bonner drew the claustral buildings from the west in 1790 (Gilyard-Beer, 13), showing parts of the south transept still standing, including the arch into the south transept chapel, which is surmounted by a tall area of bare wall and topped by a clerestory window. All this has since vanished, but apart from this, few losses have been sustained subsequently.

Excavations were carried out by MacKenzie-Walcott and Samson in 1875 and again by Eeles in 1930. The Department of the Environment has exposed the foundation walls of the church and to the south the earlier refectory with its splendid tiles.

The plan of the church is the typical early Cistercian one, and the two chapels in each transept are even separated by solid walls. Although a plan with this feature and a square-ended, aisleless presbytery would be expected around the mid-twelfth century, by the standards of Cistercian architecture of 1200 it was noticeably conservative. Even excluding the north of England, abbeys in the south

and southwest were using more up-to-date models. At Abbey Dore, for instance, work on an enlarged choir with a rectangular ambulatory and east chapel range was begun around 1185; and very shortly after Cleeve was started, ambitious eastern schemes were employed at Beaulieu, Waverley, and probably Forde.

The two-story elevation in the transepts, shown in the Bonner sketch, was also conservative, as was surviving detailing such as the remaining respond against the south wall in the south transept. The latter originally formed the opening into the east chapel and has chamfered setbacks; it rests on a chamfered plinth without a base molding. The doorway into the cloister from the south aisle was also chamfered. Similarly austere is the wall of the south aisle, which lacks any articulation and is built of irregularly coursed masonry.

A campaign break in the first bay of the nave suggests that only the east end of the church was finished by the time Henry III granted the abbey wood for stalls. Little remains of the nave; the piers were cylindrical like those at Buildwas, and one surviving base at the west end shows a typical waterholding form. Eeles reported that the arches had two-order chamfered moldings.

The plan, masonry, elevation, and few surviving details are notable, then, for their extreme conservatism. So distinctive is this quality that it suggests a deliberate archaism. Cleeve was not alone in this; the same occurred at Buildwas, though somewhat earlier, and somewhat less forcefully.

T. Hugo, "The Charters and Other Archives of Cleeve Abbey," *Proc. SAS* 6 (1855): 17-73.

F. Warre, "Old Cleeve Abbey," *Proc. SAS* 6 (1855): 74-97.

E. C. MacKenzie-Walcott, "Old Cleeve Abbey," *Trans. RIBA* (1876), 103-27.

F. W. Weaver, "Cleeve Abbey," *Proc. SAS* 52 (1906): 1-41.

VCH: Somerset 2 (London, 1911): 115-18.

F. C. Eeles, "Cleeve Abbey; Recent Discoveries," *Proc. SAS* 77 (1931): 37-47.

R. S. Simms, "Cleeve Abbey," *Arch. Jnl.* 107 (1950): 118-19.

Sir Nikolaus Pevsner, *BoE: South and West Somerset* (London, 1958): 126-28.

R. Gilyard-Beer, *Cleeve Abbey* (London: Department of Environment, 1960).

COGGESHALL (Essex)

Coggeshall lay on the banks of the Blackwater River. It was founded in 1140 by King Stephen and his wife Mathilda as the thirteenth and last of the houses of the Congregation of Savigny. Included with the land was the manor of Coggeshall, both the property of the queen. The abbey became Cistercian in 1148 when the Congregation was merged with that order.

Work on a permanent church must have begun shortly after the merger. A consecration of the high altar by the bishop of London, Gilbert Foliot, in 1167 is recorded in the history of the house written in the early thirteenth century by Abbot Ralph (1207-1218). Perhaps the other essential buildings were also completed by this date since Ralph mentions that the next year (1168) the second abbot, Simon de Toni, "returned to his own house of Melrose" (*Chron. Angl.*, 16). Although it is not known when Simon took up his appointment, it may well have been when Coggeshall became Cistercian and he was sent to establish it on orthodox lines.

Ralph next mentions the abbey's buildings during the rule of Abbot Peter (1176-1194), recounting an unusual episode. One day the assistant hosteler, Robert, found in the guest house several persons dressed as Templars. Realizing they were men of importance, he hastened to arrange for them to dine with the abbot in his private quarters. When he returned, however, the Templars had vanished, and the porters reported that no such persons had passed through the gates (ibid., 134). The story reveals that the abbot had already separated himself from the community and was living in his own accommodations at this early date.

Although the principal buildings belong to the 1160s, it is clear from the existing remains that work continued through the late twelfth and into the early thirteenth century; the guest house and abbot's lodging date to about 1190, as do parts of the monks' dormitory undercroft and an open corridor to the east with three bays of rib vaults. The *capella extra portas* stands complete, though restored,

and belongs to about 1220. Subsequently, the abbey's history is obscure. The cloister was rebuilt in the mid-fifteenth century (Gardner, 21), and by 1518 a mansion belonging to Sir John Sharpe existed adjacent to the abbey buildings.

The monastery was dissolved in 1538, and the site was sold to Sir Thomas Seymour, who resold it to the crown three years later. At that time a survey noted that the church "is clene prostrate and defaced but the cloyster and lodgings doe yet remayne untouched" (Beaumont, 61). By the late sixteenth century these too had disappeared, and a mansion belonging to the Paycocke family was raised on the site. Coggeshall remains in private ownership.

An excavation of the church was started by St. John Hope in 1914, but the Great War cut it short, and it was not resumed. Some remains were unearthed, however, including brick bases of the west nave piers and fragments of a screen wall running between them. No further work has been undertaken.

Although nothing of the church is visible above ground, in dry summers the outlines of the walls can be discerned. These have revealed the plan (fig. 22) of a five-bay, square-ended chevet with north and south aisles, transepts with one chapel each, and a nave of eight bays. The overall length was 210 feet, with the chevet measuring seventy-three feet, the nave 112 feet, and the transepts eighty feet from north to south and twenty-five feet in width.

It is likely that the aisled chevet was a late twelfth- or early thirteenth-century addition, the presbytery of the 1167 church being almost certainly aisleless. Originally each transept probably contained two chapels, but the inner ones would have been sacrificed to provide aisles in the extension. In the nave the piers were cylindrical and measured four feet in diameter; unusually, they are made of brick and are among the earliest of this material known (Gardner, 31). At the Cistercian abbey of Ter Duin (Belgium), however, brick piers were used, and it could be that it was from this part of Flanders that the idea spread to Coggeshall.

Surviving fragments from the cloister show a scalloped capital and early waterholding base (ibid., plate 6, no. 2). These details date to *circa* 1170

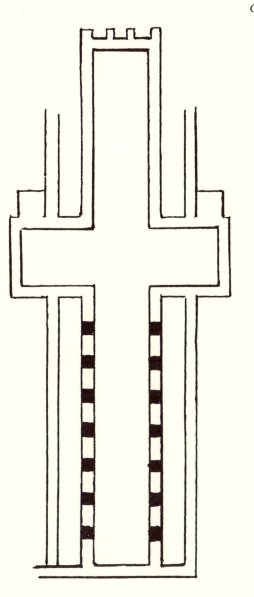

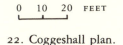

0   10   20   FEET

22. Coggeshall plan.

and suggest that the consecration of 1167 may have marked the completion of the claustral buildings as well as the church.

J. Stevenson, ed., *Radulphi de Coggeshall, Chronicon Anglicanum, Rolls Series* 66 (1875).

E. L. Cutts, "An Architectural Account of the Remains of Coggeshall Abbey," *Trans. EAS* 1 (1858): 166-85.

B. Dale, *Annals of Coggeshall* (London 1863).

VCH: Essex 2 (London, 1907): 125-29.

G. F. Beaumont, "The Remains of Coggeshall Abbey," *Trans. EAS*, new ser. 15 (1921): 59-76.

RCHM: Essex 3 (London, 1922): 165-67.

J. S. Gardner, "Coggeshall Abbey and its Early Brickwork," *Jnl. BAA*, 3rd ser., 18 (1955): 19-32.

Sir Nikolaus Pevsner, *BoE: Essex* (London, 1954), 251-52.

COMBE (Warwickshire)

Combe was founded by Richard de Camvill in 1150 as a daughter house to Waverley. It was the wealthiest of the Cistercians' three foundations in Warwickshire.

Little has emerged about the history of the buildings at Combe. One late document only records the gift of £30 in 1509 from Sir Edward Raleigh to build the south side of the cloister and to glaze it (Dugdale, 530).

Dissolved in 1539, the abbey was converted before the turn of the century into a country house by Lord Harington. He used three sides of the cloister to form the nucleus of the building, leveling the fourth side occupied by the church and taking its stone for construction. By the early seventeenth century the estate was in the hands of the Craven family, and it was from them in the 1950s that the estate was purchased by the city of Coventry for use as a public park.

The abbey was illustrated in Dugdale's first edition of the *Monasticon* (1655-1673), and many of the claustral buildings can be recognized. Although a new house was begun for the Cravens around 1680, the medieval parts were retained and are visible in Buck's 1729 engraving (*Antiquities* 1, sec. 5, plate 9). This house was replaced by a large Victorian mansion designed by Eden Nesfield in the 1860s. Most of this Victorian building has since been demolished.

The present courtyard was originally the cloister of the abbey, with the church lying to the south in the area now occupied by the moat. When the moat was being dug in 1864, local newspapers reported that the foundations of the church had been unearthed but gave no details. Parts of the fifteenth-century cloister remain on the north and west sides of the courtyard, while its east side is formed by the fronts of the original twelfth-century range. This includes the handsome round-headed doorway to the chapter house with deep twin windows on either side; and on the north and south, respectively, remain the passage and slype entrances, the latter with a pointed profile. The stone is a warm red sandstone; detailing includes waterleaf, volute (plate 138), and unusual twisted-incised capitals, and roll moldings, some with chevron applied to the outer rolls. In the wall of the passage is a small door with chamfered angles that once led into the day room and just beyond, in what is now the gentlemen's lavatory, is a fragment of arch respond with a reset arch with a gorged outer roll. Behind these façades are parts of Nesfield's Victorian building, which employed profiles identical to the twelfth-century ones.

From the evidence of the east range, a date around 1180-1190 is suggested for the twelfth-century building.

W. Dugdale, *The Antiquities of Warwickshire* 1 (London, 1730): 222-26.

VCH: Warwickshire 2 (London, 1908): 73-75; and 6 (London, 1951): 72-73.

Sir Nikolaus Pevsner and A. Wedgewood, *BoE: Warwickshire* (London, 1966), 236-38.

COMBERMERE (Cheshire)

Randle Blundeville, earl of Chester, founded Combermere in 1133 as part of the Congregation of Savigny. He endowed the abbey with property and revenues that included income from salt houses, from a quarter of the town of Nantwich, and from rectorial rights to the church there. These sources seem to have continued to supply Combermere after it became Cistercian in 1148. Men were apparently attracted to the monastic life at Combermere, and patrons supported the community, for in 1153 a colony was established at Poulton, in 1172, another at Whalley, and in 1219, a third at Hulton.

No documents have come to light on the history of building at Combermere.

Dissolved in 1539, the abbey was sold to Sir George Cotton, who incorporated some of the monastic buildings into a country house that he built over the site. When Buck visited the abbey in 1727, some parts of the claustral buildings were recognizable immured into the house (*Antiquities* 1, sec. 3, plate 11). The house has since been demolished, however, and nothing is visible on the site.

J. P. Earwaker, *East Cheshire: Past and Present* 2 (London, 1880): 432-33.

G. Ormerod, *History of Chester* 3 (London, 1882): 402-19.

J. Hall, ed., "The Book of the Abbot of Combermere," *Record Society for Lancashire and Cheshire* 31 (1896): 1-74.

Sir Nikolaus Pevsner, *BoE: Cheshire* (London, 1971), 181-82.

CROXDEN (Staffordshire)

The monastery at Croxden had one false start; first settled at Cotton in 1176, the monks left after two years and moved to Croxden. The original community had come from Aulnay-sur-Odon in Normandy under the patronage of Bertram de Verdun whose family earlier had founded Aulnay. Croxden remained Aulnay's sole foundation in England.

According to William de Shepished, the author of the abbey's late thirteenth century *Chronicle*, building began under Abbot Thomas of Woodstock (1178-1229) (Lawrence, 30). A consecration was recorded in 1181, but this was a *dedicatio loci* (*Mon. Angl.* 5:661). Another consecration is noted in 1232. Under the fifth abbot, Walter of London (1242-1268), described as *strenuissimus*, the monastery was enlarged by "the half of the church," presumably meaning the west nave bays and west end (Hills, 298). A third consecration by Bishop Roger Weseham of Coventry and Litchfield took place in 1254. Extensive work on the monastic buildings was also carried out by Abbot Walter; he finished the chapter house and refectory and was entirely responsible for building and equipping the kitchen, the whole of the infirmary with its great hall, chapel, and kitchen, and the novitiate (Lawrence, 30-31). In his "latter days" he began the enclosure wall around the monastic precincts, and before he died he had completed half its length and erected the great gates at the main entrances of the monastery.

Under Walter's successor, William of Howton (1268-1274), work continued. William is credited with the two-storied abbot's house that faced south (ibid., 31). In 1313 the great bell of the monastery was accidentally broken on Holy Saturday, and in 1332 a great wind blew off the roofs of the conventual buildings (ibid., 43). Repair on the latter began at once, and the abbot, Richard de Shepished (1329-1335), retiled all four roofs of the cloister (the accounts specify that this took 25,550 tiles), the roofs of the refectory and belfry (19,000 tiles), and finally the monks' dormitory and abbot's house (30,000 tiles). He also extended the monks' dormitory and began rebuilding the abbot's house (ibid., 43-44). In 1369 some of the buildings adjoining the church collapsed and were rebuilt the next year. In 1374 the cloisters were repaired (ibid., 63).

By 1377 Croxden's fortunes had suffered a sharp reverse for reasons unknown; that year the population of the abbey included only the abbot and six monks, and the same number are mentioned in 1381 (VCH: Staffordshire 3:228). Recovery took place slowly; in the fifteenth century under the register of the twenty-second abbot, Dom John de Checkley-Walton (circa 1460-1506), it was noted that "the good abbot . . . roofed the monastery, the great barn and the bakehouse, and many other buildings about the monastery, in particular the cloister and the room which is called the parlour" (Lawrence, 16). Finally, in the early sixteenth century it was remarked of Abbot Walton that he was engaged in building.

The monastery was dissolved in 1538, and the contents inventoried for sale. Among the lots was one for the "roffe of the churche," another for the "loft under the organs," and a third for "all the old tymber in the cloister" (T. Wright, ed., "Three Chapters Relating to the Suppression of the Monasteries," Camden Society, 1st. ser., 26 [1843]: 164-65). In 1731 when Buck visited the site, the remains looked much as they do today, except for the disappearance of the west wall of the cloister (Antiquities 1, sec. 7, plate 14). At some time afterwards a country road was allowed to run diagonally through the church, and this now awkwardly separates the chevet and north transept from the remains of the claustral buildings. In 1936 Croxden was placed under the guardianship of the Department of the Environment, which has cleared the site. No excavation has been undertaken.

From the Chronicle it is clear that a permanent church was built in the twelfth century. The only traces of this are some masonry courses in the south transept (exterior wall) and the exposed pier base in the north transept with its setting out design clearly visible (P. Fergusson, "Notes on Two Cistercian Engraved Designs," Speculum 54 [1979], plate 3). The rebuilding in the thirteenth century occurred over the plan of the original transepts, as may be deduced from the unusual relation of the transepts to the impressive ambulatory and radiating chapel scheme. It is possible that the twelfth-century east end was of the rectangular ambulatory type used at Byland.

Almost all the extensive remains on the site, then, date from the thirteenth century. What is mysterious is the thoroughness of the replacement of the twelfth-century work.

G. Hills, "Croxden Abbey and its Chronicle," Jnl. BAA 21 (1865): 294-315.

C. Lyman, "Croxden Abbey," in R. Plant, ed., A History of Cheadale (London, 1881): 259-76.

W.H.G. Flood, History of Croxden Abbey (London, 1893).

C. Lyman, The Abbey of St. Mary, Croxden, Staffordshire (London, 1911).

P. K. Baillie Reynolds, Croxden Abbey (London: Department of Environment, 1946).

M. Lawrence, "Notes on the Chronicle and other Documents relating to St. Mary's Abbey, Croxden," Trans. of the North Staffordshire Field Club 85-87 (1951-1953): 1-27, 27-50, 51-74.

P. K. Baillie Reynolds, "Croxden Abbey," Arch. Jnl. 120 (1964): 278.

VCH: Staffordshire 3 (London, 1970): 226-30.

Sir Nikolaus Pevsner, BoE: Staffordshire (London, 1974): 111-13.

FLAXLEY (Gloucestershire)

Flaxley lies in the heart of the forest of Dene in a valley sealed to the west by steep hills. It was founded in 1151 by Roger, son of the earl of Hereford, reputedly on the site where his father had been killed in a hunting accident on Christmas Eve eight years earlier. The monks came from Bordesley.

The abbey's charters were confirmed between 1151 and 1154 by Henry, duke of Normandy, and were confirmed again in 1158 by Henry as king. On the latter occasion he gave the monks the right to take wood and other materials "ad domos suas et ad aedificia sua facienda," but without committing waste in the forest (*Mon. Angl.* 5:590). According to Leland (1545), whose source is lost, the abbey was greatly helped initially in its building by a bishop of Hereford; this was most likely Gilbert Foliot before his transfer to London in 1163 (*Chart. F.*, 11). A third confirmation was obtained from Pope Celestine III in 1192 (ibid., 178-80, no. 77). Before 1200 various gifts of candles and hosts were recorded (ibid., 130-31, no. 2), along with one by Gilbert Monmouth and his wife, Berta, who gave five shillings from the mill at Hope (two miles from Flaxley) for the purchase of wine for Mass but stipulated that if money were left over, the residue could, with the consent of the whole chapter, be spent for the repair of books (ibid., 133 no. 6). Taken together these gifts suggest completion of the church before the turn of the century. Under Henry III Flaxley received grants of wood in 1218, 1222, and 1223 (ibid., 24). In 1230 the king allowed the abbot two oaks for the roof of the aisle (*CR: Henry III, 1227-1231*, 354), and more wood was granted the next year (ibid., 565). In 1232 the king gave the abbey ten more oaks "ad ecclesiam suam et domos abbatie sue reparandus" (*CR: Henry III, 1231-1234*, 98), but the abbot could obtain only four, and later the same year six more were allowed for the repair of the church. Two years later more oaks were given for the repair of the abbot's houses (ibid., 397).

When the Dissolution commissioners came to Flaxley in 1536, they found the house in ruins and the church damaged by fire. They reported that to raise money for the repair of the church, the monks had melted down the bells and sold the metal. The abbey was granted to Sir William Kingston, Constable of the Tower of London, who earlier in 1536 had superintended the execution of Anne Boleyn; the grant specifies the "church, steeple and churchyard" along with other properties (*L. and P. Henry VIII* 12, pt. 1, no. 795, p. 42).

Today the country house that keeps the monastery's name covers two sides of the former cloister and incorporates part of the conversi's quarters in its west wing. All that survives of the church is a stretch of the north aisle at the west end (about ten feet) now forming one side of a back courtyard, and part of the south aisle (about sixty feet), the latter immured into the eighteenth-century orangery. The masonry consists of roughly shaped stones laid with heavy mortar infilling, and there is no articulation on either the inner or outer faces. At the east end of the orangery the doorway that went from the cloister into the south aisle is visible in its lower parts. It is made of well-cut soft red sandstone; the bases are not yet waterholding, but the shafts have fillets. The upper parts of the doorway have been walled up and plastered over, but according to Crawley-Boevey, the arch moldings were round-headed (1921, 58). In the same article he mentions that the south and west walls of the south transept had been found but gives no details; these are not visible and are covered by a new garden scheme (1981). A sizable number of rib molding fragments, probably from the church, have been collected in the garden as a result of landscaping changes; they are of two kinds, a chamfered form and a single roll flanked by hollows. Both would fit a date around 1160-1170.

Of the claustral buildings, impressive parts of the original west range remain, with five spacious rib-vaulted bays and a fine late twelfth century doorway with re-worked capitals that led into the cloister. A clearance in 1788 reported that the chapter house was polygonal with a central column whose base remained (*Chart. F.*, 60).

A plan of the abbey was published by Middleton in 1881. Only the surviving claustral parts are drawn to scale, and the remainder is schematic. The church is shown as large measuring 274 feet from east to west and 112 feet across the transepts. The length suggests an extension to the choir, perhaps in the thirteenth century.

J. H. Middleton, "Flaxley Abbey: The Existing Remains," *Trans. BGAS* 6 (1881-1882): 280-83.

A. W. Crawley-Boevey, *The Cartulary and Historical Notes of the Cistercian Abbey of Flaxley* (Exeter, 1887).

VCH: Gloucestershire 2 (London, 1907): 93-96.

Sir Francis Crawley-Boevey, "Some Recent Discoveries at Flaxley Abbey," *Trans. BGAS* 43 (1921): 57-62.

D. Verey, *BoE: Gloucestershire* 2 (London, 1970): 185-87.

FORDE (Dorset)

Richard Fitzbaldwin founded Forde in 1136 with monks from Waverley. The site lay at Brightley in Devon, but after five years the monks abandoned it and set out to return to their mother house in Surrey. They had only gone as far as Thorncombe when they encountered Adelicia, the sister of Richard the viscount, and their appearance so moved her that she gave them her manor there. The gift included a house called Westford, which the monks used while they worked on their buildings. Soon the abbey became known just as Forde because it allowed a passage across the River Axe.

The abbey quickly attracted patrons and increased in wealth. In 1171 a colony was sent out to found Bindon, and in 1201, another to Dunkeswell. Unusually for the Cistercians, Forde enjoyed a reputation for learning in the twelfth century. Its most famous abbot, Baldwin (1168-1181), went on to become bishop of Worcester and then in 1184 was anointed archbishop of Canterbury.

Little is known about the history of building at Forde. The main program was carried out under Abbot Robert de Penynton (1137-1168). Much of the fine chapter house survives from this period, as do parts of the lay brothers' range. Forde's patron, Adelicia, died in 1142 and was buried before the high altar (Rowe, 350, no. 261), but the building could hardly have risen far by then. An *obit* in 1209

records a burial "in australi parte presbiterii sepeliter" (*Mon. Angl.* 5:378). In 1239 a consecration is documented (*Ann. W*, 323), possibly for an eastern extension.

By the rule of Abbot John Chidley (1330-1354) the abbey buildings and church were in ruins (Rowe, 357, no. 271), and Abbot John's successor, Adam (1354-1373), reported that the church still required rebuilding (ibid., 359, no. 273). On the eve of the Dissolution Forde's distinguished last abbot, Chard (1521-1539), initiated an ambitious new building program on the monastic quarters. Parts of the cloister survive from this work, incorporated into the mansion built by Inigo Jones from 1647 forwards. When Buck visited the site in 1734, he found it looking much as it does today (*Antiquities* 2, plate 14).

Nothing survives of the church at Forde. Because of the slope of the ground towards the River Axe, the cloister lay on the north, and the remains of the church lie, therefore, under the lawn fronting the present impressive country house. Aerial photographs reveal no outlines of the building (D. Knowles and J.K.S. St. Joseph, *Monastic Sites from the Air* [Cambridge, 1952], 144).

There is no record of an excavation or clearance, but in 1913 Brakspear published a plan of the monastery that includes a schematic outline of the church. How this was obtained is unclear, although one method Brakspear used elsewhere was to probe for foundations with steel rods. The church is shown as measuring 224 feet in length and ninety-nine feet across the transept, with a presbytery surrounded by a rectangular ambulatory, similar to those at Abbey Dore and Byland.

J. B. Rowe, "Cistercian Houses in Devon: Forde," *Trans. of the Devonshire Association* 10 (1878): 349-70. This was published again in *Contributions to a History of the Cistercian Houses of Devon* (Plymouth, 1878): 171-92.

H. Brakspear, "Forde Abbey," *Arch. Jnl.* 70 (1913): 498-99.

A. Clapham and A. R. Duffy, "Forde Abbey," *Arch. Jnl.* 107 (1950): 119-20.

RCHM: Dorset, West 1 (London, 1952): 240.

J. Newman and Sir Nikolaus Pevsner, *BoE: Dors* (London, 1972), 208-11.

FOUNTAINS (Yorkshire)

For the history and architecture of Fountains, see chapter 3 of this study, pp. 38-48. For its later building history in the fifteenth and sixteenth centuries, see Reeve, 11-13.

Fountains was dissolved in 1539. After some years of debate over whether to turn the abbey into a cathedral for a new see of Richmond, the site was sold to Sir Richard Gresham. At the end of the sixteenth century a new owner, Sir Stephen Proctor, used stone from the monastic buildings and outer court to construct Fountains Hall, which lies two hundred yards to the west of the abbey gate. In 1768 William Aislabie incorporated the ruins into the magnificent landscape scheme of Studley Royal conceived by his father in the early eighteenth century (see appendix A). From the Aislabies, the site passed into the hands of the Vyners, whose heir sold it in 1966 to the Yorkshire West Riding County Council. They have placed the ruins under the protection of the Department of the Environment.

Clearances are recorded in the eighteenth century, but the first extensive work on the ruins was undertaken between 1840 and 1854 by John Walbran. Further work, between 1887 and 1888, was carried out by Hope. Since being placed in the hands of the government in 1966, the ruins have been extensively examined by Gilyard-Beer. Some new excavations were carried out by Roger Mercer in 1968 and 1969 and by Glyn Coppack from 1977 to 1982 on the brew house, south transept and parts of the cloister.

J. R. Walbran, "On the Excavation now in Progress at Fountains Abbey," *AASRP* 1 (1850): 263-92; and 3 (1854-1855): 54-66.

J. R. Walbran, *Memorials of the Abbey of St. Mary of Fountains, Surtees Society,* 3 vols. (Leeds, 1862-

y, Yorkshire," *Col-* 71): 251-302.

be Abbey of St. Mary 2).

tains Abbey," *YAJ*

Jnl. RIBA 3rd ser.,

A. W. Oxford, *The Ruins of Fountains Abbey* (London, 1910).

VCH: Yorkshire 3 (1913): 134-38.

W. T. Lancaster, ed., *Abstracts of the Charters and Other Documents Contained in the Chartulary of the Cistercian Abbey of Fountains,* 2 vols. (Leeds, 1915).

Sir Nikolaus Pevsner, *BoE: Yorkshire, West Riding* (London, 1959), 203-13.

A. Phillips, *Fountains Abbey* (London: Department of Environment, 1967).

R. Gilyard-Beer, *Fountains Abbey* (London: Department of Environment, 1978).

FURNESS (Lancashire)

Monks from the Congregation of Savigny first settled at Tulketh near modern-day Preston in 1124, under the patronage of Stephen, count of Boulogne, soon king of England. For reasons that are unrecorded, the community moved north to Furness four years later, and Tulketh was reduced to a dependent grange. Along with all other Savigniac houses, Furness became Cistercian in 1148.

The abbey quickly amassed large landholdings with the help of its royal patron. These were confirmed by Henry II in 1158 and by Richard I between 1189 and 1194 (W. Farrer, *The Lancashire Pipe Rolls* [Liverpool, 1902], 209-10, 315-16). In 1316 a Scottish raid devastated the abbey, but no details of damage survive.

For the architecture, see chapter 4 of this study, pp. 54-61.

Furness was dissolved in 1538, and the site passed into private hands. Dismantling began at once. By the early eighteenth century topographical prints and drawings like Buck's 1727 view (*Antiquities* 1, sec. 3, plate 1), show the ruins much as they are today. Clearance of the church and some of the monastic buildings was begun by Beck in 1840, with further work carried out between 1880 and 1882. St. John Hope excavated the presbytery and transepts between 1896 and 1898. In 1923 the owner, Lord Cavendish, gave the site to the government.

F. Evans, *Furness and Furness Abbey* (London, 1842).

T. J. Beck, *Annales Furnesienses* (London, 1844).

L. Delisle, "Documents Relative to the Abbey of Furness, Extracted from the Archives of Savigny," *Jnl. Arch. Assoc.* 6 (1851): 419-24.

E. Sharpe, "The Ruins of the Cistercian Monastery of St. Mary in Furness," *Jnl. BAA* 6 (1851): 304-17, 358-74.

R. S. Ferguson, "Masons' Marks from Furness and Calder Abbey," *Trans. CWAAS* 6 (1883): 357.

J. C. Atkinson, ed., *The Coucher Book of Furness Abbey*, Chetham Society, new ser., 9 (1886); 11 (1887); 14 (1887).

W. H. St. John Hope, "The Abbey of St. Mary in Furness, Lancashire," *Trans. LCAS* 16 (1899): 221-302.

H. Brakspear, "On the First Church at Furness," *Trans. LCAS* 18 (1901): 70-87.

W. H. St. John Hope, *The Abbey of St. Mary in Furness* (Kendal, 1902).

F. M. Powicke, "Furness Abbey," *VCH: Lancaster* 2 (London, 1908): 114-31.

W. H. St. John Hope and S. C. Kaines-Smith, "Furness Abbey," *VCH: Lancashire* 8 (London, 1914): 285-305.

J. Brownbill, ed., *The Coucher Book of Furness Abbey*, Chetham Society, new ser., 74 (1915); 76 (1916); 78 (1919).

S. J. Garton, *Furness Abbey* (London: Department of Environment, 1943).

J. C. Dickinson, *Furness Abbey* (London: Department of Environment, 1965).

J. C. Dickinson, "Furness Abbey, An Archaeological Reconsideration," *Trans. CWAAS* 67 (1967): 51-80.

Sir Nikolaus Pevsner, *BoE: North Lancashire* (London, 1969), 123-27.

J. C. Dickinson, "Furness Abbey," *Arch. Jnl.* 127 (1970): 267-69.

GARENDON (Leicestershire)

Robert "le Bossu," earl of Leicester, founded Garendon in 1133 with monks from Waverley. Along with the site, the monks received 690 acres of land and revenues from the town of Stockton (*Mon. Angl.* 5:382). Further income came from the earl's sister, Margaret, dowager countess of Winchester, who endowed the house with the town of Henley, and from her son, Robert de Quensey, earl of Winchester, who gave additional landholdings in Belgrave, Halthern, and Thorpe. With these resources and the continuing support of the de Beaumonts, Garendon was in a position to expand, and colonies were sent to found Bordesley in 1138 and Biddlesden in 1147.

No documents on the history of building at Garendon have come to light.

The monastery was dissolved in 1536. The previous year it had been reported that the "large old monastery was partly ruinous" (*VCH: Leicestershire* 2:6). From the materials for sale mentioned in the Dissolution inventory, it is clear that the church was large (Nichol, 797-98), though no details of its form are given. The abbey passed into private hands, but some buildings remained when Sir Ambrose Phillips, the owner from 1683 to 1706, demolished them and dug up the foundations to build his country house, Garendon Hall. This house was taken down in 1964, and no trace of the abbey is presently visible. An excavation by Williams in 1969 revealed details of the dorter and chapter house (Hurst, 246). The latter had a five-sided east apse built around 1360.

J. Nichol, *History and Antiquities of the County of Leicestershire* 3, pt. 2 (London, 1804): 786-841.

VCH: Leicestershire 2 (London, 1954): 5-7.

Sir Nikolaus Pevsner, *BoE: Leicestershire and Rutland* (London, 1960), 106.

D. G. Hurst, "Garendon Abbey," *Med. Arch.* 13 (1969): 246.

HOLMCULTRAM (ABBEY TOWN)
(Cumberland)

Prince Henry of Scotland and Alan, lord of Allerdale, founded Holmcultram in 1150. Monks from Melrose in Scotland formed the first community. The Scottish connections are explained by the fact that the Solway was under the rule of Scotland from 1130 to 1157, and although England reconquered the territory, the abbey remained under Melrose's authority.

Holmcultram enjoyed considerable prosperity

under the long rule of its first abbot, Everard (1150-1192), and by 1175 had five dependent granges. It is not known when construction of the permanent buildings started, but judging from the remains on site, a date around 1160 is plausible. The lack of suitable stone nearby hampered work, for supplies had to be shipped in from some distance (Grainger and Collingwood, 124). But the abbey's property was confirmed by Pope Alexander III in 1175, by Richard I in 1189, and by Pope Clement III in 1190 (*Mon. Angl.* 5:599-600, 594, 600-601). In 1186 Christian, bishop of Withorn, was buried at Holmcultram (Grainger and Collingwood, 54, no. 141), meaning in the church if the order's statute relating to the burial of bishops was followed.

The Scots plundered the abbey in 1216, and shortly thereafter Alice de Romilly gave a quarry in nearby Aspatria to the monks for rebuilding. In 1322 the abbey was again ravaged by the Scots and the church desecrated, but no record of damage survives. By 1428 the abbey's buildings were in disrepair; in that year the pope granted indulgences to those who would contribute to their restoration (ibid., 149). Fifty years later, at the election of a new abbot supervised by the abbot of Melrose, injunctions were issued ordering the rebuilding of the infirmary. It was also ordered that new locks for the inner doors of the monastery should be supplied in order to keep out unwelcome visitors (ibid., 150). According to an inscription in the west porch, Abbot Chambers was responsible for its construction in 1507 and built much else at the abbey.

The monastery was dissolved in 1538, and the following year the villagers petitioned Thomas Cromwell to allow them to continue to use the church. The petition was allowed, and the entire church remained in use until 1590 when part of the tower and steeple (114 feet in height) collapsed, destroying with it much of the presbytery. Four years later the reconstructed tower and presbytery burned, the record mentioning that the fire spared only the south side of "ye low church [i.e., the nave], which was saved by means of a stone vault" (ibid., 179). The extensive history of repairs is detailed by Grainger and Collingwood (178-86). In 1703 Bishop Nicholson reported in a letter that

nine bays of the nave were standing, though the church was in a "shamefully neglected state"; moreover, fifteen or sixteen years previously the lead from the south aisle had been taken to cover the north aisle. Stephens' three etchings for the 1723 edition of the *Monasticon* show the church's west bays intact with the clerestory and aisles. But radical alterations were undertaken between then and 1739 when Buck shows the building more or less in its present state (*Antiquities* 2, no. 1). During this period the three east bays of the nave were demolished, both aisles dismantled, and the six west arches blocked. The truncated parts of the church still serve as the parish church of Holmcultram or Abbey Town.

A restoration was carried out in 1885. Excavations were undertaken by Ferguson in 1872, by Hodgson in 1906, and by Martindale in 1913. Parts of the latter two excavations are still visible, although much overgrown.

The present aisleless rectangular space (plate 60) requires some reconstruction on paper. The roof (of pre-Dissolution timbers, according to Martindale) rests on the rebuilt base of the former middle story. At the same time, the cleresteresery was eliminated; light now enters via windows in the wall of the blocked arcade.

The plan drawn by Martindale shows a typical early Cistercian form except for a deeper than usual presbytery (ninety-six feet long). That the presbytery was in fact lengthened in the thirteenth century is suggested by the excavation of part of a buttress from that date at the east end of the building. Despite the clearances, the changes to the crossing have not been sorted out, though three at least are known from the medieval period (Martindale, 245), some doubtless due to the size of the tower and steeple. The transepts each had three chapels, and there were nine bays in the nave. The overall size of the building was an impressive 279 feet from east to west and 135 feet across the transepts, dimensions that exceed those of Carlisle Cathedral seventeen miles away.

For the nave, see chapter 4 of this study, p. 62.

C. J. Ferguson, "St. Mary's Abbey, Holme Cultram," *Trans. CWAAS* 1 (1874): 263-75.

G. E. Gilbanks, *Some Records of a Cistercian Abbey: Holmcultram, Cumberland* (London, 1900).

T. H. Hodgson, "Excavations at Holmcultram," *Trans. CWAAS*, new ser., 7 (1907): 262-68.

VCH: Cumberland 2 (London, 1911): 162-73.

J. H. Martindale, "The Abbey of St. Mary, Holme Cultram," *Trans. CWAAS*, new ser., 13 (1913): 244-51.

F. Grainger and W. C. Collingwood, "The Register and Records of Holmcultram," *Cumberland and Westmorland Antiquarian and Archaeological Record Series* 7 (1929).

Sir Nikolaus Pevsner, *BoE: Cumberland and Westmorland* (London, 1967), 57-58.

JERVAULX (Yorkshire)

Jervaulx was first established at Fors in 1144 by Akarius Fitz Bardolph, who gave land to the monks of the Congregation of Savigny who were then in the neighborhood. According to the Byland *Chronicle*, which records the history of its one-time dependency, this gift was confirmed by Akarius' overlord, Alan, earl of Brittany and Richmond, who granted the monks wood from his forest and asked to be informed when the first buildings were to be erected so that he might be present. This took place the next year, and the earl proposed to help in the raising of the church with his own hands, though others in his party who had come to record the official confirmation of gifts were less willing to assist (*Mon. Angl.* 5:570, no. 2). In this way the first wooden church (*primum domum ligneum*) was built.

Why the new foundation failed to obtain recognition as part of the Congregation of Savigny is far from clear. Concern was voiced over the self-sufficiency of the abbey's economy, though a truer reason may have had to do with doubts over the leadership of the first community. In the event, direction of the community's affairs was assigned to Byland, then also Savigniac. The union of the two orders took place in 1148, and the next year Jervaulx achieved independent status. One of the founding monks at Byland, John of Kinstan (1149-circa 1185/90), was sent as first abbot. In 1156 a move was made sixteen miles down the River Ure (originally Jore, hence Jorevale) to better land and a kinder climate. Fors became a dependent grange.

For the architecture, see chapter 5 of this study, p. 84.

Dissolved in 1537, the abbey passed into private hands. Dismantling of the buildings began soon after (see appendix A). By 1732 Mrs. Pendarves made reference in a letter to Swift to "jumbled Jervaux," a state that still prevailed in 1806 when the antiquary John Carter was there (appendix A). The next year, however, the owner, the earl of Ailsbury, began clearance. He uncovered the church and established the relationship of the standing walls to the claustral buildings. An excavation was carried out in 1905 by Hope and Brakspear.

W. H. St. John Hope and H. Brakspear, "Jervaulx Abbey," *YAJ* 21 (1911): 303-44.

VCH: Yorkshire 3 (London, 1913): 138-42.

H. Brakspear, "Jervaulx Abbey," *VCH: Yorkshire, North Riding* 1 (London, 1914): 280-83.

W. L. Christie, *Jervaulx Abbey* (Ripon, 1951).

Sir Nikolaus Pevsner, *BoE: Yorkshire, North Riding* (London, 1966), 203-205.

KINGSWOOD (Gloucestershire)

Kingswood was founded by Walter of Clare, earl of Gloucester, with monks from Tintern. The first settlement was made at Kingswood sometime between 1139 and 1141, but a few years later the community moved to Hazelton, only to return to Kingswood in 1147. Shortly thereafter a third move took place, this time to Tetbury. Finally, the monks returned once more to a new site at Kingswood in 1148 (Lindley, 116-19). These migrations are most plausibly explained by either shortages of water or the unsettled conditions of the Anarchy.

Little has come to light on the history of building at Kingswood. In 1241 the monastery was in debt on account of money borrowed for the bell (Perkins, 199). The next year a gift of ten marks was acknowledged "to the work of the church" (ibid., 201), and expenses were recorded for a new hospice. The abbey was hard hit by the Black Death in 1347, and with the community's numbers severely reduced, the church fell into disrepair; in 1364 and again in 1368 a papal indulgence was obtained for all who would contribute toward its upkeep (Lindley, 120).

The abbey was dissolved in 1538, and the site sold to one of the Dissolution commissioners who used the stone from the former buildings for a new country house at Oselworth.

There is no record of any excavation. The site of Kingswood I has been established as lying a mile or so to the south of the later, permanent foundation. No above-ground remains of either are visible, although the gatehouse built in the fifteenth century survives intact. A site plan was published by Lindley in 1954 (plate 20) and shows the cloister on the north side of the church.

V. R. Perkins, "Kingswood Abbey, near Wotton-under-Edge," *Proc. Clifton Antiquarian Club* 3 (1893-1896): 217-24.

V. R. Perkins, "Documents Relating to the Cistercian Monastery of St. Mary," *Trans. BGAS* 22 (1899): 179-256.

VCH: Gloucestershire 2 (London, 1907): 99-101.

E. S. Lindley, "Kingswood Abbey, Its Lands and Mills," *Trans. BGAS* 73 (1954): 115-91; 74 (1955): 36-59; 75 (1956): 73-104.

D. Verey, *BoE: Gloucestershire* 2 (London, 1970).

KIRKSTALL (Yorkshire)

The first settlement of Kirkstall abbey was made at Barnoldswick under the patronage of William of Poitou and Henry de Lacy. Fountains supplied the monks. The site proved to be unprotected and subject to flooding, however, and in 1152 the move to Kirkstall took place (see chapter 1 of this study, pp. 8-9.

For the history and architecture, see chapter 3 of this study, pp. 48-51.

The monastery was dissolved in 1539, and the site passed into private hands. Despite a succession of owners, many of the buildings remained relatively untouched as late as 1723, as may be seen in Buck's engraving of that date (*Antiquities* 1, sec. 1, plate 10). An excavation in 1713 is mentioned in which the remains of a "tesselated pavement" were found (J. Nichols, *Examples of Decorated Tiles*

[London, 1845], vii). In 1779 the tower of the church collapsed in a gale, falling toward the northwest and destroying the first aisle bay on the south. In 1890 following the gift of the site to the Corporation of Leeds, Hope began excavations and Michelwaite the task of restoration. In the past twenty years a series of expert excavations have been carried out on the claustral buildings and guest houses.

W. Mulready, *An Historical, Antiquarian, and Picturesque Account of Kirkstall Abbey* (London, 1827).

J. W. Connon, *Kirkstall Abbey* (Leeds, 1866).

W. H. St. John Hope, *Report on the Preservation of the Ruins of Kirkstall Abbey* (Leeds, 1870).

E. K. Clark, "The Foundation of Kirkstall Abbey," *T. Soc.* 4 (1892-1895): 169-208.

J. R. Irvine, "Notes on Specimens of Interlacing Ornament at Kirkstall Abbey," *Jnl. BAA* 48 (1892): 26-30.

W. T. Lancaster and W. P. Baildon, eds., "The Coucher Book of the Cistercian Abbey of Kirkstall," *T. Soc.* 7 (1904).

W. H. St. John Hope, "Kirkstall Abbey," *T. Soc.* 16 (1907): 1-72.

J. Bilson, "The Architecture of Kirkstall Abbey Church," *T. Soc.* 16 (1907): 73-149.

VCH: Yorkshire 3 (London, 1913): 142-46.

J. Taylor, ed., "The Kirkstall Abbey Chronicles," *T. Soc.* 42 (1952): 1-133.

D. Owen, *Kirkstall Abbey* (Leeds, 1955).

D. E. Owen, ed., "Kirkstall Abbey Excavations 1950-1954," *T. Soc.* 43 (1955).

Sir Nikolaus Pevsner, *BoE: Yorkshire, West Riding* (London, 1959), 340-47.

C. M. Mitchell, ed., "Kirkstall Abbey Excavations, 1955-1959," *T. Soc.* 48 (1961).

E.J.E. Pierie et al., "Kirkstall Abbey Excavations, 1960-1964," *T. Soc.* 51 (1966): 1-66.

KIRKSTEAD (Lincolnshire)

Kirkstead was founded by Hugh Brito, lord of Tattershall, in 1139 following a visit to Fountains. Two years were spent raising the necessary temporary buildings before the monastery received a regularly organized community (*Chron. LP*, xxii). Then Fountains supplied the monks and sent as abbot Robert de Siwella, one of its own founding monks.

According to the Meaux *Chronicle*, the monastery was set out and constructed by Adam (*Chron. M.* 1:76), who is credited with the same role at Woburn and Vaudey and was also involved in building at Meaux where he was abbot from 1150 to 1160. Postulants joined Kirkstead in large numbers, and the original site proved insufficient for expansion, so in 1187 permission was granted by Hugh's son Robert for the monastery to move a short distance to its present location (*Mon. Angl.* 5:418-19). The date suggests a firm *terminus ante quem* for the start of work, but the situation is unclear. The physical evidence of the remains dates to about 1175 at the latest, and this suggests that the 1187 permission, along with the other confirmations made then, recognized the existence of the new abbey.

For the architecture, see chapter 4 of the present study, p. 66.

The monastery was dissolved in 1537 after the abbot and monks had been arrested for their part in the Louth uprising. In the same year agents were directed that the leads be "plucked down and melted," but were ordered to "deface nothing else" (*L. and P. Henry VIII, 1537* 1:297, no. 676). The subsequent history of the site is obscure. An etching by William Stuckley in 1716 (plate 72, this study) shows only the south wall and parts of the west and east walls of the south transept still standing. Most of this has since disappeared, except for the southeast angle (plate 71). The site has recently come into the ownership of the University of Nottingham.

S. Hartshorne, "On Kirkstead Abbey, Lincolnshire," *Arch. Jnl.* 40 (1883): 296-302.
VCH: Lincolnshire 2 (London, 1906): 135-38.
Sir Nikolaus Pevsner and J. Harris, *BoE: Lincolnshire* (London 1964), 287-88.

LOUTH PARK (Lincolnshire)

Louth Park was founded by Bishop Alexander of Lincoln in 1137 and first settled at Haverholm, near Sleaford. The first site was marshy, however, which made the growing of grain difficult, and two years later the community moved thirty-two miles northeast to a new site on the bishop's estates at Louth Park. The monks came from Fountains, and the first abbot, Gervase, had been one of its founding monks.

The community expanded rapidly and within a decade numbered more than one hundred men (Talbot, 37). Despite this, construction on the church was slow, and work fell into two widely separated programs. In the first, from about 1150 to 1165, the monks' church was raised, including two or three bays of the nave. Almost a century passed before the west parts of the building, those used by the lay brothers, were finished. This suggests the continued use by the lay brothers of either the early timber church or of an intermediate stone structure of which records are lost. The church was completed by Abbot Roger Dunham (1227-1246), who, in the words of the *Chronicle*, "deinde medietatem corporis ecclesie versus occidentem, sicut ex fabricatione meremii perpendi potest, magnis sumptibus et laboribus decenter complevit" (*Chron. LP*, 13).

The exact date of the completion of work on the church is lost. There is an implication, however, that it was not the first priority, since the *Chronicle* says that Dunham started by building the infirmary, a chamber for the seriously ill, and a kitchen. Later, he raised the lay brothers' cloister from the foundations, the monks' dormitory, the warming room, chapter house, and cloister, completing all we are told at much trouble and fatigue (ibid., 13). That Dunham had the resources for such extensive work was in large part due to the wealth of a prominent churchman, William of Tournay, dean of Lincoln, who had joined the abbey as a monk in 1239 following a bitter disagreement with the formidable Bishop Grosseteste of Lincoln. Such was William's position that Abbot Dunham constructed a special chamber for him (ibid., 16). When William died in 1258, he was buried in the lady chapel that he had caused to be built and dedicated. Other instances of William's generosity are recorded in the *Chronicle*; he enriched the abbey's domestic offices with necessary untensils, its sideboards with costly vessels, and its library with books (ibid., 16-17). In addition, he built the gatehouse chapel, the porter's lodge adjoining the gate, and the carpenter's shop. During Dunham's rule the community's numbers were listed as sixty-six monks and 150 lay brothers (ibid., 15).

In 1255 an altar was consecrated to Saint Hugh; then in 1260 three additional altars were consecrated to Saints Leonard, Bernard, and Katherine (ibid., 17). In 1283 a major bell was made for the church, and six years later a minor one (ibid., 20). In 1306 another small bell was made, and a new picture was placed on the altar (*tabula nova*) (ibid., 20). Three years later new work was done about the high altar, and it was painted by Master Everard; additional pictures were painted at the altars of Saint Mary Magdalene and Saint Stephen by Brothers John of Brantingham and R. of Welton (ibid., 20). In 1310 a new ceiling was made for the belfry; then five years later new choir stalls were completed (ibid., 21, 25-26). From a *compotus* roll (dated only from the fifteenth century) we learn the wages for two plumbers who were at work on the bell tower, the west part of the church, and the north aisle soldering holes and cracks in the lead roof. Other repairs are listed for the claustral buildings (ibid., appendix 31, 70-74).

The monastery was dissolved in 1536.

Buck's engraving of Louth Park in 1726 shows indecipherable walls above ground with robbed window openings (*Antiquities* 1, sec. 2, plate 16). In 1873 the owner, William Allison, made "extensive excavations" (Trollope, 22), but it is clear that large portions of the church were not exposed (Hope, lii). Although new attempts at clearance around the crossing were made in 1966, vandalism from the nearby Council estate forced their abandonment.

Some fragments of the church protrude through the sizable mounds in the present meadow. Only the general outlines of the plan are firmly established, however. It was a large building, measuring 256 feet from east to west, 116 feet across the transepts—just a few feet shorter than Fountains. The plan (see ibid., lvi) is the typical early Cistercian one, with a square-ended presbytery, three chapels in each transept separated by unbroken walls, and an aisled nave of ten bays.

The presbytery measures three feet less in width than the nave, a feature that is also found at Kirkstall. Its flanking walls were more than six feet thick, suggesting a vault of some kind. The northeast crossing pier, exposed in 1966, shows an enlargement, perhaps dating from the late thirteenth or early fourteenth century. The earlier form (in a different masonry) and the expansion in plan when the nave was reached imply that a crossing tower was not built at first. The three transept chapels had different widths. Together, then, the evidence of the east end points to changes in the first program.

According to Trollope, the ten-bay nave was supported on at least two types of piers. One of these, of which remains survive in a neighboring garden, was round in section with four attached shafts bonded in with the pier; it supported a scalloped capital. The other was compound, although confusingly, Hope shows all the piers thus in his plan. The round pier was similar to those in the day room at Rievaulx of *circa* 1150, but the shafts there were detached. The aisles were rib vaulted, the vaults being received on the outer wall by responds with scalloped capitals (Trollope, plate 2, fig. 4).

The *Chronicle*'s reference to "timber work" in Abbot Dunham's new program suggests that the nave was not vaulted, though the aisles were, to judge by the bay articulation on both the inner and outer wall surfaces. Unfortunately, the location of the rib profiles drawn by Trollope is not specified, but they suggest a date between about 1150 and 1165 (along with other architectural detailing still scattered on the site), with the closest analogies being to work at Kirkstall. The west door, of which the lower parts emerged in Trollope's clearance, dates from the thirteenth century.

E. Trollope, "The Architectural Remains of Louth Park," *AASRP* 12 (1873): 22-25.

E. Venables, "Louth Park Abbey," *AASRP* 12 (1873): 41-55.

E. Venables, ed., "Chronicon Abbatie de Parco Lude," *Lincolnshire Record Society* 1 (1891): i-xlviii, 1-85.

W. H. St. John Hope, "Notes on the Architectural History and Arrangements of Louth Park Abbey," *Lincolnshire Record Society* 1 (1891): xlix-lx.

VCH: Lincolnshire 2 (London, 1906): 138-41.

C. H. Talbot, "The Testament of Gervase of Louth Park," *ASOC* 7 (1951): 32-45.

Sir Nikolaus Pevsner and J. Harris, *BoE: Lincolnshire* (London, 1964), 303.

A.E.B. Owen, "An Early Version of the Louth Park Chronicle," *CCC* 30 (1979): 272-75.

MEAUX (Yorkshire)

William "le Gros", count of Aumale and earl of York, established Meaux in the last days of 1150 with monks from Fountains (see chapter 1 of this study, p. 19). It was the first monastic foundation in Holderness.

A wealth of information on the buildings of the abbey is contained in the Meaux *Chronicle*. Written by the nineteenth abbot, Thomas Burton (1396-1399), after his resignation, it combines accounts of the buildings raised by each abbot with a mass of unrelated *desiderata*. Taken together, the history of the buildings at Meaux provides a unique record spanning 250 years of the architectural development at a sizable Cistercian monastery.

As soon as the charters of foundation had been completed, the *Chronicle* tells us, the founder, Count William, began work to provide temporary quarters for the community: "he had a certain great house (*magnam domum*) built with common mud and wattle (*ex vili cemate*), where the mill is now established, in which the arriving lay brothers would dwell until better arrangements were made for them. He also built a certain chapel next to the aforementioned house, which is now called the cellarer's chamber, where all the monks used the lower story as a dormitory and the upper to perform the divine office devoutly" (*Chron. M.* 1:82). At some time in the next few years these buildings were deemed too small by the first abbot, Adam (1150-1160), a monk from Fountains who had previously worked on the construction of new monasteries at Vaudey and Woburn (ibid., 1:76, 105). Adam constructed new and larger buildings (*officinae*) with timber provided by the count from the castle of William Fossard at Montferant, in Birdsall, which he had leveled following Fossard's flight on discovery that he had seduced the count's daughter (ibid., 1:105).

A rapid increase in the monks' numbers—they had risen from thirteen to forty by 1160—was the reason for replacing the building in which, as the *Chronicle* puts it, they had both chanted and slept (*psallerent et pausarent*) (ibid., 1:107). The larger wooden building was another two-story structure, like the earlier one, with a dormitory below and oratory above (ibid., 1:107). Subsequently this building became the brew house.

Despite this promising start, by 1160 economic conditions at Meaux had deteriorated, so seriously, in fact, that the community had to be dispersed, and Abbot Adam resigned his office to join the Gilbertines at Watton. Exactly what caused this breakdown is unknown, but Adam was probably part of the problem, as is suggested by the appearance of a new abbot, Philip (1160-1182), when the community was reconstituted later in 1160. Work on permanent stone buildings now began; quarries were acquired at Brough and Brantingham, and out of these, the *Chronicle* states, the monastery was built (ibid., 1:171). The buildings included a stone church, the monks' dormitory, and the lavatories; the latter two buildings Philip lived to see finished (ibid., 1:178). The death of the founding abbot, Adam, is recorded in 1180; he had rejoined the Meaux monks in 1167 and was buried in the chapter house "near to the north column next to the lectern" (ibid., 1:107), a reference that suggests a vaulted interior supported on four columns. The chapter house was part of Abbot Philip's dormitory complex. At Philip's death two years later the community once again numbered forty monks.

Under Abbot Thomas (1182-1197) gifts of a new quarry at Hessle and additional quarries at Brantingham are recorded (ibid., 1:228). Surprisingly, though, the work on the church, then some ten to twenty years in building, was found unsuitable, and Thomas "began a new church and tore down whatever had been constructed in it, because it had been arranged and constructed less appropriately than was proper" (siquidem idem abbas incepit novam ecclesiam, et quicquid autea in ea constructum fuerat prostravit, quia minus congrueter quam deceret disposita erat et constructa) (ibid., 1:234). The monks also received during the fifteen years of Thomas' office a gift from William of Rule, rector of Cottingham, to build a stone refectory, and to this Abbot Thomas was able to add on either side a warming room and kitchen "bit by bit" as funds allowed (ibid., 1:217). Thomas also laid the foundations of the refectory for the lay brothers, repaired houses in the monastery and its granges, and built new ones.

For reasons unspecified Abbot Thomas resigned in 1197. His death is recorded in 1202, and he was buried "close to the south pier of the chapter house," near his two predecessors (ibid., 1:234). Thomas was succeeded by Abbot Alexander (1197-1210), who completed the refectory for the lay brothers and began their dormitory over it, constructed the monks' cloister in stone (an earlier one in wood can be assumed), rebuilt the lavatories, and completed other workshops in the abbey at great expense (ibid., 1:326). Such undertakings are easy to account for in the regular sequence of growth of a monastery, but we then read that in his tenth year Alexander turned his attention to the church and "swept away to the ground his predecessor's work and laid with his own hands on Palm Sunday 1207 the first stone of the new church which was subsequently finished to his design" (et, cum fabricam omnem quam praedessores sui fecerant ecclesiam nostram construendo penitus avulsisset, in anno Domini 1207, dominica in ramis palmarum, quae tunc fuit 17 Kalendas Maii, ad ipso abbate Alexandro positus fuit primus lapis in fundamento ecclesiae novae, et sic ecclesiam qualis modo cernitur inchoavit) (ibid., 1:326; also cf. 1:234). The *Chronicle* records additionally that he built widely at the abbey's granges and was a great collector of books (ac librorum fuerat maximus perquisitor) (ibid., 1:326). After his resignation Alexander retired to Forde, a foundation noted for its tradition of learning.

Under Abbot Hugh (1210-1220) the lay brothers' dormitory was finished, as was the monks' cloister (ibid., 1:380). Toward the end of his rule some parts of the church appear to have been brought into use; gifts for candles for private Masses are mentioned as well as others *ad fabricam ecclesiae* (ibid., 1:361).

During the rule of Abbot Richard (1221-1235) work began on the infirmary for the monks (ibid., 1:421, 433) but made small progress because of the work on the church. Richard also began the

wells and conduits to the abbey. Additional parts of the church were probably finished; further gifts for candles are recorded and others of wine for Mass (ibid., 1:419, 417, 416). But completion of the church was credited to the next abbot, Michael (1235-1240): "and in the time of this abbot our church was completed and covered with lead (ecclesia nostra consummata est et plumbo cooperta); the stalls of the monks and the all the altars were fittingly set up" (ibid., 2:64). Michael also had the buildings for the smiths and tanners removed from North Grange to within the abbey precinct and built at Waghen a stone building with a lead roof for the manufacture of woolen cloth for the community and also for gifts to the poor and pilgrims (ibid., 2:63). His interest in the granges included "the pens of the animals and other buildings necessary for various uses, {which} were built of oak that would not rot."

Under the ninth abbot, William of Driffield (1249-1269), a belfry was built and covered with lead, and the great bell called "Benedict" hung in it. Whether the structure was free-standing or raised over the crossing is not clear. The lay brothers' stalls were constructed in the west part of the church, and the *Chronicle* continues by recording that the "entire church was covered with a vault made of planks {or boards}" (totaque ecclesia asserum testudine caelata) (ibid., 2:119), and the floor was paved with tiles. This suggests therefore that the building completed under Abbot Michael was timber-roofed and that Abbot William inserted the wooden vault under it.

A second reference to the vault occurs a hundred years later when the roof of the church was set on fire by lightning. It was struck on the north side, and the wooden beams caught fire. Fortunately, the flames were spotted by the convent tailor, who woke a monk who was sleeping out of the dormitory; together by violent poundings on the door of the dormitory they managed to rouse the monks. Climbing to the roof, the monks extinguished the flames, a feat ascribed to miraculous powers, "for how else could they have safely passed over a ceiling (*super tenuem caelaturam*) scarcely able to support a boy of seven" (ibid., 3:166), carrying great brazen vessels of water.

Abbot William also built the great granary and covered it with lead and built the *infinitorium* for the lay brothers, as well as their stalls in the church (ibid., 2:119). With the last, the church was completed; it was consecrated in 1253 by Gilbert, bishop of Withorn (Bond, 1:xxxvii, n. 1). Abbot William died in 1269 and was buried in the chapter house near his predecessors "beneath a tomb in front of the pulpit" (*Chron. M.* 2:119).

The next addition to the buildings occurred under the thirteenth abbot, Roger (1286-1310), when the dean of York, Robert of Scarborough, built a great chamber (*magnam cameram*) near the cemetery on the east side. Shortly before Abbot Roger resigned, he constructed for his own special use a set of chambers on the east side of the monks' infirmary between that and their dormitory; the abbots subsequently lived in these (ibid., 3:86-87). By then, however, Meaux had fallen into debt to the Franciscan friars at Scarborough in the sum of seventy-eight marks. To settle it, the monks were forced to strip the lead from the lay brothers' dormitory, which the friars then used to cover their own church.

Under the fourteenth abbot, Adam (1310-1339), a large painted altarpiece was commissioned from Brother John of Ulram with "apparatum historiae evangelicae prophetarum et apostolorum . . . cum decenti pictura (ibid., 2:312). Shortly before his death Adam began work on a chapel over the great entrance to the abbey, but it was never carried far, and his successor, Abbot Hugh (1339-1340) dropped the project and used the stone prepared for it to construct a great brewing vat (ibid., 3:36). Hugh also covered the monks' dormitory with lead and placed a new crucifix in the lay brothers' choir. The crucifix was carved by a sculptor (*operarius*) who worked on Fridays only, fasting on bread and water; "furthermore he had a naked man standing before him to look at, in order that he might copy his shapely form and carve the crucifix all the more skillfully" (ibid., 3:35).

Abbot William Dringhow (1367-1372) repaired the damage that the church sustained in the fire referred to above and provided two sets of vestments for the high altar, one of blue velvet with gold stars, the other of green and red diaper shot with gold (ibid., 3:167).

The eighteenth abbot, William of Scarborough (1372-1396), busied himself actively with building and artistic projects—so much so, in fact, that it takes nearly five full pages of the *Chronicle* to list

them (3:222-27). In the church he decorated the altar of Saint Benedict with enamel work, tablets, and paintings, and that of Saint Peter, likewise with tablets and paintings (ibid., 3:223). Other altars he provided with plate and vestments, and he caused silver gilt pastoral staves to be made. He also had cast the great bell called "Jesus." For the chapter house he had carved three marble slabs inlaid with brass images for the tombs of his immediate predecessors; a fourth slab, apparently his own memorial, was made but lost in the water in transit and could not be recovered (ibid., 3:223). For the monks he installed benches and bedsteads in their dormitory, added backs to their seats in the refectory, furnished the house for severely ill monks with bedsteads and separate seats, and provided their infirmary with separate rooms. Various other conventual buildings were roofed with lead. Some buildings were demolished, as redundant presumably: the chamber of the old guest house, the chamber of the chaplain who served the chapel in the wood, the kitchen of the lay brothers' infirmary. Abbot William also built widely at the abbey's various granges.

Finally, Thomas Burton himself, the nineteenth abbot (1396-1399) and the author of the *Chronicle*, repaired the cloister leading from the monks' infirmary to the lay brothers' dormitory near the church and had cast three bells named "Mary," "John," and "Benedict" to add to the belfry. Other work suggests a need for tightened security: the repair of the walls surrounding the monastery, the erection of big gates on the west side of the cloister and on the east side of the monks' infirmary, the removal within the monastery gates of the smithy and other offices. Burton also erected a horse-mill but used poorly seasoned wood, which led to the building's ruin (ibid., 3:240-41).

After the busy record of building contained in the *Chronicle*, the subsequent history of Meaux in its last century and a half is strangely blank. Dissolution took place in 1539, and three years later the buildings were demolished to provide stone for fortification at Hull. The site has been privately owned since then.

Nothing visible remains of the abbey, and only mounds in the grass mark its site (plate 140). No report of any excavation has been published, but parts of the church have been investigated by the present owner, G. K. Beaulah, who has kindly provided the following information. The thirteenth-century church measured 260 feet from east to west and 130 feet across the transepts. The east end was similar in form to the one at Byland, with a three-bay presbytery east of the crossing, a surrounding ambulatory, and five east chapels. The transepts each had two chapels, and the nave was nine bays long with aisles. Some fragments of the nave piers were uncovered; they were eight-shafted fasciculated piers with four semicircular principals and four keeled minor shafts. This was the form used at Byland and Jervaulx in the late 1170s and 1180s. Ramm and Butler's recent survey of the site was able to distinguish the church, claustral buildings, gatehouse and other buildings within an outer court to the west (*YAJ* 70:185).

E. A. Bond, ed., *Chronica monasterii de Melsa, Rolls Series*, 3 vols. (London, 1866).

J. C. Cox, "The Annales of the Abbey of Meaux," *Trans. ERAS* 1 (1893): 1-45.

VCH: Yorkshire 3 (London, 1913): 146-49.

G. K. Beaulah, "Paving Tiles from Meaux Abbey," *Trans. ERAS* 26 (1929): 116-36.

Sir Nikolaus Pevsner, *BoE: Yorkshire—York and the East Riding* (London, 1972), 312.

H. G. Ramm and R. M. Butler, *YAJ* 70 (1980): 185.

MEREVALE (Warwickshire)

Robert, earl of Ferrers, founded Merevale on a site in rolling countryside in 1148. The mother house was Bordesley in Worcestershire.

Little is known about the history of building at Merevale. A general confirmation of the abbey's possessions was obtained from Henry II at an unspecified date but before 1170 (*Mon. Angl.* 5:482). Shortly before 1344 fire damaged the monastery, and Pope Clement IV added income to the abbey for compensation (*Cal. Papal Letters* 2:141). In 1401 a papal indulgence was issued for all contributing to the repair of the abbey church during the next ten years (ibid., 5:443). At the Dissolution an inventory records among the objects in the church a number of painted windows, six old altars with images, and four bells (*Mon. Angl.* 5:484-85).

The community was disbanded in 1538, and the site passed into private hands. At present it is a farm.

In 1665 Dugdale reported that the owner, Sir William Devreux, had "patcht up some part of the ruins here" (Dugdale, 782-83). Nothing more is known until 1849 when a clearance of the church was started; Bloxam published the results of this fifteen years later along with a conjectural plan (facing p. 324). The church is shown measuring 230 feet from east to west and eighty-eight feet across the transept. The presbytery (forty feet by twenty-eight feet) was aisleless, and the transept chapels were separated by solid walls. Bloxam suggested that the church was entirely rebuilt in the fourteenth century (ibid., 329). In recent years new barns have been built at right angles to the former church. No excavations were carried out.

Two parts of the abbey buildings can still be recognized incorporated into the farm's older barns. The first is a twenty-foot portion of the south aisle wall at its west end, which is made of well-cut ashlar and is plain and without articulation. The other is the south range of the cloister and includes much of the north and south walls of the refectory, which ran parallel to the cloister walk (for the plan and details see *VCH: Warwickshire* 4:143). Two well-preserved doorways remain, one from the cloister into the refectory, and adjacent, the doorway into the kitchen (both erroneously identified by Pevsner as leading into the church). They are richly molded and date to the early thirteenth century.

W. Dugdale, *The Antiquities of Warwickshire* 1 (London, 1730): 782-83.

M. H. Bloxam, "Merevale Abbey," *AASRP* 7 (1863-1864): 324-33.

VCH: Warwickshire 2 (London, 1908): 75-78; 4 (London, 1947): 142-44.

Sir Nikolaus Pevsner and A. Wedgewood, *BoE: Warwickshire* (London, 1966), 351.

NEWMINSTER (Northumberland)

Newminster was founded by Ranulph de Merlay, lord of Morpeth, in 1138 following a visit to Fountains. The monks came from Fountains and were headed by Abbot Robert (1138-1159), who was later sanctified. Newminster was the first of Fountains' twelve affiliated abbeys.

The Scots destroyed the abbey in the year of its foundation, but probably only temporary wooden buildings were then in place. Ranulph was credited with building the monastery, and Abbot Robert with "setting out the building therein after our manner" (. . . et edificiis inibi, de more, dispositis) (*Mem. F.*, 58-59). The monastery grew rapidly; within nine years three dependent houses were established, indicating substantial patronage and a large influx of recruits. At some time after mid-century the founder, his wife, and son were buried in the *boriali parte domus capituli* (*Chart. N.*, 269-70).

In the thirteenth century numerous gifts of lights for the tomb of Saint Robert were recorded, including one from "Hugo cementarius" (ibid., 225, 229-38). In 1265 the monks were given a stone quarry at Blindwell for the repair and renovation of the abbey buildings (ibid., 5). In the early fourteenth century burials near the high altar were recorded for Robert de Umfraville, earl of Angus, for Ralph, lord Graystock, and for Margery, the lady of Ulgham (ibid., 304, 298). A gift of £20 is noted in 1416 *ad opus ecclesiae* (ibid., 302), and thirteen years later the *obit* of Roger of Thornton recorded that he had covered the nave with lead (ibid., 302). In 1436 another gift of £60 is mentioned *ad opus ecclesiae* (ibid., 303).

Newminster was dissolved in 1537, but the monks apparently resisted the commissioners, who effected entry only with the help of a mob from nearby Morpeth. Some dismantlement occurred at this time. John Leland visited in 1540 but only mentions that the abbey was "plesaunt with watar and very fayre wood about it" (5:63). Enough remained in the late sixteenth century for the first landowner's son, Henry Gray, to live at the abbey. Subsequently, however, the buldings served as a stone quarry for the surrounding neighborhood. In 1769 Wallis reported that only a fragment of a portal remained (Wallis, 2:312). But a watercolor dating from 1792 shows part of the nave arcade standing (illustrated Harbottle and Salway, 88). Forty years later this too had vanished.

At least a half dozen attempts at clearance are recorded between 1800 and the early 1960s, but no reports were published. Included as part of these clearances was the reerection in the 1920s of the cloister arcade and of fragments of tracery from a large perpendicular window that was probably part of the terminal wall of the north transept. Between 1961 and 1963 a fully documented excavation of parts of the site was undertaken by Harbottle and Salway.

Scattered fragments from the church survive above ground. Some ashlar courses from the west end are visible, as is one plinth with shaft fragments from the inner pier of the south transept that was reconstituted in the 1920 clearance. The plan shows a square-ended, aisleless presbytery of three bays' length, three chapels in each transept without separating walls, an enlarged crossing, and an aisled nave of nine bays with a galilee porch at the west. A further campaign of excavation in 1965 established that the longer than normal presbytery was original (*Med. Arch.* 10 [1966]: 18); probably it copied the presbytery at its mother house, Fountains, only without the lengthened inner chapels that accounted for the depth at the Yorkshire house. In size Newminster was slightly larger than Fountains.

Excavation of the northeast crossing pier revealed that the simple square plinth of the original was encased with later masonry. Since the plinth resembles those of the nave piers, as at Rievaulx (*circa* 1140), it is likely that the nave continued through the crossing and that no tower was built in the first church. By contrast, the reconstituted pier in the south transept, sits on an unusually high plinth, has a waterholding base, and is composed of eight fasciculated shafts separated into majors and minors with keeling of all the shafts. Similar piers are found in the nave at Roche (*circa* late 1170s); the transept chapels at Roche also lack dividing walls. A date of about 1180 for the transept pier at Newminster is consonant with the reerected cloister capitals (plate 45 of this study).

What is missing at Newminster is clear evidence of an earlier building. Ordinarily a stone church would have replaced the earliest wooden one within a few years after settlement, and particularly in a successful monastery. If a date of around 1150 is accepted for the nave and crossing, and of around 1180 for the transepts, the difference between the two is most likely explained by a substantial renovation of the transepts in the 1180s, perhaps as part of a modernization scheme similar to the one at Furness (see chapter 4 of this study, p. 60).

J. Wallis, *Natural History and Antiquities of Northumberland* 2 (London, 1769): 290-313.

J. Hodgson, *A History of Northumberland* 2, pt. 2 (Newcastle, 1832): 403-19.

J. T. Fowler, ed., *Chartularium abbathiae de novo monasterio, Surtees Society* 66 (Durham, 1876).

Sir Nikolaus Pevsner, *BoE: Northumberland* (London, 1957), 262-63.

B. Harbottle and P. Salway, "Excavations at Newminster Abbey, 1961-63," *Arch. Ael.*, 4th ser., 42 (1964): 95-171.

PIPEWELL (Northamptonshire)

Pipewell was founded by William Batevileyn in 1143 with monks from Newminster in Northumberland. William appears to have been in touch with the houses of both Garendon and Newminster about supplying monks to form the first community, and by mistake a colony was dispatched from both houses. They met on the site, and after long argument the monks from Garendon withdrew, allowing those from Newminster to remain (Brakspear, 300-301).

The church at Pipewell is first mentioned during the abbacy of Andrew de Boyewell (1298-1308), at which time the choir stalls were made for the monks (*VCH: Northamptonshire*, 118). Three years after Abbot Andrew's death a dedication is documented with many local lords and people present; it included the church, cloister, and chapter house (Brakspear, 301) and suggests sizable alteration of the twelfth-century buildings. These operations may have contributed to an unstable economy at Pipewell, for shortly after the dedication the abbey was reported seriously in debt—so much so that in 1323 the entire community had to be dispersed to neighboring houses while the abbey's affairs were righted. In 1412 a petition to the pope complained that the buildings had become dilapidated (*VCH: Northamptonshire*, 119).

The monastery was dissolved in 1538, and the site was granted to Sir William Parre; but before he could begin dismantlement, trespassers carried off parts of the buildings. To investigate the thefts, a commission was appointed in 1540. Its report provides an interesting picture of the condition of the monastery two years after the Dissolution and shows that most of the buildings survived, although without their roofs and windows. The church still stood, but the "floors of the steeple had been taken away by those who had come to clear off the lead for the king" (ibid., 120-21). The inventory also mentions four chapels and five altars in addition to the main altar. Subsequently, dismantling was thorough. A drawing dated 1720 shows only mounds where the buildings had been (Brakspear, facing 299).

A clearance was undertaken in 1908 by Markham and Brakspear, which revealed the plan of the church and the outlines of the monastery. The church was medium-sized, measuring 236 feet in length (see Brakspear, facing 312). From the form of the east end, it is likely that Abbot Boyewell extended the choir, most probably by sacrificing the inner chapels from the twelfth-century transepts (thereby reducing them from three to two) in order to create an ambulatory. He also strengthened the crossing, presumably for the tower mentioned above, and included a western aisle in the transept, the latter an unusual feature that follows Byland. The four-bay choir, however, was terminated at full height in a straight east wall on the model of Jervaulx.

VCH: Northamptonshire 2 (London, 1906): 116-21.

C. A. Markham and H. Brakspear, "Pipewell Abbey," *AASRP* 29 (1907-1908): 361.

H. Brakspear, "Pipewell Abbey," *AASRP* 30 (1909-1910): 299-313.

Sir Nikolaus Pevsner, *BoE: Northamptonshire* (London, 1961), 373.

QUARR (Isle of Wight, Hampshire)

Quarr was founded in 1132 by Baldwin de Redvers, lord of Wight, as part of the Congregation of Savigny. Along with the rest of the Savigniac houses, it became Cistercian in 1148.

For the work of construction, according to Sir

John Oglander writing in 1609, the founder "browght owt of ye Lowe Counterye one Johe le ffleminge, a good Free Mason, whome he imployed abowt ye mason woorke for ye bwyldinge of Quarr" (Long, 198). A consecration of the church by the bishop of Winchester, Henry of Blois, took place in 1150 (Stone, 1:33). The next year numbers were such that a new colony could be sent to found Stanley in Wiltshire. In 1155 the founder died and was buried on the north side of the sanctuary (Long, 198). Around 1200 William Maskerel gave the abbey one acre of wheat from his mill at Brook for the making of communion hosts (Hockey, 62). In 1278 a second abbey, Buckland in Devon, was established from Quarr. Then in 1292 permission was granted to the community to quarry stone at Binstead for the monastery. Frequent attacks on the house in the mid-fourteenth century led the abbot to obtain a license to fortify the buildings with a stone wall and towers in 1365 (*VCH: Hampshire*, 138). In 1502 John Bullock requested in his will that he be buried "before the statue of Our Lady beneath the Cross" (Hockey, 62).

The monastery was dissolved in 1536, and shortly thereafter the site was purchased by John Mills, who had apparently already been living there. Demolition of the church began at once, and in 1539 much of the stone was sold to build fortifications at East and West Cowes. Just how thorough demolition was is indicated in the memoirs of Sir John Oglander, who began a search for the foundations of the church in 1607. Corn was growing over the site and the workmen Oglander hired to dig found nothing (see appendix A).

In 1891 Stone and St. John Hope examined the above-ground remains and conducted some "very summary" excavations. The cloister lay to the north of the church due to the availability of water. Parts of the conversi's buildings survive and are in use as a barn to the adjacent farmhouse. At their south end they include fragments of the former west façade of the church.

Stone's plan shows a typical early Cistercian church, with three chapels in each transept separated by solid dividing walls. The chapels flanking the north and south sides of the presbytery are almost certainly later medieval additions raised to meet the need for additional altars without embarking on a full eastern extension.

W. H. Long, ed., *The Oglander Memoirs* (London, 1888).

P. G. Stone, *Architectural Antiquities of the Isle of Wight*, 2 vols. (London, 1891).

VCH: Hampshire 2 (London, 1903): 137-40.

S. C. Kaines-Smith, "Quarr Abbey," *VCH: Hampshire* 5 (London, 1912): 152-54.

F. W. Anderson and R. N. Quirk, "Notes on the Quarr Stone," *Med. Arch.* 8 (1964): 115-17.

Sir Nikolaus Pevsner and D. Lloyd, *BoE: Hampshire* (London, 1967), 760-61.

S. F. Hockey, *Quarr Abbey and its Lands, 1132-1631* (Edinburgh, 1970).

REVESBY (Lincolnshire)

William de Roumare, earl of Lincoln, founded Revesby in 1142 with monks from Rievaulx. The first abbot was Saint Ailred, who served for four years before being recalled to Rievaulx as abbot.

The abbey buildings were probably laid out and raised by a secular master mason at some time after mid-century; in a charter gifting land to the monastery made between about 1170 and 1198 one of the witnesses signs himself "magistro Willemo Novi Operis" (Owen, 232). In the early thirteenth century two further gifts came to the monks from Lucy, widow of Walter Faber of Kirkby, who first gave them meadow land, chiefly to decorate and strew their choir ("ad chorum ecclesiae suae aspergendum et decorandum") (Stanhope, 17, no. 69; and 19, no. 56), and later under either Henry III or Edward I, gave them sixteen pence annually to maintain one candle burning always before the altar of Saint Nicholas in the abbey church (ibid., no. 109, 28).

Just prior to the abbey's dissolution in 1538 the duke of Norfolk reported to Thomas Cromwell that the house was in "great ruin and decay" (*L. and P. Henry VIII* 13, pt. 1 [1209]). The site was granted to Charles Brandon, duke of Suffolk.

At present the only visible remains are contained in a small railed area in a large meadow. A notice claims they include the stone from the high altar and the grave of the founder, William de Roumare.

In 1869 Barker conducted a clearance of parts of the south transept and nave and of the chapter house and northeast angle of the cloister. These resulted in a schematic plan (Barker, 24). A more detailed version of this hangs in the tower of the nearby parish church. The nave is shown with seven bays and measured 126 feet from the crossing to the west end; it was thirty-four feet wide with aisles of fifteen feet. The arcade rested on octagonal bases. The transepts measured 126 feet from north to south. If Barker's conjecture is correct that the east end had a rectangular ambulatory and chapel scheme, it resembles the plan of Byland. He also reported that he found capitals (ibid., 22), though he does not describe or illustrate them. They may possibly be those immured in the west tower of the parish church built in the late nineteenth century using ashlar from the abbey; these are small trumpet scallop capitals with angle leaves.

T. Barker, "Recent Excavations on the Site of Revesby Abbey," *AASRP* 10 (1869): 22-25.

E. Stanhope, *Abstracts of the Deeds and Charters relating to Revesby Abbey, 1142-1539* (Horncastle, 1889).

VCH: Lincolnshire 2 (London, 1906), 141-43.

D. M. Owen, "Some Revesby Charters of the Soke of Bolingbroke," *Pipe Roll Society Publications*, new ser., 36 (1960): 221-34.

Sir Nikolaus Pevsner and J. Harris, *BoE: Lincolnshire* (London, 1964), 341-42.

RIEVAULX (Yorkshire)

For the foundation history and early architecture, see chapter 3 of this study, pp. 31-38.

Rievaulx was dissolved in 1538, and the site was granted to Thomas, earl of Richmond (see appendix A). Some buildings, including the twelfth-century church and the west claustral buildings, were subsequently mined for their stone. By 1721 when Buck engraved his plate of Rievaulx (*Antiquities* 1, sec. 1, plate 18), the standing portions appeared much as they do today. In 1758 the remains were incorporated into the spectacular landscape scheme of Duncombe Park. In 1804 the *Gentleman's Mag-azine* mentioned that a few years earlier two sides of the crossing tower had blown down (pt. 2, p. 614). A clearance took place in 1812 (Rye, 70), but no details are known. Then in 1821 the *Gentleman's Magazine* (pt. 1, p. 297) reported that an excavation in the twelfth-century church had led to the discovery of the nave piers. The site was gifted to the nation in 1918 and came under the care of what is now the Department of the Environment. Shortly thereafter it was cleared by Sir Charles Peers who published a brief guide. There has been no systematic examination or publication of the remains.

J. C. Atkinson, *Chartularium Rievallense, Surtees Society* 83 (1889).

C. H. Compton, "Rievaulx Abbey," *Jnl. BAA* 48 (1892): 15-25.

H. A. Rye, "Rievaulx Abbey, Its Canals and Building Stones," *Arch. Jnl.* 57 (1900): 69-77.

VCH: Yorkshire 3 (London, 1913): 149-53.

W. St. John Hope, "Rievaulx Abbey," *VCH: Yorkshire, North Riding* 1 (London, 1914): 494-99.

Sir Charles Peers, *Rievaulx Abbey* (London: Department of Environment, 1934).

J. Weatherill, "Rievaulx Abbey: The Stone Used in Its Building," *YAJ* 38 (1952-1955): 333-54.

Sir Nikolaus Pevsner, *BoE: Yorkshire, North Riding* (London, 1966), 299-303.

ROBERTSBRIDGE (Sussex)

Alured de St. Martin founded Robertsbridge in 1176, with the monks coming from Boxley in Kent, itself a direct foundation of Clairvaux. Occupation of an earlier site before the removal to nearby Robertsbridge is indicated by a charter of 1314 that mentions "the chapel in the said vill [Salehurst] on the spot where the abbey was originally founded" (*VCH: Sussex* 2:72). Remains of this first foundation have not yet been found.

A general confirmation was obtained from Richard I (undated) and another from the bishop of Chichester, Seffrid II, in 1204 (Perceval, 456-59). An undated late twelfth century deed from Hugo Lunsford records the gift to the monks of one acre of meadow at the dedication of the church (Cooper, 151).

The abbey was dissolved in 1539, and the site acquired by Sir William Sidney of Penshurst, who converted the buildings into an iron forge (Ward, 79). Probably the church was demolished at this time. The monastic buildings remained until the end of the eighteenth century, however, when the forge went bankrupt. A farm now covers the site, on the banks of the Rother close to the village of Salehurst. It is owned by the brewers, Messrs. Guinness.

Salzman investigated parts of the cloister, now the farmyard, but no excavation has been carried out. Nothing of the church is visible above ground. It stood north of the present-day abbey house, and aerial photographs show the plan as cruciform with a straight-ended, aisleless presbytery (D. Knowles and J.K.S. St. Joseph, *Monastic Sites from the Air* [Cambridge, 1952], 135). Some monastic buildings are shown in eighteenth-century sketches by Grimm (illustrated by Cooper), and much of the mid-thirteenth-century abbot's house, with a vaulted crypt, survives in the building still called by that name. In addition, fragments of the refectory (running east-west in the old Cistercian arrangement) can be identified. Some architectural details also remain in the former vicarage garden at Salehurst; they include a large, plain, scalloped capital, perhaps from a nave pier, and a base with angle spurs, almost certainly from the cloister arcade. Additional fragments of window tracery and rib moldings from the thirteenth and fourteenth centuries indicate later programs of building.

G. M. Cooper, "Notices of the Abbey of Roberts-bridge," *Sussex Archaeological Collections* 8 (1856): 140-76.

C. S. Perceval, "Charters and Other Documents relating to the Abbey of Robertsbridge," *Archaeologia* 45 (1880): 427-61.

VCH: Sussex 2 (London, 1907): 71-74; and 9 (London, 1937): 218-20.

J. L. Hodgson, *A History of Salehurst* (London, 1914).

L. F. Salzman, "Excavations at Robertsbridge Abbey," *Sussex Notes and Querries* 5 (1934-1935): 206-208.

J. L. Ward, "The Restoration of St. Mary's Church, Salehurst, and a Note on Robertsbridge Abbey," *Sussex Notes and Querries* 15 (1959): 77-83.

ROCHE (Yorkshire)

Two local lords, Richard de Buili and Richard Fitz Turgis, founded Roche in 1147. It was colonized by monks from Newminster. In the gift of the land the foundation charter specified that the monks were to hold the site "on condition that they may build an abbey on whatever side they wish according to the more suitable situation of the ground" (Purvis, 390).

For the architecture, see chapter 4 of this study, pp. 62-66.

Roche was dissolved in 1538. Its actual dismantlement was described in vivid detail in an account written in 1591 (see appendix A). Buck visited the site in 1725 and drew the ruins (*Antiquities* 1, sect. 1, plate 18); he shows them much as they are today, except that more of the south wall of the south transept remained intact. In 1776 Capability Brown landscaped the site as part of the earl of Scarborough's Sandbeck Manor and moved some of the "mounds" at the west end. In 1884 Fairbank mentions "recent excavations" (p. 41) and the next year records that the rest of the nave was cleared (pp. 392-93). The government took control of the site in 1921 and has cleared and consolidated the walls, but no systematic excavation has been undertaken.

J. Aveling, *The History of Roche Abbey from Its Foundation to Its Dissolution* (London, 1870).

S. O. Addy, *Charters of Roche Abbey* (Sheffield, 1878).

J. Stacye, "Roche Abbey," *AASRP* 17 (1883): 38-54.

F. R. Fairbank, "Roche Abbey, and the Cistercian Order," *AASRP* 18 (1884): 35-52.

F. R. Fairbank, "Roche Abbey: Further Report on the Excavations There," *AASRP* 19 (1885): 392-97.

J. Bilson, "Roche Abbey," *YAJ* 20 (1908-1909): 447-54.

VCH: Yorkshire 3 (London, 1913): 153-56.

J. S. Purvis, "Seventeenth-Century Copies of Early

Yorkshire Charters," *YAJ* 29 (1927-1929): 390-91.

T. W. Hall, ed., "Roche Abbey Charters," *Hunter Archaeological Society Transactions* 4 (1937): 226-48.

W. Reewe, *Historical Notices of Roche Abbey* (Skegness, 1939).

A. Hamilton Thompson, *Roche Abbey* (London: Department of the Environment, 1954).

Sir Nikolaus Pevsner, *BoE: Yorkshire, West Riding* (London, 1959), 414-17.

P. Fergusson, "Roche Abbey: The Source and Date of the Eastern Remains," *Jnl. BAA*, 3rd ser., 34 (1971): 30-42.

D. Parsons, "A Note on the East End of Roche Abbey Church," *Jnl. BAA*, 3rd ser., 37 (1974): 123.

RUFFORD (Nottinghamshire)

Rufford was established in 1146 under the patronage of Gilbert de Gaunt, earl of Lincoln, at a site that lay in the heart of Sherwood Forest. It was the fifth and last of the daughter houses of Rievaulx.

It is not known when work began on a permanent church and claustral buildings, but from documents it seems that construction was underway around 1160. Between 1166 and 1190 a gift of a mill was made to the abbey, the profits being specified for the stonework of the church (*Chart. Ruff.*, no. 411); and between 1176 and 1196 Alice, wife of James of Kelham, gave land, a palfry, a beast for the new building works, and a gold ring to guild a chalice (ibid., no. 375). In a further gift made between 1170 and 1199 Robert of Maskham gave a half mark's worth of rent with the expectation that the new work on the church would be finished shortly, the money thereafter to be used for lights in the church (et novo operi ecclesie de Ruford' ex post expletionem ecclesie lumini ecclesie) (ibid., no. 388). This picture of activity is complemented by the names of five masons (*cementarii*) who worked at the abbey in the twelfth century and who are known from witness lists: Radulfo between 1186 and 1204 (ibid., no. 117), Gileberto, late twelfth century (no. 779), Osmundo, *circa* 1180-1200 (no. 997), Hedwardo and Roberto,

late twelfth century (no. 826). A sixth mason, Johanne, is documented in the early thirteenth century (no. 22).

Work on the church continued into the thirteenth century. Between 1210 and 1260 a total of six gifts are recorded *ad opus ecclesie* (ibid., nos. 624, 931, 935, 995, 996, and 999). In 1233 Henry III granted the monks permission to enlarge the courts of their house by taking one acre of the king's wood (*CR: Henry III, 1231-1234*, 206). In about 1240 Robert of Lexington gave land and one hundred marks for the maintenance of three monks in the chapel beside the infirmary originally built by his father (*Chart. Ruff.*, no. 947).

Dissolved in 1536, Rufford passed into private hands. In the seventeenth century a large country house was built over the site, incorporating the lay brothers' frater and cellar into its walls; these are the only visible traces of the abbey and are fine examples of early claustral buildings. Excavation of parts of the church took place in the mid-1950s, and in 1981 the Department of the Environment was rebuilding the country house with its incorporated medieval remains.

The plan of the church at Rufford (Gilyard-Beer, 162) shows a characteristic early Cistercian form with the exception of the transept chapels, where there are three on the north and two on the south. This resulted from modifications made in the later Middle Ages, when instead of lengthening the presbytery eastward, the monks enlarged it by absorbing the inner chapel of the south transept. The choir and transepts have similar proportions to those at Roche, with the transepts at both Rufford and Roche being proportionally wider than those at Rievaulx or Fountains.

Gilyard-Beer has established that after the presbytery and transepts were built, it was decided to enlarge the church; the nave and aisles were moved some feet to the north and are out of alignment with the earlier work. The nave had seven bays; on the south side the first two piers were compound, but thereafter cylindrical piers were adopted. Since the north arcade is out of alignment with the south, Gilyard-Beer has hypothesized that the first wooden church stood within the nave, with the walls of the stone church going up as an envelope around it; this would have prevented an accurate sighting for the precise alignment of the south and north arcades.

VCH: Nottinghamshire 2 (London, 1910): 101-105.

R. Gilyard-Beer, "Rufford Abbey," *Med. Arch.* 9 (1965): 161-63.

C. J. Holdsworth, ed., *Rufford Charters, Thoroton Society Record Series* 29 (1972); 30 (1974); and 32 (1980).

Sir Nikolaus Pevsner, *BoE: Nottinghamshire*, 2nd ed. (London, 1979), 301-303.

SAWLEY (Yorkshire)

William de Percy, scion of the great northern family, founded the monastery in 1148. An abbot, twelve monks, and ten conversi from Newminster in Northumberland formed the first community, which settled a site on the east bank of the Ribble.

In the founding charter William says that he constructed the monastery, but since this occurred before he summoned the monks, it is clear that his work consisted of the earliest wooden buildings (*Chart. S.* 88:1-3). A confirmation of the abbey's possessions was obtained from Pope Alexander III in 1172 (ibid., 62-64). Late in the reign of Henry II (i.e., before 1189) a lay brother witnessed a deed, signing himself "Brother Waryn, Keeper of the Works of the Church of Sallay" (R. P. Littledale, ed., *Pudsay Deeds, Yorkshire Archaeological Society Record Series* 56, no. 44 [1916]: 122-23). Also late in Henry II's reign a "Hugh the Carpenter" seems to have been working at Sawley, since the abbey oversaw the legalities in connection with a grant of land to him (*Chart. S.* 88, no. 123); he was still associated with the abbey under Richard I (ibid., no. 127).

Sawley's financial condition was far from secure. In the late 1180s a report on the abbey by three senior visitors, the abbots of Clairvaux, Igny, and Mortemer, advised either the total destruction of the abbey or its removal to some more suitable site (*Chart. S.* 90, no. 615). In 1189 a convocation of senior abbots met to decide if this recommendation should be implemented. They identified the main problem as the climate, which made the growing of grain nearly impossible. As likely a reason may

have been the poor quality of the land originally granted the monks. Sawley was saved by the intervention of the founder's daughter, Maud; she provided income from a neighboring parish and donated better lands, in order, as the chronicler tactfully put it, "to prevent her father's charity being lost." Confirmations of the refoundation were obtained at once from Richard I and Pope Clement III (*Chart. S.* 90:138-39), and in the same year the monks received a gift of stone from a quarry at Heselwold (*Chart. S.* 88, no. 101). Around 1190 a gift of land is specified "ad opus ecclesie et edificiorum suorum" (ibid., no. 274), and two others identically worded came to the monks at some time during the reign of Richard I (nos. 117 and 288).

In 1206 a gift made in fulfillment of a vow made in peril of death provided the monks with candles for all Masses (ibid., no. 187). A land grant early in the reign of Henry III was witnessed by a "Hugo cementario" (no. 608); two others around 1225-1235 and 1235-1245, by "Robert cementario" (nos. 583 and 646); and another, by "Alanus carpentarius" (no. 384). "Richard the mason" also seems to have worked at Sawley in the early thirteenth century, as implied by a land grant (no. 661). Early in the reign of Edward I, the name Thomas, referred to both as "le macon" and "cementarius," occurs six times in witness lists (nos. 586, 588, 599, 649, 657, and 662). Toward the end of the thirteenth century the Scots burned some of the buildings at Sawley, but no detail of the losses survive. Shortly after, in 1299, the monks had the gift of a quarry confirmed to them (Harland, 76). In 1381 the community numbered seventy, counting both monks and lay brothers, a relatively large number, at least in comparison with Bordesley, a wealthier house, where a total of fifteen was counted.

Sawley was dissolved in 1536, at which time the list of monks included the name James Wadyngton, carpenter. The site was then sold into private hands. When Buck visited the abbey in 1721, considerably more of the claustral buildings remained, although the ruins of the church look little higher than they are now (*Antiquities* 1, sec. 1, plate 21). In the early nineteenth century the earl de Grey, who already owned Fountains, purchased the site; and in 1848 he began its clearance (*Gentleman's Magazine*, pt. 2 [1848], 196). Thirty years later a further clearance was undertaken (Walbran [1852-1853], 166). In 1934 the abbey was given to what is now the Department of the Environment. In 1939 McNulty reported that Fattorini had conducted excavations "with excellent results," but no report was published (McNulty, 204).

Although the present remains look particularly unattractive due to the eroded and irregular appearance of the black argillaceous shale used in most of the walls, considerable portions of the church and claustral buildings survive. The plan of the twelfth-century church (fig. 23) consisted of a two-and-one-half bay, aisleless presbytery, three chapels in each transept separated by unbroken walls, and a short, aisleless nave measuring just under forty feet. Clearly, the nave was temporary, as the much longer north wall of the cloister shows, and its completion was left until such time as finances permitted work to continue westward. In the fifteenth century the presbytery was extended by four bays, but without breaking through the inner chapels of the transepts to form continuous aisles.

The twelfth-century plan is of considerable interest. The transepts are identical in dimension to those at Fountains II, and like Fountains, Sawley also lacked aisles to the nave and had an unstressed crossing. Since both features were adopted at Fountains around 1153 and at Kirkstall around 1155 and thereafter became part of Cistercian architecture, their absence at Sawley suggests a date around 1150.

The presbytery had very thick (five and a half feet) flanking walls, like those at Kirkstall, probably to accommodate vaults. The transept openings were extremely plain, each framed by a projecting rectangular shaft with chamfered angles that terminated in scroll-like spurs (plate 32). The shaft must have continued up the face of the wall dividing the elevation into distinct bays in a manner resembling the French house of Ourscamp rather than English examples like Fountains or Rievaulx.

J. R. Walbran, "On the Recent Excavations at Sawley Abbey in Yorkshire," *AASRP* 2 (1852-1853): 72-89.

J. Harland, *Historical Account of the Cistercian Abbey of Salley* (Clitheroe, 1853).

J. R. Walbran, "On the Recent Excavations at Sawley, Yorkshire," *S. Soc.* 67 (1876): 159-77.

S. D. Kitson, "Salley Abbey," *YAJ* 20 (1909): 454-60.

VCH: Yorkshire 3 (London, 1913): 156-58.

J. McNulty, ed., *The Chartulary of the Cistercian Abbey of St. Mary of Sallay in Craven*, Yorkshire Archaeological Society Record Series 88 (1933); and 90 (1934).

J. McNulty, "Sallay Abbey 1148-1536," *Transactions of the Lancashire and Cheshire Antiquities Society* 54 (1939): 194-204.

Sir Nikolaus Pevsner, *BoE: Yorkshire, West Riding* (London, 1959), 430-31.

SAWTRY (Huntingdonshire)

Simon de St. Liz (or Senliz), earl of Northampton and later earl of Huntingdon, founded Sawtry in 1147, with monks from Warden forming the first community. Litigation over the original land grant resulted in its being reduced by half; apparently the earl had given the monks land that was not his. The abbey never became large or wealthy, and its landholdings remained small.

The founder was credited with erecting the monastery, although this probably means only the earliest wooden buildings. The next documentary mention come in 1238, when a dedication of the church by Robert Grosseteste, bishop of Lincoln, is recorded (Ladds, 371). Sawtry was dissolved in 1536, and among buildings mentioned at this time were the church, gate house, bell tower with four bells, and a stone house, possibly the parish church, at the gates (ibid., 308-18). At an inquiry held six years later, William Angell, who had been the last abbot, said that he had paid for the glazing of a new window at the west end of the church and had borrowed £20 for timber for building the church.

In the early nineteenth century it was reported that the foundations of the former buildings had been dug through to provide road building materials. Excavations were carried out around 1850, but no report was published (ibid., 342); excavations by Ladds from 1907 to 1912 provide much of what is known about the buildings.

Today only the earthworks surrounding the site

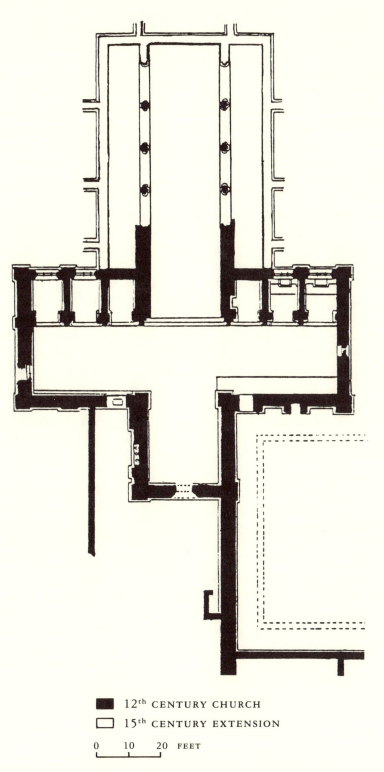

■ 12ᵗʰ CENTURY CHURCH

□ 15ᵗʰ CENTURY EXTENSION

0   10   20   FEET

23. Sawley, plan of church and later choir extension.

are visible. From the trenches left when the foundations were removed, a plan of the buildings has been worked out (*RCHM: Huntingdonshire*, 230). The church was typically early Cistercian in form, comprising a two-bay, aisleless presbytery, transepts, each with two chapels separated by unbroken walls, and an aisled nave of seven bays. It was relatively small, measuring 190 feet from east to west, ninety-eight feet across the transepts, and thirty-two feet across the presbytery. A record from the excavations describes the piers as round in section (Ladds, 346-47) but gives no other details.

Numerous fragments remain at nearby Manor and Grange Farms, in the garden of the Old Rectory at Sawtry, against the east wall of the Sawtry church, and in the gardens of a number of houses in the vicinity (ibid., 348-53).

S. I. Ladds, "Sawtry Abbey, Huntingdonshire," *Cambridge and Huntingdonshire Archaeological Society Transactions* 3 (1914): 295-322, 339-74.
VCH: Huntingdonshire 1 (London, 1926): 391-92; and 3 (London, 1936): 203-204.
RCHM: Huntingdonshire (London, 1926), 230.
Sir Nikolaus Pevsner, *BoE: Bedfordshire and the County of Huntingdon and Peterborough* (London, 1968), 342.

SIBTON (Suffolk)

William de Cayneto, hereditary sheriff of Norfolk and Suffolk, founded Sibton in 1150 with monks from Warden in Bedfordshire. With William's help Sibton accumulated extensive landholdings in East Suffolk and Norfolk and soon commanded sizable resources (Denney, 11).

Little is known from documents about the history of building at Sibton. But the names of two secular masons have survived, both of sufficient status and means to have been very likely in charge of work. The first, "Waltero le Mascun," occurs as a witness to a charter between 1160-1170; the second, "Randulfus cementarius," occurs around 1200 (Brown, 73 and 75). A mid-fourteenth-century *compotus* contains detailed accounts of routine building

repairs as well as the materials and cost of one new undertaking, the building of a new hall (*Nova Aula*) in 1368, complete with the names of the six masons employed and their wages (Denney, 29, 118ff.).

At the Dissolution, Sibton was listed among the larger houses; most unusually, the abbot and monks sold the monastery to the duke of Norfolk in 1536, though it was not due for suppression.

Notice of some finds at the site is made in 1806 (*Gentleman's Magazine* 99, pt 1, 17), but without providing helpful details of architecture. An excavation was carried out in 1892, but no report was published.

Of the church the only visible remains are of the south aisle wall, much overgrown (for a plan, see Hope, facing p. 56). There was no internal articulation. The nave measured 126 feet from east to west. Of much greater interest is the refectory, which ran parallel to south walk of the cloister (i.e., in the older Cistercian arrangement). It has scalloped and early foliate capitals with beading at the angle of the leaves, both motifs plausible around 1175. They support abaci of developed form and arch moldings with a keeled section.

W. H. St. John Hope, "Sibton Abbey," *Proceedings of the Suffolk Institute of Archaeology and Natural History* 8 (1894): 54-60.
VCH: Suffolk 2 (London, 1907): 88-89.
A. H. Denney, ed., "The Sibton Abbey Estates," *Suffolk Record Society* 2 (1960): 1-160.
R. A. Brown, "Early Charters of Sibton Abbey, Suffolk," *Pipe Roll Society Publications* 36 (1960): 65-76.
Sir Nikolaus Pevsner, *BoE: Suffolk*, 2nd ed. (London, 1974), 419-20.

STANLAW (Cheshire)

Stanlaw was founded in 1172 by John, constable of Chester, on an isolated site on the Mersey estuary close to the River Gowy. The monks came from Combermere. After occupying Stanlaw for 107 years, the main body of monks moved in 1279, according to the *Chronicle of St. Werburgh*, to Whalley in Lancashire, where they had been accumulating property for some time. Repeated flooding of the monastery and its granges was given as the reason. Stanlaw thus became a grange. But the move was not free from controversy; the abbot resigned and stayed at Stanlaw, and with him remained five of the monks. In 1287 the great tower of the church was blown down (Hulton, vii), and further calamities occurred in 1289 when fire destroyed the greater part of the abbey and the sea again inundated the site.

In an inventory at the Dissolution in 1536, there is a reference to buildings still standing at Stanlaw, and this was borne out when the site was visited by Buck in 1727; he shows some immured twelfth-century details in the standing buildings (*Antiquities* 1, sec. 3, plate 12). Ormerod mentions that a farm covered the site of the twelfth-century foundation but that built into its barns were four columns, some fragments of architectural detailing and two doorways (Ormerod, 400). The site is now covered by the giant Ellesmere Port oil refinery complex.

W. A. Hulton, ed., *The Coucher Book at Whalley*, *Chetham Society* 10 (1847).

M.E.C. Walcott, "Inventory of Stanlaw," *LCHS*, new ser., 12 (1871): 53-56.

G. Ormerod, *History of Chester* 2 (London, 1882): 398-404.

VCH: Lancashire 2 (London, 1908): 131.

Sir Nikolaus Pevsner and E. Hubbard, *BoE: Cheshire* (London, 1971), 337.

STANLEY (Wiltshire)

Henry II and his mother, Maud, established Stanley in 1151. Monks from Quarr (Isle of Wight) settled a first site at Loxwell, or Lockswell, but in 1154 they moved two miles northeast to Stanley.

Work on permanent buildings began shortly after settlement (Brakspear, 544), but the documents tell us nothing of their form. In 1212 a serious fire destroyed the twelfth-century church and probably many of the claustral buildings. Shortly thereafter, the monks obtained two quarries and rights to another, as well as help a little later from the bishop of Salisbury, Richard Poore (1217-1228). These resources were augmented by Henry III, who granted the abbey wood and stone for rebuilding (*VCH: Wiltshire* 3:274). Despite this, work seems to have proceeded slowly. In 1241 the monks exchanged quarries with Lacock Abbey, and three years later Henry III gave them money "in constructione fundamenti ecclesie de Stanl' ad operationem ejusdem ecclesie" (*CR: Henry III, 1242-1247*, 191). In 1246 the king gave the abbot oaks in the forest of Cippenham and Melkesham "ad stalla ecclesie sue facienda" (ibid., 461), and later in the same year, more oaks "ad fabricam ecclesie sue" (409).

In 1247 it was recorded that the monks entered the new monastery (Lehmann-Brockhaus, no. 4291). That this meant only the east parts of the church emerges from later documents, however. The bishop of London, Fulk Basset (1244-1259), issued indulgences to anyone contributing toward the completion of the building. Work finished in 1266 when the king donated a tun of wine to mark the dedication by the bishop of Salisbury, Walter Wyle (*CR: Henry III, 1264-1268*, 165).

In 1270 the new refectory was finished. In 1290 Edward I gave stone to build a chamber in the abbey for his own use (*CR: Edward I, 1279-1288*, 9), and two years later he licensed the monks to dig stone at the king's quarry in Pewsham Forest for building the abbey houses and a wall about them (*Cal. Pat., 1281-1292*, 484). In the fourteenth century new cloister alleys were raised, and mention was made of building in the church but without details (Brakspear, 494). Just prior to the Dissolution it was recorded that the abbey was "newe buylded."

In the late summer of 1536 while the abbey was being closed down, it was inspected by the county commissioners, who were moved to praise the buildings (*VCH: Wiltshire* 3:272). The site was sold to Sir Edward Baynton, who used the stone to construct his country house at Bromham. John Aubrey visited the site in 1665 and recorded: "here is now left scarce any vestigium of church or house" (Brakspear, 495).

Today the only visible remains are some architectural details that line the path at the back of

Brimhill Court (two miles southwest), some fragments preserved in the Trowbridge Museum, and a number of thirteenth-century tiles built into the newly constructed Catholic church of St. Edmund at Calne.

The information about the buildings at Stanley comes from an excavation undertaken in 1905 by Brakspear. This showed the cloister and domestic buildings lying to the north of the church. The excavations revealed that the church was entirely rebuilt in the thirteenth century, except for some courses of wall at the west end and in the north transept that date to the twelfth. The thirteenth-century plan shows a building of modest size (214 feet from east to west, 118 feet across the transepts), with a three-bay presbytery with flanking aisles, transepts with one chapel on the north and two on the south, and an aisled nave of eight bays. Except for the presbytery, the church seems to have been rebuilt over the foundations of the former church, and a number of features of this building can be recognized in the plan. The monastic buildings to the north prevented enlargement of the church on this side, so to provide room for an expanded presbytery while at the same time utilizing the old footings, the monks probably sacrificed the inner chapel of the north transept of the twelfth-century church to make the aisle for the presbytery. On the south side where nothing hindered expansion, two chapels could be built in addition to the aisle. It is likely, then, that the first church had two chapels in each transept, a square-ended, aisleless presbytery, and a nave of eight bays. It would thus have resembled Buildwas and Bindon.

All the architectural detailing found by Brakspear was thirteenth and fourteenth century in date. The one area of the monastery that was not rebuilt was the lay brothers' quarters, doubtless because they escaped the 1212 fire. This building was divided into two aisles with a row of columns down the center and was rib vaulted.

C. Eddrup, "Stanley Abbey," *WANHM* 24 (1889): 271-81.

H. Brakspear, "The Cistercian Abbey of Stanley, Wiltshire," *Arch* 60 (1907): 493-516.

H. Brakspear, "Stanley Abbey," *WANHM* 35 (1908): 541-81.

H. F. Cheetle and J. L. Kirby, "Stanley Abbey," *VCH: Wiltshire* 3 (London, 1956): 269-75.

Sir Nikolaus Pevsner, *BoE: Wiltshire*, 2nd ed. (London, 1975), 127.

STONELEIGH (Warwickshire)

A community was first established around 1140 at Red Moor (or Radmore) by two devout hermits and their followers. Their life was disturbed by foresters, however, and they requested of their patron, Queen Mathilda, a change of site. This she agreed to, on the condition that they adopt the Cistercian Rule. A charter was drawn up and confirmed by Henry, duke of Normandy, in 1154 that granted the monks the right to build a church and claustral buildings (Hilton, 12). Shortly thereafter, the new community believing their knowledge of the Rule to be too imperfect, requested from the neighboring Cistercian abbey, Bordesley, two brethren who might instruct them. A close bond was thus formed between the two houses. Within some months a move was made to a new site at Cryfield, and then in 1155 to Stoneleigh. There, on April 13 of that year, the bishop of Coventry, Walter Durdent, laid the first stone of the new church and consecrated the churchyard.

In 1241 fire burned the monks' dormitory, and the king granted the abbot forty oaks from his forest at Kenilworth for the rebuilding (*CR: Henry III, 1237-1242*, 302). Under Abbot Robert de Hockele (1310-1349) the east end of the church was rebuilt, new choir stalls made for the monks, carved work completed under the steeple (a rood screen?), a large east window inserted, and the building newly decorated and covered with lead; these renovations necessitated a rededication (Dugdale, 257).

The monastery was dissolved in 1536, at which time the commissioners described the house as ruinous. With its bells and lead, however, the worth of the abbey was fixed at £214.19s.4d. The site was granted in 1539 to Charles Brandon, duke of Suffolk, whose heirs sold it to Sir Thomas Leigh in 1562; his lineal descendant, Lord Leigh, still lives there. In the late sixteenth century a country house was built over the east portions of the cloister and over the south transept and south aisle of the church. A much larger mansion was raised between 1714 and 1726, partly utilizing the west ranges of the monastery; the contract for this undertaking specified construction with "the stone of the Old building." There is no record of any excavation at Stoneleigh.

Since the south aisle and south transept of the former church were incorporated as residential quarters (which they still remain), their disentanglement is difficult. They are easiest to recognize from outside the house, where it is possible to trace the southeast and southwest crossing piers and four of the nave arches, the latter with much building around. The church was not large, for the crossing piers were only twenty-six feet apart. The piers had plain faces with rectangular setbacks. Fragments of the crossing arch from the southeast pier are visible; it was carried by scalloped capitals with plain abaci. Inside the house the entrance from the south transept into the south aisle remains; it was carried on a single half-round column with scalloped capitals and supported on a base with angle spurs. All the detailing indicates a date around 1170. The present courtyard is essentially the old cloister, and it preserves two original doorways, one into the south aisle, the other into the chapter house. Both have three orders of moldings, the former with an unusual chevron decoration on the outer roll, the latter supported by waterleaf and scallop capitals.

Of the east claustral buildings (for a plan, see *VCH: Warwickshire* 6:232), the chapter house, slype, passage, and undercroft can be recognized. All were vaulted, the chapter house from a single central pier (which survives in the present kitchen) with an undecorated capital, the slype and passage with barrel vaults, and the undercroft with rib vaults with chamfered profiles and *congés* at their springers.

Some original details are reset to form the present entrance to the house; they include scallop capitals, moldings with triple rolls, and bases with angle spurs. They are all consistent with a date around 1165-1175.

W. Dugdale, *The Antiquities of Warwickshire* 1, 2nd ed. (London, 1730): 257.

J. M. Gresley, *The Cistercian Abbey of Stoneley* (Ashby-de-la-Zouche, 1854).

VCH: Warwickshire 2 (London, 1908): 78-81.

J. T. Smith, "Stoneleigh Abbey," *VCH: Warwickshire* 6 (London, 1951): 229-36.

R. H. Hilton, ed., "The Stoneleigh Leger Book," *Dugdale Society* 24 (1960).

Sir Nikolaus Pevsner and A. Wedgewood, *BoE: Warwickshire* (London, 1966), 407-408.

STRATFORD LANGTHORNE (Essex)

Stratford Langthorne was founded by William de Montfichet in 1135 as part of the Congregation of Savigny. The monastery was perhaps first settled at Burstead (*Mon. Angl.* 5:586), but this is not altogether clear. In 1148, along with other Savigniac houses, Stratford became Cistercian. Wealth came to the community rapidly; it counted among its dependencies almost a score of manors, and it owned 1,500 acres within the limits of West Ham. A reputation for social prestige became associated with the abbey, and Chaucer singled it out in the fourteenth century as a model of French language pronunciation, albeit satirically.

Nothing is known about the twelfth-century architecture at Stratford, but rebuilding of the church, or parts of it, in the thirteenth century has left some record. In 1241 the king ordered the constable of the Tower of London to permit the abbot of Stratford "emere petram in civitate Lond' ad operationes ecclesie sue," provided this did not impede the functioning of the Tower (*CR: Henry III, 1237-1242,* 291). In the late fourteenth century the monastery was damaged by floods, and the king, Richard II, paid for its restoration (*VCH: Essex,* 113). In 1400 a great west window is mentioned as being newly added to the church, the gift of John Belhous, who gave money "ad opus cujusdam magne fenestre de novo constructe versus occidentem pro vitracione ejusdem" (Challenor Smith, 309).

Dissolved in 1538, the abbey was granted to Sir Peter Mewtas. Weaver mentions remains in 1631, but these had vanished by 1784 when the land was bought by Thomas Holbrook, who dug up the foundations of the buildings, reused some of the stone, and sold the rest. No trace remains of the abbey today, and the site is occupied by railway sidings, small factories, and a sewage works. Some thirteenth-century fragments survive in All Saints church, West Ham. In 1973 Powell worked out a precinct plan of the monastery (Powell, 113).

J. H. Round, "The Abbeys of Coggeshall and Stratford Langthorne," *Trans. Essex Archaeological
Society*, new ser., 5 (1894-1895): 139-43.
J. C. Challenor Smith, "Some Additions to New-
court's Repertorium vol. II," *Trans. Esssex Archaeological Society*, new ser., 6 (1898): 308-10.
RCHM: Essex, Central and South West 2 (London,
1921): 252.
Sir Nikolaus Pevsner, *BoE: Essex*, 2nd ed. (London,
1966), 343.
W. R. Powell, "Stratford Langthorne," *VCH: Essex*
6 (Oxford, 1973): 112-15.

SWINESHEAD (Lincolnshire)

Swineshead was founded by Robert de Gresley as part of the Congregation of Savigny, with the first monks coming from Furness. In 1148 Swineshead became Cistercian, and the community received as abbot Gilbert of Hoyland (*c.* 1150-1167), one of Saint Bernard's intimate friends and a writer of considerable literary merit. He came to Swineshead direct from Clairvaux.

Nothing is known about the history of building at Swineshead, although a hint of the size of the church is suggested by the Dissolution inventory in which the bells and lead were alone valued at £274 (*VCH: Lincolnshire*, 145).

There are no visible remains of the monastery. A deserted country house built in 1607 for Sir John Lockton using stone from the abbey stands over the site.

VCH: Lincolnshire 2 (London, 1906): 145-46.
Sir Nikolaus Pevsner and J. Harris, *BoE: Lincolnshire* (London, 1964), 690.

THAME (Oxfordshire)

Robert Gait founded Thame in 1138 on a site at Otteley and accompanied his gift with a modest grant of land. The abbey's cartulary says he built an abbey there (*construxit ibi abbatiam*), having first obtained from Waverley a promise to furnish monks for a monastery (Salter, 26:83). The site was subject to flooding, however, and the move to Thame was made in 1140. Bishop Alexander of Lincoln donated the new site from his park of Thame.

A consecration is recorded in 1145, perhaps of the east parts of the church, but as might be expected, building continued well past mid-century; between 1170 and 1184 a grant of land was witnessed by "Johanne cementario" (ibid., 100). In 1232 new choir stalls were given to the community by Henry III (*CR: Henry III, 1231-1234*, 38), and four years later he presented thirty oaks for a kiln to help in the rebuilding of the presbytery which had fallen down (*CR: Henry III, 1234-1237*, 245). A letter written in 1507 by William Wood, a monk of the abbey, to Pope Julius II (1503-1513) contains the information that Furness and Thame have almost identical dimensions (*VCH: Oxfordshire* 2:85). In 1526 Bishop Longland of Lincoln in the course of a visitation reported that the abbey's buildings were in ruins through neglect (Pewy, 705).

The monastery was dissolved in 1539, and the neighborhood quickly used it as a local source for building stone. Later the Wenman family obtained the site and raised the country house of Thame Park over parts of the monastic buldings. Sections of the abbey's buildings are now incorporated into the kitchen wing and include reused thirteenth- and fourteenth century stone (see *VCH: Oxfordshire* 7:168). The fine early sixteenth century abbot's quarters survive, as does the *capella extra portas* of about 1250.

The church lay to the north of where the country house now stands. An examination of 1840 by William Twopenny revealed that it measured 230 feet from east to west with a lady chapel extending an extra 45 feet to the east. It was later reported that the nave was seventy feet wide with eight bays. The bases of the piers were found in Twopenny's excavation, and traces of the chapter house and other claustral buildings were also unearthed (Lee, 455).

From these dimensions, it is clear that the twelfth-century church was modest in size but that an ambitious extension was undertaken in the thirteenth century. A nave of eight bays would measure around

120 feet from east to west. And assuming a crossing of about twenty feet, the east parts would have extended about eighty or ninety feet (at Byland, by comparison, they measure eighty-five feet).

F. G. Lee, "Thame Abbey," *Building News* (30 March, 1888), 455.

G. G. Pewy, "The Visitation of the Monastery of Thame, 1525," *English Historical Review* 3 (1888): 704-22.

VCH: Oxfordshire 3 (London, 1907): 83-86; and 7 (London, 1962): 168-69.

H. F. Salter, ed., *The Thame Chartulary, Oxfordshire Record Society* 25-26 (1947-1948).

J. Sherwood and Sir Nikolaus Pevsner, *BoE: Oxfordshire* (London, 1974), 809-14.

TILTY (Essex)

In 1153 Maurice Fitz Geoffrey founded Tilty, the Cistercians' third and last house in Essex (following Stratford Langthorne [1135], Coggeshall [1140]). Monks from Warden formed the first community.

Tilty's early years seem to have been troubled. The *Dunmow Chronicle* records that the work on St. Mary of Tilty was begun on March 16, 1188 (*VCH: Essex*, 134). This means that the church, and unless an extension was referred to, also the earliest wooden buildings, continued in use for well over thirty years. Ralph of Coggeshall credits the second abbot Simon (*circa* 1188-1214) with building the whole monastery and says that he transformed what had been little more than a grange into a beautiful and prosperous abbey (quasi de pauperrima grangia pulcherrimam et opulentam instituit abbatiam) (*Chronicon*, 169). A confirmation of the abbey's rights and properties was obtained from Richard I in 1199 (*Mon. Angl.* 5:625). But on Christmas Day 1215 soldiers of King John broke into the church and ransacked it during the conventual Mass (*Chronicon*, 177). Damage must have been considerable, since five years elapsed before a new consecration. In 1361 the abbot and community were granted license to acquire land for the maintenance of two lamps in the church and one in the dormitory (*VCH: Essex*, 134).

The monastery was dissolved in 1536, and the inventory taken then mentions a low tower over the crossing and "a payer of organes" in the church (Waller, 288). The site was granted to Margaret, marchioness of Dorset, who had been living in the abbey's guest house for some years already. Soon after the community left, the neighborhood mined the buildings for their stone, leaving only the *capella extra portas* to serve as the parish church, as it still does.

Partial excavation of the church was carried out by Galpin in 1901 and by Steer in 1942. With the help of aerial photography, Dickinson published a plan in 1963, although details remain conjectural. The church was small (174 feet from east to west, 90 feet across the transepts), dimensions close to those of Buildwas, and lay to the south of the cloister. The building was typically early Cistercian with a two-bay, aisleless presbytery, two chapels in each transept with solid dividing walls, and an aisled nave of seven bays.

Portions of the conversi's buildings still stand on the site, but only fragments of the exterior walls of the church can be traced. Steer reported that thirteenth-century columns exist in the walls of a nearby barn and mentioned that among other fragments are some of brick (Steer, 95, 100). Use of brick also occurs at Coggeshall.

Radulphi de Coggeshall, *Chronicon Anglicanum, Rolls Series* (London, 1875).

W. C. Waller, "Records of Tilty Abbey," *Trans. EAS*, new ser., 8 (1903): 353-62; and 9 (1906): 118-21, 287-89.

VCH: Essex 2 (London, 1907): 134-36.

RCHM: Essex, North West (London, 1916), 321-22.

F. W. Galpin, "The Abbey Church and Claustral Buildings of Tilty," *Trans. EAS*, new ser., 18 (1928): 89-95.

F. W. Steer, "A Short History of Tilty Abbey with an Account of some Excavations on the Site in 1942," *Essex Review* 58 (1949): 169-79; 59 (1950): 39-50, 95-100, 113-21.

Sir Nikolaus Pevsner, *BoE: Essex* (London, 1954), 359.

P.G.M. Dickinson, *Tilty Abbey and the Parish Church of St. Mary* (Chelmsford, 1963).

VAUDEY (Lincolnshire)

William, count of Aumale and earl of York, founded Vaudey in 1147 with monks from Fountains. An initial site at Bytham had to be abandoned, probably due to lack of water and the poor nature of the land, and the monks were rescued by one of William's tenants, Geoffrey de Brachecourt, who gave them a better site at Vaudey (see chapter 1 of this study, p. 19). Expansion followed, and by the end of the century the landholdings of Vaudey were considerable.

Little is known about the history of the architecture. Adam, a monk from Fountains, is credited with building the monastery (*Chron. M.*, 82), and he was at work there in 1149 when the count made the visit that led to the establishment of Meaux. In 1532, just before the Dissolution, Vaudey was visited by three senior Cistercian abbots who deposed the incumbent abbot, William Stile. Appealing their verdict to Thomas Cromwell, Stile listed the problems he had faced when taking up his office, including that "the body of my church fell down and the rebuilding cost me £100" (*L. and P. Henry VIII* 5:621, no. 1477).

The monastery was dissolved in 1536, and the site granted to the earl of Suffolk, who used the stone to expand his house at nearby Grimsthorp Park. When Leland visited the abbey in 1543, he already spoke of "the ruins of Vaudey." Stukeley was there in 1736 and wrote that the abbey's surrounding wall was intact and that foundations remained of abbey buildings. In 1871 Wild reported that some remains could still be seen though "they are fast crumbling away" (Wild, 114). At present only a few tumbled stones are visible on the densely overgrown site.

Excavation was undertaken in 1831 and again in 1851. The intention of the latter was to provide building material for the repair of Swinestead church, but some information was recorded about the finds (*Gentleman's Magazine* 121, pt. 1 [1851]: 647; and 122, pt. 2 [1851]: 155). The nave piers were made of clustered columns, and a free-standing pier with sixteen shafts that measured eleven feet in diameter is illustrated. This presumably came from the crossing. The distance between the crossing piers is mentioned as being twenty-five feet. Other piers

were found in the south transept and presbytery, and the latter had aisles. Aisles indicate an extension of the choir eastward, probably in the late twelfth century.

E. Richardson, "Vaudey Abbey," *Arch. Jnl.* 8 (1851): 210-11.
J. Wild, *The History of Castle Bytham, Vaudey Abbey* (London, 1871).
VCH: Lincolnshire 2 (London, 1906): 143-45.

WARDEN (Bedfordshire)

Walter Espec founded Warden in 1136 on land he owned at Old Warden. Four years earlier he had founded Rievaulx, and the Yorkshire house supplied the first monks.

Warden quickly attracted men and patrons, and within seventeen years three daughter houses had been established: Sawtry (1147), Sibton (1150), and Tilty (1153). A dedication is recorded for some date within the third quarter of the twelfth century (*Chart. W.*, no. 87). A number of gifts to the community bear out this general date. Between about 1152 and 1172 and again between about 1170 and 1180 funds were received for the maintenance of lights "super altare Sancte Marie" (ibid., nos. 324 and 299). Three similar gifts were made between 1170 and 1180 for the "super magnum altare" (nos. 35, 31 and 195), and one between 1180 and 1190 for a light to burn before the pyx (no. 320). Shortly after 1200 a gift of land was confirmed that Robert de Blaini had made when he was admitted as a *conversus* and of one acre of land that his father had made to the abbey church as dower when it was dedicated (no. 87). Also around 1200 "Gaufrido cementarius" witnessed a further gift of land (no. 52). From the early and middle thirteenth century come additional endowments intended to maintain a lamp before the altar of the Virgin (nos. 66 and 220).

The population of Warden in the late thirteenth century was around fifty. As much may be deduced from an incident involving the notorious Fawkes de Bréauté, who became so enraged at the abbey that he stormed its buildings and dragged thirty of the monks through the mud to imprisonment at Bedford Castle.

A new church was begun in 1323, but money ran short, and the monks were forced to request a license for soliciting alms to pay for its completion (*VCH: Bedfordshire* 1:362). Work was finished in 1366. Most likely the new building was an elaborate choir extension rather than an entire new structure.

The monastery was dissolved in 1537, and the site passed into the hands of the Gostwick family, who raised a mansion over the east claustral buildings, incorporating some of them into it. Buck's view of Warden in 1730 shows some traces of medieval work (*Antiquities* 1, sec. 6, plate 13). These ruins were demolished around 1790 (cf. illustration in *Gentleman's Magazine*, pt. 1 [1815], 577). The site of the monastery is at present a farm, with parts of the ruined mansion adjacent.

An excavation was conducted by Rudge in 1839 and revealed part of the south wall of the presbytery from the fourteenth-century rebuilding. This showed that the presbytery was aisled and vaulted. Many of the records of the finds from this excavation survive in the Bedford Record Office. Excavations by Rudd and West in 1960, 1961, and 1974 showed that the abbey was large. The church had only one transept chapel on the north transept, suggesting that the fourteenth-century extension took the inner chapel as an aisle for the presbytery. Tile pavements were also found.

C. H. Compton, "Kirkham Priory and Warden Abbey," *Jnl. BAA* 50 (1894): 283-94.

VCH: Bedfordshire 1 (London, 1904): 361-66; and 3 (London, 1912): 251-53.

E. H. Fowler, ed., "Cartulary of the Abbey of Old Warden," *Bedfordshire Historical Record Society Publications* 13 (1930).

G. T. Rudd and B. B. West, "Excavations at Warden Abbey in 1960 and 1961," *Bedford Archaeological Journal* 2 (1964): 58-72.

Sir Nikolaus Pevsner, *BoE: Bedfordshire and the County of Huntingdon and Peterborough* (London, 1968), 132.

Med. Arch. 19 (1975): 233.

WAVERLEY (Surrey)

Waverley was the first Cistercian house established in Britain. It was founded in 1128 by William Giffard, bishop of Winchester, with monks from L'Aumône in Normandy.

Documents throw little light on the first buildings. For the twelfth century the *Annals* of the abbey record only the completion in 1179 of a new lavatory for the monks and new aqueducts (*Ann. W.*, 241). The size of the monastery sixty years after foundation is specified; at the election of Abbot Christopher in 1187 mention is made of 120 lay brethren, seventy monks, and around thirty plough teams at work on the estates (ibid., 244). Work on a new church began in 1203 under the direction of Dan William Bradewatere, who "coepit jacere fundamentum novae ecclesiae" (ibid., 255).

Eleven years later Bishop Albin of Ferns dedicated five altars, namely, those in the east chapels and choir, and he also blessed the cemetery (ibid., 282). In 1222 Dan William's death is recorded, and he was honored with burial by the south wall of the church. In 1225 the monastery was visited by Henry III, and on January 17 of that year the king was admitted as an associate of the order (ibid., 301). The next year two more altars were consecrated (ibid., 301), probably those in the north transept, and the king's forester, John de Venuz, was directed to allow the abbot to take five oaks out of his bailiwick (*VCH: Surrey* 2: 80). More building material came in 1231 when Henry III ordered the constable of Windsor to allow the abbot to cut timber in his wood of Wanbrough *ad operationem ecclesie* (*CR: Henry III, 1227-1231*, 491). By June of that year two altars in the south transept were dedicated (*Ann. W.*, 309), and later in the year three more (ibid., 310). Finally, on December 21, 1231, the monks "entered their new church from the old" (intraverunt in novam ecclesiam de prima veteri ecclesia) (ibid., 310). Thus after twenty-eight years of work the eastern end was finished, leaving much of the nave of the old church intact. As was often the case, the new structure had been raised as an envelope around the east end of the first church.

Work on the new nave dragged on slowly. Serious floods damaged the abbey buildings in 1233 (ibid., 312), and a few years later one of the principal masons, if not the master mason, a lay brother called John of Waverley, was ordered by the king to make the queen's chamber in Westminster Palace (Harvey, *English Medieval Architects*, 288). He was gone two years. Later he was five years at Hailes, and he was back in the king's service in 1251. In 1245 Eleanor, the sister of Henry III and wife of Simon de Montfort, gave twenty-five marks and a further sum of eighteen marks *ad fabricam ecclesiae* (*Ann. W.*, 336). In 1248 an accident was recorded during construction of the tower, when a workman fell from the top but miraculously escaped injury (ibid., 340). In 1270 the king granted permission to John of Eton, the abbey's subprior, to take six oaks in Aliceholt forest for timber (*CR: Henry III, 1268-1272*, 215). The church was finished in 1278 and consecrated by the bishop of Winchester (ibid., 390). During the nine days of celebration permitted by statute for a dedication, women were permitted to enter the monastery, and at a great feast given on the first of these days the unlikely figure of 7,066 people is recorded in the Worcester *Annals* as sitting down to meat (*Ann. Monastici* 4:474-75). The Waverley *Annals* stop in 1291, and no further information on the buildings from documents is known.

For the architecture of Waverley, see chapter 2 of the present study, pp. 25-29ff.

Waverley was dissolved in 1536, and the site granted to the treasurer of the king's household, Sir William FitzWilliam, who built a house incorporating portions of the former monastic buildings. His heirs sold it in the early years of the seventeenth century to the Cobham family under whose ownership the ruins are said to have undergone "great dilapidations" (E. W. Brayley, *History of Surrey* 5, pt. 1 [London, 1850]: 287). Briefly owned a century later by William Aislabie, brother of the owner of Fountains, Waverley was sold in 1725 to Mr. Child of Guildford for £13,000. He built a new house to the northwest and reorganized the landscape. Buck's print of 1737 (*Antiquities* 2, sect. 12, plate 13) shows both the new house and the ruins, the latter looking not too unlike those that stand today, though Brayley mentions further mutilations for building materials in the 1770s

when annexes were built to the house (ibid., 287).

The site was excavated by Brakspear between 1899 and 1905. It came into the guardianship of what is now the Department of Environment after the Second World War. It has recently been consolidated (1980-1981) by the department, though without exposing the foundations.

W. C. Smith, *History of Farnham and the Ancient Cistercian Abbey of Waverley* (Farnham, 1829).

H. R. Luard, ed., *Annales monastici, Rolls Series* 2 (London, 1865).

F. J. Baigent, "The Abbey and Church of the Blessed Mary at Waverley," *Surrey Archaeological Collections* 8 (1880-1882): 157-210.

VCH: Surrey 2 (London, 1905): 77-89.

H. Brakspear, *Waverley Abbey* (London, 1905).

Sir Nikolaus Pevsner and I. Nairn, *BoE: Surrey*, 2nd ed. (London, 1971): 502-505.

WOBURN (Bedfordshire)

Monks from Fountains settled at Woburn in 1145 under the patronage of Hugh de Bolebec, who is described in the Fountains *Narratio* as "powerful and of great wealth" (*Mem. F.*, 88). To expiate his worldliness, Hugh was persuaded to found Woburn by the abbot of Fountains, Henry Murdac. The *Narratio* continues that Hugh "consecrated to divine use a certain village called Woburn, in the diocese of Lincoln, together with the adjacent lands. The holy abbot took the gift from the hand of the rich one and when the usual buildings had been erected [*et aedificiis, de more, constructis*] chose according to rule brothers to send to the place."

Apart from the mention in the Meaux *Chronicle* that Woburn was built by Adam (abbot of Meaux, 1150-1160), no documents on the history of building have come to light. The deeds and charters of the monastery have disappeared (Thomson, 154ff.). A confirmation of the abbey's possessions is recorded at some date before 1162 (*Mon. Angl.* 5:479).

A vivid account of the last years of Woburn and the human dilemmas facing the community there in the face of pressure to concur in the matter of the king's divorce has been preserved (*VCH: Bed-*

fordshire, 367-69). Woburn was dissolved in 1538, and the site granted nine years later to John Lord Russell; his descendants, the dukes of Bedford, still own it.

In 1627 Inigo Jones' new mansion for the fourth earl was built over the site of the church, incorporating some parts of the abbey, probably the claustral buildings, in the foundations. This house was replaced by the present building in the mid-eighteenth century. No decipherable details of the medieval period can be recognized, although some parts of the basement may be constructed of reused masonry.

VCH: Bedfordshire 1 (London, 1904): 366-70; and 3 (London, 1912): 459.

G. D. Thomson, "Woburn Abbey and the Dissolution of the Monasteries," *Royal Historical Society Transactions*, 4th ser., 16 (1933): 129-60.

Sir Nikolaus Pevsner, *BoE: Bedfordshire* (London, 1967), 166-67.

APPENDIX A

The Dissolution and After

AT THE Dissolution the fate of the buildings of the Cistercians, as with those of other religious orders, varied widely from region to region. Whereas a few Cistercian houses largely escaped dismantlement, elsewhere destruction was nearly total. Why some abbeys were spared and others were not is often difficult to account for. Officially, the Dissolution commissioners of Henry VIII were to see that "all the walls of the churches, stepulls, cloysters, fraterys, dorters, chapter howsys" were pulled to the ground.[1] But success varied widely. In the first place, implementing such a policy cost money, usually more than was realized through the sale of materials from the demolished buildings. In Lincolnshire, for instance, John Freman proposed merely defacing the churches and making the conventual buildings uninhabitable by removing stairs and roofs, and then offering long-term leases to use them as quarries. At Kirkstead in the same county, however, the king's agents were directed to see that the leads be "plucked down and melted" but were to "deface nothing else."[2] As often as not, demolition was an ad hoc affair. Sometimes cost was secondary, as at Quarr and Beaulieu, where the king ordered destruction as an act of State to provide material for coastal defenses on the Isle of Wight. At Furness, by contrast, it was a more private matter; there a Mr. Holcroft was rewarded for his "diligence" by being put in "trust to pluck downe the church."[3]

When the commissioners themselves did not accomplish demolition, a condition of lease or sale specified that the new owner or occupier should do so within a fixed period. A frequent pattern was for sale (or occasionally bestowal as gift) to be made to the gentry, whereupon the abbeys were often pulled down to provide stone for a nearby country house. From Stanley, for example, ashlar was carted away to build Sir Edward Baynton's Bromham Hall. To hasten demolition of the church, the foundations were mined, costing the life of a workman.[4] At Bindon Viscount Howard constructed a Tudor mansion near the old monastery, using its stone, and at Boxley the Wyatt family did likewise. Even so, a large monastery offered much more stone than was needed; at Fountains the west ranges alone provided Sir Stephen Proctor with all the material to build his late sixteenth century Fountains Hall.

In some instances, rather than demolish the fabric, the new owner actually adapted it for domestic residence. Buckland in Devon is the classic example, where the purchaser, Sir Francis Drake, using treasure taken in his voyage round the world, built a mansion within the actual framework of the former church—kitchen in the choir, entrance hall in the crossing, and so on. Stoneleigh underwent a similar fate, although the conversion was less pointedly mocking, the south aisle being turned into the great hall of the new house and the south transept into the dining room and, with an inserted floor, two bedrooms. More usually the church was demolished but the conventual buildings left. At

---

[1] See J. Gairdner, ed., *L. and P. Henry VIII* 11, no. 242 (London, 1888), 105. The best survey is D. Knowles, *Bare Ruined Choirs* (Cambridge, 1976); see also M. Aston, "English Ruins and English History: The Dissolution and the Sense of the Past," *Jnl. WCI* 36 (1973): 231-55; S. Piggott, *Ruins in a Landscape: Essays in Antiquarianism* (Edinburgh, 1976); D. Knowles and R. N. Hadcock, *Medieval Religious Houses:*

England and Wales, 2d ed. (London, 1971), esp. 1-6.

[2] Gairdner, ed., *L. and P. Henry VIII, 1537* 1, no. 676, p. 297.

[3] T. A. Beck, *Annales Furnesienses* (London, 1844), 360.

[4] H. Brakspear, "The Cistercian Abbey of Stanley, Wiltshire," *Arch* 60 (1907): 493-516, esp. 495, 502.

Coggeshall the monastery was sold to Sir Thomas Seymour in 1538, and when three years later he resold it to the crown, a survey noted that the church "is clene prostrate and defaced but the cloyster and lodgings doe yet remayne untouched."[5] In any case adaptation of the claustral buildings with their two-story arrangement sensibly met the residential requirements of a domestic household. At Cleeve, Rufford, Kirkstall, Flaxley, Thame, Stoneleigh, Forde, and Combe new owners carried out such transformations, in the last three instances leaving the chapter houses relatively untouched where they still survive, as a private chapel at Forde, a kitchen at Stoneleigh, and a municipal tea room at Combe.

For some monasteries more ambitious proposals were made. Sir Arthur Darcy suggested establishing the royal stud of mares at Jervaulx, using the former monastic buildings as stables. The abbot at Rewley, a thirteenth-century foundation, offered £100 to have the abbey converted into a college. And Fountains was to become the cathedral of a new diocesan see extending from Richmond into Lancashire. None of these projects was carried out. But at Tintern the claustral buildings were converted into a wire manufactory, and at Robertsbridge, an iron forge.

In rare cases abbey churches were spared in order to serve a new function as a parish church. This occurred at Quarr, although use was brief and the building was then demolished. But Abbey Dore and Holmcultram survive to the present day in this changed role, albeit in truncated form. At Holmcultram, in the disputed border country, motives of defense were as strong as those of devotion, however. Petitioning Cromwell, the townspeople pleaded for the church, which was a ". . . grete ayde, socor, and defence for us ayenst the Scotts."[6]

Some owners tackled the disposal of monastery and contents systematically. The purchaser of Rievaulx, Thomas, earl of Richmond, ordered an inventory of materials to be made and issued instructions regarding their safekeeping. The pavement, iron, and stained glass from the church were to be "layd up under lok and key and out of danger of wastyng and stelying."[7] Once secured, the glass was to be graded into three sorts and only the last category was to be "taken out of the lede and the lede molten."

More typically, the commissioners disposed of an abbey's fittings and furnishings by auction, the sale occurring in the chapter house or cloister. Orderly disposal was not guaranteed, however. At Bordesley an unauthorized sale occurred soon after the monks were ejected in late July of 1538, and it took until September before the lots could be newly organized. Their division reveals the thoroughness of the sale; for instance, the tiles on the east walk of the cloister were sold to "a servaunt of the busshopes of Worceter," while to a Mr. Markeham went "the iron and glasse in the wyndowes of the north syde of the cloyster."[8]

Sometimes disposal was accompanied by uglier, even violent, incidents. At Roche a system of bidding for the fabric was agreed upon among the neighboring landowners, but the local populace descended on the abbey before dismantlement could begin. The ensuing free-for-all was described in poignant detail some years after the episode itself by Michael Sherbrook, an Elizabethan clergyman. The sack began with the church, and the only buildings to escape ruin were the abbey's barns; country people respected their utility. As a record of a Cistercian monastery's last hours and a graphic description of its contents, Sherbrook's account is without equal in the entire Dissolution:

---

[5] See G. E. Beaumont, "The Remains of Coggeshall Abbey," *Trans. Essex Arch. Soc.*, n.s., 15 (1921): 61.

[6] H. Ellis, ed., *Original Letters Illustrative of English History*, 1st ser., 2 (London, 1825): 90.

[7] *Chart. R.*, 334-43, esp. 338-39. The inventory lists furnishings in the church and conventual buildings and is the fullest to survive for a Cistercian house. It may be compared with inventories of Cistercian abbeys in Staffordshire: Dieulacres, Croxden, and Hulton (see F. A. Hibbert, *The Dissolution of the Monasteries as Illustrated by the Suppression of Religious Houses*

in Staffordshire [London, 1910], 237-44, 255, 257); or that of the sale at Bordesley (see n. 8 below). See also the inventory at Stanlaw (M.E.C. Walcott, "The Inventory of Stanlaw," *Lancs. and Ches. Hist. Soc. Proc. and Pap.* 23 [1872]: 53-56); and at Pipewell (H. Brakspear, "Pipewell Abbey," *AASRP* 30 [1909-1910]: 299-313).

[8] T. Wright, ed., "Three Chapters of Letters Relating to the Suppression of the Monasteries," *Camden Society*, 1st ser., 26 (1843): 266-67, no. 132.

The Suppression of an abbey, hard by me, called the Roche Abbey; a House of White Monks; a very fair builded house all of Freestone; and every house vaulted with Freestone; and covered with Lead (as the Abbeys was in England as well as the Churches be). At the Breaking up whereof an Uncle of mine was present, being well acquainted with certain of the Monks there; and when they were put forth of the House, one of the Monks, his Friend, told him that every one had given to him his Cell, wherein he lied; wherein was not any thing of Price, but his Bed and Apparell, which was but simple and of small price. Which Monk willed my Uncle to buy something of him; who said, I see nothing that is worth Money to my use: no said he; give me two pence for my cell door which was never made with five shillings. No said my Uncle, I know not what to do with it (for he was a Young Man unmarried, and then neither stood need of Houses nor Doors). But such Persons as afterward bought their Corn or Hay or such like, found all the doors either open or the Locks and Shackles plucked away, or the Door itself taken away, went in and took what they found, filched it away.

Some took the Service Books that lied in the Church and laid upon their Waine Coppes to piece the same: some took Windowes of the Hay laith and hid them in their Hay; and likewise they did of many other Things: For some pulled forth Iron Hooks out of the Walls that bought none, when the yeomen and Gentlemen of the Country had bought the Timber of the Church: for the Church was the first thing that was put to the spoil; and then the Abbat's Lodgine, Dorter, and Frater with the Cloister and all the Buildings thereabout, within the Abbey Walls: for nothing was spared but the Ox-houses and Swinecoates and such other Houses of Office, that stood without the Walls; which had more Favour shewed them than the very Church itself. . . . It would have pitied any Heart to see what tearing up of the Lead there was, and plucking up of Boards, and throwing down of the Sparres; and then the Lead was torn off and cast down into the Church, and the Tombs in the Church all broken (for in most Abbeys were diverse Noble Men and Women, yea and in some Abbeys, Kings; whose Tombs were regarded no more than the Tombs of all other inferior Persons: For to what end should they stand, when the Church over them was not spared for their Cause) and all things of Price, either spoiled, carped away or defaced to the uttermost.

The persons that cast the Lead into foders, plucked

up all the Seats in the Choir, wherein the Monks sat when they said service; which were like to the Seats in Minsters, and burned them, and melted the Lead therewithall: although there was wood plenty within a flight shot of them: for the Abbey stood among the Woods and the Rocks of Stone: In which Rocks was Pewter Vessels found that was conveyed away and there hid: so that it seemeth every Person bent himself to filch and spoil what he could: yea even such Persons were content to spoil them, that seemed not two days before to allow their Religion, and do great Worship and Reverence at their Mattins, Masses and other Service, and all other their doings: which is a strange thing to say; that they could this day think it to be the House of God and the next day the House of the Devil: or else they would not have been so ready to have spoiled it. . . . For the better Proof of this . . . I demanded of my Father thirty years after the Suppression, which had bought part of the Timber of the Church, and all the Timber in the Steeple, with the Bell Frame, with other his Parteners therein (in the which steeple hung viii, yea ix Bells; whereof the least but one, could not be bought at this Day for twenty pounds, which Bells I did see hang there myself, more than a year after the Suppression) whether he thought well of the Religious Persons and of the Religion then used? And he told me Yea; for said He, I did see no Cause to the contrary: Well, said I, then how came it to pass you was so ready to destroy and spoil the thing that you thought well of? What should I do, said He; might I not as well as others have some Profit of the Spoil of the Abbey? For I did see all would away; and therefore I did as others did.[9]

Sherbrook's account captures the mixture of motives and moods that was part of the Dissolution. At the space of some generations, the troubled responses continued to be felt. Particularly puzzling was the speed with which the local populace could turn from the acceptance of a religious institution to its pillage in a matter of days. On occasion a regretful note may be detected even in the commissioners' reports, at least toward the buildings they were dooming if not toward the institutions they were destroying. Writing to Cromwell in 1537, Sir Arthur Darcy recorded of Jervaulx that the abbey was wholly covered in lead and noted that "ther is oon off the ffayrest churches that I have seen, ffayre medooze, and the ryver runnying by ytt, and

    [9] A. G. Dickens, ed., "Tudor Treatises," *YASRS* 125 (1959): 123-26.

grett demayne," though his intention, like that of the county commissioners at Stanley who registered their regard of the architecture, was doubtless as much appraisal as praise.[10]

The destruction of buildings was by no means simple, as the accident at Stanley and as Sherbrook's account indicate. Other sources show as typical the sequence in which Roche was quarried down. The roof, especially if lead-covered, went first. The timbers themselves—as well as the choir stalls in the case of Roche—fueled the furnaces to melt the lead, and the metal was sold with the proceeds going directly to the king. At Jervaulx, Richard Bellasis wrote to Cromwell: "I have taken down all the leade of Jarvaxe and maid it in pecys of half foders." But they did not all reach the market; working late in the year, Bellasis complained of carting problems, "for the ways in the cowntre are so foule and deep that no caryage can passe in wyntre"; he proposed postponing "takyn down the howse" until the following spring.[11]

Given the nearly total destruction in the midlands and the south of England, it is a wonder that anything survived at all. That more remains in the north is probably explained by a variety of factors. The particular attitude of the owner was crucial. A powerful man such as the earl of Rutland at Rievaulx could prevent scenes such as those at Roche, or unauthorized sales like those at Bordesley, or thefts as at Pipewell, where, a commission of investigation was told, trespassers had carried off part of the buildings. A further factor slowing dismantlement was opposition to the Dissolution, which ran higher in some regions, such as Yorkshire, than others.

Inevitably, the traumatic events of the Dissolution produced a reaction. With the accession of Mary and the restoration of Catholicism, there was discussion about reopening some religious houses, although little is known of its effects, if any, on the process of destruction. The new owners prob-

ably adopted a wait-and-see attitude, and as Mary's reign was brief, no consistent policy was ever implemented. Sherbrook's interrogation of his father about the events at Roche also reflects the next generation's search for explanations.

Earlier, in the 1530s and 1540s, sporadic efforts had been made to rescue historical records, even as the hundreds of religious institutions were torn apart. John Leland (d. 1553), working for Henry VIII, began collecting manuscripts and books; his itineraries including a visit to the library at Rievaulx, where he recorded works (now lost) by Walter Daniel, Ailred's biographer.[12] His travels also prompted him to collect material relating to topography and monuments, although insanity prevented him from publishing his work.

On the whole, Tudor antiquarianism followed nontopographical lines, focusing instead on history, place names, and genealogical matters. Rarely is detailed information given about the fate of specific Cistercian buildings or sites, the references in Leland, for instance, being limited to noting at Pipewell that of ". . . the late abbey . . . there be faire buildinges at this place" or of Newminster that it is ". . . plesaunt with watar and very fayre about it."[13] Yet at least Leland's itineraries reflect an embryonic interest in going out and looking, in traveling and recording, despite the difficulties made so evident in his title: *Laboriouse Journey and Serche of Johan Leylande for Englandes Antiquitees*. The same spirit of inquiry surfaces a little later in men like Humphrey Lhuyd (d. 1568) in Wales, and William Lambarde, whose *Perambulation of Kent* (1576), the first county history, relates with relish the scandal of the automata image on the rood at Boxley (shown to have been operated by the monks with wires). Topographical interest based on personal observation, however small-scale, marks the start of the transition from despoiling to conserving. The first topographical history, Camden's *Britannia*, appeared in 1589 (first English edition 1610), and

[10] Wright, ed., "Letters Relating to the Suppression of the Monasteries," 164-65, no. 77. For Stanley, see catalog.

[11] Wright, ed., "Letters Relating to the Suppression of the Monasteries," 165; see also G. C. Denning, "A Lead Ingot at Rievaulx Abbey," *Ant. Jnl.* 32 (1952): 199-202. For some mysterious reason, not all of Bellasis' lead was transported out. In 1923 some of the pigs were discovered still lying by the

west wall of the church and were reused for the leading of the windows in York Minster (see Aston, "English Ruins and English History," 242).

[12] See J. Leland, *Commentarii de Scriptoribus Britannicis* (Oxford, 1709), 200-201.

[13] For Pipewell and Newminster, see L. T. Smith, ed., *The Itinerary of John Leland* (Carbondale, 1964), 1:13, and 5:63.

although it stressed Roman rather than medieval remains, it stimulated a broader curiosity about the past. As early as 1607, at Quarr, Sir John Oglander undertook a search for the former abbey church: "I went to Quarr, and inquyred of divors owld men where ye greate church stood. Theyre wase but one, Father Pennie, a verye owld man coold give me anye satisfaction; he told me he had bene often in ye church whene itt wase standinge, and told me what a goodly church it wase; and further sayd that itt stood to ye sowthward of all ye ruins, corn then growinge where it stoode. I hired soome to digge to see whether I myght find ye fowndation butt could not. . . ."[14]

Oglander's search was probably atypical, although it is hard to gauge the degree to which such interests were held. Some encompassed medieval remains, and they were sufficiently well known in the early seventeenth century to be satirized. In his *Microcosmography* John Earle describes the antiquary as: "a man strangely thrifty of time past . . . a great admirer of the rust of old monuments, [who] reads only those characters where time has eaten out the letters. He will go you forty miles to see a saint's well or a ruined abbey; and there be but a cross or a stone footstool in the way, he'll be considering it so long, till he forget his journey."[15]

In the seventeenth century scholarship both reflected interest in the past and helped form it. Besides Camden, men like Speed (1611), Dugdale (and Dodsworth)(1655-1673), Aubrey (1670s), and Thoresby (1695) began publishing lists and charters of pre-Reformation houses.[16] On occasion this writing gives a glimpse of the condition of a Cistercian house. Dugdale, for instance, reported in 1656 that at Merevale the owner, Sir William Devreux, had "patcht up some part of the ruins here"; a year or so later Aubrey noted of Waverley that:

This abbey is situated, though low, in a very good Air, and in as Romantik a Place as most I have seen. Here is a fine Rivulet runs under the House and fences one side; but all the Rest is wall'd. . . . Within the Walls of the Abbey are sixty acres: the Walls are very strong and chiefly of Ragg-stones ten feet high. Here also remain Walls of a fair Church the walls of the Cloyster and some Part of the Cloysters themselves, within and without are yet remaining. Within the Quadrangle of the Cloysters was a Pond, but now it is a Marsh. Here also was a handsom Chapel (now a stable) larger than that at Trinity College in Oxford. . . . The Hall was very spacious and noble with a Row of Pillars in the middle and vaulted over Head. . . .[17]

Much of this new scholarly movement was court oriented, with the College of Heralds serving as a center for antiquarian research. In the course of their work, the heralds made regular visitations touring the countryside to register the names and arms of those entitled to use arms. They also recorded inscriptions, studied tombs, and from stained glass drew donors or arms. Camden had been a herald, as had Dugdale.

By far the most enduring of these seventeenth-century works was Dugdale's and Dodsworth's three-volume *Monasticon Anglicanum*. It collected a selection of charters for each house preceded by a synopsis of its history. Organized by religious order, the *Monasticon* thus assembled for the first time documentary material on the Cistercians.[18] It was also illustrated, earning the book the added distinction of being the first medieval history of specific sites with illustrations. For the Cistercians the authors chose plates of Fountains and, more strangely, Combe. Like Camden's *Britannia*, the *Monasticon* reveals an attitude that is factual and descriptive, qualities that influenced its artists, Daniel King and Wenzel Hollar, whose work is stiff and literal;

[14] W. H. Long, ed., *The Oglander Memoirs* (London, 1888), 199.

[15] John Earle, "Microcosmography: Or A Piece of the World Discovered in Essays and Characters" (1628), in R. Aldington, ed., *A Book of Characters* (London, n.d.), no. 9.

[16] J. Speed, *A History of Great Britain* (London, 1611); R. Dodsworth and Sir William Dugdale, *Monasticon Anglicanum*, 3 vols. (London, 1655-1673). John Aubrey's *Monumenta Britannica*, although written in the 1670s, was not published until the nineteenth century. Ralph Thoresby's inclusion may

be permitted for his role in the reissue of Camden's *Britannia* in 1695, for which he contributed the account of the West Riding of Yorkshire. Later expanded, this was published separately as *Ducatus Leodiensis* (London, 1715).

[17] For Merevale, see Sir William Dugdale, *The Antiquities of Warwickshire*, 2nd ed. (London, 1656), 2:782-83. For Waverley, see John Aubrey, *Natural History and Antiquities of Surrey* (London, 1718), 3:360.

[18] See *Mon. Angl.* 1:695-945; volume 2 dealt with the Scottish houses of the order (see pp. 1,027-1,035).

the same style continues into the early eighteenth century in the engravings of the Buck brothers (1711-1725 and forward).[19]

Both Dugdale and Dodsworth knew Lord Fairfax (as did Thoresby's father), and through him, the poet Andrew Marvell. Marvell's poem, "Upon Appleton House," written after his appointment as tutor in 1651 to Fairfax's daughter, is a long and complex work set at Nunappleton in Yorkshire, a former Cistercian nunnery established in 1150. The stanzas on the ruin mix satire on the conventual life with nostalgia for a past whose physical fragments stir emotions:

> While with slow Eyes we these survey,
> And on each pleasant footstep stay,
> We opportuny may relate
> The progress of this Houses Fate.
> A nunnery first gave it birth.
> For Virgin Buildings oft brought forth.
> And all that Neighbour-Ruine shows
> The Quarries whence this dwelling rose.[20]

Although detailed information about the individual sites is lacking, the necessary first steps were taken in the seventeenth century to eventually form a new attitude toward the past. It was with the making of lists and the publication of documents that an increasing historical consciousness about the country's former monastic institutions began to take shape. Although Marvell's "neighbour-ruine" was still the quarry whence a great house rose, owners slowly realized ruins could provide something more than stone. Properly set off, they could evoke a whole set of emotions, and more surprisingly, could even assume pictorial and scenic interest. With the advent of the Romantic period began the great vogue for incorporating ruins as culminating objects in landscape garden schemes. Easy as it is now to mock this aestheticizing treatment, the taste for

the picturesque served as a certain form of conservation.

For the Romantics, Cistercian ruins came to be the quintessential Gothic ruin, though this involved a turn of taste that would have startled the order's founders. The customary location of the abbeys in isolated and steep-sided valleys, originally for reasons of seclusion, now provided the perfect setting for the Romantic's taste in natural scenery. At Roche, where Sherbrook had lamented the Dissolution, Horace Walpole produced the most fashionable compliment of the day by describing the ruins as ". . . hid in such a venerable chasm that you might lie concealed there even from a squire parson of the parish. Lord Scarborough, to whom it belongs, neglects it as much as if he was afraid of ghosts." Two years later, in 1774, when work finally began on Capability Brown's redesigning of the grounds, the new contract specified completion "according to the ideas fixed on with Lord Scarborough (with Poet's Feeling and Painter's Eye)."[21] Not everyone approved. William Gilpin grumbled: "Mr. Brown is now at work in the center part of the three vallies near the ruin itself. He has already removed all the heaps of rubbish which lay around, some of which were very ornamental and very useful in uniting the two parts of the ruin."[22] He accused Brown of giving the ruins a "too tailored look," whereas the governing ideas should be "solitude, neglect and desolation."

Hard on the heels of critics like Gilpin came artists to sketch—Turner, Sandby, Girtin, Flaxman, Cotman, and others—while the gentry embarked on travel tours armed with treatises on the sublime and picturesque. Before long, sites like Fountains, Rievaulx, and Tintern were widely known and extravagantly praised. It is easy to forget, in fact, that these eighteenth-century enthusiasms and the landscape changes resulting from them, still condition the way we see some of the most famous

---

[19] Daniel King illustrated the plates of Fountains and Combe. In the two supplemental volumes, published by John Stevens in 1722-1723, views of Kirkstall, Rewley, Holmcultram, and Tintern were added. The publications of S. Buck and N. Buck, *Antiquities of England and Wales*, 4 vols. (London, 1711-1753), illustrated 428 views of abbeys, castles, towns, etc., and were issued in sets of twenty-four each from 1711 on. The first two sets covered Yorkshire and included five Cistercian sites (By-

land, Fountains, Kirkstall, Rievaulx, and Sawley).

[20] H. M. Margoliouth, ed., *The Poems and Letters of Andrew Marvell*, 3d ed., 1 (Oxford, 1971): 65.

[21] Quoted by M. Girouard, "Sandbeck Park, Yorkshire, III," *Country Life* (Oct. 21, 1965), 1,024-27.

[22] W. Gilpin, *Observations Relative Chiefly to Picturesque Beauty Made in the Year 1776* (London, 1789), 24.

abbeys. Fountains, for instance, is unthinkable without John Aislabie's canals, cascades, and lawns (begun 1716), or Rievaulx without Thomas Duncombe's terraces, temples, and wooded slopes (begun 1758).

The Romantic passion for ruins was not, of course, a static sensibility. As the concept changed, the physical appearance of sites was altered to conform. At Fountains the rough outline of these changes can be followed. Early in the eighteenth century the abbey had to induce a sense of melancholy and gloom, so trees were planted in the cloister, chapter house, and refectory and ivy encouraged up the walls. Thomas Gent effused:

With piteous Wonder here we may bemoan
Magnificence into Confusion thrown
Whose venerable Ruins plainly show
The Mutability of things below.[23]

Different "improvements" followed. When William Aislabie purchased the abbey in 1767 for £18,000, he united it with his father's landscape and embarked on changes: the cloister was transformed into a parterre, and architectural fragments pieced together to diversify the scheme; ". . . in the center part of the church a circular pedestal was constructed out of fragments of the old pavements and surmounted by a heathen statue." Gilpin who reported this was shocked. Earlier he had noted that the ruins were full of trees, but now he angrily commented: ". . . a Goth may deform when it exceeds the power of art to amend." He castigated the sacrifice of the site's "soothing melancholy" and accused Aislabie of violently tearing away the "outworks of the ruin" and subjecting its "main body" to the "hand of decoration."[24]

The sorry fate of the monastery—unkempt, abandoned, ravaged by nature—fired the picturesque imagination. If a site lacked these qualities, writers provided them, and owners hastened to match fact to fiction. Who would recognize Kirkstall,

dour and dirty as it is today in a Leeds suburb, from Hall's 1797 description: ". . . the blended vegetation everywhere dispersed, on the crown of the dormitory and other places, like the airy gardens of Babylon, of which historians speak, seems to familiarise the wonders of those days; while the cells below, made more subterraneous from accumulated ruin without, join in giving the whole all the peculiarity and air of ancient fiction, or fairy enchantment."[25] But the picturesque did not save everything. At Biddlesden the ruins of the church, including parts of the tower, were in "good part standing" when Browne Willis visited in 1712. But when he returned in 1735, he recorded that the proprietor, Henry Sayer, had "totally demolished everything" and "leveled the site."[26] Similarly, the *Gentleman's Magazine* of 1796 described at Buckfast the ". . . walls and foundations of this once splendid seat of superstition," noted the "abbey church and remains of its tower all lying around in such massy fragments that it is scarcely to be conceived by what power so vast a fabric could be joined," and predicted that they would "remain unmolested for ages to come."[27] Yet within ten years everything had disappeared.

A more critical approach can be discerned by the late eighteenth century, however. The aesthetic efforts of the Gothic dilettante came to be seen as a disguise, even as a parody, of the past. Attention now turned to the remains less for inspiration than for information. The exposure of bare walls was now prized over their enhancement with ivy or plantings. The switch in attitude can be illustrated in two reports made by the antiquarian John Carter. Visiting Jervaulx in 1806, he was moved to write: "Hard is thy destiny indeed, havocked down to unintelligible masses of ruins, barely discriminating where the Abbot lodged, where the brethren took their pittances, where they paced in pious contemplation, where they studied, or where they inclined to soft repose. . . ."[28] Lyric as this is, it tells us little about the abbey. Fifteen years later

[23] T. Gent, *Ancient and Modern History of the Loyal Town of Ripon* (London, 1733), 23.

[24] W. Gilpin, *Observations on Mountains and Lakes of Cumberland and Westmorland* (London, 1792), 2:177-80.

[25] H. Hall, *A History of the Town and Parish of Leeds* (London 1797), 23.

[26] B. Willis, *The History and Antiquities of the Town and Deanery of Buckingham* (London, 1755), 152-53.

[27] *Gentleman's Magazine* 66 (March 1796): 194-96. Compare with the report in the 1792 issue under the signature of Antiquarius secundus (pp. 891-92).

[28] For the quotation, see ibid., 76 (1806), pt. 2, pp. 626-

Carter was back at Jervaulx, and his tone is now quite different. He briskly gives the measurements of the church and buildings, mentions tombs, lists moldings, and assigns periods to the work. A clearance made this possible, one of the earliest, undertaken by the earl of Aylesbury in 1807. Responsible care of discoveries was another matter; within a generation of the earl's work, the tile floor of the church, discovered entire, had completely vanished.

With the clearing and recording of the ruins, a modern attitude toward the architecture of the past emerges. Yet this too embodies a distinct sensibility, complete with its disciples and detractors. Present attitudes in fact organize our response to medieval ruins just as single-mindedly as those of earlier generations. Some ingredients of this result from a shift in the character of ownership. Whereas from the Dissolution through the nineteenth century monastic remains were regarded as private property and thus subject to the whims of eccentric owners, since 1918 Cistercian sites began passing into the hands of the government: Rievaulx in 1918, Byland in 1921, Roche in 1921, Furness in 1923, Buildwas in 1925, Croxden in 1936, Sawley in 1947, Kingswood in 1950, Cleeve in 1951, Rufford in 1959, Fountains in 1966, and Waverley in 1967. At present, about eighty percent of Cistercian abbeys with important above-ground remains are in the care of the government Department of the Environment. Conservation is now the full-time concern of professional experts. But under their supervision the sites have assumed a uniform tidiness, an unmistakable clean-surfaced look, even a bare linearism—features set off by a landscaping that consists of shaved lawns and manicured verges.[29] Such neatness suggests a touch of machine age and Bauhaus doctrines, an extreme version of the "too-tailored" look that Gilpin much earlier discerned and deplored. Yet so persuasive is this topographical style that to find a site that has escaped such treatment is very rare. Of Cistercian abbeys in the north, for instance, only Jervaulx conveys a sense of earlier tastes. There, wild flowers grow in the walls, long grass covers buried foundations, and seats invite rest and contemplation. Though such features may not guarantee Gilpin's prescribed "solitude, neglect, and desolation," they can touch us in a way that the stripped appearance of other sites does not.

---

27. Unintelligible they certainly were, leading Mrs. Pendarves, a century earlier, to coin the phrase, "jumbled Jervaux." For Carter's second visit, see ibid., 91 (1821), pt. 2, pp. 603-606.

[29] Sir Charles Peers (1868-1952) was important in establishing the appearance of the sites; he also supervised the clearance of Rievaulx and Byland. His obituary (*Ant. Jnl.* 33 [1953]: 149-50) notes: ". . . his love of gardens rejuvenated the neglected piles of castles and abbeys with mown lawns and bright flowers. No ivy mantled towers were left for owls to lament in. . . ."

APPENDIX B

The Builders of Cistercian Monasteries in England

WHO BUILT the monasteries of the Cistercians? Was it the monks and lay brothers of each house? Or was the work contracted out to secular professionals at all levels, from the master mason, who formed the design and organized and directed work, to the quarrymen who prepared the stone? Behind these questions lies a considerable literature, which goes back over a hundred years and has often generated an abrasive, polemical tone. In the mid-nineteenth century, for instance, scholars like Lenoir (1851), the Abbé Texier (1856), Springer (1861), and the Comte de Montalembert (1877) argued that the monasteries were raised by the monks with their own hands.[1] This view remained unchallenged for nearly half a century before the nearly opposite position was advanced by Hamilton Thompson (1920), Coulton (1928), Swartwout (1932), Knoop and Jones (1933, and later editions 1949, 1967).[2] They held that monastic building was the work of secular craftsmen. Knoop and Jones put it typically: "Some instances could be cited of monks who were craftsmen, but they are so exceptional as to be negligible"; and writing of the Cis-

tercian lay brothers, "though it would be rash to assert that no masons were to be found among [them], it is in the highest degree improbable that any considerable amount of building was carried out by them."[3] This revisionist position has held firm ever since.[4]

As is to be seen in the text of this study, the first wooden buildings that the founding community occupied were not normally built by either the monks or lay brothers. One of the earliest legislative acts of the Cistercians, the *Summa cartae Caritatis*, written around 1119, ordained: "No abbot shall be sent to a new place without at least twelve monks and . . . without the prior construction of such places as an oratory, a refectory, a dormitory, a guest house, and a gate-keeper's cell, so that the monks may immediately serve God and live in religious discipline."[5] The sound common sense of this ordinance was observed in general, and the usual practice was for the patron to raise the first structures after consulting with the founding house.[6]

Following settlement, the development of the site became a prime consideration for any com-

[1] A. Lenoir, *Architecture monastique* (Paris, 1852); L'Abbé Texier, *Dictionnarie d'orfevrerie, de gravure et de ciselure chrétiennes*, vol. 27 of J. Migne's *Troisième encyclopédie archéologique* (Paris 1856); A. H. Springer, *De Artificibus Monachis et Laiciis Medii Aevi* (Bonn, 1861); Comte de Montalembert, *Les Moines d'Occident*, vol. 4 (Paris, 1877).

[2] A. H. Thompson, "Medieval Building Documents," *Proceedings of Somerset Archaeological and Natural History Society* 66 (1920): 1-25; G. G. Coulton, *Art and the Reformation* (New York, 1928); R. E. Swartwout, *The Monastic Craftsman: An Inquiry into the Services of Monks to Art in Britain and in Europe North of the Alps during the Middle Ages* (Cambridge, 1932); D. Knoop and G. P. Jones, *The Medieval Mason: An Economic History of English Stone Building in the Later Middle Ages and*

Early Modern Times (Manchester, 1933); and J. Harvey, *The Medieval Architect* (London, 1972).

[3] Knoop and Jones, *The Medieval Mason*, 95.

[4] J. Harvey, *The Medieval Architect* (London, 1972), 174-75, is equally forthright and the same view surfaces in W. Braunfels, *Monasteries of Western Europe* (Princeton, 1972), 79.

[5] See J. de la Croix Bouton and J.-B. Van Damme, *Les Plus Anciens Textes de Cîteaux* (Achel, 1974), 121. The translation is by B. K. Lackner in J. L. Lekai, *The Cistercians: Ideals and Reality* (Kent, OH, 1977), 448.

[6] P. J. Fergusson, "The First Architecture of the Cistercians in England and the Work of Abbot Adam of Meaux," *Jnl. BAA* 136 (1983), 74-86.

munity, particularly as new postulants joined. Some, even much, of this work was done by the monks and lay brothers. This would make sense as a matter of economy—the survival of the early communities was frequently marginal—and also as a matter of discipline—manual labor was an essential part of the Rule of Saint Benedict, which, in turn, was basic to the Cistercian reform; it not only ensured self-sufficiency for the community, thereby minimizing contact with the outside world, but it was also recognized for its spiritual value. To suppose that the Cistercians excluded building as a category of manual labor is inherently unlikely, and as will be seen below, there is indisputable evidence that certain monks and lay brothers worked on building projects. Thus when the Norman historian Ordericus Vitalis, writing in the early 1130s, remarked that the Cistercians built their monasteries "with their own hands," he was reporting fact, not repeating myth.[7]

Other documents confirm Ordericus' observation. One of the clearest early accounts comes from the *Vita Prima*, the life of Saint Bernard, written between 1150 and 1170 by William of St. Thierry, Arnold of Bonnevaux, and Geoffrey, abbot of Clairvaux. One passage describes the events leading to the enlargement of the monastery in the mid-1130s, a decision critical in the evolution of the order's architecture from small to large scale. It relates that while Bernard was away in Italy the prior, Godefroid de la Rochetaille, Bernard's cousin, worked out plans for a new and larger set of buildings.[8] Presented to Bernard on his return they met with resistance, however. The prior, in an attempt to justify the project, pointed out that "although there were no woods surrounding the new site to make an enclosure (as was the case with the property they occupied at present), it would be easy to build walls down there because of the great abundance of stone." In answer Bernard argued: "a house of stone is something that requires a great deal of money and labor, and if we were to put up any such, men

might think ill of us, or say that we cannot be satisfied in any one place. Or they might think we had great riches (although admittedly we have nothing) and that wealth had gone to our heads." Eventually Bernard was won round to the idea. The local nobility helped with gifts and these were used to buy "abundant supplies of building material." The text then goes on to say "the monks supplied the labor themselves. Some cut down trees, others squared stones, and a mill was set up on the river. Some worked at this and others at that—carpenters, tanners, bakers, and the rest set up their workshops. . . . In an unexpectedly short time the walls were built, encircling a large monastery and enclosing all the work places. And the newly-born church grew and flourished rapidly."

Taken literally the account is not without problems. It does not actually say that the monks did more than square the stones and construct the encircling wall of the monastery; other roles may be implied, but they are not specified. Clouding the issue at Clairvaux is the fact that the monks were assisted in the work by outside labor whose participation in the building of the church is recorded.[9] Building at Clairvaux was, then, a cooperative effort involving the community and outside labor. But to what extent was this typical?

Outside labor had been employed by the Cistercians from the early years of the order. There are four references to the needs of "hired workers" in the *Exordium Parvum* (cap. xv) and the *Summa cartae Caritatis* (cap. xiii, xx, xxiv). And confirmation of their use comes from a number of early sources. Besides at Clairvaux, the monks at Fountains were using lay craftsmen by 1134, two years after the settlement of the site, as may be deduced from the reference to the greater need for food of the *operarii* and *carpentarii* than that of the rest of the community.[10] Regulation of these outside masons crops up in the legislation of the General Chapter meeting at Cîteaux; in 1134 a statute permitted them to eat meat, a food otherwise proscribed to the

[7] M. Chibnall, ed., *The Ecclesiastical History of Orderic Vitalis, Vol. IV, Books VII and VIII* (Oxford, 1973), 327.

[8] See G. Webb and A. Walker, eds., *Saint Bernard of Clairvaux* (London, 1960), 87-89. The quotations that follow come from the same source. On the precise date of the project, see

E. Vacandard, *Vie de Saint Bernard* (Paris, 1927), 1:413.

[9] For Clairvaux, see M. Aubert, *L'Architecture cistercienne en France* (Paris, 1947), 1:64.

[10] *Mem. F.* 1:50.

community, and somewhat later, in 1157, another authorized their attendance at some offices in the church and permitted them to wear mittens.[11]

Taking this evidence together in the context of the scholarly dispute mentioned at the beginning of this appendix, it is clear that the issue is not whether outside masons worked in Cistercian monasteries, or whether the monks and lay brothers did also. It is beyond question that both did. The issue is the degree and nature of the work done by those inside and those outside the monastery. The documentary evidence from the English houses of the order in the twelfth century, though still not complete, provides some useful information on the matter. A first step is to list the recorded names of masons working at Cistercian monasteries in the twelfth century, their ranks, and any further mention of their work. Considerably more names can, in fact, be found than the three in John Harvey, *English Medieval Architects: A Biographical Dictionary Down to 1550* (London, 1954) (see table). This listed information can be broken down into various categories and augmented from other sources. One approach to categorization is by broad rank within the monastic hierarchy, that is, abbot, monk, and lay brother.

Abbey	Name	Date	Rank	Additional Reference
Byland[a]	Henry Bugge	1139-1143	lay brother	"custos operis abbaciae"
	Godwyno	1170-1190	sec. mstr. mason	"magister cementario"
Fountains[b]	Robert	1170-1200	mason	
	Ivo	1180-1200	mason	
	Jordan	late 1100s	mason	
	Gregory	late 1100s	carpenter	
	Adam	late 1100s	cementarius	
	Ucted	late 1000s	mason	
Kirkstead[c]	Adam	c. 1140	monk	"in aedificiis construendis monasteriorum"
Kirkstall[d]	Dan Alexander	1152	abbot	"basilicam erigit . . . et dispositis ex ordine humilibus officinis monasterium suum"
Meaux[e]	Adam	1150-1160	abbot	"Adam et monachi aedificaverunt magnam illam domum"
Newminster[f]	Robert	1138-1140	abbot	"edificiis inibi, de more, dispositis"
Quarr[g]	Johe le ffleminge	c. 1150 (?)	free mason	"employed for building"
Revesby[h]	Willelmo	1170-1198	sec. mstr. mason	"magister novi operis"
Rufford[i]	Radulfo	1186-1204	cementarius	
	Gileberto	late 1100s	cementarius	
	Osmundo	1180-1200	cementarius	
	Roger	1180-1200	artifex	
	Hedwardo	late 1100s	cementarius	
	Roberto	late 1100s	cementarius	

[11] *Statuta* 1 (1134:xxiv): 18; and (1157:56): 67.

Abbey	Name	Date	Rank	Additional Reference
Rufford cont.	Peter of Clune	late 1100s	cementarius	
	Ralf	late 1100s	cementarius	
	Simon of Southwell, with his son, Henry	late 1100s	cementarius	
Sawley[j]	Waryn	before 1189	lay brother	"Keeper of the works of the church"
	Hugh	1180s	carpenter	
Sibton[k]	Walter	1160-1170	mason	
	Radulfus	c. 1200	cementarius	
Thame[l]	Johanne	1170-1184	cementarius	
Vaudey[m]	Adam	1147-1149	monk	"in aedificiis construendis monasteriorum"
Warden[n]	Gaufrido	c. 1200	cementarius	
Waverley[o]	Dan William de Bradewatere	1203	rector	—"coepit jacere fundamentum novam ecclesiae" —"inchoavit novam ecclesiam"
Woburn[p]	Adam	c. 1145	monk	—"aedificiis de more constructis" —"in aedificiis construendis monasteriorum"

[a] For Bugge, see *Mon. Angl.* 5:350; for Godwyno, see W. Farrer, ed., *Early Yorkshire Charters* (Edinburgh, 1916), vol. 3, Charter no. 1850, pp. 460-61.

[b] For Robert, see B. L., Add. MS. 37779, fol. 116v, and Univ. Coll., MS. 170, fol. 43r; for Ivo, B. L., Add. MS. 37770, fols. 12v and 13r, and Univ. Coll. MS. 170, fol. 47r; for Jordan, see Rylands MS. 224, fol. 118v, and Oxford, Bodelian, MS. Rawlinson B. 449, fol. 134r; for Gregory, B. L., Cotton Tib. MS. 112, fol. 204v; for Adam, B. L., Add. MS. 40009, fol. 289v; for Ucted, B. L., Cotton Tib., MS. 112, fols. 286v-287r. I would like to thank Miss Joan Woodward of Oxford for drawing my attention to these mentions.

[c] *Chron. M.* 1:76.

[d] *Fund. K.*, 178.

[e] *Chron. M.* 1:107.

[f] *Mem. F.* 1:58-59.

[g] W. H. Long, ed., *The Oglander Memoirs* (London, 1888), 198.

[h] D. M. Owen, "Some Revesby Charters of the Soke of Bolingbroke," *Pipe Roll Society Publications*, new ser., 36 (1960), 232.

[i] *Chart. Ruf.*: for Radulfo, no. 117; for Gileberto, no. 779; for Osmundo, no. 997; for Hedwardo, no. 826; for Roberto, no. 826; for Peter of Clune, no. 830; for Ralf, no. 826; for Simon, no. 826. For Roger, see Harvey, *English Medieval Architects*, 227.

[j] For Waryn, see R. P. Littledale, ed., *Pudsay Deeds, Yorkshire Archaeological Society Record Series* 56 (1916), no. 44, pp. 122-23; for Hugh, see *Chart. S.* nos. 123 and 127.

[k] See R. A. Brown, "Early Charters of Sibton Abbey, Suffolk," *Pipe Roll Society Publications* 36 (1960): 65-76, esp. 73, 75.

[l] *Chart. T.*, 100.

[m] *Chron. M.* 1:76.

[n] E. H. Fowler, ed., "The Cartulary of the Abbey of Old Warden," *Bedfordshire Historical Record Publications* 12 (1930), n. 52.

[o] *Ann. W.*, 91b, and 113.

[p] For the first mention, see *Mon. Angl.* 5:479, but compare *Mem. F.* 1:86; for the second mention, see *Chron. M.* 1:76.

There are three recorded cases of abbots who engaged in the design and construction process. Two of them—Robert of Newminster, later canonized, and Adam of Meaux—had similar backgrounds. They had begun their monastic lives at the Benedictine abbey of Whitby before moving south within the Benedictine family to St. Mary's York in the late 1120s or early 1130s. Together with Dan Alexander of Kirkstall, they were monks at St. Mary's in 1132 during the turmoil that led to the establishment of Foundatins.[12] Robert and Alexander are named in the *Narratio* as among the original founding monks, and according to the Meaux *Chronicle* Adam left St. Mary's shortly afterwards to join the new community. These details are important because they establish all three men as being at Fountains in the spring of 1133 during Geoffroi of Ainai's visit. Geoffroi had been sent to Fountains from Clairvaux by Saint Bernard because the new community had not been established in the traditional manner and needed instruction in the customs of the Cistercians. Architecture can be assumed to have been among the subjects of instruction; Geoffroi was skilled and experienced in building, and the *Narratio* states that he taught the monks singing and chanting and that they "built houses and set out workshops" during his stay.[13] Other sources establish Geoffroi's role as similar to that of a master mason and show that he was one of the principal figures in the architecture of the order. He is named (with Archardus) as the master of the second church at Clairvaux, begun two years after he was in Yorkshire; he is credited with building Clairmarais in French Flanders in 1140; and he probably worked at other sites that were founded in parallel circumstances to Fountains if the mention that "he set in order and established many monasteries" is taken to include building.[14]

Geoffroi most likely trained other monks in architecture, and specifically Robert, Alexander, and Adam during the time he spent at Fountains. This is not surprising given the new community's ignorance of Cistercian life and the expectation of

growth for the house in the years ahead. Subsequently, it is documented that all three men "set out" monasteries—Newminster in Robert's case, Kirkstall in Alexander's, Woburn in Adam's—"after our manner," a phrase that may be taken to mean after the Cistercian manner or, perhaps, more explicitly after the manner of the Clairvaux filiation to which the three houses belonged. About Robert and Alexander's further building activity nothing more is known, but for Adam the picture is much fuller. Adam built four monasteries and seems, in fact, to have duplicated Geoffroi's role as an itinerant monastic master mason. The Meaux *Chronicle* says he was occupied in constructing the buildings (*occuparetur et esset sollicitus . . .*) at Kirkstead (founded 1139), Woburn (1145), and Vaudey (1147).[15] He is mentioned specifically as being at work at Vaudey in 1149 when he had his famous encounter with William, count of Aumale and earl of York, which led to the foundation of Meaux with Adam as first abbot.[16] During the period from 1133 to 1150 Adam was a monk at Fountains, but after his appointment as abbot of Meaux his building activity continued for the ten years of his rule. One of his buildings is described in the *Chronicle*; it was a two-story timber structure of larger size than an earlier one on which it was modeled, with the lower story serving as a dormitory for the monks, and the upper as their oratory. About this building the text explicitly states that both "Adam et monachi aedificaverunt magnam illam domum."[17] It should be noted, however, that the building in question was wooden, that is, it belonged to the first family of buildings rather than to the stone and thus more constructionally complex permanent buildings.

Several monks who were not abbots, are known to have engaged in building from the order's early years in a capacity similar to that of Robert and Adam. Within the family of monasteries affiliated to Clairvaux, in addition to Geoffroi of Ainai, Archardus is documented as being the master in charge of the building at Himmerod in 1138 and a Robert is mentioned as being sent from Mellifont in Ireland

[12] For the accounts, see *Mem. F.* 1:9 and *Chron. M.* 1:74.

[13] The two memories are combined into one sentence by Serlo (see *Mem. F.* 1:47).

[14] For Geoffroi's work at Clairvaux and Clairmarais, see M. Aubert, *L'Architecture cistercienne en France* (Paris, 1947),

1:97; for Serlo's mention of Geoffroi's other work, see *Mem. F.* 1:47.

[15] *Chron. M.* 1:76.

[16] See p. 19 of this study.

[17] *Chron. M.* 1:107.

in 1142 to oversee work there.[18] Later, and outside England, two monks, Jordan and Berthold, laid out the plan and supervised construction of the new abbey church at Walkenreid in Germany, begun in 1207, and used twenty-one lay brothers who worked as masons, wallers, and carpenters.[19]

Monks also filled other building roles, such as those of supervisor or administrator of building operations (see below), which would have required some literacy and the ability to supervise men. In fact, Saint Bernard's own brother, Gérard, the first cellarer at Clairvaux, was, we are told, "skilled in directing the work of masons, smiths, farmers, gardeners, shoemakers, and weavers."[20] Additional references show the monks' involvement in building in more direct terms and even, touchingly, of this activity as sometimes outrunning their skill. For instance, it is recorded that the monks at Obazine (Corrèze) began work under Abbot Stephen around 1150 to enlarge the monastery.[21] But they were not competent to do the work, and the abbot, who took an active role in supervision, was obliged to engage a number of lay masons to complete it.

The texts are less revealing than might be supposed concerning the work of the lay brothers. Lay brothers outnumbered the monks in all twelfth-century foundations and, bound by a lighter rule, undertook a larger degree of the manual labor. One would imagine their playing a central role in construction of the monasteries. Yet few texts mention them. One rare early reference comes from Byland around 1140. This abbey's troubled early history included settlement on four sites before its eventual establishment at Byland. Among these settlements was one at Hood where the community lived for the four years between 1139 and 1143. During this stay Philip, whose account of the abbey's history dates to about fifty years later (*circa* 1197), records that Henry Bugge was *custos operis abbaciae*. Fortunately, a little is known about Bugge. He was a knight attached to the household of the Mowbrays,

a powerful family in the north of England who were the patrons of the Byland monks. It was presumably through the pious support of the Mowbrays that Bugge came in contact with the community and decided to join them. His status as a knight indicates capacity for responsibility and command. A second mention of a lay brother's association with the construction process also concerns a Yorkshire house, Sawley in the West Riding. At some time before 1189 Brother Waryn is described as "Keeper of the works of the church at Sallay." Whether both Bugge and Waryn engaged in building is debatable, however. John Harvey believes the term *custos* meant warden and signified a resident substitute for the master mason.[22] A famous example of this position's being used occurs at Canterbury, where Gervase, in his account of the rebuilding of the cathedral between 1178 and 1185, mentions the monk *qui cementarius praefuit*.[23] Subordinate to the master mason, William of Sens, he was "overseer of the masons" and was clearly appointed on a temporary basis as William's deputy for giving directions during a period of major work pressure. Gervase adds that the appointment excited much envy and malice on the part of persons in a position to criticize, probably the other senior masons.

On the other hand, Knoop and Jones point to the use of the title *custos* in the later Middle Ages and in nonmonastic contexts to mean the sacrist, i.e., the treasurer of the fabric fund.[24] Such a position was largely supervisory, with responsibility for making payments for materials and labor. If the titles used for Bugge and Waryn represent this latter function, they furnish further proof of the presence of outside labor, which would have required payment for piece work and firm on-the-spot regulation of work crews.

Despite the relative scarcity of references to the lay brothers, their role in building was doubtless considerable. Only a small percentage would have specialized in the various building roles, perhaps

[18] See H. Hahn, *Die frühe Kirchenbaukunst der Zisterzienser* (Berlin, 1957), 80, 253; for Robert, see A. Schneider et al., *Die Cistercienser: Geschichte, Geist, Kunst* (Cologne, 1974), 58.

[19] R. Dohme, *Die Kirchen des Cistercienserordens in Deutschland während des Mittelalters* (Leipzig, 1869), 34-35.

[20] M. H. D'Arbois de Jubainville, *Etudes sur l'état intérieur des abbayes cisterciennes* (Paris, 1858), 229.

[21] Swartwout, *The Monastic Craftsman*, 80.

[22] Harvey, *English Medieval Architects*, xi.

[23] R. Willis, *The Architectural History of Canterbury Cathedral* (London, 1845), 51.

[24] Knoop and Jones, *The Medieval Mason*, 27-31; see also R. Branner, "*Fabrica, Opus*, and the Dating of Medieval Monuments," *Gesta* 15 (1976): 27-30.

ten to fifteen percent, and the vast majority would have been occupied on the abbey's granges, farms, and in other tasks within the monastery proper. A text from the French houses at this period throws light on the matter. At Clairmarais (Pas-de-Calais) during a period of active building around 1150, Abbot William is recorded as employing lay brothers for the work and also as "collecting from the various monasteries of our order all those who were skilled in the art of building."[25] The same practice can be illustrated at Viktring in Carinthia. Among the first community were five lay brothers from Clairvaux who came from Villers in Lorraine in 1147 and are referred to as "conversi barbati diversis artibus periti."[26] So widespread was the practice that the General Chapter moved to regulate it in 1158. A statute legislated that the monks and lay brothers could only work at their own monasteries, and in others of the order, but might not engage in outside work.[27]

For the employment of hired labor within the community, the documents may be analyzed by the rank of the individual in the building trade: master masons, masons, and carpenters. The earliest instance of the name of a master mason occurs at Quarr on the Isle of Wight, a foundation of the Congregation of Savigny established in 1132 by Baldwin de Redvers. The source records that Baldwin "employed for the building of the monastery" Johe le ffleminge, who is described as a "good Free Mason." Unfortunately, it is not clear if Johe was at Quarr during its Savigniac years (1139-1147) or after 1148 when the house became Cistercian.

In two other cases the names of master masons occur as witnesses to monastic documents. At Revesby a charter dated between 1170 and 1198 was witnessed by Willelmo, who is described as "magister novi operis," and at Byland a deed of land was witnessed by "magister Godwyno cementarius" at some time between 1170 and 1192. Both names appear in years when active construction was underway at the house, and their use as witnesses may

plausibly be connected with their work as master masons. Certainly the increasing complexity and scale of the new buildings of the Cistercians from about 1170 forward implies the employment of specialists; design and setting out called for high standards of what has been called "constructive geometry" and would have required a degree of professionalism, in fact, unlikely to have been found within a monastic community. Clear proof that secular masters were used comes from the early thirteenth century. At Waverley the first church was replaced in 1203 by a vastly larger and more elaborate building, and the abbey's *Annales* record that the foundations were laid in that year by Dan William of Broadwater, who is described as "rector ecclesiae de Bradewatere." Mention of his death in 1222 and subsequent burial at the abbey suggests a period of eighteen years in which he had charge of the work there.[28]

More difficult to interpret are the documents that refer to the last category of men—the *cementarii*, masons, and carpenters whose names surface every now and then in the charters of individual houses. Mostly they occur as witnesses to deeds of land or other gifts to the house. Whether their association with building at the abbeys can be assumed on this basis is difficult to establish, however. At Sibton, Walter and Radulfus, both referred to as *cementarius*, were men of substance to whom the abbey granted land, the gifts suggesting their connection with work on its buildings.[29] Similarly, the willingness of Sawley to oversee the legalities relating to a grant of land to Hugh the carpenter implies his work at the abbey.

Elsewhere the situation is more ambiguous. At Fountains the names of six masons and carpenters recorded in the last quarter of the twelfth century may or may not belong to men actually working at the abbey. Arguing for their association with building is the practice at Fountains going back to 1134 of employing outside labor to help with work, and the fact that the period in which their names

[25] H. de Laplane, "Les Abbés de Clairmarais," *Mem. de la Soc. des ant. de la Morinie* 12 (1868).

[26] V. Mortet and P. Deschamps, *Recueil de textes relatifs à l'histoire de l'architecture et à la condition des architects en France au Moyen Age XII-XIIIe siècles*, 2 (Paris, 1929): 21.

[27] *Statuta* 1 (1157:47): 66; in the early thirteenth century

examples are known of Cistercians taking charge of building for lay patrons (see Harvey, *English Medieval Architects*, 288).

[28] *Ann. W.*, 113, under 1222.

[29] The suggestion is made by R. A. Brown, "Early Charters of Sibton Abbey, Suffolk," *Pipe Roll Society Publications* 36 (1960): 68.

occur was one of major activity and expansion, involving the construction of large structures like the refectory and west claustral ranges. On the other hand, construction itself might have attracted increased benefactions as people seeing a successful enterprise underway were prompted by the very activity to make additional gifts; in turn, witnesses would have been needed to validate them. Thus it could be argued that the names are merely those of free men brought to the abbey as legal witnesses of the gifts. If complications arose subsequently, such men could be easily found and could be appealed to in a court of law.[30] Their presence as witnesses was not, therefore, anything more than a legal matter and does not necessarily imply any professional activity. This interpretation would mean that in a case like Rufford, where the names of ten masons and carpenters are recorded from the late twelfth century, all that can be deduced is that an ample supply of such free men existed in close proximity to the abbey. A thriving town and big collegiate church at Southwell seven miles away, whence Simon and his son are mentioned as coming, would have provided livelihood for a number of masons and carpenters who might then have been summoned to the abbey to witness a gift as occasion arose.

The above material tells us much about the wider debate of who conducted monastic building in the twelfth century. At least in Cistercian monasteries, both monks and lay brothers took an active part in construction, to a degree far greater than the mere "amateur cooperation" that Swartwout was prepared to concede to them.[31] But they also worked from the start with hired labor from outside the community. Apart from the documentary evidence, the presence of outsiders could be inferred from the large number of masons' marks still visible on the sites, which were necessary for the calculation of wages. Building was not, of course, constant; when funds were in hand, work would be actively pushed forward with a combination of help from both inside and outside the abbey. Even then, to imagine monastic and secular craftsmen working side by side on the same scaffolding raising walling or turning vaults is inherently unlikely. Such a situation would render chaotic the mundane but necessary aspects of building contracting as the calculation of task work, or the meeting of specifications, and would lead inevitably to friction and disputes. But any monastery was a complex of buildings and when work was contracted out, it is only sensible that it would be for a specific project or parts of one requiring particular skills.

That most of the names of secular master masons and of individual craftsmen occur in the last quarter of the twelfth century may best be explained by the rise of a new professionalism. A similar trend has been noted in the production of manuscript painting and metal work. For architecture Early Gothic was marked by a sharp rise in technological complexity and by an increased sophistication in design, both features that fostered specialization. Yet to infer that building became the exclusive preserve of secular master masons and masons by the thirteenth century simplifies the situation. In England, for instance, it is likely that at Waverley the secular master who had begun the large new church, Dan William of Broadwater, was replaced at his death by a member of the monastic community, a lay brother, John of Waverley.[32] And in Germany throughout the thirteenth century there are a number of references to both monks and lay brothers serving as masters of the works.[33]

[30] I am indebted to Professor Christopher Holdsworth for pointing this out to me.

[31] Swartwout, *The Monastic Craftsman*, 86.

[32] For John of Waverley's career in royal service as well as at Waverley, see Harvey, *English Medieval Architects*, 288.

[33] See Aubert, *L'Architecture cistercienne* 1:98-99.

APPENDIX C

Temporary Foundations: Twelfth-Century Cistercian Houses in England

Original Site	Date Founded	Date Dissolved	New Location
Barnoldswick (Yorkshire)	19/5/1147	1152	Kirkstall (Yorkshire)
Brightley (Devon)	3/5/1136	1141	Forde (Dorset)
Bytham (Lincolnshire)	23/5/1147	1147-1148	Vaudey (Lincolnshire)
Calder I (Cumberland)	10/1/1135	1138	Hood (Yorkshire)
Cotton (Staffordshire)	1176	1178	Croxden (Staffordshire)
Cryfield (Warwickshire)	1154-1155	1154-1155	Stoneleigh (Warwickshire)
Fors (Yorkshire)	1145; 10/3/1150	1156	Jervaulx (Yorkshire)
Garendon I (Leicestershire)	(?)	1133	Garendon II (Leicestershire)
Haverholme (Lincolnshire)	1137; 1139	1139	Louth Park (Lincolnshire)
Hazelton (Gloucestershire)	1139-1141	1147-1148	Tetbury (Gloucestershire)
Hood (Yorkshire)	1138	1143	Old Byland (Yorkshire)
Kingswood I (Gloucestershire)	7/9/1139	1139	Hazelton (Gloucestershire)
Kingswood II (Gloucestershire)	1147	1148	Tetbury (Gloucestershire)
Kirkstead I (Lincolnshire)	2/2/1139	1187 (?)	Kirkstead II (Lincolnshire)
Loxwell (Wiltshire)	1151	1154	Stanley (Wiltshire)
Old Byland (Yorkshire)	1143	1147	Stocking (Yorkshire)
Otley (Oxfordshire)	22/7/1137	1140	Thame (Oxfordshire)
Poulton (Cheshire)	12/5/1153	1214	Dieulacres (Staffordshire)

Original Site	Date Founded	Date Dissolved	New Location
Red Moor (Staffordshire)	1141	1154	Cryfield (Warwickshire)
Robertsbridge I (Sussex)	29/3/1176	c. 1200	Robertsbridge (Sussex)
Stocking (Yorkshire)	1147	1177	Byland (Yorkshire)
Tetbury (Gloucestershire)	1148	1149–1150	Kingswood III (Gloucestershire)
Tulketh (Lancashire)	4/7/1124	1127	(Furness (Lancashire)
West Lulworth (Dorset)	1171 (?)	1172	Bindon (Dorset)
Wyresdale (Lancashire)	1193	1204	Arklow (Ireland)

SELECT BIBLIOGRAPHY

Aylmer, G. E., and R. Cant. *A History of York Minster*. Oxford, 1977.

Atkinson, J. C., ed. *Cartularium abbathie de Rievalle Ordinis Cisterciensis. Publications of the Surtees Society* 83 (1889).

Aubert, M. "Existe-t-il une architecture cistercienne?" *Cahiers de civilisation médiévale* 1 (1958): 153-58.

———. *L'Architecture cistercienne en France*. 2 vols. Paris, 1947.

Beck, T. A. *Annales Furnesienses: History and Antiquities of the Abbey of Furness*. London, 1844.

Beuer, H. V. "Evolution du plan des églises cisterciennes en France, dans les pays Germaniques et en Grande-Bretagne." *Cîteaux in de Nederlanden* 8 (1957): 268-89.

Bilson, J. "Fountains Abbey." *Journal of the Royal Institute of British Architects*, 3d ser., 8 (1901-1902): 365-68.

———. "The Architecture of Kirkstall Abbey Church, with Some General Remarks on the Architecture of the Cistercians." *Publications of the Thoresby Society* 16 (1907): 73-141.

———. "Roche Abbey." *Yorkshire Archaeological Journal* 20 (1908-1909): 447-54.

———. "The Architecture of the Cistercians, with Special Reference to Some of their Earlier Churches in England." *Archaeological Journal* 66 (1909): 185-280.

Boase, T.S.R. *English Art, 1100-1216*. Oxford, 1953.

Bond, E. A., ed. *Chronica monasterii de Melsa*. 3 vols. *Rolls Series* 43. London, 1866-1868.

Bony, J. "French Influences on the Origin of English Architecture." *Journal of the Warburg and Courtauld Institutes* 12 (1949): 1-15.

———. "Origines des piles gothiques anglaises à fut en délit." In M. Kühn, ed., *Gedenkschrift Ernst Gall*, 95-122. Munich, 1965.

Bouton, J. de la Croix, and J.-B. Van Damme. *Les Plus Anciens Textes de Cîteaux*. Achel, 1974.

Brakspear, H. "On the First Church at Furness." *Transactions of the Lancashire and Cheshire Archaeological Society* 18 (1900): 70-87.

———. *Waverley Abbey*. London, 1905.

———. "The Cistercian Abbey of Stanley, Wiltshire." *Archaeologia* 60 (1907): 493-516.

———. "Stanley Abbey." *Wiltshire Archaeological and Natural History Magazine* 35 (1908): 541-81.

———. "Pipewell Abbey." *Associated Architectural Societies Reports and Papers* 30 (1909-1910): 299-313.

———. "Forde Abbey." *Archaeological Journal* 70 (1913): 498-99.

———. "Jervaulx Abbey." *Victoria County History: Yorkshire, North Riding*. London, 1914. 1:280-85.

Branner, R. "Gothic Architecture 1160-1180 and its Romanesque Sources." In vol. 1 of *Acts of the XX International Congress of the History of Art*. 92-104. Princeton, 1963.

Brigode, S. "L'Abbaye de Villers et l'architecture cistercienne." *Revue des archéologues et historiens d'art de Louvain* 4 (1971): 117-40.

———. "L'Architecture cistercienne en Belgique." *Aureavallis: Mélanges historiques remis à l'occasion du neuvième centenaire de l'abbaye d'Orval*, 237-45. Liège, 1975.

Brooke, C. *The Monastic World, 1000-1300*. London, 1974.

Browne, J. *A History of the Metropolitan Church of York*. 2 vols. Oxford and York, 1847.

Bruzelius, C. A. "Cistercian High Gothic: The Abbey Church of Longpont and the Architecture of the Cistercians in the Early Thirteenth Century." *Analecta Cisterciensia* 35 (1979): 1-204.

———. "The Twelfth-Century Church at Ourscamp." *Speculum* 56 (1981): 28-40.

———. "The Transept of the Abbey Church of Châalis and the Filiation of Pontigny," in

B. Chauvin, ed., *Mélanges à la mémoire du Père Anselme Dimier* (Arbois, 1982), 3:447-54.

Bucher, F. "Le Fonctionalisme de Saint Bernard et les églises cisterciennes Suisses." *Actes du XIXᵉ congrès international d'histoire de l'art* (1958), 49-56.

———. *Notre Dame de Bonmont und die ersten Zisterzienser Abteien der Schweiz.* Bern, 1957.

———. "Cistercian Architectural Purism." *Comparative Studies in Art and Literature* 3 (1960): 98-105.

Buck, S., and N. Buck. *Buck's Antiquities, Venerable Remains of Castles, Monasteries, Palaces in England and Wales.* 4 vols. London, 1711-1753.

Burger, S. "Architettura Cistercensa Primitiva." *Critica d'arte* 5 (1958): 450-69.

Butler, L.A.S. "The Cistercians in England and Wales: A Survey of Recent Archaeological Work, 1960-1980." *Studies in Cistercian Art and Architecture* 1 (1982): 88-101.

Bynam, C. W. *Docere Verbo et Exemplo: an aspect of twelfth-century spirituality.* Harvard Theological Studies 31 (1979).

Canivez, J. M. *Statuta capitulorum Generalium Ordinis Cisterciensis ab anno 1116 ad annum 1786.* Bibliothèque de la Revue ecclésiastique. 9 vols. Louvain, 1933-1941.

Clapham, A. W. "The Architecture of the Premonstratensians, with Special Reference to their Buildings in England." *Archaeologia* 73 (1923): 117-46.

———. *English Romanesque Architecture after the Conquest.* Oxford, 1934.

Clark, E. J., ed. *Fundacio Abbathie de Kyrestall.* Publications of the Thoresby Society 4 (1895).

Clay, C. T. "The Early Abbots of the Yorkshire Cistercian Houses." *Yorkshire Archaeological Journal* 38 (1955): 8-43.

Colvin, H. *The White Canons in England.* Oxford, 1951.

Cothren, M. "Cistercian Tile Mosaic Pavements in Yorkshire: Context and Sources." *Studies in Cistercian Art and Architecture* 1 (1982): 112-29.

Curman, S. *Cistercienserordens Byggnadskonst.* Stockholm, 1912.

D'Arbois de Jubainville, M. H. *Etudes sur l'état intérieur des abbayes cisterciennes.* Paris, 1858.

Dimier, A. "Saint Etienne Harding et ses idées sur l'art." *Collectanea Ordinis cistercensium reformatorum* 4 (1937): 178-93.

———. "Architecture et spiritualité cisterciennes." *Révue du Moyen Age Latin* 3 (1947): 255-74.

———. *Recueil de plans d'églises cisterciennes.* 2 vols. Paris, 1949. Supplément. Paris, 1967.

———. "La Règle de Saint Benoit et le dépouillement architectural des Cisterciens." *L'Architecture monastique.* Numéro spécial du Bulletin des relations artistiques France-Allemagne (1951).

———. "L'Eglise de L'abbaye de Foigny." *Bulletin Monumental* 118 (1960): 191-205.

———. *Les Moines bâtisseurs.* Paris, 1964.

———. "Eglises cisterciennes sur plan bernardin et sur plan bénédictin." In vol. 2 of P. Gaillais and Y.-J. Riou, eds., *Mélanges offerts à René Crozet,* 697-704. Poitiers, 1966.

———. *L'Art cistercien hors France.* Paris, 1971.

———. "En Marge du centenaire bernardin, l'église de Clairvaux." *Cîteaux—Commentarii cistercienses* 25 (1974): 309-14.

———, and J. Porcher. *L'Art cistercien en France.* Paris, 1962.

Donkin, R. A. "The Cistercian Order and the Settlement of Northern England." *Geographical Review* 59 (1969): 403-16.

———. *The Cistercians: Studies in the Geography of Medieval England and Wales.* Toronto, 1978.

Duby, G. *Saint Bernard: L'Art cistercien.* Paris, 1976.

Dugdale, Sir William. *The Antiquities of Warwickshire.* 2d ed., 2 vols. London, 1730.

———. *Monasticon Anglicanum.* 6 vols., new enlarged ed. by John Caley et al. London, 1846.

Eames, E. S., and G. K. Beaulah, "The Thirteenth-Century Tile Pavements in the Yorkshire Cistercian Houses." *Cîteaux in de Nederlanden* 7 (1956): 264-77.

Enlart, C. *Monuments religieux de l'architecture romane et de transition dans la région picarde.* Paris, 1895.

Esser, K.-H. "Die Ausgrabungen der romanischen Zisterzienskirche Himmerod als Beitrag zum Verständis der frühen Zisterzienserarchitektur." *Das Münster* 5 (1952): 221-23.

———. "Über den Kirchenbau des Hl. Bernhard von Clairvaux." *Archiv für mittelrhenische Kirchengeschichte* 5 (1953): 195-222.

———. "Les Fouilles de l'abbatiale d'Himmerod et la notion d'un plan 'bernardin,' " *Bulletin Monumental* 111 (1953): 29-36.

———. "Les Fouilles de l'église romane de l'abbaye cistercienne d'Himmerod." In *Mémorial d'un voyage d'études de la société nationale des antiquaires de France et Rhenanie*, 171-74. Paris, 1953.

———. "Les Fouilles à Himmerod et le plan bernardin." *Mélanges à St. Bernard*. Dijon, 1954.

Eydoux, H. P. "L'Abbatiale de Moreruela et l'architecture des églises cisterciennes d'Espagne." *Cîteaux in de Nederlanden* 5 (1954): 173-207.

Fergusson, P. J. "The Cistercian Churches in Yorkshire and the Problem of the Cistercian Crossing Tower." *Journal of the Society of Architectural Historians* 29 (1970): 211-21.

———. "Roche Abbey: The Source and Date of the Eastern Remains." *Journal of the British Archaeological Association.* 3d ser., 34 (1971): 30-42.

———. "The Late Twelfth Century Rebuilding at Dundrennan Abbey." *Antiquaries Journal* 53 (1973): 232-43.

———. "The South Transept Elevation of Byland Abbey." *Journal of the British Archaeological Association.* 3d ser., 38 (1975): 155-76.

———. "Notes on Two Cistercian Engraved Designs." *Speculum* 54 (1979): 1-17.

———. "The Earliest Architecture of the Cistercians in England and the Work of Abbot Adam of Meaux." *Journal of the British Archaeological Association* 136 (1983), 74-86.

Fraccaro de Longhi, L. *L'Architettura delle chiese cisterciensi italiane, con particolare riferimento ad un gruppo omogeneo dell'Italia settentrionale.* Milan, 1958.

Gantner, J. *Kunstgeschichte der Schweiz.* 2 vols. Frauenfeld, 1947.

Gilyard-Beer, R. *Abbeys.* London, 1958.

———. "Fountains Abbey: The Early Buildings, 1132-1150." *Archaeological Journal* 125 (1968): 313-19.

———. *Fountains Abbey.* London: Department of the Environment, 1978.

Hahn, H. *Die frühe Kirchenbaukunst der Zisterzienser.* Berlin, 1957.

Harbottle, B., and P. Salway. "Excavations at Newminster Abbey, Northumberland, 1961-1963." *Archaeologia Aeliana*, 4th ser., 42 (1964): 85-171.

Hearn, M. F. "The Rectangular Ambulatory in English Medieval Architecture." *Journal of the Society of Architectural Historians* 30 (1971): 187-208.

———. "On the Original Nave of Ripon Cathedral." *Journal of the British Archaeological Association*, 3d ser., 35 (1972): 39-45.

———. "Postscript: On the Original Nave of Ripon Cathedral." *Journal of the British Archaeological Association* 129 (1976): 93-94.

Héliot, P. *Les Eglises du Moyen-âge dans le Pas-de-Calais.* Vol. 7 of *Mémoires de la commission départementale des monuments historiques de Pas-de-Calais.* Arras, 1951.

———. "Les Oeuvres capitales du gothique français primitif et l'influence de l'architecture anglaise." *Wallraf-Richartz Jahrbuch* 20 (1958): 85-114.

———. "La Diversité de l'architecture gothique à ses débuts en France." *Gazette des Beaux-Arts* 69 (1967): 269-306.

Hill, B. *English Cistercian Monasteries and Their Patrons in the Twelfth Century.* Urbana, 1968.

Hockey, S. F. *Quarr Abbey and its Lands, 1132-1631.* Leicester, 1970.

———. *The Beaulieu Cartulary. Southampton Record Series* 17. Southampton, 1974.

Holdsworth, C. J., ed. *Rufford Charters.* 2 Thoroton *Society Record Series* 29 (1972); 30 (1974); 32 (1980).

Holtmeyer, A. *Cisterzienserkirchen Thüringens.* Jena, 1906.

Hope, W. H. St. John. *Report on the Preservation of the Ruins of Kirkstall Abbey.* Leeds, 1870.

———. "Notes on the Architectural History and Arrangements of Louth Park Abbey." *Lincolnshire Record Society* 1 (1891): xlix-lx.

———. "Sibton Abbey." *Proceedings of the Suffolk Institute of Archaeology and Natural History* 8 (1894): 54-60.

———. "Byland Abbey." *The Builder* 71 (Oct. 3, 1896): 270-71.

———. "Fountains Abbey." *Yorkshire Archaeological Journal* 15 (1898-1899): 269-400.

Hope, W. H. St. John. *The Abbey of St. Mary in Furness*. Kendal, 1902.

———. "Kirkstall Abbey." *Publications of the Thoresby Society* 16 (1907): 1-72.

———. "Rievaulx Abbey." *Victoria County History: Yorkshire, North Riding* 1 (London, 1914): 494-99.

———, and H. Brakspear. "Jervaulx Abbey." *Yorkshire Archaeological Journal* 21 (1911): 303-44.

Janauschek, L. *Originum Cisterciensium*. Vienna, 1877.

Kidson, P., and P. Murray. *A History of English Architecture*. London, 1962.

Kinder, T. N. "Some Observations on the Origins of Pontigny and its First Church." *Cîteaux—Commentarii cistercienses* 31 (1980): 9-19.

Knowles, D. *The Monastic Order in England; A History of its Development from the Times of St. Dunstan to the Fourth Lateran Council, 943-1216*. 2d ed. Cambridge, 1963.

———. *The Religious Orders in England*, 3 vols. Cambridge, 1948-1959.

———, and C.N.L. Brooke. *The Heads of Religious Houses: England and Wales, 940-1216*. Cambridge, 1972.

———, and R. N. Hadcock. *Medieval Religious Houses: England and Wales*. 2d ed. London, 1971.

———, and J.K.S. St. Joseph. *Monastic Sites from the Air*. Cambridge, 1952.

Krönig, W. *Altenberg und die Baukunst der Zisterzienser*. Bergisch Gladbach, 1973.

Leask, H. G. *Irish Churches and Monastic Buildings*. 3 vols. Dundalk, 1955-1960.

Leclerq, J. *Bernard of Clairvaux and the Cistercian Spirit*. Kalamazoo, 1977.

Lefèvre-Pontalis, E. *L'Architecture religieuse dans l'ancien diocèse de Soissons au XIe et au XIIe siècles*. Paris, 1894.

Lekai, L. J. *The Cistercians: Ideals and Reality*. Kent, OH, 1977.

Lorenzen, V. *De danske cistercienserklosters bygning historie*. Copenhagen, 1941.

Luard, H. R., ed. *Annales monastici*. Rolls Series, vol. 36, pt. 2. London, 1865.

McNulty, J., ed. *The Chartulary of the Cistercian Abbey of St. Mary of Sally in Craven*. *Yorkshire Archaeological Society Record Series* 88 (1933): 90 (1934).

Mélanges Saint Bernard, XXIVe Congrès de l'Association Bourguigonne des Sociétés Savantes. Dijon, 1953. Dijon, 1954.

Negri, D. *Abbazie cistercensi in Italia*. Pistoia, 1981.

Nicholl, D. *Thurstan, Archbishop of York, 1114-1140*. York, 1964.

Oursel, C. "L'Abbatiale de Fontenay." *Cîteaux in de Nederlanden* 5 (1954): 125-27.

Panagopoulos, B. K. *Cistercian and Mendicant Monasteries in Medieval Greece*. Chicago, 1979.

Powicke, F. M. *Ailred of Rievaulx and his Biographer Walter Daniel*. London, 1972.

Rahtz, P., and S. Hirst. *Bordesley Abbey, Reddich*. 2 British Archaeological Association Reports, no. 23. Oxford, 1976.

Reeve, J. A. *A Monograph on the Abbey of St. Mary at Fountains*. London, 1892.

Rose, H. *Die Baukunst der Cistercienser*. Munich, 1916.

Ruttimann, P. H. "Der Bau- und Kunstbetrieb der Cistercienser unter dem Einflusse der Ordensgesetzgebung im 12 und 13 Jahrhundert." *Cistercienser-Chronik* 23 (1911): 1-13, 50-57, 69-88, 100-114.

Salter, H. F., ed. *The Thame Chartulary*. *Oxfordshire Record Society* 25-26 (1947-1948).

Schlink, W. *Zwischen Cluny und Clairvaux*. Berlin, 1970.

Schmoll, J. A. "Zisterzienser-Romanik: Kritische Gedanken zur jüngsten Literatur." *Formositas Romanica*, 153-80. Basel, 1958.

Schneider, A., W. Bickel, and A. Wienaud. *Die Cistercienser: Geschichte, Geist, Kunst*. Cologne, 1974.

Serbat, L. "L'Architecture des cisterciens dans leur plus anciennes églises en Angleterre." *Bulletin Monumental* 74 (1910): 434-46.

Sharpe, E. "The Ruins of the Cistercian Monastery of St. Mary in Furness." *Journal of the British Archaeological Association* 6 (1851): 304-17, 358-74.

———. *The Conventual Churches of the Cistercian Abbeys of St. Mary at Fountains and Kirkstall*. London, 1870.

———. *The Architecture of the Cistercians*. London, 1874.

Stalley, R. *Architecture and Sculpture in Ireland, 1150-1350*. Dublin, 1971.

————. "Mellifont Abbey: Some Observations on its Architectural History." *Studies* 64 (1975): 347-67.

Swartling, I. "Cistercian Abbey Churches in Sweden and the 'Bernardine Plan.'" *Nordisk medeltid: Konsthistoriska studier tillängnade Armin Tuulse. Stockholm Studies in the History of Art,* no. 13, pp. 193-98. Uppsala, 1967.

Swiechowski, Z., and J. Zachwatowicz. "L'Architecture cistercienne en Pologne et ses liens avec la France." *Nadbitka z biuletnyu historii stuki* 20 (1958): 139-73.

Tester, P. "Excavations at Boxley Abbey." *Archaeologia Cantiana* 88 (1973): 129-58.

Thompson, A. Hamilton, A. W. Clapham, and H. G. Leask. "The Cistercian Order in Ireland." *Archaeological Journal* 88 (1931): 1-36.

van der Meer, F. *Atlas de l'ordre cistercien.* Paris-Brussels, 1965.

Venables, E., ed. *Chronicon Abbatie de Parco Lude.* 2 *Lincolnshire Record Society* 1 (1891).

Wagner-Rieger, R. *Die italienische Baukunst zu Beginn der Gotik.* 2 vols. Graz-Koln, 1956-1957.

Waites, B. "The Monastic Grange as a Factor in the Settlement of Northeast Yorkshire." *Yorkshire Archaeological Journal* 40 (1959-1962), 478-95.

Walbran, J. R., ed. *Memorials of the Abbey of St. Mary of Fountains. Publications of the Surtees Society* 42 (1862); 67 (1876).

Walsh, D. "Measurement and Proportion at Bordesley Abbey." *Gesta* 19 (1980): 109-13.

————. "The Changing Form of the Choir at the Cistercian Abbey of St. Mary, Bordesley." *Studies in Cistercian Art and Architecture* 1 (1982): 102-11.

Webb., G. *Architecture in Britain: The Middle Ages.* Harmondsworth, 1956.

Williams, D. H. *White Monks in Gwent and the Border.* Pontypool, 1976.

Zakin, H. *French Cistercian Grisaille Glass.* New York, 1979.

INDEX

Library of Congress Cataloging in Publication Data

Fergusson, Peter, 1934-
Architecture of solitude.

Bibliography: p.
Includes index.
1. Architecture, Cistercian—England. 2. Abbeys—
England. 3. Architecture, Medieval—England. I. Title.
NA5463.F4 1984   726'.7'0942   83-43072
ISBN 0-691-04024-9

PLATES

1. Rievaulx, from south.

2. Rievaulx, nave looking east.

3. Rievaulx, south aisle.

4. Pontigny, south transept.

5. Clermont, nave.

6. Fountains, from west.

7. Fountains, south transept.

8. Clermont, south transept.

9. Ourscamp, south transept.

10. Fountains, nave.

11. Fountains, south aisle looking east.

12. Fountains, exterior south transept from east.

13. Fountains, west doorway moldings.

14. Fontenay, chapter house doorway.

15. Trois-Fontaines, west façade.

16. Fontenay, nave looking east.

17. Clairvaux, engraving by Israel Sylvestre.

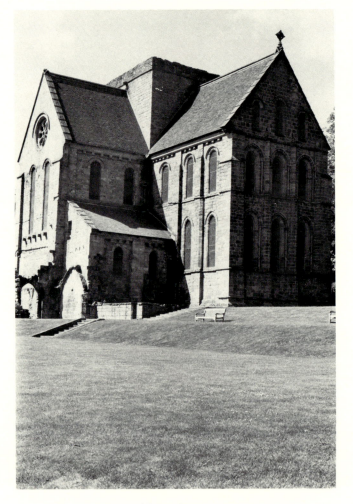

18. Brinkburn, from southeast.

19. Kirkstall, from south.

20. Kirkstall, south transept and choir.

21. Kirkstall, choir vaults from crossing.

22. Kirkstall, nave pier, base molding.

23. Kirkstall, southeast crossing pier.

24. Kirkstall, north transept.

25. Kirkstall, nave looking west.

26. Kirkstall, north aisle.

27. Berteaucourt-les-Dames, nave looking east.

28. Fontenay, chapter house.

29. Fountains, east guest house, drawing by George Cuitt.

30. Kirkstall, west façade.

31. Lillers, Collegiale St. Omer, west façade.

32. Sawley, north transept.

33. Clairvaux III, St. Bernard holding model of church.

34. Fountains, capital, south aisle, *c.* 1152-1155.

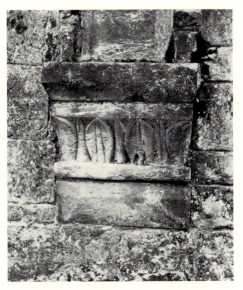

35. Byland, capital, lay brothers' range,
c. 1155-1160.

36. Jervaulx, capital, lay brothers' range, *c.* 1160.

37. Fountains, capital, parlor, *c.* 1160.

38. Fontenay, capitals, chapter house, *c.* 1155.

39. Fountains, galilee porch, *c.* 1160.

40. Kirkstall, nave, west doorway into cloister, *c.* 1160-1165.

41. Kirkstall, capital, lay brothers' range, *c.* 1160.

42. Fountains, capital, chapter house interior, 1160s.

43. Fountains, capitals, chapter house doorway, 1160s.

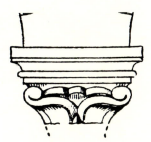

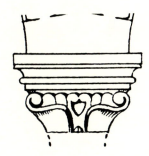

44. Kirkstall, capitals, from cloister, *c.* 1165.

45. Newminster, capitals from cloister arcade (reerected), *c.* 1170.

46. Stoneleigh, capitals, chapter house, *c.* 1165.

47. Furness, nave looking east.

48. Furness, south aisle, east bays.

49. Furness, north transept.

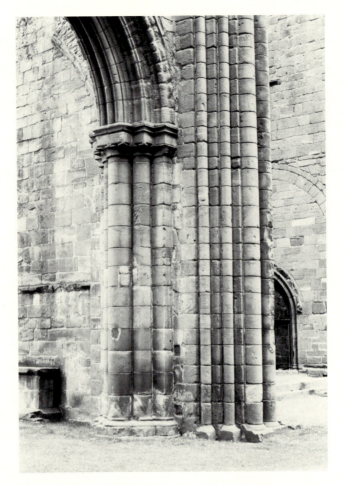

50. Furness, northeast crossing pier.

51. Furness, corbel, northeast crossing pier.

52. Furness, north transept chapel from east.

53. Lillers, Collegiale St. Omer, nave.

54. Nouvion-le-Vineux, nave looking west.

55. Durham, doorway of Bishop Pudsey's Chapel.

56. Furness, north transept doorway.

57. Calder, from northwest.

58. Calder, west doorway.

59. Holmcultram, west doorway.

60. Holmcultram, nave looking west.

61. Roche, transepts.

62. Roche, choir from east.

63. Preuilly, choir.

64. Clermont, north transept, west wall.

65. Preuilly, south transept.

66. Mortemer, north transept.

67. Acey, north transept and choir.

68. Creil, St. Evremond, nave (destroyed).

69. Gournay-en-Bray, Ste. Hildevert, nave looking west.

70. Bellefontaine, choir entrance.

71. Kirkstead, south transept.

72. Kirkstead, south transept.

73. Dundrennan, south transept.

74. Laon, St. Martin, nave looking west.

75. Roche, capital, north transept, 1170s.

76. Roche, capital, choir, 1180s.

77. Kirkstead, capital, south transept, vault springer, 1170s.

78. Byland, south transept, southeast angle.

79. Byland, south transept, southeast angle, detail of clerestory.

80. Byland, drawing attributed to Paul Munn, view from northwest.

81. Byland, drawing after John Sell Cotman, view of south transept.

82. Ste. Marguerite-sur-Mer, nave.

83. Pogny, nave.

84. Byland, west end of nave.

85. Byland, west façade.

86. Tynemouth Priory, choir.

87. Jervaulx, nave, south door, west bay.

88. Jervaulx, south aisle, west bay.

89. Old Malton Priory, nave looking east.

90. Ripon Cathedral, choir, north side view to west.

91. Ripon Cathedral, north transept, north and east walls.

92. Rievaulx, refectory, inner wall, cloister end.

93. Fountains, parlor, vaulting respond, 1160s.

94. Byland, south transept, arch respond, c. 1170.

95. Berzé-le-Sec, capital, nave, c. 1160.

96. Dommartin, capital, *c.* 1165.

97. Vaucelles, capital, chapter house, *c.* 1165.

98. Fountains, capital, chapter house, *c.* 1165.

99. Byland, capital, chapter house, *c.* 1170.

100. Byland, capital from nave pier (abbey museum), 1170s.

101. Dommartin, capital, *c.* 1165.

102. Furness, south aisle, west bay, vaulting respond, *c.* 1175.

103. Old Malton Priory, capital, south transept, *c.* 1175.

104. Jedburgh, pier capital, nave, *c.* 1175-1180.

105. Byland, capital, west end of nave, *c.* 1190.

106. Buildwas, view to east.

107. Buildwas, south transept, east wall.

108. Buildwas, chapter house.

109. Forde, chapter house.

110. Bindon, chapter house, respond, north side.

111. Buildwas, northwest crossing pier.

112. Buildwas, nave looking west.

113. Abbey Dore, exterior from southeast.

114. Abbey Dore, north transept.

115. Abbey Dore, south transept.

116. Le Bourg-Dun, nave looking west.

117. Abbey Dore, nave arch, east bay.

118. Abbey Dore, nave, view from west.

119. Abbey Dore, nave elevation, east bay, north side.

120. Abbey Dore, chevet exterior.

121. Abbey Dore, choir, north side, west bay.

122. Abbey Dore, choir view looking east.

123. Abbey Dore, choir, south aisle looking west.

124. Abbey Dore, ambulatory chapels looking north.

125. Hereford Cathedral, lady chapel looking east.

126. Buildwas, capital, chapter house, *c.* 1160.

127. Buildwas, capitals, southwest crossing pier, 1160s.

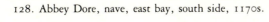

128. Abbey Dore, nave, east bay, south side, 1170s.

129. Stoneleigh, former south transept chapel respond, 1160s.

130. Buildwas, crocket capital, west façade,
exterior, c. 1185.

131. Buildwas, vault departure capital, choir, c. 1190.

132. Abbey Dore, capitals, southeast crossing pier, 1170s.

133. Abbey Dore, capital of soffit of east arch of south transept arcade, 1170s.

134. Abbey Dore, capital, nave pier, c. 1175-1180.

135. Abbey Dore, capitals, chevet, north aisle, c. 1190.

136. Le Bourg-Dun, capitals, nave, 1170s.

137. Mortemer, capitals, west façade, center doorway, c. 1180.

138. Combe, capital, chapter house, *c.* 1185-1190.

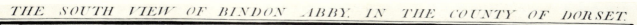

To Edward Weld Esq.

Proprietor of these Remains.

This Prospect is gratefully Inscrib'd by
Yr most Humble Servants
Saml. & Nathl. Buck

Bindon or Bynedone a Cistercian Abby dedicated to the Virgin Mary; founded and endow'd by Roger de Newburgh and his Wife Maud An. 1172. We find that K. Hen. III at the latter End of his Reign & his Queen Eleanor undertook the Patronage of it.

Saml. & Nathl. Buck Delin. et Sculp. 1733.

139. Bindon, nave, north arcade as standing in 1733.

140. Meaux, buried remains as of 1970, view from northeast.